Up from the Village

An Autobiography

Peter Adwok Nyaba

Cover design, typesetting and layout : Africa World Books

Africa
World Books
Pty Ltd

Table of Contents

Foreword

*I*f I was writing a book of fiction and was looking for a story full of drama, I would look for a protagonist who would scare away people by his mere threatening appearance and by his long wooden stick. I would impress my readers by the deeply black colour of his skin, by a skull full of bumps, by brilliant silky eyes, a powerful voice, and a strong body of gigantic dimensions (with a height of 2.24 metres, at least), and I would make my hero to be born in poverty. Let him grow up naked in a boundless, dangerous wilderness of shining rivers, elephant grass, and treacherous swamps in the middle of vultures, beasts, and large herds of cattle. But I would eventually bless him with the miracle of finding a place for education, allow him to travel, to experience hardship, to have exciting though often painful adventures in countries like Hungary and Austria, and to let his study of geology be rewarded by the title of PhD.

In order to bring some more turbulence and action into my story, I would change my hero's identity several times and make him to play, in succession, the role of an aggressive rebel, a fearless guerrilla fighter, a strong-minded political agitator, and, eventually, a fierce advocate for human rights. And, of course, I would have to give my

*Fig. 1a. Adwok Nyaba with Kwacakworo's
nearly 100-year-old mother (2009)*

story a solid historical frame, situate it in wartime, fill it up with all kinds of horror and bloodshed, and eventually add a touch of tragedy by making the tall man lose one of his long legs during the fighting, and disrupt his happy family life by the loss first of his young boy and later his brilliant daughter. If I wanted my story, moreover, to be of existential significance and touch the reader's sensibility by the drama's social, cultural, and human dimensions, and if, eventually, I didn't fear that my story would become over-loaded by the great number of emotional events, political battles for power, and personal misfortunes, I would surely copy the different elements found in Peter Adwok's life story and use them as the script for a novel, a thriller, or even a film.

I always thought that Peter Adwok shouldn't waste all his energy on only writing sharp political analyses and aggressive pamphlets. I thought he should take the time to write about his life, about his simple childhood in the beautiful land of the Shilluk, his parents and relatives, his education at universities abroad, and the long years spent with the liberation army; about his wife and his children, his friends, and his numerous journeys to foreign countries; about his feelings, his sorrows, his fears, his love, his anger, his hopes, his ideals, his doubts, his regrets, his beliefs, and his visions—not forgetting his never-ending struggle to find a less painful prothesis for his amputated leg!

I wanted that the coming generations of South Sudanese to have the privilege to read the testimony, to read about the personal life, of one of its most devoted freedom fighters while at the same time gaining insight into the background of the long war for the liberation of South Sudan from the North. The life of any fighter is surely full of interesting stories, but the story of Peter Adwok is of an exceptional significance, because he was not only a brave fighter (the only commander to lose a leg in battle!) but one of the most outspoken personalities in the long struggle for freedom and human rights, a political activist of great intellectual power.

Peter Adwok is an old and trusted friend, and surely one of my best friends in South Sudan. We first met some thirty years ago, but our friendship and cooperation are not much more than fifteen years old. Our collaboration during those intense years was very close, fruitful, mutually inspiring, and always pleasant. I spent many happy hours in his home in Nairobi or Juba, and he visited my hometown of Davos many times, becoming a friend of my family and my close friends. We often met at workshops inside or outside of the Sudan. In January 2020 we met in Juba, possibly for the last time. When I look back on our cooperation, Peter Adwok stands up in my private and professional life in South Sudan as a source of inspiration, energy, and joyful feelings of friendship. But to work with Peter Adwok was not only a constant challenge, it was also entertaining, encouraging, and often full of fun. In his presence, I would never feel alone, abandoned, or helpless.

I have always admired Adwok's psychological strength, his physical bravery, his courage and determination, his intelligence, his knowledge, and his capacity to focus on human welfare, even under stress and in extremely harsh circumstances. Adwok has a strong body and a strong mind, and he has a loud voice when attacking oppressors of all kinds. If he has been feared it was because he was known to be fearless and brave. He is respected because he didn't worry for his own life when—physically or intellectually—fighting the so-called 'common enemy' during the liberation war. People and readers may have liked or disliked Peter Adwok's opinions, but no one could ever doubt his selfless intentions and strong love for his country.

At long last, however, Adwok gave in to my pressure and began to write this book, the long-awaited autobiography. And of course, I should now be very happy about this late decision. I *should* be happy, indeed, and yet I feel terribly frustrated! By taking so long to fulfil my wish, at such a late time in our lives, my younger brother Adwok put me in a very awkward position: he dared to ask me to write a foreword for a book he knew I would never be able to read. With the passage of time, my eyesight has become so bad that I can't read anymore, let alone recognise the faces of people in the street. Considering my visual handicap, I first wanted to decline to comment on Adwok's autobiography; to me, it seemed an impossible task. But when Adwok suggested I simply focus on our common work and our personal relationship, I eventually had to give in.

Peter Adwok's autobiography surely does not need my comments, and I have most probably little to add to his own explanation of our common work. All I could possibly do is to enlarge the reader's

Believing of the historic relevance of Adwok's life, and quite serious myself when it comes to realising important projects, I spent years trying to convince him to write his autobiography. But all my efforts were in vain. He stubbornly refused and postponed the realisation of my suggested project to a later time. Adwok seemed to believe that the most important goal of a fighter was to succeed in his fight, without looking back, and that, compared to the political goal, the personal destiny of a fighter was not that important.

Fig. 1b. Peter Adwok Nyaba in Davos (2005)

understanding of the important role he played in the history of his country, and complete his account by adding some information which could not find a place in his memoir because he was only indirectly a part of it.

Writing about own achievements and to place oneself inside the historic context is an almost impossible task for anyone who has some sense of modesty, and in particular for a person like Adwok Nyaba who had never thought about himself, never worried about his personal security, his reputation or his professional career, but exclusively concentrated on practical, social, political, and humanitarian issues. By definition, an autobiography doesn't look at a person from the outside; the author may be self-critical and confess to regretting some of his decisions, but he would hardly give evidence to certain features of his character (such as a good, or a bad, temper). And he wouldn't praise himself for his deeds, for his kindness, or for the personal sacrifices he made while fighting for his people.

In spite of being by nature aggressive and fearless, Adwok was never haughty or hurtful. He was always open-minded, respectful, and even kind to interlocutors, ready for dialogue and seeking understanding—including me! Over the last thirty years, we never quarrelled. I therefore thought that in my foreword, I should, first of all, give some emphasis to Peter Adwok's personal qualities and express my gratitude for all he has done for his country, including supporting my own work as a peace advisor.

Because cultural and not political issues were the basis of my relationship with Adwok, I want to highlight some of his work in the field of culture in general and the promotion of peaceful ethnic co-existence in particular. Adwok's military engagement and his political career have been impressive. Looking back on his life, it would not be possible for him to avoid to outline and to comment on the political context which forced him to stand up against dictators and to fight for his convictions. The story of Adwok's work as an activist of the South Sudanese civil society is surely captivating and of historic importance. But to me, his greatest intellectual achievements, and perhaps his greatest purpose, were his activities as an advocate for the House of Nationalities peace project, his work for the Gurtong peace website, and his inventory and description of the material and immaterial culture of all the ethnic groups living in South Sudan. Tribalism was never a concept in Adwok's mind: respect for all cultures was the guideline for his actions and the motor of his activities as a speaker, writer, and political analyst.

The struggle for the independence of South Sudan from the northern part of the Sudan lasted more than fifty years. It was a seemingly endless history of suffering, bloodshed, and misery, without hope for any kind of economic and social development. I dare to ask the question: Was it all a misunderstanding? The people of

South Sudan were fighting for independence from the North, but the real reason for the rebellion against the rulers in the North was not political: it was essentially human. The fight for independence was of course a fight for a better country and for freedom, but it was essentially a fight for the respect of the peoples' cultures and identities, a fight for dignity, liberty, justice, and development. It was an uprising against oppression, racism, and exploitation. At the beginning, there was a strong belief that the liberation of the country would change everything to the better, that people could enjoy their independence, and find relief through development and respect for human rights. That's what the people were fighting for—and thousands lost their lives to reach this goal.

The dream of peace, harmony, and development was soon disrupted by the pitiless realities of the war. When fighting, one had to focus on the movements of the enemy, and there was no time to think of the time that would come after a victory. Moreover, the strength of the liberation armies was—right from the beginning—weakened by internal rivalries about the leadership, and even about the political directions of the different movements. This was the case during the Anyanya rebel movement, as well as during the time of the SPLA: leaders were killed and replaced, and the internal schisms led to resistance and fuelled further ethnic unrest. While the SPLA, the liberation army, was fighting the army of the government in the North, it also had to cope with the armed opposition of a great number of Southern tribal militias.

In 1992, somewhere near Nasir on the Sobat River, I met with Dr. Riek Machar and Dr. Lam Akol. That was at the time when the SPLA had split into two rival military groups. Discussing the situation in the country, I encouraged the two leaders to try to unite the people of South Sudan: 'You shouldn't only focus on your "common enemy", as you call your brothers in the North, but first of all you should work for the unity of your own people. Tell them what they can expect from you after the victory, how you will bring peace and progress to their villages, how you will create a feeling of nationhood by uniting the ethnic groups. People want to be sure that their cultural identity will be respected and that their voice will be heard. At present they are witnessing a reckless dictatorship by you, the military leaders.'

The two men looked stunned but, fortunately, didn't get angry. Eventually they answered: 'You are right. But at the moment, we have to make sure to win the war and to gain independence from the North. That is our priority. After the victory, we shall work for unity among the ethnic groups and prepare for a peaceful future. We shall make sure that our cultural diversity will be respected and that development will reach even very remote areas. There will be democracy in the country, with political parties, workers' unions, women's groups, and a strong civil society. But this is not the time yet for those plans.'

Thus, the original goal of the fight was postponed to the time after independence. Yet, hoping that unity would result out of a military or political victory was wishful thinking. Even after independence, personalities and their fight for power would continue to split the country for a long time to come and fuel further ethnic conflicts. At the end of the war there was great jubilance about the gained national identity, but after only a short time frustration grew over the continuous state of unrest and the lack of development.

It was during the mentioned period of the violent internal split of the SPLA that I met Peter Adwok for the first time. I was then leading the delegation of the International Committee of the Red Cross (ICRC) in Lokichogio in northern Kenya. The radical split inside the liberation movement had resulted in terrible military clashes between the two factions, and hatred and ethnic violence had spilled over from South Sudan to the ICRC hospital for war-wounded soldiers in Lopiding near Lokichogio: the mainly Dinka followers of Col. Garang de Mabior had started to attack the mainly Nuer and Shilluk followers of Dr. Riek Machar and Dr. Lam Akol.

To solve the conflict, the ICRC asked leading members of the two factions to come and speak with the patients in an effort to end the attacks; the hospital was far too small to physically separate the wounded soldiers. In reply to the ICRC's demand, the humanitarian agencies of the two factions (the Sudan Relief and Rehabilitation Agency [SRRA] and Relief Association of Southern Sudan [RASS]) sent some of their leaders to mediate. One member of the Nasir faction's delegation happened to be an impressively tall man with only one leg, a man called Dr. Adwok Nyaba. That was when we met for the first time.

One year later, at a time where clashes between the two factions had resulted in further bloodshed, I was working as an advisor to Operation Lifeline Sudan (UNICEF was coordinating forty-two NGOs working in South Sudan). When I was asked by the head of UNICEF, Philip O'Brien, to organise workshops for the NGOs in order to provide them with information on the many tribes living in South Sudan, I rejected his idea. 'I can lecture about the people living in South Sudan when I am in Europe, but not here,' I argued. 'Here it would be better to invite personalities from different tribes and to let them provide the foreigners with competent information.' The NGOs would not only learn about the tribes, but they would also even be able to meet personally with members of the various ethnic groups.

Philip agreed and allowed me to organise a few workshops in Lokichogio. For each workshop, I invited about seven personalities (they were all prominent men or women known to me from the time of my work for the ICRC) and asked them to introduce the foreigners to the culture of their people. Each time, I invited two members of the bigger tribes (Dinka and Nuer, from different areas), together with five members from smaller and less known tribes. Each workshop was to focus on a different main topic (such as agriculture, cattle and fish, medicine, material and immaterial culture etc.) and was to provide general information about the location, the environment, the livelihood, the language, the customs, and the major problems of the speaker's tribe. Thus, the participants from the NGOs could receive first-hand information and get competent answers to their specific questions. While this informative aspect of the workshops was expected to be of great benefit for the NGOs, another result came rather as a surprise: the information provided by the speakers was not only completely new and often surprising for the members of the NGOs, but even for the representatives of the other tribes. Upon hearing about another group's customs, some of them would exclaim, 'But we also have this tradition and that belief. We are the same.'

The 'discovery' of the other's human and cultural identity eventually led to greater mutual understanding, sympathy, and a feeling of brotherhood. Political opinions and allegiances became suddenly less important than this awareness of cultural unity. At the end of each workshop, I would invite the speakers from South Sudan to a farewell evening in my home. This was always a joyful event which showed that different political opinions lose their importance when people meet on a personal level. The meetings had not been organised for making peace between the participants, and yet the split between the spirits had disappeared, was forgotten and had made space for friendship.

This practical experience showed that ethnic and political hatred can vanish when people get to know each other as simple human beings. All peoples in South Sudan live in material poverty, but they are all very proud of their cultures and their identity as human beings. Indeed, respect of the other's identity is the key to understanding and peace, in South Sudan as much as elsewhere.

My experiences with hosting meetings of South Sudanese from different ethnic and political sides would soon be tested on a higher level. The Swiss Ambassador in Kenya, Josef Bucher, a thinker and visionary with a great sense for practical issues and cultural sensibilities, got the idea to invite some of the most important political and social leaders of the two factions of the liberation movement of South Sudan to a brainstorming meeting. The hope was that solutions to the peaceful settlement of the ethnic and political problems of South Sudan could be discussed. The meeting was to last three days and take place at the resort of Aberdare in Kenya. Willy Matunga, the well-known human rights activist (later the chief justice of Kenya), was invited to facilitate the meeting. The twelve participants were all standing on different sides of the armed conflict in South Sudan.

Among them were such prominent personalities like Prof. Bari Wanji, Dr. Simon Lukare Kwaje, Telar Deng, Prof. Peter Nyot Kok, William Ajal Deng, Dengtiel Ayuen Kur, Mario Muor Muor, Simon Kun Puoc, Anna Kima Hoth, Monica Nyabol Aleu, Prof. George Nyombe, Gabriel Gai Riam, Oiyok David Oduho, Martin Ohuro Okeruk, Father Kinga George Dalku—and Dr. Peter Adwok Nyaba. Some of these participants were known to be particularly violent: they were referred to by such names as 'Unguided Missile,' 'Loose Cannon,' or 'Gun Out of Control'—and Peter Adwok was considered to be one of them!

Because there was the possibility that the meeting between enemies could become physically violent, the embassy sent me to Aberdare as a kind of peacemaker—just in case there should be any necessity to cool down tempers. Because of my long experience in South Sudan, my good reputation both in Dinka and Nuer territories and my role in the epic escape of the so-called 'lost boys' to safety in Kenya, I was well known and respected by South Sudanese across the board. My mere presence at the meeting could resulting in an atmosphere of calm, peace, and confidence.

The meeting in Aberdare allowed me to meet Dr. Adwok Nyaba for a second time. It would become the starting point of many years of fruitful and pleasant cooperation. To the surprise of all participants, the Aberdare meeting of declared enemies ended peacefully and had a promising outcome. Prof. Bari Wanji's idea to create a forum (he called it 'House of Nationalities'), where all ethnic groups and sections would be represented in order to discuss their problems and to find nonviolent solutions to their conflicts, was unanimously adopted as the only possible way of bringing lasting peace to South Sudan.

After the successful Aberdare meeting, with its optimistic outcome, the Swiss government decided to play a more active role in the Sudan and appointed Ambassador Bucher as its extraordinary ambassador for the Sudan; I was to become the ambassador's special peace advisor. Ambassador Bucher and his assistant, Salman Bal, would be masterminding the whole project from a distance and make use of my cultural knowledge and my popularity in South Sudan for testing and implementing their ideas on the ground, during workshops, meetings, and travels abroad.

After Ambassador Bucher's transfer to Finland, Ambassador Daniel Bieler was appointed as special ambassador to the Sudan. Assisted by Salman Bal, he made sure that Switzerland continued its substantial support to the idea of a House of Nationalities; all the workshops and meetings in five states of South Sudan and in

Fig. 3. House of Nationalities workshop, Nyeri Club,

the Nuba Mountains, as well as the trip through African countries would take place under Ambassador Bieler's farsighted guidance.

The outcome of the Aberdare meeting needed to be put in writing, and since Peter Adwok was known to be a good and fast writer, Ambassador Bucher asked him to turn Prof. Bari Wanji's proposal into a concrete project. Without delay, Peter Adwok wrote a small draft on the House of Nationalities project and published it. But because this first draft was written in a fighting spirit, Ambassador Bucher found it far too aggressive to be a convincing inspiration for making peace. Peter was asked to write a more neutral, sober, and less emotional second version of the peace project. To do this, he was invited to Davos, my hometown in Switzerland. Here in the mountains, undisturbed by events at home, he could perceive things from a distance and write in peace. Napoleon Adok Gai, my still very young close friend, joined us in Davos. He had just obtained his master's in information technology at Leicester University in England and was now free to get engaged in the implementation of the project. Ambassador Bucher accepted my proposal to employ Napoleon; he was happy to see that the peace project got an early and enthusiastic support from members of the younger generation.

Peter Adwok spent a few weeks in Davos, discussing details of our project with Napoleon and composing his second, now very balanced, version of the 'House of Nationalities' booklet. As an introduction to the concept of peaceful co-existence, I wrote a short foreword to the pamphlet. To facilitate understanding, a summary of the concept was distributed as a leaflet of two pages in 2003; it listed all the ninety ethnic groups or tribal sections found in South Sudan.

The final concept of the House of Nationalities was the result of thorough discussions at many meetings. The idea was the creation of a forum where one elected representative of each of the ethnic groups (a section would be considered to be a tribe by itself) living in a state would meet on a regular basis to discuss their practical problems (these were conflicts about grazing lands or access to water,

Fig. 3 House of Nationalities meeting at the Panafric Hotel in Nairobi. Peter Adwok is in the middle of the top row, two rows behind Ambassador Bucher; Napoleon Adok is sitting in front on the left side.

occasionally armed conflicts due to cattle raids, and theft of children) in order to reach a lasting settlement. Questions concerning local development (planning of roads, placement of hospitals and higher schools etc.) would be discussed in the forum as well. The practical, cultural, and political worries, and needs of the communities would be brought to the attention of the local government.

The elected representative could be a chief, a man, or a woman. Once established in the states, the ten forums, representing all ethnic groups of South Sudan, would meet periodically and function as a kind of second chamber in the parliament (the political and legal authority of such a chamber would need to be decided on at a later stage). Cooperation between ethnic groups would enhance peace and facilitate the work of the government, in the states as well as on the level of the nation; the cultural identity of all ethnic groups would be recognised officially and receive substantial support from the government.

Peter Adwok's final booklet on the concept of the House of Nationalities was distributed among South Sudanese and discussed by the participants, first in two very big meetings in Nairobi which were attended by stakeholders of the social, political, and military life in South Sudan, and later on in meetings for the youth (in Nairobi, Kampala, Akon, and Panyagor); for women (in Lokichogio and in three refugee camps in Uganda); in Magui in Eastern Equatoria; in the Nuba mountains (in Lwere and Dilling); and eventually in five of the then ten states of South Sudan. Napoleon Adok organised these meetings, except the meetings in the states which were organised by Acuil Malith. Peter Adwok was present at all the big meetings held outside of South Sudan. At a later stage, Switzerland sponsored an educational trip through three African countries (South Africa, Botswana and Ghana); it was organised for chiefs and governmental officers to make them familiar with similar and successful concepts of peaceful tribal cooperation.

Fig.4. Visiting Kwacakworo's home in Davos (2005): James Oryema, John Luk, Peter Adwok, Mrs. Perner, Marie, King Adongo Akway, Marko, Kwacakworo, Amer Ajok and Omot

The biggest of all these meetings was held in Neuchâtel in Switzerland in 2005. The more than sixty very prominent participants (leading women and men from South Sudanese civil society, paramount chiefs, the king of the Anywaa, leaders of NGOs and UN organisations, human rights activists, researchers, intellectuals, politicians, and ambassadors from various African and western countries) adopted the House of Nationalities project as a model for peaceful existence even in countries other than South Sudan. Peter Adwok was one of the participants.

The South Sudanese who attended promised to do all they could to implement the House of Nationalities project. 'We shall stand for the House of Nationalities in all weathers, if there is rain or sunshine,' Dr. Lam Akol said. But not everybody in South Sudan welcomed the peace project. John Garang, the leader of the SPLA mainstream, probably thought that the House of Nationalities project was just an attempt to split the unity of his own followers. Since many Dinka supported the House of Nationalities, Garang was fearing for his authority and power. 'Are you with the SPLM or with the House of Nationalities?' was the question asked by Garang's followers. The question deliberately ignored the fact that the House of Nationalities was intended to unite rather than split the people of South Sudan. Unsurprisingly, nobody could explain why peaceful talks between representatives of ethnic groups would be harmful or dangerous.

I may illustrate the fearful attitude of those opposing the peace project on purely military grounds, or for reasons of personal enmity, by a small anecdote from the Nuba Mountains.

In January 2002, the special Swiss ambassador for peace-building in the Sudan, Josef Bucher, had organised a meeting between the Nuba rebels and the Sudan government on the Bürgenstock in Switzerland. The result of the talks was the Nuba Mountains ceasefire which led to the creation of a military peacekeeping force (Joint Military Commission) which consisted of officers from many European and non-European countries and had the task of separating the fighting forces of the Sudan government and the Nuba rebels.

In the framework of this mission, I worked for some months as a commander [[is "commander the correct word here? Thanks]] in the rebel-held areas of the Nuba Mountains and became a trusted friend of the Nuba. When working in the Nuba Mountains, I discussed the House of Nationalities peace project with the Nuba rebel leader Abdel Aziz el Hilu and the SPLA General Daniel Kodi. Abdel Aziz commented on the booklet enthusiastically, saying, 'I have thought so much about how to bring unity and peace to South Sudan, but here, in Peter Adwok's booklet, I have found the solution: it's the House of Nationalities!' But when I asked the SPLA commander Daniel Kodi if he had read the pamphlet, he replied, 'No, I have not, and I will not read it. When I see the name of Peter Adwok on a book, I know already what is inside.' Daniel Kodi's attitude was typical of those who rejected the House of Nationalities project without even wishing to know the ideas behind it and the benefits expected from it. Instead, they suspected that people like Peter Adwok were using the project to weaken the power of the military.

When I later discussed such superficial positions with the Nuba rebel leader Abdel Aziz, who was himself militarily linked to the SPLA, he explained: 'As you know, we are all officers and have to obey the orders of John Garang. What can we do?' Like all South Sudanese, Garang would be very proud of his own ethnic origins but wouldn't see the need to respect the cultural identity and to recognise the dignity of other ethnic groups. Garang had simply perceived the programme of cultural diversity and ethnic peace as a threat to his own authority and military power.

The House of Nationalities project was planned to bring people of different ethnic origins and cultures together to create a sense of unity and nationhood. Once implemented, political leaders would find it more difficult to split people along ethnic lines. At a time when more than twenty local militias were opposing the liberation army, unity of the people would make it much more difficult for the 'common enemy' in the North to divide the rebel movement. During the war, the government in the North of the Sudan was just too happy to see that the people in the South could get so easily be divided by internal schisms and ethnic rivalries.

But it was not only the ambitions of military leaders which were responsible for the fighting amongst the South Sudanese. Members of the South Sudanese diaspora contributed actively to the divisions in the South: they were sending messages full of hatred, spreading wrong information, wild accusations, and crude slander. Divided itself by ethnic tensions, the diaspora was constantly fuelling tribal unrest, calling for violence and revenge. Indeed, the violent voices of the South Sudanese diaspora were a very serious obstacle to any attempt to bring peace to the country. Their goal was the exact opposite of what the House of Nationalities project was trying to promote. What to do?

Napoleon Adok Gai, the IT expert, got the idea of creating a website which would spread the message of peaceful co-existence to the people living outside of the country by providing them with unbiased information on the situation in South Sudan. The platform would allow people to enter into dialogue and exchange opinions without insulting each other. It was designed to become a kind of virtual meeting point for civil society and all people who were not physically engaged in the military or political conflict and who were sincerely striving for peace.

Ambassador Bucher supported Napoleon's idea and asked him to create a peace website. Later on, the well-known journalist Jacob Jiel Akol and Amer Ajok assisted Napoleon in his daily work, and a board of directors fed the site with new ideas. Peter Adwok was one of these directors. As usual, his presence on the board was a constant source of inspiration and ideas. The website was called 'Gurtong,' an Anywaa term which refers to making peace between former enemies when there has been a loss of life.

Gurtong immediately became very popular both in the diaspora and among intellectuals inside South Sudan, not only because it allowed people to speak out or to comment in a polite manner but also because it provided unbiased, 'objective' information about current political topics and about matters of a more general and cultural interest. Lengthy and intellectually more demanding papers and analysis written by scholars and researchers living inside and outside of South Sudan were published on the website and, thus, made accessible to everybody. Gurtong was fighting gossip. It was a place of serious cultural and political exchange.

When still living in England, Napoleon decided to transport the concept of Gurtong even physically to the places of the diaspora. He thought that it was important to enhance the website by holding forums where South Sudanese men and women could meet and discuss face to face the problems that were dividing the people both at home and abroad. The participants at those meetings would carry the spirit of peace to their friends and tribesmen, thereby creating a sense of togetherness even among members of the diaspora. Within a short time, the mainly young friends of Napoleon founded a number of such 'Gurtong satellite groups' in countries where resident South Sudanese had been particularly active in dividing people at home along ethnic or political lines, including the United States, Australia, England, Germany, Sweden, Norway, and Finland. The beneficial effect of these diaspora groups was well reflected on the website's very popular Gurtong Discussion Board, where the opinions expressed became much more moderate, more reflective, and less aggressive than had been the case before.

Napoleon's role in the House of Nationalities project became important in another programme: John Luk Jok had submitted a proposal to the Swiss Embassy, seeking educational support for young Nuer schoolchildren. Asked by the Swiss ambassador for my opinion, I suggested to replace John Luk's proposal with a scholarship programme for children from disadvantaged ethnic groups (tribes or tribal sections), girls and boys who had no access to educational facilities. For the implementation of the House of Nationalities project, it was vital that the representatives of the tribes could read and write, or were at least able to communicate in a language known to others.

Ambassador Bucher and the Swiss Development Agency accepted my proposal. The selection of the children was difficult. Unfortunately, tribes which had nobody who had ever gone to a primary school had to be excluded. In case of the Murle, even an adult man would get the chance to be further educated (it was Akot Maze, later on a well-known commissioner in Pibor County). After a difficult selection process, twenty-one girls and boys from the Anywaa, the Jiye, the Didinga, the Larim, the Lolubo, the Lugbwara, the Luo, the Päri, the Lango, and some children from very remote Dinka and Nuer areas were selected (by Anasia Achieng, Ines Islamshah Napoleon, John Luk, and myself) and sent to secondary schools in Kenya. Napoleon and I were taking psychological care of the students who often felt very lonely. Of course, not all the students were successful (some felt homesick and never came back after school holidays), but some of the children made it up to university and a few were quite successful in their future professional careers.

Peter Adwok was not involved in the scholarship programme, and yet he contributed to the education of future generations by compiling an overview of all the tribes living in South Sudan. Because the House of Nationalities was designed to unite all cultural identities ('tribes') living within the borders of South Sudan, it was of course of fundamental importance to know them by name and to locate them. This study was a big academic and practical challenge, not only because there were/are so many ethnic groups but because many of them were not even known by name, let alone recognised as a cultural group. Peter Adwok agreed to make the needed research, conducted plenty of interviews, and established a list showing each and every tribe living in South Sudan: he found sixty-six distinct ethnic groups, this without counting the various sections of bigger tribes living in separate areas.

Peter Adwok's list showed a tribe's location, related its history, explained its material and immaterial culture, and hinted at the various problems the people of that ethnic group faced. When I printed Peter Adwok's information from Gurtong, I got a book (illustrated by pictures, maps, information on the relation of all languages spoken in South Sudan, and enriched by a lecture by Prof. Wani Gore on ethnic groups in South Sudan) of not less than 300 pages! Even if this information had no scientific ambition and surely would need corrections and updates, this work of Peter Adwok is of tremendous importance for the cultural awareness of the people living in South Sudan and will save many ethnic groups from formal disappearance. Since the so-called 'cultural pages' will be a book of reference for all generations to come, it should be enriched, published, and made available to the public.

The Gurtong website, because of lack of funds, is on the way to disappearing, and the House of Nationalities has not yet formally embraced. In consequence, fighting and bloodshed continue, and ethnicity is still a source of discord. But the idea of an institution which brings ethnic groups together will not die soon. There will be no peace without the respect of the dignity of all cultural identities. Eventually, the South Sudanese' struggle for recognition of their human rights will be successful. During our last meeting, Peter Adwok concluded our discussions by saying: 'Only a revolution will bring change.' I can only hope that further bloodshed is not needed to bring people to reason.

This is all I could say about my friendship and fruitful and pleasant cooperation with Peter Adwok Nyaba during the last years of my work as a peace advisor in South Sudan. Even if it has taken him a long time, I am happy that my old friend has—finally! —written his memoir. It is a precious and historic document, left behind by one of the most devoted figures from South Sudan's fight for independence and human rights.

Kwacakworo
Davos, Switzerland
November 2021

Introduction

This is a story about my personal interaction, call it experience, with society, in all its different sociological and cultural configurations. It's a daunting endeavour to condense seventy-six years, even more, of life activities in a small book like this one. What worries me is how the reader will receive the book's objectiveness and truthfulness, given that many of the persons I have mentioned, some of whom were very close friends, are no longer around in this life. I hope I am not being oversensitive. An individual's story is just a narrative, and nothing exponentially significant should be attached to it. But of course, I was an actor in a life full of political episodes and drama, some of them tragic, and indeed did publish books depicting or analysing those events, and therefore these narratives must at least consistently add up.

Not everything about my person comes out overtly in the autobiography. This was deliberate. This introduction, therefore, is an opportunity to mention some of these omissions. Without beating my own drum, as they would say, I am conscious of my shortcomings. I was, for some people, intolerably controversial, while for others I was a nuisance and notorious but not dangerous. Some people resented and did not tolerate my politics, including my ideological orientation. However, through all of this, I had many people I would categorize as friends, and I don't remember having made personal enemies, whether at the political or social level. I make no apologies, for that is life in its totality. I would add, however, that what I did, or didn't do, was more often than not dictated by the prevailing circumstances.

In the family, I must admit that I was hard on my children. I wanted them, and indeed sometimes forced them, to go over the top at school. My late daughter Keni would confirm that; I insisted that she complete her BA studies in the United States International University without a holiday break. This was, in my opinion, necessary to compensate for the time she had lost as a result of shifting education systems: from Sudanese schools in Juba and Khartoum, to an Ethiopian school in Debre Zeit, and then to the East African school system in Kenya and Uganda. The results of her BA (International Relations) could have been much higher had I allowed her to study at her own pace.

My life partner, Hon. Abuk Payiti, epitomizes the dictum that beside every successful man stands a strong woman, but I am not implying that I am or have been successful. But I don't think I would have made it without her, particularly at difficult moments when my life was on the edge. I am happy that as a family we have enjoyed nothing but love and complete solidarity. Pito, Kut, and Suzan have made their families. I wish them, and especially their children, good health and every success in life. Agyedho, now working for the African Union, is beginning to be independent and I wish her all success.

Since this is a testimony that will live on after I am gone, I would like to mention a few friends and relationships we developed at the family level. There were times when our residence became like an international club. We developed close friendships with two Dutch families in Nairobi: Dr. Simon Simonse and his wife Mercedes, and their children Afalis, Elias, and Camille; and Koert and Margaret Lindyer and their two sons, Kevin and Marvin.

Simonse and I taught together in the University of Juba when I came back from post-graduate studies in Hungary. We had a nice adventure travelling by road from Juba to Nairobi in December 1982. I was travelling to attend the third conference of the African Geological Society. Koert Lindyer, long-time Africa correspondent for NRC Handelsblad in Amsterdam, the Netherlands, has been a frequent traveller to the Sudan since the eighties of the last century. Koert visited and wrote a newspaper piece about me in 2008, when I was appointed minister in Khartoum, and was with me in Malakal during both the midterm elections in 2010 and the referendum on South Sudan's independence in 2011.

I recall vividly the two friends who worked for Pax Christi Netherlands and Radio Hilversum. In 2000 they sought my advice for choosing a local non-governmental organization to manage Radio Voice of Peace, donated to South Sudan to mark the seventy-fifth anniversary of Radio Hilversum. They agreed with my recommendation and selected the New Sudan Council of Churches. Their friendship and that of Prof. Eisei Kurimoto was a source of great strength to my family and I thank them all.

In the region of the Horn of Africa and Great Lakes, and in the context of academic and political activism, I developed friendships at the personal, social, political, and ideological levels. In Uganda, there was the late Prof. Dani Nabudare who became almost a mentor, and the late Hon. Omwony Ojwok, both of whom I had met in the house of Dr. Lam Akol in Khartoum in 1985; they were in the struggle against Obote's regime. Prof. John Ryle, who was recently awarded the Order of the British Empire, and Philip Winter were indeed wonderful friends. I would say almost the same of the so many former Sudanese friends and colleagues in study, work, and partying. It is sad that we are citizens of different countries.

In Kenya, I came to know Hon. Nganga Mwandawiro, Benedict Wachira, Booker Ngesa, and Gacheke Gachihi, all of whom were members of the Communist Party of Kenya. I also met former Chief Justice of Kenya Dr. Willy Matunga, Prof. Peter Anyang'

Nyong'o, John Githongo, Dauti Kihara, Dr. Atsango Chesoni, and others who were involved in the struggle for a second liberation in Kenya. I had the opportunity to interact with Hon. Raila Odinga, Hon. Cyril Ramaphosa, and the late Ato Seyoum Mesfin in the context of the South Sudan crisis.

Finally, two individuals stand out in special and different ways. Dr. Conradin Perner (Kwacakworo) defeated my obstinacy and had to acquiesce to writing this autobiography. He remains my elder brother. I will never forget our days in Nairobi, Davos, and in southern Sudan. I knew Dr. Carol Berger by name since the early eighties of the last century, when she succinctly reported on the events in the Sudan, but I only met her in May 2016. She is a wonderful person, as well as being my editor. We have since become good friends. I thank her and wish her all the best of life in the Mediterranean area.

Up from the Village speaks to my humble beginnings and my modest contribution to the struggle of the people of South Sudan for freedom, justice, fraternity, and prosperity. It ends on a sad note as I was part of the phenomenal failure of the SPLM's political and military elite to realise people's aspirations for socioeconomic and cultural development. The centuries-old conditions of abject poverty, ignorance, and superstition show no sign of coming to an end. I only hope that the present context, into which the people have been thrown, contains the seeds of its own destruction and, with it, the means for a transformation.

Peter Adwok Nyaba
Juba
July 2021

Chapter 1

Life's Early Years

Birth & the Village

When I read through biographies and autobiographies of many Africans, I usually come across striking similarities, across the board, in the rural environment in which many of us were born and raised. Whether speaking about the south, west, or east of Africa, rural life appears uniform, except in parts where European colonialism or capitalism have profoundly permeated and penetrated to transform the traditional and indigenous order. Sudan and South Sudan have until recently been largely rural. Even after nearly two hundred years of contact with the rest of the world, modernism characterised by urbanisation and civility is yet to take root. Many of us in government, as ministers and senior bureaucrats, epitomise the dictum that you can take a person out of the village, but you cannot take the village out of him. This may explain, in part, why our towns remain largely extended villages.

I was born in the village. My parents were both rural folks, living in close proximity to the bustling colonial town of Malakal. I would add that this proximity had little impact socially or culturally on their lives, except for the few consumer commodities they purchased from the Arab merchants. They were both illiterate and I don't think that status bothered them. They lived off the land, tilling as much as their capacity permitted to give them their livelihood. They did not have the support of modern technological innovations and depended on the vagaries of nature. It was much later in life that I learned that land could be privately owned, in the manner that we find in Uganda and Kenya. But even today, the land of my ancestors is communal land held by Wad Nyikango, the Chollo sovereign, in the name of the Chollo people.

At the time I was born, the Chollo people were subjects of the Anglo–Egyptian Condominium. My father, Nyaba Tor, although a royal—at the rank of *Kwanyireth* (a baron)—was in reality an ordinary Chollo peasant. The Chollo royalty no longer lived parasitically off the labours of the rest of Chollo peasantry, or the neighbouring ethnicities like the Dinka, Nuba, Maaban, and Arab northern Sudanese. My father lived by tilling the land. He was the only male of six siblings and half siblings; his father, Tor Ajak, was polygamous. The tradition of marrying many wives was and is still common among the Chollo, and indeed among many other nationalities in South Sudan. It is seen usually as an expression of one's wealth and stature in society. And now it has political dividends; in a polity like South Sudan where national state and local politics is organised on the basis of community, then those communities with large demographic indicators control political power. This is how the Dinka and the Nuer came to dominate power.

Like his father, Nyaba was married to two wives: the eldest wife, Akolong Titagany, may her soul rest in peace, hailed from Dot, a hamlet of Watajwok. That my stepmother gave birth to girls must have impelled my father to marry a second wife. My mother, Nyaywach Achonglith, may her soul rest in peace, hailed from Makal village and was the last of four siblings. I did not have the opportunity to see my maternal grandfather, grandmother, or my uncle. In fact, I never knew my uncle's name. But I met and interacted with my mum's other siblings: Nyator and Nyatyeno Achonglith. Aunt Nyator never liked me, although her daughter, Nyathow, was my sitter as a baby. She had grudges against my father, who was always uncomfortable whenever she came to visit my mum. Aunt Nyator saw my father in me and at times transferred her resentment and hostility to me, which angered my mother. Aunt Nyatyeno lived in Anagdiar, and we saw her less frequently. I remember the time in 1963 when my father and I visited her. She was such a lovely lady and my father liked her.

Because of this rural background, I did not, and indeed would never, know the date of my birth. In the village, date of birth is of no consequence and therefore no one refers to it in the way that I know the exact time of birth of my children. It was sufficient that the *gaami* (traditional birth attendant) declared that the child delivered was of a particular gender and was healthy. Chollo tradition dictates that the gender of the new-born is announced by the side of the door where the umbilical cord is buried for a girl, it was usually on the left side. There was no room for ambiguity. Should there be a deformity in the new born that raises doubts about its gender or future physical fitness, the traditional birth attendant has the discretion to immediately eliminate the foetus and pronounce it *apoodh* (dead).

It invariably took some days before the child-naming ceremony was performed. This was always a function of the economics of the family, which in turn depended on the last harvest. If the family sorghum store, *okodo,* was large enough, they made an elaborate child-naming celebration in which sorghum beer was served to the elders and *kwon* served to the hamlet's children. The Chollo people have no tradition or custom of a predetermined naming system, as with the Anywaa, Bari, and others. The exceptions are in the case of twins, whereby gendered names (Ngoor/Angar, Bol/Nyabol/Nyibol, Acwil, Otuk/Nyatuk) that the Chollo share with their Dinka cousins are invoked; in the case of physical deformity (Nyikango); and when the birth follows a death in the family, names like Obur/Nyaburu, Adwok, Aywok, Chol/Achol, and Aban/Nyaban are invoked to mark the event.

When I reflect on my own situation, life for me was somehow full of omens. "He has returned," must have been my father's reaction when the village's traditional birth attendant, Adwok Nyadolek, broke the news that it was a baby boy. I was the third child. My elder siblings were Ciro, a girl, and a male who had died a few days into his life. In the rural environment, and village settings for that matter, the causes of infantile death are predictably linked to poor hygiene, lack of pre- and post-natal medical care, and the lack of vaccinations against such fatal children's diseases as diphtheria, polio, typhoid, and tuberculosis. In such circumstances, not so many Chollo children live to celebrate their fifth birthday. I must count myself among the lucky ones. Because my elder brother had not lived, the sentiment was that my birth marked his "return."

The Chollo people in the villages, including some townsfolk, believe that certain bad traits like greed, cruelty, jealousy, and many other instinctual drives that we find in society are there from the time of birth, and inculcate in the child during the gestation. They know that these traits trigger conflict and social disharmony and are not surprisingly frowned upon in Chollo society. Excessive greed, for instance, could lead one to steal. In order to cleanse the new-born of these attributes, a ceremony to dispel or weaken these spirits (*chedi p l*) is conducted. The ceremony requires that the mother, after she has sufficiently recovered her physical strength, brew sorghum beer for the elderly and cook a special kind of *kwon* for the children in the village.

My father, and indeed the rest of the family, must have been devastated by the loss of my elder sibling. Apart from the general feeling of grief over losing a child, the reason for this sorrow was obvious. Like his father, my grandfather Tor wad Ajak, and his sister Ayileew, who were the only siblings of their mother, Nyaba was the only male of the six siblings born to Tor wad Ajak by his two wives. Ajak wad Lathnyal married four wives and so, in addition to my grandfather and his sister, Ajak had seven other sons and daughters. The name of my father, Nyaba, connotes a state of perpetual despair and grief over the recurrent deaths in the family.

Being patrilineal, the Chollo people attached enormous importance to the male members of the family. This is because the male carries the family lineage in perpetuity through his descendants. The girls are equally valued, but only because they bring cattle in bride price to the family. Because the girl is expected to move to her marriage home in the community of her husband and her offspring count on their husbands' side, she is not treated in the same way as a son. Without a son, a family's existence and lineage end with the patriarch. In this respect, the Chollo people would say, *"Kál wije apath,"* literally translating to "The family became extinct." The death of my sibling, the only male in the family, therefore, was more than a tragedy, and my birth was received with joy.

As I grew up in the village, and much later when I was married and we had time to converse, my mother used to tell me stories about my childhood. It seems that I had a difficult growth on account of frequent ailments, including bouts of malaria, intestinal complications, and malnutrition. I was tall for my age, very skinny, and somewhat weak. But I was articulate and had a sharp tongue, probably a defensive mechanism to compensate for my weak muscles. I received so much love and affection from my parents, elder siblings, and relatives in the village and neighbouring areas. Everywhere in the immediate environ of my home, people, particularly elders, poured their blessings on me, usually in the form of saliva or the sprinkling of water on my body when they found out that I was the son of Nyaba. They also praised God that he had blessed my father with a son. All of this spoke to the sociocultural tradition of the Chollo people, which particularly venerates the single son with supplications that providence will preserve his life.

My great-aunt, Ayileew nya-Ajak, was very fond of me. I would spend much of my time sitting and listening to the fairy tales (wathi-*ngu*) she told with passion. It was important to her that I would continue the family line of her brother, Tor wa-Ajak. To this day, I still remember how she spoiled me every afternoon when I returned home with the goats and sheep. She would have saved something for me to eat. Every time she went to Malakal town, which she usually called *kal obwonyo* (meaning "the camp of the red people") she brought back dates and groundnuts for me. It was the saddest day of my life when in 1957 I came back home from boarding school in Dolieb Hill to find that she had passed on.

My date and place of birth had relevance only in school and other governmental institutions. I was always in trouble when it was necessary to record one's age or birthday. It took me a long time to decipher when my birth had occurred. Even my father could not remember precisely when I was born. In all my documents, including academic ones like the Sudan School Certificate, my BSc from Khartoum University and PhD from the Hungarian Academy of Sciences, my date of birth is recorded as 1 January 1948. But this was only a guess. The practice in the Sudan then, and even now in South Sudan, was that one went to the Medical Commission to obtain an "assessment of age" certificate. It was a subjective exercise, usually made to the nearest five years by the medical officer. It was obligatory for me and other students to have that certificate before we could sit for the Sudan School Certificate Examinations in March 1968 or gain employment in government.

But I never stopped trying to figure out my date of birth. Every time I came back from Dolieb or Atar I would ask questions. My father, if he was in a good mood, would tell me, "Ah, it was on a Friday afternoon when you were born." As there would be fifty-two or so Fridays in a normal year, I found it a serious challenge to link that Friday to a particular month as I tried to compute the date of my birth. On another occasion, I believe we were walking back to the village from a fishing expedition, he said, "You were born before the rains, at a time when the clouds begin to form, and Rath Dak was still an *ochollo* in Debalo awaiting his coronation." This information had elements that could be corroborated with known facts in order to clear the confusion. In Upper Nile, the clouds start to form around the month of March. Dak Padiet Kwathkier was enthroned in Pachodo as the thirty-first *rath* of the Chollo people in 1945, a few months after the passing on (*k thi l g naam*) of Rath Aney Kur Nyidhok. This meant that I must have been born on a Friday in March or April 1945, a full three years before my official birth year of 1948.

Amongst the Chollo people, as it would also be with some Luo groups albeit with some variations, *adwok* translates to "has come back." It means that a departed person has returned or perhaps the new-born is an incarnation of the departed one. I believe, from my current level of understanding and knowledge of tradition and culture, had I been born a girl, my birth wouldn't have been seen as consequential. It would not have invoked the memory of my departed sibling. My family was already crowded with female siblings when I was born. Piero was the eldest, while Adiang, Arek, Nyakoth, and Achol were all from my stepmother's side. On my mother's side, Ciro was also a girl, whom I followed. Therefore, I doubt my father would have had much consideration for me if I had been another daughter. This digression demonstrates the attitude and behaviour of patriarchal communities towards their children and explains why my father was determined to send me to school.

Kwanyireth Ajak wad Lathnyal, our great-grandfather, was the head of the clan tree or lineage. He had four wives and founded the hamlet we all came to live in. In most cases, Chollo hamlets are named after their founders. Travelling from Malakal southwards to Dolieb Hill, using the dirt road or footpath on the east bank of the White Nile, one passes through the line of hamlets that make up Watajwok village: pa-Aywok Nyalabo, pa-Jago Kai-Chok, pa-Pamet, pa-Awang, pa-Akolakany, pa-Lwal, pa-Ajak, pa-Anyakway, pa-Kuchgor, pa-Denyibong, pa-Adorwin, pa-Amonding and pa-Damlai. The "pa" means "hamlet," making pa-Aywok Nyalabo, for example, Aywok Nyalabo's hamlet. To the right side, across the floodplain lies a low-lying ridge dotted with hamlets. As we travel southwards from its northern end, we find pa-Kudit, pa-Akwoch wad Nyikayo, pa-Amum Adolek, and pa-Nyikango Kuleke adjacent to it, pa-Adung Kur-nyal and pa-Kwoj, and finally pa-Nyodho and then the bush school in its southern end.

It may be said with some degree of confidence that all the people in these hamlets knew each other. In only rare cases would the residents not know a person domicile in any of the hamlets. The elders usually met and socialised in work parties, fishing parties, and other community activities to which all were obliged to attend. The women also had their own activities that brought them together. Children and adolescents had the most opportunities to meet and engage with each other. In this way people knew themselves even by names and character.

Watajwok, on the east bank of the White Nile, had a history of resisting the British colonial administration, particularly after the establishment of Malakal as the capital of Upper Nile Province. It is difficult to know when Kwanyireth (KT) Ajak founded the village that became known as Malakal. By the middle of the eighteenth century, the Chollo had colonised the east bank and there were villages on the northern bank of Sobat River (known as Atul-pi among the Chollo). In my assessment, it must have during the reign of Rath Yor-nyakwaci wad Kudit (1780–1820).

The contradictions, indeed, power struggles between the reigning sovereign and the princes (*nyiradh*) *and* between the princes themselves, on account of ascendency, were the main drivers of this migration to the east. In fact, Chollo call the east bank and the settlements that grew there, founded by the princes, *L g Jiango* ("sanctuary"). It was also where the Chollo retreated during the tensions and conflict with the Turkish administration (1824–1881). But this eastwards movement and habitation was also the result of the explosion of the population on the west bank. The British colonial administration, having named Malakal as its capital, destroyed the Watajwok hamlets to create space for Malakal town and later to settle the Arab nomads known as the Misseriya. I will come back to this story in a moment.

Rath Dhokoth wad Bwoch, who reigned over the *podhi* or provinces of Chollo (1670–1690), founded Watajwok village. It was tradition that each Chollo sovereign reigned from his village, suggesting that Watajwok must have been among the oldest of Chollo villages. Nevertheless, there is little in Watajwok to reflect its long history except the oral history. Laaki Nyikango (the Chollo Kingdom) is situated where such materials as stone, sand, cement, and steel for the construction of permanent structures hardly exist. The Chollo people used mud, wood, and grass to build their huts (*t*) and cattle byres (*lwak*).

The distinguishing feature of Watajwok village has long been the mud-walled and grass-thatched roof of Dhokoth's shrine, which is refurbished every five years. Between 1837 and 1881, the village and the shrine were razed to the ground several times by the Turks as they carried out raids for slaves. Nor were the hamlets on the east bank spared. In the 1920s the British colonial administration destroyed the homesteads there, forcing the people to leave, and settled the Misseriya nomads in their place.

Why would the British colonial authorities want to settle the nomadic Misseriya tribe in Upper Nile, far away from their traditional lands in Kordofan? The conflict between the authorities and the people of Watajwok that prompted the colonial wrath and punitive actions must relate to Chollo animal husbandry, which is shrouded in myths and metaphysical beliefs about cattle and traditions surrounding the use of their by-products. The Chollo people keep small herds, and the manner in which they care for their livestock speaks to the importance they attach to their cattle. For instance, they don't allow adolescents, neither boys nor girls, to drink milk. In the same vein, they wouldn't offer milk to strangers:

they believe that giving milk to unknown people could affect the health and fertility of the cows.

Malakal, a Turkish distortion of Makal, the Chollo village located north of today's airport. Makal was founded by Diwad wa Ochollo; it connotes a temporary abode suggesting Chollo spirituality. As a colonial settlement, it was first situated in the Turkish fort of Tufakiyia, about eight kilometres to the south. The pacification of large parts of Upper Nile provinces to include Nuer, Dinka and Murle areas necessitated the transfer and relocation of the provincial capital from Kodok to Malakal. Apart from being an administrative centre, it was a place of settlement for former slaves who were emancipated after the defeat of the Mahdist state and who had become used to urban life. The need for a constant supply of milk for the town dwellers forced the decision to import and settle Misseriya Arabs in Watajwok village. When Chollo people resisted accepting the Arabs, the colonial authorities burned down the hamlets, forcing the Chollo people back to the west bank or to the banks of the Sobat River.

But the people's resistance continued: every time the police burned down the houses, they would come back and erect new ones. A settlement was later made with Paramount Chief Yieljak that restricted the Arab pastoralists to a small northern part of the floodplain and separated by a barbed-wire fence, leaving the larger southern part to the cattle of Watajwok. By the time I had come of age, rearing my sheep and goats on the floodplain, the barbed wire fence was gone. Relations between the Chollo people and the Misseriya Arabs had become cordial and, indeed, Misseriya pastoralists regularly came to the area during the winter (December to May or June) for pasture and water.

I spent most of my early childhood life in our hamlet of Watajwok village. The only time I was absent was when my father decided to take me to Kwogo village to stay for a short period with my sister Piero. Our hamlet, pa-Ajak, lies almost in the middle of the stretch of villages on the dirt road between Malakal and Dolieb

Hill. The road to Dolieb is passable only during the dry season, between December and June. By the beginning of December, the villagers were forced to clear the grass and level all the spots with free labour.

The vehicles plying this route to Dolieb Hill, and further south to Ayod, Duk, Bor, and Juba, were a kind of attraction for the children. When the village children heard the sound of an approaching car they would run to the roadside to wave at the vehicle. Sometimes this exercise proved fatal. A child in the hamlet next to ours, oblivious of the danger, ran towards a speeding car. He was lucky because the driver managed to quickly apply the brakes, sparing his life. More often, if an elder was present in the hamlet, he or she would see to it that no child played carelessly on the road. The rainy season brought respite as the government stopped road transportation and shifted to river transport. The road became our playground by day and a place to dance during the moon-filled nights.

The first thing my mother did every morning was to warn me against running towards an approaching car lest it crush me. The repeated warnings against engaging in what others did, sometimes with threats that I would be lashed, instilled a fear that bottled up in me and prevented me from socialising with my peers. In the early evening, when other children went to play and dance, I would be forced into the house to sleep. As a result, not only did I miss many childhood entertainments, but I started to loathe them. When it was hot, I would sit alone under the neem tree in front of hamlet. One day, in the mid-afternoon, I was sitting in my usual place. The air was still and it was really hot. One could see a mirage very close to the hamlet. In spite of the noise the chickens made, I dozed off in the small shade of our hut until I was abruptly woken up by the noise of a passing car. I stood up to run to the safe spot from which we usually watched passing vehicles when all of a sudden everything turned dark.

I laid in hospital bed unconscious and for the next five days. When I was able to talk, my mother told me I had had an accident.

But I had not been struck by a vehicle. In my panic, I had tripped on one of the pegs for our livestock. When I fell, I hit my head on another of the pegs, breaking my skull. Instead of rushing me to the hospital about six kilometres away in Malakal to get emergency attention, my father went to Makal village, further north, to look for a traditional skull surgeon. He was well known in the area for saving people who had fractured their skulls. The Chollo are fond of stick duels and other violent conflicts as a means of resolving their differences. Wad Odan, as he was known, inherited this trade from his father, and was quite skilled in resetting fractured skull bones using simple implements. Relatives would take the victim first to Wad Odan, and only after his "operation" would they then take him or her to the hospital in Malakal for treatment. My father did just that.

Probably because I had been comatose, I could not feel the pain of the operation on my head, carried out without the service of anaesthesia. It was only on the third day after the accident that I was taken to the hospital in Malakal, where paramedics worked on my head. The sharp sting of iodine applied all over my head caused me to sneeze and show signs of life. This was to the delight of my father, mother, and all the relatives who accompanied me to the hospital and were waiting outside the theatre. I had survived the terrible accident. I stayed for a week in the hospital and was discharged to go back to the village.

The Chollo people seldom ignore such grave accidents and don't count them as bad luck or anything of the sort. But they must at least consult a sorcerer who will in a clever way attribute the accident to something mysterious, ostensibly to demonstrate his spiritual powers. I use the word "clever" because the sorcerers invariably gather intelligence and out of that information come to their conclusion. My father went to consult the local sorcerer, whose guess was that the restless spirit of my elder sibling who had died shortly after birth must have caused the fatal accident. My father slaughtered a ram in sacrifice and paid the sorcerer a goat for his services. Three months after my discharge from the hospital, Wad Odan came to visit me. He examined my head without any sedation and it was another painful experience. Even crying would not stop the pain. He told my father that my skull had healed, but warned that the skin on my head was very thin and I should be very careful to avoid being hit on the head. Because of this, I was no longer allowed to play with my peers.

For most of the time, I kept a distance from where my peers played or trained with stick fights, for fear that I might accidentally be hit on the head. It was customary that a Chollo male must learn those skills for defence purposes. To enforce the sorcerer's advice, my father decided that I should be taken to stay with my sister in Kwogo village. It was one of the constituent hamlets of Watajwok on the west bank of the White Nile River, directly opposite Malakal town. A large floodplain separated the village from the White Nile, but it was possible from Kwogo to see the trees and buildings of Malakal, especially the colourful lights in the town by night. The day when I was to leave our hamlet, I could hear my parents arguing. My mother did not countenance of the idea of me going to Kwogo but my father was adamant and carried me off on his shoulders.

Still young and naïve, I could not quite differentiate the difference between pa-Ajak and pa-Ajamaiker in Kwogo. As somebody new in the village, I was confined to my sister's house. This was partly because I had not acquainted myself with the village children and partly to keep a distance from others until my head healed properly lest I ran into another accident. After a few days, I learned that the next village, pa-Yowin, was the village of my Great-aunt Nyangong Ajak, the stepsister of my grandfather, Tor Ajak. I started to frequent her house, and she also became fond of me.

She liked answering my questions about our clan. Of course, she was excited that I knew about not only my father but the father of my father, and the relations between her and my grandfather. She couldn't believe it when I counted my lineage up to Nyadway, which became the talk of the village. I could not say how I had pieced it together, or who had been of assistance in the process. Perhaps, I got it from different sources, for I had many relatives who had married in Kwogo. It is possible that I gathered the information from them. It fascinated my sister and her husband that I could recite my clan lineage at such a tender age. They thought I must have been possessed by some spirits and had become a medium. They sent a message to my father.

The ability to know my clan lineage was an excuse for those who wanted to tease me or test my brain, asking me aggressive and provocative questions, some of them completely unrelated to my clan knowledge. Inadvertently, some of those questions did improve my arithmetic skills of adding and subtracting. I tried to avoid my peers as I attached myself to the elders, listening attentively to their conversations to extract any information of interest. I would run errands for them, doing it as quickly as possible, to come back before some important facts had been spoken. Hamlet elders usually liked children who accepted to run errands for them, especially fetching items from their homes or elsewhere. They didn't like the noisy or recalcitrant kids.

One day I ran into another tall and skinny boy. It was as if we already knew that we were blood relatives. Samuel Otieno, as he later became known, was my cousin, the son of my aunt, Jwodho nya Ajalwong. We grew up to be close friends and, indeed, some who saw Otieno and I walking together thought we were twins for we looked alike in terms of our physique and appearance. He was my companion throughout the time I spent in Kwogo and sometimes helped deal with a bully from an adjacent hamlet.

My father was following my growth and physical and psychological development in Kwogo and wanted me to remain there until the time it was appropriate to bring me back to Watajwok. My brother-in-law, Ogawi, worked for a Greek merchant in Malakal. That was the time when the Greeks and Arab merchants controlled economic life in Malakal. Besides retailing merchandise, this Greek owned a small bottling industry that produced carbonated soft drinks. My brother-in-law ran this Pepsi-Cola plant, and sometimes he came home with one or two bottles of Pepsi-Cola, which gave us a funny feeling after drinking it.

Time went by and I was beginning to like the life in Kwogo, especially the consumer items my brother-in-law brought for us from the Greek's shop. My nephew, Arop Ogawi, was growing and became a friend. Together we enjoyed the things from town like bread, pancakes, dates and groundnuts, cheese, Pepsi-Cola and others, which his father brought for us from time to time. One day my father came to visit us. When the two of us remained in the room, in what appeared like an interview, he asked me if I knew who he was. I told him he was my father. "What is my name?" he asked, and I said Nyaba. "What is my father's name?" I told him that his father's name was Tor wad Ajak wad Lathnyal wad Kwickwajo wad Dyel Gwoth wad Nyadway wad Tugo. I was about to add "wad Dhakoth" to the list of ancestors but stopped when I saw tears running down my father's cheeks. I was shocked. My first thought was that I had said something which my father did not like. But if that had been the case, he would have lashed me, as the elders often do. I failed to understand this attitude, which contrasted with that of Great-aunt Nyangong, who enjoyed reciting the names of her clan. I asked my father what the matter was but he would not reply. I got frightened and ran out of the room, leaving him alone.

That evening my father did not return to Watajwok. He spent the night in the house of Deng wad Nyangong, who was his second cousin. By tradition, my father could sleep in his daughter's house only if there was no alternative accommodation in the neighbourhood. In the morning my father went to another village and came back with a man I came to know later was a sorcerer. They summoned me to a tree they were sitting under. I wanted to sit down, but they directed me to stand. They then placed a slightly loose steel ring around my right ankle, ostensibly to deflect evil spirits. My father had made up his mind to take me back to Watajwok. It must have been a Sunday, because my brother-in-law had not gone to work that morning.

Before the day had begun to warm up, my father and I hit the road to Watajwok. It about an hour's walk because I could not walk as fast as he did. My father usually took just fifteen minutes to walk from Watajwok to Kwogo. We found someone with a canoe to take us to the east bank, leaving us to wade through the two-ki-lometre-wide floodplain between our village and the White Nile River. It must have been four years since I had been taken to Kwogo. Everything was completely different and only with difficulty did I remember the people I had known before I left the hamlet. My mother was so excited when she saw me. She welcomed me with tears of joy in her eyes. The family and village elders came around and in short time they performed Chollo prayers of welcome, with my Great-aunt Ayileew leading the rituals.

Returning to my hamlet in Watajwok was a kind of relief from the detestable bullying of a certain Olwak who resided in the next village. He was shorter, a little older than me, and had strong and developed muscles. I developed a psychological fear of this boy. If there was anything I feared or hated in Kwogo, it was the sight of this cruel brute. No number of complaints against him would bring me any sympathy and support from my sister or her husband, who thought I should pull myself up and just beat him. Of course, in Chollo villages, bullying among boys, as long there is no marked age difference, was tolerated as a means of encouraging valour and courage. One was expected to prove oneself by demonstrating courage and perseverance against an adversary.

After a few days I became used to pa-Ajak hamlet and found myself in good company. There were four of us who were around the same age: Olir Olwangi Ajak, Gwang Nyikango Ajak, Bol Ding Ajak, and myself. Those three boys were fraternal uncles to me. They were my father's first cousins, but that was inconse-quential as we grew up together as equals. As I was now around eight years of age, my father was obliged to find a stick for me that befitted my height and weight. It was an age when one was expected to learn village life and practices. This included caring for goats, sheep, and calves. One learned where the animals were tethered, and their particular pegs and ropes. One also learned to recognise and differentiate the wild fruits. The stick could be used to dig out wild sweet carrots (*yienho*), or in self-defence to protect one's head in case a peer attacked, and when playing Chollo polo (*akwardigo*), either amongst ourselves or in competition with boys from neighbouring hamlets or distant villages. I enjoyed rearing our goats and sheep, which we did in the floodplain (*agu*) or high grassland ridge (*odur*) east of the line of hamlets. The idea was to prevent the livestock from sneaking into gardens to graze on crops. This was done in turns. Sometimes out of negligence the animals destroyed crops, and that afternoon we all would be punished. My experience was that goats, more than sheep, were usually notorious and liked eating corn and sorghum leaves, and other vegetables in the fields.

It was in the autumn of 1953, in October, just before the beginning of winter, when my father brought me home to Watajwok. The gardens close to the hamlets had already been harvested and so the animals were free to roam about. There was not much work to look after them. One day I saw a strange man arrive in the hamlet. My father welcomed him warmly and took him to a hut in my stepmother's compound. They took some time, I believe they were enjoying sorghum beer (*athabobo*), before my father called for me, saying, "This is *jal-pwonyo* [teacher] Adiang" He was the teacher at the Watajwok Bush School, one of the satellite bush schools the American Presbyterian Mission established in some selected villages. I saw the teacher nod his head, as though in approval that I could be accepted to his school. The bush school was in pan- Amujo, a series of hamlets on the ridge separating the main floodplain (*tor*) from *agur*. It is worth explaining the meaning of *agur*, the small floodplain that separates pan-Amujo from pa- Maan. Local people still spoke about the flood that covered (*nyayo*) the plain with Nile perch (*gur*) in the year Ajak wad Lathnyal passed on. The people of Watajwok believed that this very rare occurrence (*nyayi gur*) was Ajak's blessings to the people of Watajwok.

I look back on those days with nostalgia, sometimes in amazement, that although it was a life of extreme difficulties, the village was a traditional school of life. I am amazed that after nearly seven decades of statehood, Sudanese people in the south, east, west, and centre are still living this primitive and often unproductive rural life. During my childhood there was little to celebrate. I lived at the mercy of nature, especially when I slept on an empty stomach. I could have died like my elder sibling. The women and girls carried the brunt of this difficult life. They fetched water from the river, about three kilometres away from the hamlet. When they returned, they had to pound and grind the sorghum beans into a paste from which they made food for morning and evening meals.

During the rainy season, nature provided plenty in terms of wild and cultivated green vegetables like *achwobo, anywoch, ad l-par, odhunyo*, and *athidho*, prepared either with fresh or dried meat or fish. It was difficult to get fish because Chollo environmental conservation practices prohibited fishing during the spawning period. My mother later used to tell me that as a child I did not like green vegetables at all, and that every time I came back from looking after the animals, the first thing I did was to rush to the cooking place and open the cooking pot to see what was being cooked. If it was neither meat nor fish, I would run away crying or refuse to tie down the animals. If I found meat or fish on the fire, I would be happy and quickly tie down the animals. In order to satisfy my appetite for *gi kayo*, my mother sometimes collected firewood to sell in Malakal, and this enabled us to have beef or fish in our meals. It was because of this that my nickname in pa-Ajak hamlet was *Nyaringo*, meaning "piece of meat."

In order to assist my mother, I would join others who went to make grass mats. I learned the art of mat-making, and indeed was able to produce one or two a day, which my mother would sell in Kal-Liir, the Misseriya Arab camp on the way to Malakal. Through this, I ensured that we had beef, mutton, or fish at least three times a week. I am sure if it were today, this would be counted as child labour or child abuse. In fact, the concept of child labour does not exist in Chollo villages as long as it is not linked to capitalist extraction, expropriation, or profiteering. In the rural environment in which we grew up, all labour at the family level was a contribution to the common good. I think of this as training and preparing one for future responsibilities.

In a polygamous family, the mother tries her best to take care of her children in every aspect. My mother, nya-Achonglith, was a hard-working woman. She would do anything to put food on the table for us. That was how I decided to make woven mats, to save her going to fetch firewood in the forest. One day she hurt her foot while trying to chop wood; the axe landed on her foot, almost severing two toes. She had to be rushed to the hospital in Malakal. It was a sad day for all of us children: Ciro was the eldest, Otuk followed me, and Nyadhok followed Otuk. Later on, Oboch (a boy) and Nyagaak (a girl) were added. By 1984, however, only Ciro and I were still alive. All of the others had died of natural causes. My brother Otuk did not go to a formal school. I remember how adamant my mother was that he should remain in the hamlet to help her, since she considered me a lost person. Later, while living in Khartoum and working for a plastics company, Otuk managed to enrol in evening classes and passed the Sudan School Certificate Examination in 1982.

The life in the village was one of perpetual agony and inconvenience, particularly due to the inability to bridge the gap of inequality, or to reciprocate injustice in a manner that would prevent aggression from my peers. I also saw this injustice in the way my mother laboured in her garden while my stepmother basked in the comforts of the village. Those situations of injustice tormented me psychologically and left me feeling miserable for most of the time.

The other thing I really detested in the village life was the lack of solidarity at the family level. Individuals minded their own business when it came to gross violations, as in domestic violence, and there was never an opportunity for retribution, unlike life in the urban centres where legal counsel existed. The man was ever-powerful. He could beat his wife or wives at will and no one would intervene. It sometimes resulted in murder, which could have been prevented. In the hamlet, what I observed and appreciated was when the eldest or head of the clan would supervise all the homesteads to ensure that all the children were fed. He saw to it that each household had a lit fire, and if none were present, he would mobilise other homesteads to contribute to the home that was in need.

The wars and conflicts over the last forty years have completely destabilised Chollo rural areas. People have been displaced to distant places in the Sudan, Equatoria, and even to Uganda and Kenya, and further afield to Australia, the United States, and Europe. I am not sure they will ever come back. If they did return, they could contribute to the change of the indigenous Chollo life-style. They would come back with new ideas and technology that could contribute to social economic and cultural development.

Chapter 2

Going to School

The Danger of Touching a White Woman

The time must have been around the Christmas season, or a little before it, in the year 1953. My father had just brought me back to the hamlet. It was an eventful time in Watajwok village. A new *bány* (commander), Akoch Awakier, had been approved by the elders, and the ceremony for his installation was to take place, including formation of a *ngoli kál* (a village army, militia, or vigilante group). Each of the fifteen Chollo provinces (*podh*), or a group of them, from time to time establish what may be categorised as an army (*kál*) over which the *bány* commands, as in regular armies. More often than not, the reigning Rath form his own and his known as *kál Rath* literally King's men. Rath Dak Padiet (1945–1952) had a *kál* called Myem (meaning "sticky mud"), while Rath Ayang (1974–1992) called his *kál* Chwom. Akoch

Awakier named his *kál Ngu* (lion) for Watajwok village, including people living in hamlets on the Sobat River. The *kál* included all the initiates, young adults, and some elders who might have missed the *kál* before *Ngu*.

In the Chollo tradition, the times of *ngoli kál* are references remembered in lieu of calendar points. The *bány* stands out as someone who is physically competent and a great sorcerer in the village. He must have defeated all those who competed for the position. It is worth mentioning that once a boy has been initiated into adulthood, he automatically becomes a potential soldier in the village army (*yáy podh*) or the king's army (*yáy Rádh*). The ceremonies of *ngoli Ngu* coincided with an event that also became part of the ceremonies. Three wild elephants had strayed into Watajwok area. This event counted as good luck for *Bány* Akoch Awakier, and exalted his image as a great oracle or sorcerer who was revered far and wide in the Chollo Kingdom. The youth of *kal Ngu* landed with their spears on the three elephants, killing them. This was well received in Watajwok and the neighbouring villages of Obwaa and Dhothim, but not so much by the British colonial authorities in Malakal, although no one was reprimanded or punished.

The beginning of *wudo*, when the cold dry northerly winds blow freely over the land, chilling everything in its path, was the time when Chollo hamlets erected windshields (*ayiæg*) to protect the animals and the young boys who tended them in the morning from the cold wind. It was also the time immediately after the harvesting of crops grown close to the villages, when the monotonous task of protecting crops from goats and sheep had been left behind, and every boy and adolescent in the hamlet had time for leisure. The village boys had only the task of cleaning the byres and tying the goats and sheep in the evening. There was enough time to do nothing except play. In Kwogo, that would be the time when we went fishing for mud fish left behind by the receding floodwaters. Sometimes we engaged in the dangerous game of hunting for bush rats in the grass.

Since my return to the hamlet, my father had been constantly speaking with me about education. He would tell me how people who had gone to school became important individuals in society, including the local schoolteacher and some of his acquaintances who were working as government officials in Malakal. He encouraged me to go to the bush school in pan-Amujo. I was to learn later that the bush school in Watajwok constituted one of the education catchment areas for the American Mission-run Dolieb Hill Elementary School. The decision to have satellite bush schools must have been driven by economic considerations. The British southern policy gave the Christian missionaries, whose primary objective was Christian proselytisation, a monopoly over education and the school system. The American Presbyterian Mission perhaps wanted to throw its net far and wide, which would best be served by a satellite system of bush schools. It reduced the economic cost of running such a system by allowing the children to first learn in their villages, then travel to Dolieb Hill to attend class three and four.

The bush school was, therefore, a preparatory institution to introduce the children to basic arithmetic and vernacular Christian scriptures while remaining in their villages. This cost the Mission absolutely nothing save the little salary or incentive paid to the bush schoolteacher. This system did not completely remove the children from the traditional village mores, like raising animals and respecting social and cultural obligations. This was also appropriate for parents who did not want their children to go far from the village. The Chollo have the practice of revenge, with violent acts carried out on extended kin to avenge an earlier attack. Children could easily become the victims of revenge as they passed through the territory of hostile hamlets on the way to or from the school at Dolieb Hill.

My father wanted me by all means to become a modern, educated person. I can vouch, he would have risked sending me even if the school was in a distant place. Now that the school was nearby in pan-Amujo, it was even better for him. I could at the same time take care of our animals. He saw to it that I never missed going to pan-Amujo, although I informed him that I had not been admitted into the class. I believe that must have informed his decision to relocate to pa-Adung wa Kur-Nyal, only a few metres from the school, building a hut there for my mother and her children. This was to make it easier for me during the rainy season. To go to the bush school from Pa-Ajak we had to wade through the waters of *agur*, which was more than three hundred metres wide and half a metre-deep. During the rains and as the perennial floods invaded the area, the *agur* would become a metre or more deep in some parts. At this time of the year, it was very uncomfortable to cross the *agur* early in the morning, when the northernly winds had chilled its waters. As children, we went about without clothes.

By late 1953, the Anglo–Egyptian Sudan was on its way to self-government, a prelude to independence. The American Mission must have been aware of the political developments and therefore had to adjust their policies. In this context, they decided to close the satellite bush schools in Watajwok, Anagdiar, Ogot-Konam, and Nyijwado in Tonga by the end of 1953, leaving only those in Palo, Pathworo, Adhidhiang, and pa-Naam in Pajur. No children would again be admitted to those bush schools. The class at Watajwok School, already filled with adolescents, would be last batch of pupils. The schoolteacher, Jal-pwonyo Obedayo Adiang Akujok, must not have known about the planned closure of his school when he promised my father that I would be taken in to learn. Thus, since my father did not know the situation in regard to the bush school, he pushed the idea that I should continue going to the school in pan-Amujo, even though I was not allowed to enter the class.

At first, I found walking alone to the bush school very scary. The grass towered over my skinny body, making it difficult sometimes to find my way, and this conjured all kinds of images of dangerous animals attacking or eating me. So, I decided I would go in the company of adolescent boys from pa-Lwal, our neighbouring hamlet. From that hamlet came Obyeny Jago, Opaki Thanyjok, and Ogwok Lith, while Aywok Nyikwech came from pa-Akolakany. They were older than me and were already enrolled in the bush school. It meant leaving my hamlet early in order to catch up with them and walk together to pan-Amujo. The bush school was a single round room in a mud-walled, grass-roofed building. The room also served as the office of Jal-pwonyo Obedayo Adiang. It had been built by the village community.

In this American education system, there were no first- or second-year classes at Dolieb Hill Elementary School; there were only third- and fourth-year classes. This meant that those who passed from the third year in the bush school went to join the third year in Dolieb. In this way, a pupil spent at least five to six years at the primary level before moving to the next level, intermediate school. This American system was completely different from the systems in the Catholic and the Anglican mission-controlled areas in Malek, Mundri, Rumbek, Detwok, and Tonga, which did not have satellite bush schools.

The bush school system was configured in such a way that the village (bush) school system was managed by what were called "slate" teachers. The slate teachers were individuals who had failed to pass to Class Six in the Obel (Protestant) or Owechi (Catholic) primary schools. They were not qualified to work as clerks, police, or nurses in hospitals, or to train as teachers in one of the teachers' training institutes to become "approved" teachers. Being a slate teacher, therefore, was a kind of insecure employment, which the missionaries exploited for the purpose of proselytisation and propagation of the Christian faith. This explained the exponential emphasis in the bush school on Christian scriptures and the blind belief in them.

The bush school in Watajwok had no desks or chairs for the pupils. They sat on the ground and wrote on their laps. Since it was a one-roomed building, they learned or were taught in batches by the same teacher. When the third-class pupils were inside learning, the rest would be playing outside. Only the third-class pupils had exercise books and pencils. For the rest, the learning was basically oral and the subjects were vernacular Chollo, Christian scriptures, and arithmetic. As I was not enrolled in the school and indeed it was too late to enrol, I was not permitted to enter when the first- and second-year pupils were called into the class. I was left outside, although we had come together from the hamlets. I would sit outside, beside the window, and listen attentively to what was being taught. The Bible stories were so fascinating that I developed a keen interest in always being there to listen. It did not bother me that I was not a bona fide pupil and I continued going to school, braving the chilly waters of *agur*, to the delight of my father.

One day something spectacular occurred to interrupt my daily routine of going to school together with the other pupils. When I reached pa-Lwal, I did not find the older boys. They had left for school earlier without warning me. When I asked Angar Jago, Obyeny's younger sister, she informed me that her brother had told her that a certain white woman was coming to school. My heart sank and I was so discouraged that I almost went back to my hamlet. What would my father say if I did not go? Maybe I would end up being lashed, I said to myself. The thought of being beaten scared me so much that I decided to run to school, forgetting about the cold water I waded through.

The pupils were seated in groups under the mahogany tree outside the class-cum-teacher's office. Through the window where I always sat, I saw a white woman sitting at the teacher's desk. It was my first time ever to see a white person. Without knowing what I was doing, I found myself touching her hairy hands and body. Then suddenly, without warning, Jal-pwonyo Adyang hit me so hard in the face that I fell down under the desk in serious pains and began crying loudly. I had never been treated like this before so I thought the teacher was really cruel.

Miss Dorothy Rankins, for this was her name, pulled me up from under the table and spoke to me in the Chollo language.

"Sorry. Don't cry," she said. From her bag she took out something unwrapped the plastic and gave it to me, with the word "eat". It was sweet and this made me smile. I could see that Jal-pwonyo Adyang was furious and wanted me out of the room but Miss Rankins restrained him. She was happy when I started smiling and could speak clearly again. "What is your name?" she asked. Adwok wad Nyaba, I replied. "What do you want?" she asked. I told her I wanted to know how to read and to write. Then came another question, "Do you know the scriptures?" to which I responded in the affirmative. She asked me to recite the Lord's Prayer and the Apostle's Creed, which I did without difficulty. I had memorised them while sitting outside the class. Then she turned to ask Jal-pwonyo Adyang, "What do you think would be the age of this boy?" About eight years old said the teacher. Then she turned to me and said, "You will next year go to school in Dolieb Hill. I will come to pick all of you in April." And then she told me to go out.

I had never realised how dangerous it was to touch a white woman. Still hurting from Jal-pwonyo Adiang's murderous slap, I emerged from the classroom to a jeering crowd of pupils. They had no sympathy for me. They only considered that I had imposed myself after only recently appearing at the school. Nevertheless, I felt a sense of gratitude to Miss Rankins as I was still enjoying the sweetness of the Carmella sweet, she had given me. It really quenched my anguish and resentment towards the teacher who had struck me.

I later learned that Miss Rankins had come to the bush school in Watajwok for two reasons: to conduct exams for the third-year pupils and to select a certain number of pupils who would join the first year at Dolieb Hill when the schools opened in April 1954. It confirmed that the American missionary system of satellite bush schools was being changed, and the school in Dolieb henceforth would admit pupils directly from the villages whose bush schools had been closed. I was to be one of the first-year pupils.

I came home to inform my father about my ordeal with

Jal-pwonyo Adyang, how he had cruelly slapped me for touching the white woman, the questions the white women asked me, and how I had answered those questions. Then I told him that the white woman promised to come back to take me and others to school in Dolieb Hill. He was happy that I had made it, but made no comment about the slap I had received from his friend, Jal-pwonyo Adyang. It was as if he was telling me that there was nothing, he could do about it and, after all, I had been accepted and would be going to school. My father was not concerned about the slap I had received from the teacher. Perhaps he believed it was part of disciplining a child.

However, it took me a while before I could forget about it. In reflecting about the attitude Jal-pwonyo Adiang had demonstrated that morning, I concluded that the teacher must have feared that my behaviour with the white woman could cost him his job as a teacher. This explains the force with which he reacted, with a slap that could have killed me. Anyway, the opportunity of being accepted to school outweighed the blow received for touching a white woman. Thirty-six years later, in September 1989, I and my family met Dorothy Rankins in Addis Ababa, Ethiopia. She looked at me with astonishment as I related in detail this long-ago episode.

As the American missionary promised in December, on the first day of April 1954, a vehicle arrived in the bush school compound to pick up those pupils who had passed the examination and been accepted to Dolieb Hill Elementary School. Once Miss Rankins had finished boarding them, she turned to pick seven others. She first looked around to locate me, and directed me to the car. When all were on board, the vehicle took off, leaving the unlucky ones behind, some of whom had picked grudges against me. It was a promise made good.

Dolieb Hill was a distance away and I was glad that we did not have to walk through the villages. The missionaries had experience with pupils from Konam (Chollo villages along the Sobat River). Unless a vehicle went to pick them up, they would not come to school, and indeed many of them prematurely terminated their schooling. I vividly remember our arrival. It was a Saturday and that night we slept on empty stomachs and the next day had to depend on dried food we had brought from home. The cooks, girls drawn from the surrounding villages, would only come to prepare food for us on Monday. On our second day in Dolieb Hill, the school overseer, Abba Nyawet, punished us for breaking the biblical law forbidding labour on Sunday, simply because we had gone to clear a piece of land in a nearby thicket, which we intended for a garden to cultivate maize. Those difficult times have remained embedded in my memory.

The American Presbyterian Mission opened the Dolieb Hill Mission in 1902 to proselytise the Chollo people and make them Christians. The school must have opened much later because the story goes that it took the Americans fourteen years before they baptised the first Chollo convert. The missionaries managed both the boys' and girls' schools. By 1954, the Anglo–Egyptian Sudan was moving towards self-government; it was understood that the schools would be handed over to the Sudan government. Thus, although both were boarding schools, the missionaries maintained a Chollo environment in terms of schoolteachers, workers, cooks, and cuisine. The dress for the first- and second-year pupils was the Chollo *lawo*. The school served only two meals, perhaps to not alienate us too much from our home environment. Acwil Lwal Jok and Dorothy Rankins were the respective headteachers. After the episode at Watajwok Bush School, I never spoke with Miss Rankins again and only saw her on Sundays when we all attended a single church service.

The classes started in earnest. We were issued with slate plates and pencils and spent four to five weeks learning to read what we had scribbled on the slate. Of the thirty-five pupils in the class, and indeed in the whole school, five of us — Gwang Akich, Tipo Ajwet, Otor Kwathkier, Amum Othow, and I — were the youngest. The school was about acquiring knowledge, learning the art of writing and reading, sports, and personal hygiene. At Dolieb Hill, as part of school activities, they made us continue such village pursuits as making handicrafts like mats and hats. In the first year, life evolved into a perfunctory routine, organised in such a mechanical manner that we soon became used to it. There was no piped water so on waking we hurried to the banks of Sobat River to wash ourselves before the bell rang for the school parade. We did not have the luxury of taking tea, and breakfast was served only after the first two lessons in the morning. At that time there was neither flag raising nor a national anthem to sing in the missionary schools. I am not sure if there was a tradition of raising the condominium or British or Egyptian flags at the school.

After breakfast we would return to the class until about noon. After about fifteen minutes of rest, the final lesson ended around one o'clock. There was no lunch served so after the classes the pupils went straight to the so-called "schoolwork," which was separate from "classwork" and "homework". The schoolwork included manual labour ordered by the headteacher. This lasted for an hour and was undertaken immediately after class. After the schoolwork we played football, volleyball, and American baseball. On Sundays we visited relatives in the surrounding villages of Palo, Pathworo, Paju, and Adhidhiang on the southern banks of Sobat River. The school year ended about the second week of December and we were then sent home for a three-month holiday.

While in Dolieb Hill Elementary School, I remember events and episodes that had a historical impact on the social, economic, and political development in the Sudan and on the people of South Sudan in particular. In April 1955, we were promoted to second class or class two as they would then say. We had just come back from the mid-term holidays in August when the headmaster announced that the school was again closing for an indefinite period. I was too young to understand what had happened.

The story ran that the first company of the Equatoria Corps of the Sudan Defence Force (SDF) had mutinied in Torit on 18 August.

The "disturbances" as they were officially called, spread quickly through Equatoria and parts of Bahr el Ghazal provinces. Two days later there was a shooting in Malakal in which some people were killed. It explained why some Equatorians, mostly civilians and families of former soldiers and police, walked through the school on their way southwards while we were still at Dolieb Hill.

The gravity of the *"southern disturbances"* could be gleaned from the reaction of the Azhari's government and the British colonial administration, which still effectively had sovereignty over the Sudan. It utilised all means of the government's propaganda machinery to discredit the mutineers. The government flew a plane low over villages in the Chollo Kingdom, broadcasting on a loudspeaker the voice of Rath Kur Papiti Yor Akoch appealing for peace and calm. Rath Kur asked the Chollo people to not join the rebellion because he wanted the people and their livestock to reproduce and increase in number. I was on the ground in our hamlet in pan-Amujo when the plane passed overhead, repeating the message over the loudspeakers. It was dramatic watching the elders bow their head in reverence, as though Rath Kur himself was in the plane. It was the first time that a Chollo sovereign had addressed his subjects from a government platform.

It was a really long holiday, from August 1955 until April 1956. My parents had shifted villages and we now domiciled in pa-Adung in pan-Amujo. This was the village of Bol Adung, who was my elder, a senior at the school, and acted as my guardian at the school. A relative of ours, Obur Ador Nyawello, came one day to visit my parents. He hailed from the Watajwok hamlet, on the west bank of the White Nile River. I don't know what he discussed with my father but I was soon called and ordered to sit down. Someone caught my head and Obur began cutting the Chollo traditional facial markings. I protested and shouted, but to no avail. In a matter of three minutes my forehead was bleeding. I never liked Obur again, until the time of my initiation into adulthood, in 1963, when I stayed at his homestead.

As time went by, I could feel myself growing up and developing my muscles and bones. I started to engage in some manual work, weaving reed mats and looking after the sheep and goats, jobs that all the village boys undertook. I wove mats, some of which went to fencing our homestead, while my mother carried others off to be sold in Malakal. My cousin, Amos Ajak Adung, who had only completed Class Four at Dolieb Hill School, was now working with the government dairy farm in Malakal. On a visit to the hamlet, he advised my father to buy me some books to read so I wouldn't forget what I had learned in the school. So, one morning we took the two-hour journey to the American Bookshop in Malakal. The shop was full of books. I was mesmerised, so much so that I could not decide which book I wanted. My knowledge of the English language was still not to the extent of reading titles I had not seen before. Shyly, I asked if there were any books in the Chollo language.

The shop attendant brought the two books: one had a yellow cover and pictures, *The Story of Joseph*, part of a series of Bible stories; the other had a red cover, *Rath Nyadway*, and offered stories of the Chollo king and the grandson of the founder Watajwok village. My father paid the money and we left for the village. When there was nothing to do I would sit under the tree, surrounded by the village folks who were captivated by these stories. They had not heard about Rath Nyadway testing local sorcerers. In the book, Rath Nyadway is seen tricking the sorcerers until one of them, hailing from a distant village, who otherwise could have been tipped off by a relative, found out that it was a pot of beans on fire. Rath Nyadway punished the other sorcerers, who failed the test. Published by the American Printing Press in Malakal, the story of Rath Nyadway resonated with the story of Prophet Elijah and the priests of Baal and attempted to discount African beliefs of witchcraft and sorcery.

The Watajwok hamlets, on the east bank of the White Nile, were on average three to four kilometres from the centre of Malakal town. In reality, that distance seemed like a billion light years, so different were the two places. Watajwok and Malakal did not communicate on the same frequency in terms of national events that took place in the town. On 1 January 1956, people in Malakal, like other towns in the Sudan, celebrated the independence of the country from the Anglo–Egyptian Condominium. Most people in Watajwok knew nothing of this and therefore were not part of the celebrations. None of the village elders, not even the chief, knew or was invited to attend the independence celebrations in the town. It was indeed a reflection of the socio-political divide between the urban and the rural parts of the country. It also reflected another reality: the town's government, security forces, and mercantile class—the *jellaba*—were dominated by northern Sudanese and the southern peasants were marginalised, excluded, and discriminated against.

In fact, ever since the colonial Closed District Ordinance which sealed, insulated, and isolated southern Sudan from the civilised world, Sudan has never been socially integrated. The two parts of the country were administered separately until 1946. Because of this, the nationalist movement for independence took root first in northern Sudan while it lagged in south. In fact, the southern disturbances, as mentioned above, can be attributed to the politics of disparity in the socioeconomic, political, and cultural development between northern and southern Sudan. It was in this context that South Sudanese continued the struggle until they attained their independence, or rather secession, from the Sudan in 2011. I have always preferred the use of "secession" to "independence" on account of historical continuity.

By the time the schools reopened in April 1956 throughout southern Sudan, the country seemed to have recovered from the August events. I don't remember how the information was relayed to us in Watajwok. We left the village on a Sunday afternoon and walked for four hours to Dolieb Hill. In the morning, the pupils were called to a parade in the compound in front of the school. The blue, yellow, and green tri-colour—the new flag of the Republic of the Sudan—flapped in the wind in front of the school, marking the new reality of Sudan's independence as the flag was a symbol of its sovereignty. A new teacher who had just graduated from the Maridi Teachers' Training Institute had been assigned to the school. He was quite fluent in the Arabic language, and therefore, sang the national anthem. The headteacher then welcomed us back from the long holiday. He announced that the government had decided to freeze the previous school year 1955, and that we would repeat the class. I am not sure whether the announcement by the headteacher meant anything to some of us. Our understanding of such issues was still at a rudimentary stage.

What did the independence of the Sudan really mean? In his announcement, the headteacher also said that the government was waiving the token fifteen piastres our parents paid annually as school fees. He failed, however, to explain that it was now universal free primary education. This mattered a great deal to our parents who each year had to sell a goat or ram to raise the fifteen piastres. Although the school was nationalised, some of the American missionaries remained at Dolieb Hill performing religious functions. But the school administration shifted into the hands of Sudanese. Other visible changes were that each pupil was issued with a bed; hitherto the pupils had slept on mats spread on the ground, and has provided school uniforms. This was a development. The cuisine also changed to become uniform throughout the same education level; hitherto we had been served the same food as in the Chollo villages.

The school syllabus now included, in addition to the English and Arabic languages, hygiene and arithmetic. Geography was also taught, which introduced us to ways and means of living in different parts of the Sudan. The quality of teachers improved as a new batch of primary schoolteachers replaced the missionary-approved teachers. The provincial education officer, a northern Sudanese based in Malakal, visited the school once, ostensibly to affirm the government's nationalisation of the schools and to oversee the transition from missionary education. At least once a month the provincial mobile cinema unit would pay a visit to entertain the pupils, schoolteachers, and their families. The films shown were by Sudanese producers and usually about the achievements of the national government.

For some of us, time had gone by without us hardly noticing. Suddenly we were in Class Four, marking the end of our stay at Dolieb Hill Elementary School. It was in early October 1958, a few weeks before the time of "general December", when pupils throughout the southern provinces sat for the Intermediate School Entrance Examination. The school administration announced that anyone who had not been baptised would not be allowed to sit the examination. In retrospect, I believe this must have been a trick by the missionaries still at the school. It must have been out of the assumption that all the students in the school were Christians. I still had on my ankle the steel ring put there by the sorcerer in Kwogo some five years before, and although I learned Christian scriptures in class and went to church every Sunday, I believed I needed my father's permission to convert to Christianity.

The announcement distressed me so much and filled me with worry about what would happen if I refused to be baptised. Did I have to go home to seek my father's permission? The village was far away and the school administration would not allow me to go. Baptism involved adopting a European name, preferably that of one of the apostles, to make one appear to be a good Christian. It also involved removing the steel ring on my ankle, signifying that I didn't believe in witchcraft and so forth. The issue of the steel ring was resolved when one of the teachers suggested that he would inform my father that the school regulation did not permit wearing such things, whether on the wrist or on the ankle.

Until that point in time, I had been known by the two names Adwok and Nyaba, being my father's and mine in reverse. After pressuring, arm-twisting, and blackmail, I agreed to be baptised but on the condition that I would retain my name as it was. On baptism day, set for 8 October, I still resisted taking on another name on account that my father would not accept it. William Adair, the American elder of the church, consulted with Elder Bwogo Kiir Akaiding, who dismissed my concerns and gave me the name Peter. Out of respect, for he was my aunt's husband, I consented and with others was baptised in the Sobat River, according to the tradition of American Presbyterian Church. Henceforth, I was known as Peter Adwok Nyaba. To my surprise, when I went home after completing my exams, everyone in my family happily called me Peter; they had not converted to Christianity yet welcomed the name as if I had achieved something in life adopting a Christian name.

The school would only close after the Intermediate Entrance Examinations. On the twelfth of December, a military scout Comer pulled up to the school at about seven o'clock in the morning. A southerner went up to the headteacher's office and we quickly learned he was Paulino Lado Waden, a teacher at Atar Intermediate School. He had come to supervise the examination. The church was the only building large enough to accommodate the candidates, allowing space between the students to avoid cheating. It was just half a day's exercise in which the candidates sat for English, Arabic, and arithmetic, after which the school administration released us to travel to our homes.

The independence of the Sudan was a matter of great interest to all Sudanese, and the headteacher in Dolieb Hill announced with pride in April 1956 that we (the Sudanese) were free from colonialism. Nevertheless, until we saw the military vehicle bring the invigilator to the school, we were not made aware of the change of government from civilian to military that had occurred. The military had overthrown the democratically elected government of Abdalla Bey Khalil on 17 November 1958. According to the popular narrative, the Umma Party had won the majority of seats in the parliamentary election of 1957, trouncing the National Unionist Party (NUP) of Sayed Ismail el Azahri. The NUP had dominated the first national government, and Azhari was the Sudanese who had lowered the Condominium flag and raised the Sudanese flag on the morning of 1 January 1956.

It later became clear that, afraid of losing a vote of no confidence in parliament, the Umma Party prime minister, Abdalla Bey Khalil, invited Gen. Ibrahim Abboud to take over power in the hope that Abboud would surrender it back after six months, once the political storm had subsided. It took the Sudanese people six years of relentless struggle, armed rebellion in the southern provinces, and strikes and civil disobedience by workers and students to overthrow the military in a popular uprising in October 1964, returning Sudan to liberal democratic governance.

That year, 1958, eight pupils from Watajwok village sat for the Intermediate Entrance Examination. We agreed that we would hit the road together to go back home as soon as we had finished the examination. In fact, there was no school property to be handed over and we wanted to arrive home before sunset. It was late for Adwok Bol to cross to the west. In the morning we conducted a small get together to celebrate the homecoming in the homestead of the elder among us, and after that we dispersed to our hamlets to wait for the results. We were now back to the usual village mores.

It was time for the animals and the boys to be sent to the cattle camp. It would perhaps be my last time to participate in the cattle camp. I was now about twelve years old. After initiation into adulthood, one would not again go to the cattle camp. My classmates—Obyeny, Aywok, and Opaki—had already been initiated and therefore would not join me in the cattle camp. Our camp was located on an island in the middle of the White Nile River. There was sufficient pasture and water for the cattle, and lots of milk and fish for us, some of which we took home to the elders and young children.

There were three of us in our camp: Olir, Bol, and myself. The camp itself was a territory where we pegged our sixteen cows and a small circular enclosure we built from weeds and grass. Inside this enclosure we daily lit a huge heap of cow dung to heat the enclosure as it was usually chilly at night. With time, the ash would cover the enclosure in a thick layer, making it comfortable to sleep on since we did not have mattresses or blankets in the camp. At the beginning of the cattle camp season it was difficult for me, but as time went on I became used to this rough life, where we had to cook our own food, run errands to the village to bring milk for children, and sometimes catch fish in the small streams on the island. Because going to the village involved crossing the White Nile and walking a distance of six kilometres, nobody would voluntarily undertake the journey. We had therefore to agree to alternate between ourselves. Thus, each of us went to the village every third day.

It was on one of those days, as I was returning to the cattle camp and somewhere before the Jonglei rice scheme, that I met one of the teachers from the girls' school at Dolieb Hill, Ustaz Timothy Aban Agany-Amon. I felt embarrassed that he had seen me naked; my whole body, including my head, was covered in red ash. I almost passed by him, pretending to have not seen him. But he knew the trick and called out loudly, using my nickname, "Ah, is it you, Nyaringo? You have gone back to the village?" "We are on leave, teacher," I told him politely and apologetically. I was ashamed that he had found me in such poor condition. He smiled and said, "Well, go and tell your father you have been accepted to Atar Intermediate School." I thanked the teacher, who was already a few metres away.

The day was growing late so there was no time to go back to the hamlet to inform my father and then come back to cross to the river. A certain lone hippo in the area became aggressive and attacked people from about six o'clock, as the sun set. To avoid being assaulted, we sometimes carried a large piece of burning wood, big enough to last half an hour, when we crossed after seven or eight in the evening. In the morning I told my peers what happened as I was returning from the village and that I needed to immediately convey the news to my father.

Although it was not my turn, they readily agreed and prepared all that needed to be taken home in terms of milk and fish for the families. I duly informed my father that I had passed the examination and been accepted to Atar Intermediate School. By this time, he knew that after Dolieb Hill there was something called intermediate, and something called secondary school after that. He did not want me to remain in the cattle camp. He instructed me to take supplies to the camp but that in the morning I should meet him in Dangershopi. I was now to spend the rest of my time before the school opened in Kwogo village, staying with my sister.

I failed to see the logic of uprooting me from the village life in Watajwok and sending me to another village life in Kwogo. This was what I told my father when I met him in Dangershopi, but he insisted I should go, saying that he had his reasons. We walked together to the town centre where he bought me a new *lawo* and a jumper. Kwogo village was not as it had been when I lived there as a boy. At the age of twelve, I had to tread carefully to observe the many Chollo traditions and customs. Having been to school was not an excuse for committing a misdemeanour.

Luckily enough, my cousins Owor and Tipo Ajwet, who had been my classmates at Dolieb, had come home on holiday. I believe this was the reason why my father wanted me to be in Kwogo, so I could link up with them once more and enjoy the life of enlightened boys. What my father did not know was that the two had not passed and would not be able to attend intermediate school, so our time together was filled with envy, jealousy, and quarrels.

Chapter 3

Atar Intermediate School

Atar is a Chollo name for the wide stagnant body of water connected to the White Nile River by a small stream. Chollo legend has it that Atar is a collection of waters that the main river, the White Nile, cannot keep and, therefore, does not qualify to be called a river or stream (*naam*). In the kingdom, apart from the a*tar* which separates the feuding Chollo villages of Nyiyar (to the north) and Pakwar (to the south), there is another *atar*, found north of Káldoro (Kodok). A third *atar* is found eight kilometres from Atar's confluence with the White Nile. This is where the Dinka hold their court. Added to the name *atar* is *ardieb*, being the tamarind tree, under which the Dinka convene for their annual courts. Atar Ardieb falls under the administrative jurisdiction of Fangak District.

Notwithstanding its historical totality as Chollo land, the area of Atar became the epicentre of a land dispute between the Chollo and the Padang Dinka, which escalated into a violent conflict in

1980s and thereafter. The Atar Intermediate School was eventually destroyed as a result of the competing claims and the civil war that spanned twenty-one years. However, for the records, it is imperative to write the story of Atar Intermediate School as an educational institution that helped raise the social awareness and political consciousness of southern Sudanese who studied and taught at the school.

Many of the teachers and students of Atar Intermediate School later became political leaders in the subnational, or regional, self-administered Southern Region, as well as the independent Republic of South Sudan. Of the teachers I knew in Atar between 1959 and 1962, Othwonh Dak Padiet became minister of state for local government (1975–76), deputy speaker of the People's National Assembly, and joined the High Executive Council (HEC) as minister of finance and planning (1981–83); Joshua Dei Wal became the commissioner of Upper Nile (1978); and Thomas Kume Khan was a minister in the HEC in 1980. Some former students of Atar Intermediate School, including the author, held positions in the government of the independent South Sudan.

In 1959, when I entered Atar Intermediate School, it was the only intermediate school in Upper Nile Province. It took pupils from the elementary schools of Abuong (Dinka), Akobo (Anywaa and Lou Nuer), Detwok (Chollo), Dolieb Hill (Chollo), Leer (Nuer), Lul (Chollo), Malek (Bor Dinka), Obel (Chollo), Tonga (Chollo), and Wanglel (Nuer). To be in a class of forty students hailing from different parts of Upper Nile Province, all of whom had passed the Intermediate Entrance Examination in December 1958, one counted as being among the cream of Upper Nile Province.

It was the second spot in my life outside my village, and the first outside an entirely Chollo ethnic environment. Although the school was located in the middle of Chollo hamlets, it had a modern configuration in terms of the architecture and design of its buildings. The school population was multi-ethnic and international. The school had two foreign Christian priests: an Egyptian Coptic pastor, whose name I recall as Dr. Swilliam Dhiom, and an Irish Catholic priest called Slater, who later in the year was replaced by a Dutch priest, Fr. Alwin Meyer. At the height of Abboud's policy of Islamisation and Arabisation of the southern provinces, the foreign Christian missionaries were expelled.

The school had five northern Sudanese teachers: Headmaster Abdel Gadir el Mardhi, from Kordofan; and Ustaz Gassim, Ustaz Senada, and Ustaz Bakri, all of whom were from what is usually known as the Gezira triangle. The fifth teacher was Ustaz Mohammed Saleh, who introduced himself as coming from "a very far, far country between Egypt and the Sudan—Wadi Halfa." And so the class gave him the nickname Mr. Far Country. There were also southern Sudanese teachers: Ustaz Paolino Lado Waden, a Bari who hailed from Juba in Equatoria; Ustaz Joshua Dei Wal, a Nuer from Nasir in Upper Nile; and Ustaz Thomas Kume Khan, a Nuer from Bentiu, Upper Nile. Later, Ustaz Othwonh Dak joined the teaching team on a temporary basis; he had postponed for a year his admission to the University of Khartoum. The other school staff were Awak Ayik-mal, the school clerk; Marko Kur, the school store-keeper; Fadalmulla, an ex-army soldier, who was the school's *sole* (an Arabic word connoting a military rank) or guard; and Abaker Ahmed, a Bargo from Dar Fur, the school cook; Abdalla Thok, a Nuer from Fangak, assisted Abaker. There were about fourteen workers, mostly Chollo, who looked after the school garden and school compound. All but one of them, a man called Okech from Pakwar, were brutally murdered by the Sudanese army at the height of Anya-nya insurgency in 1964.

The school comprised teachers' houses to the north, set in an row on the banks of the White Nile River and Khor Atar. Immediately south of the senior teachers' compound was the school compound, comprising the main hall, which opened in an east–west direction, flanked on the south by Class One and a teachers' office, and to the north by the second teachers' office and that of the headmaster. On the right side of the main hall was the store, Class Two, Class Three, and Class Four. The dormitories— named Jur, Sobat, Zeraf, and Pibor—were arranged in two compounds with the dining hall in the middle. Further to the south was the junior teachers' compound, and beyond it were quarters for workers and officials. The school had a clinic run by a certified nurse, Stanslaus Amum, and occasionally a medical assistant would be present in the school to take care of serious ailments.

Atar was then, by the standards of southern Sudan, a small town. It had a small police post, a market run by northern merchants, a bakery, and a butcher that slaughtered twice a week for the school and the small workforce living around the school. The town became lively between April and December, when students were back from holidays and the school was open. The southern pattern schools, whether primary or intermediate (formerly run by the missionaries), operated on a different calendar from the national pattern schools, including Rumbek and Juba commercial secondary schools; they opened between July and March, recognising the different seasons in southern Sudan.

My first journey to Atar started from Kwogo rather than Watajwok, where I could have told my peers about my new place of learning. I arrived in Malakal at about ten o'clock. My father and mother had come from Watajwok, so we sat on the riverbank near the quay to talk. She had prepared the dry food Chollo travellers take on their journeys (*okew*). Other town folks had prepared *ayodo* (a type of dried bread) for their children who were leaving for boarding school. My parents had brought only one pound, despite the school fees being two pounds, and there was nothing left to cover the steamer fare to Atar. I protested loudly at this stinginess. It was agreed that I would come back to collect the other pound. For the fare, I could take ten piastres from the one pound and buy the ticket. I refused to do this and chose to walk to the next station, at a place called Obel, where I would join the other students coming from Panyidway [Palo, Pajur, Pathworo and Adhidhiang] also travelling on the same boat to Atar.

The steamer, or post-boat, that plied between Malakal and Juba left Malakal punctually at four o'clock. That meant that I must reach Obel ahead of its arrival, otherwise I would have to walk all the way to Atar. Carrying my belongings on my head, I set a fast pace and reached Obel station as other students were coming in from the villages of Panyidway. These older students had completed their studies at Dolieb Hill. They recognised me and called me by my nickname, Nyaringo. The student leader had a steamer warrant for forty students. There were about thirty-two when the steamer arrived and we all boarded. It was the first time I had ever travelled on a steamer, and I felt so proud of myself for having made an achievement. We sat on the deck to enjoy ourselves in the evening breeze. The moon was already shining above the horizon.

Just before we reached Atar I ran into two boys, Paul Odhong Luigi and Venansio Twong Deng. Innocently, and without thinking, I asked them if they were travelling to Tonga. "Why do you want us to go to Tonga?" asked one of them in an angry voice. "Where are you going?" I told them I was going to Atar Intermediate School. This infuriated them and they began to a quarrel with me. I was lucky that some older students intervened to quell the feud. In no time, we saw the corrugated roofs of Atar Intermediate School, lit up by the moonlight's reflection. To the amusement of the passengers and the crew, the older students began to sing the school song:

> *Atar now will shine, will shine,*
> *When the sun goes down and the moon comes up*
> *Atar will shine, will shine.*

The steamer hooted to signal its arrival and shone its bright spotlight, moving from left and right on the riverbank, trying to locate an appropriate docking place. There were already many people at the quay. It was expected that there would be students on-board. The school authorities were there, waiting to welcome the students back from the holidays. The arrival of the Juba-bound steamer was also an opportunity for local people to earn some cash. At the quay were hawkers from the neighbouring Pakwar village, waiting to sell charcoal, fish, vegetables, eggs, and chickens to the passengers. Soon after disembarking we were taken to the dormitories. There were about sixty-five of us coming from Malakal. The students from Akobo, Bor, and Fangak were already in place and were delighted to receive us.

Compared to Dolieb Hill, Atar Intermediate School was a completely different environment. Boarding was a general feature of the education system in the southern provinces, necessitated by the fact that students came from distant locations. It was the one good thing that the colonial administration did to bring together the different nationalities of the southern provinces. In fact, it was through the boarding school system that a generation of southern leaders was formed. By bringing together peoples from many ethnicities, the boarding schools helped create a national awareness.

The dormitories in Atar were permanent structures and the students slept on wooden beds with woven-grass mats. The school provided each student with two blankets to serve as a mattress and a mosquito net. Some richer students brought in cotton mattresses and slept more comfortably. In Atar, students ate bread baked from wheat flour; in Dolieb it was *akello* or *apoto*, traditional Chollo dishes made from sorghum. Like many places in Upper Nile Province, Atar was mosquito-infested, which explains why the administration provided each and every student with a mosquito net.

In Dolieb Hill we never experienced bats or their strong foul scent. Our first day in Atar was spent chasing and killing the bats and cleaning the rooms. The school encouraged us to kill as many bats as possible to reduce their population. The school even had a "swimming pool" where the students bathed. The riverbank pool had been carved out of the White Nile using strong poles and bamboo barriers to keep out the crocodiles. These reptiles are capable of reading the minds of humans. They would sometimes come out of the river and enter the pool. Because of this, every time we set off to bathe someone would throw a large mudstone into the pool to check whether or not there was crocodile.

Like in Dolieb, each of us cleaned and tidied up our space in the room, and washed ourselves in the White Nile River. We fetched our cups of tea from the kitchen rather than from the dining hall, usually before the bell rang for the school parade. On the first day of school we were given textbooks, exercise books, a pen and ink-pot, a pencil, and an eraser. We were informed that tailors would be coming to make school uniforms. Although nearly all of the students had arrived, the teaching would not start fully until after a week.

Apart from the school calendar, which differentiated the southern and national patterns of education, the curriculum was also different. The subjects taught in southern schools were English and Arabic languages, mathematics, biology, geography, and Christian scriptures. As a matter of policy, history and civic education were excluded from the curriculum. It is worth mentioning that the promulgation of the Closed District Ordinance, which virtually insulated the southern province from the civilised world and the rest of Sudan, was intended to create an uncritical mass of obedient and subservient people. Thus, the education provided by the Christian missionaries was designed to serve that objective. It was not an education that could generate social awareness or a national consciousness. It was also anti-Islamic and anti-Arab in content, and therefore spurred a hatred of northern Sudanese and a feeling of inferiority among the southern Sudanese when it came to dealing with their northern compatriots.

Even four years into independence and national government, students in the southern pattern schools continued to learn only neutral subjects, which dampened their social awareness as compared to the northern Sudanese. At Dolieb Hill Elementary School we had learned the English and Arab languages at the same time. But by the time we sat for the Intermediate Entrance

Examination, we had progressed more in English than Arabic. We were surprised to find in Atar the same Arabic textbooks we had finished studying in Dolieb Hill.

But more spectacular was the fact that although the military government had decreed a law for the complete Arabicisation and Islamification of the people of southern Sudan, the teaching of the Arabic language in southern pattern schools remained quite backward. In hindsight, could it have also been a policy to deny knowledge of Arabic and Arab history to southerners in the same way that German colonial administrators discouraged the use of the German language in Tanganyika, and instead promoted Swahili as a means of preventing the Africans from knowing the German language? Indeed, later-on in Hungary, my Hungarian instructor used to tell me that knowing a language means knowing the way those people think and behave, suggesting that it could be a double edge knife.

The first two weeks of school were exciting. We were introduced to completely new subjects like science (biology), algebra—the funny combinations of letters and numbers—and geography, which was different from the "Ways and Living in the Sudan" we had learned in elementary school. With delight, we were informed that there would be no "schoolwork," the after-class labour activity we had done at Dolieb Hill, which we extremely detested. Since there was nothing academic to do after classes, there was time to play. The Catholic priest, Father Slater, hosted indoor games in his compound. So we went there to spend the whole of the afternoon, up to dinner time at six o'clock, playing games. One day while we were playing dominoes, the priest appeared in front of us and asked me directly whether I was hungry and wanted some food. I told him I was not hungry and that I had my lunch. He was not quite convinced because the other students started laughing at me, as if I was not saying the truth. The appearance of malnourishment displayed by my tiny body must have prompted the father's question.

One would not be wrong to think that Atar Intermediate School was mainly for the people of Upper Nile Province as the Chollo (from Detwok, Lul, Dolieb Hill, Obel, and Tonga elementary schools) formed the largest single group. In our Class One, we were twenty-eight Chollo out of forty students. The Nuer (from Nasir, Akobo, Wanglel, and Leer elementary schools) followed; the Ngok and Bor Dinka (respectively from Abuong and Malek elementary schools); and Anywaa (Akobo Elementary School). There was a noticeable absence of Murle (Pibor District), and Maaban and Dinka - Abailang, Ager, and Nyiel- (Renk District), as well as Koma (Nasir District). The absence of students from these districts was evident affirming the fact that virtually no schools existed in their areas. However, six students, all fourth years, of the Moro ethnicity from the Mundi/Maridi districts in Equatoria, arrived by steamer from Juba, giving the school a further glimpse of the peoples of southern Sudan, although there were still no students from Bahr el Ghazal.

It was understandable that the authorities did not want students at that tender age to travel far from their homes. While at Dolieb Hill in 1957, one student, Isaac Odhong Laa, passed the Intermediate Entrance Examination and was accepted at Nugent School Loka, located in the Yei District of Equatoria. He had to be returned and admitted to Obel Intermediate School, just three kilometres from his home in Paalo. He was too young to be so far away from home, living among people he had never known. This raised questions as how these Moro students were admitted to Atar.

It turned out that they were the products of a private school run by the Moro community in Malakal. In fact, the Moro as a community dominated the police, prisons, and medical services, as well as tailoring, masonry, and carpentry work in Malakal. They were well organised and could afford to run a school. The idea of bringing together different ethnic groups in a place like Atar Intermediate School must have had something to do with the government's objective of nation building. Indeed, we all came from schools predominantly made up of our ethnic compatriots. It was the first time in my life that I started to socialise with people of Dinka, Nuer, Anywaa, and Moro nationalities. It was something of a liberation, breaking with the ossified ethnic sociocultural barriers. We were now forced to speak in English or Arabic all the time, even when addressing a fellow tribesman or woman.

It was also important to cultivate and inculcate a sense of commonality, which is one of the cornerstones of nation building. In an effort to enforce this imperceptible rule, the school authorities secretly planted a wooden or plastic ball marked "D" with one of the biggest students in the class. He was given express instructions to hand it over to the first student he found speaking in his own ethnic language. It was not easy for some of us first year students who came from a closed community background where neither English nor Arabic was spoken. In fact, in my village, a few kilometres from Malakal, the capital of Upper Nile Province and an economic centre, one was frowned upon for speaking Arabic, reflecting the deep suspicion of and distaste for anything Arab. The Chollo people harboured these sentiments which emanated from their bitter experience with Arab slave traders during the Turkiya.

In the beginning it was difficult to speak English without making grammatical mistakes. Speaking English became like a drama among the first-year students. We enjoyed teasing, jeering, and laughing at anyone who was shy, particularly the ones who made grammatical errors. I vividly remember an incident from those early days in Atar. A classmate, Paul Tap, a Nuer from Nasir District, came into our room in a pensive mood, as though aware we would judge whatever he said. "Who tore my book?" he asked. His posture and body language made all of us laugh. Paul thought he had made a grammatical mistake, so he changed the question to "Who torn my book?" It was now incorrect, and this made the laughter even louder. Confused, Paul Tap asked again, "Who tear my book"? When we again laughed at him, he became angry and started to utter aggressive words, intending to provoke a fight. Luckily enough, a senior student who was standing around cooled down the situation. He pointed to Paul and told him that he had not, after all, made any mistake when he first asked the question. In fact, judging each other helped us to master communication in English, which was not the case for the Arabic language.

The four years in Atar were the most formative years of my life, though punctuated by some serious events which impacted my life. I was in late childhood and the only goal was to study hard and pass my examinations. It was a competitive environment, all the more so because the class comprised the former tops of their respective elementary schools. One had to work hard to keep up with the rest of the class. The year 1959 ended without much to raise concerns and the school was closed for a three-month holiday.

The school closed in early December, and it was back to the village. I was not sure whether I would spend the leave in Watajwok. It was also Christmas season and celebrating Christmas had almost become part of Chollo culture, marked by youth and elders, even though they were not avowed Christians. Shopping for new clothes, brewing sorghum beer, and general plastering of the huts and their decoration were under way in all the hamlets in anticipation of Christmas Eve and the following days. It was the season when youths exchanged invitations to spend time together in dancing and other social activities. I informed my father that I wanted to celebrate Christmas with my friends and colleagues at Dolieb Hill. I was not sure he would accept my request. To my delight, he gave me permission to go. Not only that, he gave me an ebony walking stick—some kind of overvaluation of a son. An ebony stick or mace is a symbol of Chollo aristocracy or possession of magical powers. I was so embarrassed going about with this stick that I hid it in the roof of our house before I left the hamlet with my peers.

I spent Christmas Eve at my aunt's house in pa-Ding Oki; in fact, I went to sleep immediately after dinner as I was tired from walking from Watajwok and, moreover, I was not interested in dancing and other games. In the morning we went for church service and in the afternoon went to the school playing grounds where athletic games and a football match were in progress. It was during the games that I ran into Prince Kwongo Dak Padiet, who was a relative through his mother and was, in fact, my nephew. He wanted my friendship, which I accepted willingly, although I was rather apprehensive when he said we would travel to his village on the west bank of the White Nile. But it was too late.

He had already informed his mother, Bareth Nyathow, who was excited about meeting me. I was a bit worried what my parents would think when my peers, with whom I had travelled, arrived in Watajwok without me. We spent two weeks in Prince Kwongo's village of Kwijo, which was founded by his father, Rath Dak Padiet Kwathkier after he was installed as the king in June 1945. It was a sharp learning experience for me. It was even more dramatic when both of us later arrived at my village. I thought I was going to reciprocate the hospitality I had enjoyed in Kwijo. But this was not to be. On the contrary, the village elders captured Prince Kwongo and made an elder watch over the prince. They rebuked my father for allowing me to befriend the prince and move about freely with him.

because a Chollo prince is a potential *rath* (king) he must be protected wherever he goes in the kingdom. And that was, indeed, the prince's fate: on 31 August 1993 Prince Kwongo Dak Padiet was installed as Rath Chollo. It was considered a great risk for the people of Watajwok to have the prince as a guest and in the company of his peers in the village. If anything should occur, like the prince being hurt or killed, the whole village would face collective punishment by Pachodo. My village's elders, therefore, took over the responsibility as soon as they informed the chief that there was a prince in the village. I don't know to what extent Prince Kwongo liked being hijacked by the village elders. It was not long before he was expected to return to school—Jonglei Primary School—in Malakal. But it seemed that Prince Kwongo was aware and used to the traditions and rituals that surrounded him. He was hardly surprised when the village elders acted the way they did. We were to meet later in life to consolidate our friendship.

In April 1960, the schools reopened, and we went back to Atar. It was only then that we became aware of policy changes. In line with the military government's policy to Arabise and Islamise the people of southern provinces of the Sudan, an order had been issued to change the weekly day off from Sunday to Friday, to conform with the supposed Arab and Islamic character of the country. The senior class students may have been privy to this information as both Rumbek and Juba Commercial secondary schools had gone on strike and were closed. We were to follow suit in protest of this policy change.

It must be mentioned that when it came to challenging government policy, the students, rather than the government employees, were usually the vehicle, and their actions invariably received support and solidarity from the southern masses. Student strikes throughout the southern provinces constituted mass political action against the military dictatorship. Nevertheless, due to its unorganised nature, the protest remained at the level of students. It did not translate into a major political change in the country. It was when combined with military action in the bush, in the form of the Anyanya Land Freedom Army, that these protests yielded political results.

The senior students were aware of the possible consequences, and so on Saturday night the decision to strike was circulated in secret and orally. The message was clear that no student should report to class the next day. It would have been our first Sunday attending school. At about ten o'clock the school gong was sounded but no students responded. The acting headmaster and the teachers all assembled in parade in front of the school hall. Both the Catholics and Protestants had finished their Sunday services and were relaxing in the dormitories, ignoring the repeated sounding of the gong. It later transpired that five students had responded and sneaked into their classroom. They were all Class Three students and hailed from the same ethnic group.

We were to learn later that one of the teachers, a South Sudanese, had approached the students because they all hailed from the same place. He did not want them to participate in the strike. The teacher, by trying to break the strike, hoped to get some favours from the school's Arab administration. Following school regulations, those who participated in the strike were each given five strokes of the cane. The students in fourth and third year rejected the punishment, and as they passed next to our class, shouted, *"Black legs, black legs."* The teacher had already lashed some of us. We had somehow missed the message that we were to reject the mass punishment and stage a class walkout.

That experience was a sharp learning curve for many of us. It was the first time I had heard of "black leg," the insult hurled at an individual or group of individuals who voluntarily or under pressure refuse to join peers in a mass action to support a particular demand against the administration or political system in the country. The "Sunday Strike," as it came to be known, was observed one hundred percent by the fourteen intermediate schools in southern Sudan. The government responded by closing all the schools and sending the students to their home. It is worth stating that the government policy of Arabisation and Islamisation of southern Sudan stemmed from a false definition of the Sudan as an Arab and Islamic country, ignoring its racial, religious, and cultural multiplicities. The Arab-dominated northern political elite, whether civilian or military, considered the Sudanese nationality as a transition to full integration of the Africans in the Sudan into Arab nationhood. It echoes the belief that to Islamise a non-Muslim one wins a place in heaven.

As a corollary of this definition of the Sudan, Islam and Arab culture had to be imposed by force of arms and the law. The northern Sudanese administrators who inherited the colonial positions embarked on changing traditional African, Christian, and European names to names that were Arab and Islamic. Sayyed Ali Baldo, a Dar Furi zealot and governor of Equatoria, threatened the government-appointed chiefs with dismissal unless they converted to Islam. In 1960, the people of southern provinces of Bahr el

Ghazal, Equatoria, and Upper Nile were still beginning to understand the meaning of independence. Unlike in northern Sudan,
southern Sudan was under complete military occupation and all
civil and political rights were denied.

Racial relations between the Arab northern Sudan and African
southern Sudan had not improved since the Torit mutiny of the
Equatoria Corps of the Sudan Defence Force (SDF) in August 1955.
The implementation of the Arabicisation and Islamisation policy
saw the deployment of the most brutal, ruthless, and backward
sections of northern Sudanese society in southern Sudan. The
implementation of the policy also meant that all southern teachers,
government officials, and elements of the army and security forces
were transferred out of the south and sent to work in northern
Sudan. The result was that the army, police, administrators, and the
merchant class in southern Sudan were now red-skinned northern
Sudanese. The result was inevitable: an escalation of anti-northern
sentiments.

As mentioned above, the Sunday strike was a success. It achieved
its objective of raising people's awareness in respect to the deliberate government policy to deny the people of southern Sudan
their basic civil and political rights. The strike's ring-leaders at
Rumbek Secondary School, people like Matthew Obur Anyang,
were arrested, tried, and convicted of treason. A number of the
parliamentarians, senior government employees, and students
preferred to go into exile to continue the political struggle from
East African countries, while some joined the ranks of the Anya-nya
Land Freedom Army. Three months after the strike, the government
decided to reopen the schools. While most of the adult students
would not return to school, those of us who were still young and
perhaps unconcerned about political matters chose to return to
school to continue our studies. The endgame of the government's
Islamic policy was the eventual expulsion from southern Sudan
of all Christian missionaries, most of whom were American or
European.

During the Sunday strike, Atar Intermediate School had an acting headteacher called Gassim. This was because Abdelkader el Mardi, the English-style, pipe-smoking headmaster refused to return to Atar. It was said that he was not comfortable with the military government and its policies. Ustaz Ali Babiker, now the new headmaster, was openly political and pan-Arabist in his views. More often than not he would clash with the students over some of the policies he advocated at the school. Ustaz Ali Babiker favoured the teaching of Arabic language as it was taught in northern Sudan, and therefore ordered more classical Arabic textbooks to be brought to Atar. We owed much to him because of that decision. We were not only able to command some knowledge of Arabic grammar when we were in the fourth year, but also to learn about colonialism, nationalism, and other ideas current at that time. Either before or after each Arabic class, Ustaz Ali Babiker would give us a lecture on the politics of the Sudan. He usually spoke disparagingly about southern politicians, putting off many of us.

The year 1961 was a relatively calm period. There were no serious adverse developments, although there was industrial action, mainly by the Railways Workers Trade Union, which combined the railways and river transport unions. The school opened in 1962, as in other years, in the month of April. Just two days into the school year, and after we had been provided with books, we were informed to get ready to travel; lorries were waiting on the eastern bank of the Atar River. Nobody dared ask where we were travelling to, or what we were going to do when we reached our destination, or for how long we would be gone.

As soon as the last student had waded across the river, the lorries started off towards the ferry at Khor Falus, which took us to the other side of the Sobat River. The lorry passed by my village but would not stop so I could tell my parents that I was off to somewhere. We passed through Malakal but were not allowed to alight. After about ten hours we arrived at Birkat el Agab, a cotton irrigation scheme in the Renk District of northern Upper Nile Province.

We were each given a bag and paraded in front of a farmer who gave us five minutes of instruction on how to pick cotton. He told us to hang the bag in front and to put the cotton we picked in it. When the bag was full, we were to offload the cotton into a place specially prepared for it. The teacher informed us that this was a government assignment: all the schools in the Sudan were picking cotton. As it was the country's foreign exchange earner, we were to work as diligently as possible in order to raise the image of Atar Intermediate School. The idea of working for a common good had never struck me as it did while I was picking cotton. Back in the village we did things together, like rearing goats and calves and going to fish together, which would classify as common good.

But we undertook these activities in self-interest: preventing the goats and calves from entering other people's gardens would forestall any punishment. Working for the country was therefore something new: it was labour without remuneration. Students from Obel Intermediate School were picking cotton in the Abu Gathra scheme, lying between Geiger in the north and Renk in the south. The whole exercise was to last for forty-five days, the work to be completed before the rains could destroy the cotton. It was a timely intervention to involve the school boys as hiring workers would have required more funds.

By the middle of June, we had finished the fields and set off on the journey back to Atar. It was exciting to return and settle down to our books. The teachers had to make up for the lost time and introduced evening classes in order to finish the syllabus before the secondary school entrance examinations, scheduled for December 1962. Headmaster Ali Babiker and his assistant, Paulino Lado Waden, were upbeat, saying that we had performed well in the national cotton-picking programme. The provincial authorities must have informed them because, sometime in August, the military governor of Upper Nile Province, Brig. Osman Nasr Osman, returning from commissioning the Bentiu Hospital, made a stop in Atar to convey the thanks of Minister of Education Gen. Talat Fareed and the greetings of President of the Republic Gen. Ibrahim

Abboud. In a ceremony that lasted one hour, the famous Sudanese musician and singer Ibrahim Awad entertained an audience of teachers, students, and workers at the school. The governor thanked the students and expressed his happiness that Atar had done well in the cotton picking. As a reward, he ordered the provincial mobile cinema unit to remain in Atar and entertain the school for three days. The three days of mobile cinema and films were memorable days in Atar. Not only did they show the government propaganda films about development schemes and visits of President Abboud to different parts of the country, they also showed some cultural films about neighbouring Ethiopia. The most interesting was a film of the performance of the Haile Selassie I Cultural Troupe at the National Theatre in Omdurman two years earlier. By the end of three days, nearly everybody in the school was practicing the Ethiopian shoulder dance and thanking the military government. And then we settled down to study for the examinations.

In a situation of civil war in one part of the country, no matter how remote the disturbance, its ramifications show up in different forms in other parts of the country. While there was only low-level in the border areas of Upper Nile, in Equatoria, and Bahr el Ghazal, civil disobedience simmered in northern Sudan. It showed up in delayed arrivals in Atar of the steamers, whether north- or south-bound, which was meant to undermine the military government. This never worried us much in the school as we concentrated on our studies. Then out of the blue skies came a letter announcing a strike.

Like the Sunday strike before it, the drivers of the strike were based far from Atar Intermediate School. Nevertheless, we were obliged to execute it. Notwithstanding the disadvantages it caused students preparing for their final exam, no one wanted to be branded a black leg. It was a matter of personal pride to join the strike. Though the reasons for the school strike were not well thought out, student leaders were adamant that we should take part and offered flimsy reasons. The school closed, studies were suspended, and the students sent home.

I did not go straight to Watajwok but opted to stay in Dangershopi with my cousin, William Kak, a former policeman with some political ideas. I learned from him that the Sudan African Closed Districts National Union (SACDNU), later renamed the Sudan African National Union (SANU), had ordered the strike. The liberation movement in exile planned to harvest some of the older students to fill the ranks of the Anya-nya Land Freedom Army. Rumours spread in Malakal that a 45,000-strong force was coming from East Africa to liberate southern Sudan from the Arabs. But it was only wishful thinking. It was true, however, that the strike made it easier for the Anya-nya to recruit students from primary, intermediate, and secondary schools throughout southern Sudan.

I knew my father would not appreciate the nature of the problem that had led to the closure of the school. I therefore let William explain the reasons for the strike. The story of a foreign army coming to liberate southern Sudan did not impress my father, but there was little he could do. I could only glean from his face that he was depressed. He knew that only a few weeks remained for us before we were to sit the school leaving examinations. He saw this interruption as just another waste of time. It was not known how long the school closure would last, but it was clear that the military government would not allow the strike in the southern schools to link up with the political unrest spearheaded by the workers' trade unions in northern Sudan. In the first week of December, the fourth-year students were called back to sit for their final examinations.

That the school reopened was good news for my father. He had never liked me lingering in Malakal. The news came that he did not have the money required for travel by boat, so he had to walk me the twenty-five kilometres to Atar. The journey to Atar took us two days of walking and wading through the seasonal streams. On returning to school after the strike, each student received a punishment in the form of lashes or strokes of the cane. When we reached Atar, my father made sure I had received the six lashes of the cane before he travelled back to Watajwok, underscoring his determination that I must complete school.

The exams, originally scheduled for 6 December, were postponed for one month, until 6 January 1963, giving us more time to revise our subjects. We spent the few weeks studying and working on the previous examination papers in the hope of spotting from their frequency which of the questions were likely to appear on our exams. We had enough time to study and conduct mock exams among ourselves as a means of building self-confidence. As was to be expected at that time of the year, some of our colleagues from Bor, Nasir, and Akobo found it difficult to find transport and therefore missed the examinations.

Finally, on 6 January 1963, we sat the examinations. The school was then closed and it was time for us to leave for our homes. Atar had been an interesting place compared to Dolieb, and this was enforced more by the fact that I had come of age and was now an adolescent. I had developed different perceptions of things and had strong relations with my colleagues at school and the number of friends I had made there, as well as in the neighbouring Pakwar hamlets. I was very sensitive and did not want to leave Atar without going to greet and bid farewell to my friends.

I was coming back from Pakwar and was about to enter the small shopping area a few hundred metres from the school when I heard a gunshot and saw smoke rising from the roof of the hut of a jellaba by the name of Athaya. We used to go to his shop to spend time listening to his wisdom, as he spoke fluent Chollo language. In fact, we knew the three merchants in Atar and they were very friendly with the students. I rushed to ask Ibrahim what had happened and he told me that Athaya had committed suicide. He had placed the shotgun at his throat and blown out his brains. It was a traumatising experience for his Chollo wife and very young daughter.

Events like suicide make people curious. We later learned that Athaya had been trading other people's merchandise to raise money for himself. This is what most jellaba from northern Sudan did, giving a false impression to southerners that northerners were always rich. But sometimes something goes wrong in these business deals, resulting in Athaya's tragic demise. He had extravagantly overspent his profits. When the debts came due, he had only four piastres to his name. He could not absorb this reality and therefore took his life.

Looking back on those years in Atar, from the vantage point of advanced age, I can say with confidence that my parents made the right decision. In their respective graves, I really owe them much on account of the sacrifices they made for me. At seventy-five years of age, of my four uncles, my peers with whom I grew up in pa-Ajak, I am the only one who is still alive. Over the span of my life, I managed to transcend the borders of Watajwok, of the Chollo Kingdom, and Upper Nile Province, and went into the wider southern and then Sudanese society, and into the world. I am sure had my father not decided to send me to school, my fate would have been that of my peers in the village.

The importance of education as a vehicle for social mobility cannot be overemphasised. Late ambassador Philip Obang Ojway related his debate with officials of the World Bank and IMF when they visited him when he was deputy governor of Upper Nile State. The international bureaucrats insisted that education was expensive and therefore the government must cut down on its spending. Philip would respond that if education was expensive then let them try ignorance, suggesting that the country could only develop and advance if it was run by educated people.

Chapter 4

Events That Transformed My Life

The path of a life is linearly unidirectional, but over the course of time certain episodes occur that mark qualitative changes in the life of a person. When these changes come in quick succession of each other, whether they are positive or negative developments, one is usually advised to take care. Up until the time I left Atar, I can't deny that I used to accept and believe in miracles and myths. Of course, I then still had faith in the Christian religion, which proselytises these ideas. The Chollo caution people, particularly parents, that happiness can easily turn to sadness and despair, thus every prospective initiate into adulthood or suitor in marriage must take extra care when conducting himself.

When the school closed for a long vocation, and when my father freed me from tending the livestock, I would sometimes go to Malakal to look for domestic jobs. I needed to raise money to purchase school necessities that the administration did not provide or my father wouldn't purchase. These included some fancy clothes, shoes, and extra pens and pencils. Engaging in domestic service was allowed as long as one had not reached the age of initiation. When I returned from Atar in January 1963, I showed visible signs of entering adolescence, so it was no longer permissible for me to take domestic jobs. My plan was to look for a job as a messenger in a government office, rather than menial labour on a construction site. The holiday was six months long and I really wanted to be engaged in something useful. I no longer needed my parents' permission to leave home. I could go to places like Malakal and Kwogo at my leisure. Like my peers at school, I went looking for temporary employment with government ministries but to no avail.

One day I was loitering between the government offices and the market when I met my brother-in-law Nyijak Agog, the husband of my stepsister Arek Nyaba. He asked me whether I would accept to work as a timekeeper in Melut. I did not know Melut, or even where it was, but I agreed to take the job. He accompanied me to the Department of Information and Labour, where jobs for the Melut Agricultural Scheme were advertised. The information clerk, a "de-tribalised southerner", as they called such people, were usually worse than the northerners in their treatment of southerners who were perceived to be Christian and anti-Islam. He did not seem enthusiastic about giving me the job. He assumed that I did not know Arabic and was surprised, even taken aback, when I told him I could write and read Arabic. He gave me a piece of paper and a pencil and asked me to write the Arabic word for certificate and my name, which I did correctly and diligently. He had no choice but to give me the job, even though it was only a temporary employment.

I was to travel immediately that afternoon to Melut, and this posed a big problem. How could I travel to such a distant place like Melut? I needed my father's agreement. My brother-in-law intervened to say that he would take the information to my parents. He assured me that he would explain to my father why I had to travel to Melut before getting his consent. He also gave me some money to cover my first few days away. I climbed onto the waiting lorry that would take me to Melut. It would be the furthest away from home that I had ever been, and I doubted that my parents, particularly my mother, would have countenanced such a trip. In fact, two weeks later, my father arrived, ostensibly to check on whether or not I had gone to Melut or to some other location. He was happy to find me in the company of some people he knew, and that I had conducted myself responsibly with them. He took a large portion of my first salary and went back to the southern part of the Chollo Kingdom; Melut was in the northern part of the kingdom.

The Melut Agricultural scheme was a Sudan government project under the Ministry of Trade and Industries, but the contract for construction belonged to the Ministry of Irrigation and Water Resources. It was one of the social and economic development projects the military government had planned. The strategic political objective was to support the policy of Islamising and Arabising southern Sudanese people. The primary goal was to produce cane sugar, filling a gap in production after the Ginad Sugar Project became economically unfeasible. The government chose Melut instead of Mangalla, despite studies carried out since 1948 that had shown that Mangalla was the most appropriate place for sugar-cane production.

This underlined the fact that economic projects are necessarily political decisions. Since the Arab-dominated northern political establishment remained suspicious of southern secessionism, it would only locate such a project in a place close to northern Sudan. To prove this point, construction of the physical infrastructure, including installation of the power-generating plant, at the Melut Agricultural Scheme was not commissioned and production never started. Meanwhile, the insurgency in the southern provinces escalated and the military regime was overthrown in the October 1964 popular uprising. An indecisive civilian government took over, which a leftist military coup overthrew in May 1969. The project in Melut stalled and its machinery was later transferred to the White Nile Sugar Company in Rabak.

It became apparent that the information officer in Malakal who recruited the workforce in Malakal had not followed instructions. He was supposed to recruit southerners who were devout Muslims or had Arabic names, as part of executing the government's policy of Arabicisation and Islamisation. This became clear when we were paraded in front of the project engineer, a certain Mohammed Ahmed Ibrahim. Many of us carried Christian or traditional ethnic names and this infuriated the manager as he read the names. He looked into our faces with extreme disdain clearly marked on his face. He spoke to the foreman in a manner that suggested that it was going to be only a short time before we were laid off, and quickly dispatched us to our assignments without allowing us to ask questions.

My initial assignment was to oversee a group of fifty casual workers who cut grass for building workers' camps. A tractor dropped me off some six kilometres from the camp. The labourers had walked from Melut town to the grass catchment area. I was to conduct a roll call and mark as present all those who had come. They worked until three in the afternoon. This continued for about two weeks, after which I was shifted to the building site.

Two ethnic communities inhabited Melut and its environs. The Dinka (Ager and Nyiel sections) were mostly agro-pastoralists who lived in solitary settlements far away from the river, and the Chollo, whose villages occupied both banks of the White Nile River. The two ethnic communities constituted the group of casual workers whom I oversaw on the grass project. They were now confirmed to continue working as manual workers in the building section. In the early days of grass cutting, I had a rough time with the Chollo workers. They had a false perception that being a fellow Chollo, I would show some leniency when they came late for work. It took time for us to develop cordial working relations.

I found out later that they were mainly from Manyo and did not like educated Chollo individuals from southern Chollo. They would without shame tell me in the indigenous language, "You southerner [southern Chollo] will return to your province in the south under the soil," suggesting that I would be murdered and return as a corpse to be buried. It was a kind of sensitivity arising from the belief that the government had marginalised and neglected the northern part of the kingdom. Except for Detwok Elementary School, south of Melut, there were no schools or medical centres in the whole of Manyo, a territory covering more than a hundred fifty square kilometres.

On the other hand, I had cordial working relations with the Dinka labourers. They were usually punctual and undertook their assignments without complaint. Their only concern was that I spoke to them in Arabic; they demanded that I speak to them in their own language, in the same way that I spoke Chollo to the Chollo labourers. In fact, one of them was so bold that he asked me, "Why is it that you don't know Dinka language while you can read and write?"

Actually, I could understand most of what he said as the Dinka language has many common words with the Chollo language. Moreover, I had a close association with my Dinka colleague in Atar. My problem was how to articulate my response, which required sufficient vocabulary. I found this psychological configuration of some of our people rather strange. I laughed it off, believing that it made no great difference whether one was a Chollo or a Dinka. We were all in a situation where we were forced into another different sociocultural reality and had to speak Arabic or English.

One of the timekeepers who came with me from Malakal was Abdullah Chuol Deng, who hailed from Fangak district. He was a student at the Islamic Institute in Kodok and, therefore, a Muslim by persuasion. The northerners treated Abdullah Chuol completely differently from us because of his Islamic faith. For instance, they included him in their mess and invited him to play cards with them. When we travelled to Malakal in the middle of February to cele-brate Eid el Ramadan, Abdullah was given space in the Land Rover while I was dumped with the rest of the workers into the back of a lorry. When we were laid off from the work at the end of April, Abdullah was retained. Years later, at the height of rebellion in southern Sudan, Abdullah converted to Christianity and renamed himself William Abdullah Chuol Deng. He later became one of the leaders of Anya-nya II rebellion against the Nimeri regime, and was unfortunately martyred in 1985 in a battle with SPLA forces.

The government policy of Islamicisation translated into the expulsion of the Christian missionaries from southern provinces, as well as the Nuba Mountains and southern Blue Nile. The Sudan Interior Mission was located in Melut, with another station in Abayat, located east of Paloich, and manned by Americans. These missionaries came to Melut to catch the steamer to Khartoum. One day, towards the end of April, the resident engineer called me to his office. Speaking in English, he informed me that my employment was temporary and that I would be laid off. My supervisor, with whom I had developed friendly relations, tried to intervene on my behalf but to no avail. The resident engineer was adamant. I thanked him and left.

It was my first experience with what had become a general feature of life in the Sudan, whereby one's sociocultural identity defined one's relations. Until that material point in time, when I met the resident engineer, social discrimination on the basis of race, religion, and language was not obvious to me, or perhaps I must have been naïve about it. It could have been a general practice in society but I had not conceived it in this way. It hit me like a sledgehammer to the head. I suddenly realised that an Arab and a Muslim had a better chance to get a job than a non-Arab Christian or pagan. I experienced first-hand the process we know as social discrimination. I got my last pay and caught the steamer to Malakal.

The temporary work with the Melut agricultural scheme gave me a real-life experience, and had a transformative impact on me in terms of attitude and perception of reality. I started to engage with the wider aspects of things. In fact, I had changed. This was evident when it came to engaging with my village peers. Some envied me for having gone to earn money for my parents in a place of which they couldn't dream. After a few days of answering their queries, they simply concluded that I was lucky and had a chance because my father had sent me to school. To their minds, I could now go anywhere I wanted to.

I had hoped that the temporary work in Melut would last until the end of June. This would have enabled me make some more money to cover my school fees and other expenses. As a timekeeper, I was paid twenty-five piastres a day. But because I worked over-time every day of the week, and each day was calculated as two, I was paid something between twelve and fifteen Sudanese pounds a month. Now back in the village, during the driest part of the year before the rainy season, I had nothing to do and there was no hope of finding casual labour in Malakal.

It was time for the peasants to start preparing their gardens for cultivation. Instead of going to loiter in the town, I would help my mother. She was adding an extension to her garden, and needed me to cut and clear the thicket. My stepmother did not have to culti-vate; she relied on the generosity of her children. My father was virtually grounded; he had lost his sight and was no longer engaged in cultivation. I would give myself rest on Sundays and attend the service at the Presbyterian church in Malakal. On one such day, I decided to patronise the tea shop where some of my colleagues from Atar and Obel intermediate schools came to spend time. I wanted to meet my colleague Francis Amum, who had temporary employment as a messenger for the Provincial Education Office. I believed he would have information about our results, as they were usually sent to the Provincial Education Office.

It took Francis Amum a long time to come to the tea shop. I had almost given up on waiting for him when I saw him coming. We greeted each other and from the expression on his face I could tell that he carried good news for me. "You have passed the exam-ination and have been accepted in Rumbek Secondary School," he said. I was so excited and thanked him. I asked him whether he had also made it to Rumbek and he answered in the affirmative. I then asked about our other colleagues. They were many so he took the paper out of his pocket. It was the *Upper Nile News Bulletin* published by the Department of Information and Labour, and it carried the results of students accepted to Rumbek and Juba Commercial secondary schools. Nearly three quarters of our class had passed and been accepted into secondary school.

It was still late morning and a bit too early to return to the village. But I really had nothing to do in the town and had already used up the few piastres I had brought from home. So I decided to go back to the village and give my father the good news. The excitement was so visible in my face that some acquaintances I met on my way eagerly asked me what had happened. But I was not ready to divulge anything until I had shared the news with my parents. I was lost in my thoughts, which I would say were a mixture of anxiety and happiness. I was anxious about my father's reaction to the news that I had been accepted in Rumbek, and what it would mean to him. There was a nagging fear that after having tasted the money I earned in Melut; my father might instead want me to find government job. There were cases where instead of allowing a son to pursue education, the parents forced their son to find a job in order to continue earning money for the family. Many individuals I knew ended up becoming policemen, prison wardens, or nurses in the hospital. I was determined to pursue my education.

I was of course very happy that I had passed the examination and was among the one hundred and sixty students in southern Sudan accepted to Rumbek Secondary School. That year, due to a growing number of intermediate schools and a corresponding number of students, the intake into Rumbek was raised to four streams instead of three. This instilled in me a sense of pride and hope for the future. On arrival in the village, I found my father seated alone under the neem tree in front of our homestead. I sat down close to him so he would feel my presence; cataracts had so impaired his sight that he could only recognise people by their voices.

"Who is this?" he asked. I greeted him and from my voice he knew who I was. "Why did you come back so quickly from the town?" he asked. I told him I had gone to pray in the Presbyterian church as usual, and after that I had gone to the tea shop to wait for my colleague who worked in the Provincial Education Office, who informed me that I was among the students in Atar who passed the examination and were accepted in Rumbek. "Yes, something told me you will pass your examination and that you will be accepted in Rumbek. I am very glad that you made it and I thank my ancestors for that." He then asked my mother to bring some water in a gourd. As we waited for the water, a few village folks assembled around us and praised me for my success. My mother brought the water and the elders spat into the water, performed a short Chollo ritual, and sprinkled the water and the sputum on me as a blessing.

A few days later, word went around the villages that the paramount chief of Watajwok, Jago Otong Agok, intended to beat the drum of Dhakoth, the founding *rath* of Watajwok. This was a coded message to the parents of adolescent boys to prepare them for the process of initiation into adulthood. Initiation into adulthood is a very important event in the life of every male Chollo adolescent. It marks his transition away from childhood and the village mores of rearing sheep and cows. Initiation into adulthood was the pride of every family whose male child had come of age, and they will do everything possible, without reservation, to make it a success. The initiation items include at least five to six r k (singular, r k), beads made from ostrich eggs, and *wiin*, a necklace woven from the tail hair of a giraffe. The initiation is a one-day event. After initiation, the young men join the world of adults and are expected to start a family. The mother will provide separate utensils, different from those used by younger siblings, until one is married and has his own homestead, either in the hamlet or outside of it.

In 1963 my peers in Watajwok hamlets numbered about sixty-two. This was a large number waiting for initiation, and this must have encouraged the chief to call the drum of Dhokoth. There were about twenty hamlets on the east bank. In pa-Ajak alone, four of us—Olir Olwangi Ajak, Gwang Nyikango Ajak, Bol Ding Ajak, and me, Adwok Nyaba Tor Ajak—were ready for initiation into adulthood. There was no way one could miss this occasion. We had to start collecting the ritual elements. My father sent me to his friend in Opathi-wan village on the Sobat River. It was necessary to procure the elements before somebody else came to borrow them. Because it was the initiation season, there were many competing prospective initiates. Luckily enough, I managed to find all the items that I needed.

As part of the initiation ritual, the four of us—Olir Olwangi Ajak, Gwang Nyikango Ajak, Bol Ding Ajak, and I—were inducted into the shrine of Rath Papiti (Gwang) Yor Akoch in pa-Damlai hamlet. It is Chollo tradition that upon initiation one is taken for prayers on the grave, tomb, or shrine of the person one was named after at a certain stage in one's childhood. It may happen that a child, perhaps suffering pains in the stomach or some other ailments, cries continuously. The parents consult a sorcerer whose guess is taken for truth. It seemed the four of us were named after Rath Gwang Papiti Yor (1917–1944) because our individual sorcerer had said so. It was a field day for the shrine custodian. Each of our parents presented a white sheep. In turn, the custodian and the village folks tied white beads on our right ankles, sprinkled royal waters, and prayed that we would have good luck.

In preparation for our induction at the shrine of our great-grand-father, Kwickwajo wad Delguth, we spent the days before the ceremony rehearsing and practicing the *bul* dance. One day before the grand ceremony we crossed the White Nile to the west bank, where we dressed in our full initiation attire. We were paraded in front of Kwickwajo's shrine and the custodian invoked his name to take care of his grandchildren. On the following day all the prospective initiates from Watajwok, a few dozen of us, were paraded in front of Dhokoth's shrine. It was a ceremony addressed by the custodian and Paramount Chief Otong Agok, marking the climax of our initiation into adulthood. This automatically, in the words of the paramount chief, transformed us into part of Dhokoth's army or militia, which by extension also meant the army or militia of Rath Kur Papiti, the then reigning Chollo sovereign.

The other part of the initiation was *ch ng* (dance), essentially known as *Chong ki bul*, which is the youth part of the initiation ceremony. While the drum is being beaten at different rhythms, the initiates parade themselves in anticipation of the girls they will choose. In most cases of initiation into adulthood, the ground—in terms of prospective girls with whom to dance—is prepared for the new initiates by their village's preceding generation. In our case, we did not have a preceding generation of initiates so did not have particular village girls with whom to dance at our initiation ceremony. It was just sheer luck that we were chosen by girls to dance.

The idea of jumping around to the beat of the drum was not of much of interest to me, though the dance was considered an important event for the initiates to prove their worth. Thus, on the second day, I decided I would sit and become a spectator (*aneeno*), like the older village folks. It was enough that I had fulfilled the tradition. The value of initiation, besides confirming and conferring adulthood manhood, lies in certain traditional rituals performed at the time of death. A deceased man is buried with his initiation regalia and, depending on his social status, a ram or bull is slaughtered. The village drum is beaten at a certain rhythm to announce his death. I did not wait for the conclusion of the four-day dance and crossed to the village on the eastern bank of the White Nile River. I had important matters to attend to in Malakal.

Being accepted to attend Rumbek Secondary School was an important event in my life which my school peers could appreciate, but not those of the village. We were already in the first week of July and it was time to start the long journey to Rumbek. Because there was no direct route to Rumbek, the journey was normally undertaken in two legs. The first leg was by steamer, travelling the length of the White Nile River from Malakal to Juba in

Equatoria Province. The second leg was by car from Juba through Lianya, Mundri, and Mvolo to Rumbek in Bahr el Ghazal Province. If students were sure of finding a government vehicle, they took another route, disembarking from the steamer in Shambe and continuing by road to Rumbek through Yirol and Akot.

The school administration in Rumbek sent a telegram directing the new students to collect their travel warrants at the office of the provincial education officer in Malakal. At the River Transport Authority, the information available was that the river channel was blocked by weeds between Adok and Shambe, and therefore no steamers would be sailing until further notice. It was almost three weeks before the channel was declared open and ready for navigation. When we finally left for Juba, all of the steamer's barges were so full that the authorities had to use the police to force some passengers to get off, their reservations notwithstanding, in order to give room to the students of Rumbek and Juba Commercial secondary schools. There were also female students enrolled at Kator and Maridi intermediate schools. They were among the few female passengers travelling to Juba.

The journey was like a school picnic. In fact, from sunrise to sunset we engaged in conversation and joking, or playing dominoes on the deck. The girls did the cooking and would call us only to eat. It was such an enjoyable journey that the six days passed quickly. The trip by boat from Malakal fascinated me. When we arrived in Bor the soil started changing to laterite and became rocky when we reached Mangalla. It was my first time to see a mountain. Equatoria was mountainous and ever green. It was all valleys, streams, hills, and huge mountains that seemed to be moving away as one approached them by vehicle. It was a scenery that made me appreciate nature. We arrived in Juba on a Thursday evening and were taken to Juba Commercial while the girls were taken to Kator Girls' School. Arrangements had already been made to transport us to Rumbek, a journey that would last two days.

In Juba we went to the office of the director of education to collect our subsistence allowances for the journey to Rumbek. As we negotiated a corner turning into Juba's commercial area, we passed a woman with unusually fat lower limbs. I had never before seen something like that. I got so scared that I started screaming, as if the sight of her threatened me. My colleagues calmed me down and, after she was out of sight, told me that the woman was likely suffering from a disease called elephantiasis. They warned me that it was common in Equatoria and I would likely meet more cases. That afternoon the vehicle was readied and we began our journey, breaking for the night in Mundri, and in the morning continuing to Rumbek.

The students from Equatoria and Bahr el Ghazal were already at the school and had indeed started learning. The school was located in a forest of mango, mahogany, neem, and shea trees. There was no perimeter wall enclosing the school and so it was not unusual to see villagers and their livestock trespassing between the school buildings. The student population at Rumbek Secondary School would be expected to represent the different parts of southern Sudan. However, in practice, there were no students from certain parts like southeast (Murle, Kachipo, Jie, and Nyangatom) or the northwest (Aja, Bai, Ngulengule, Forege), which although geographically part of the Sudan, were nevertheless outside the precincts of the Sudanese state in terms of the provision of social services and economic development.

This reflected the uneven character of socioeconomic and cultural development in the Sudan. It was also a reminder that even within southern Sudan, differentials in educational opportunities existed between districts. Yei River District had the highest literacy rate in southern Sudan, and for that reason the majority of Equatoria students hailed from the Juba–Mundri–Yei corridor; Bor and Chollo districts also boasted high rates. I am sure that in 1963, not a single Maaban, Koma, or Murle student was among the ethnicities from Upper Nile Province represented at Rumbek Secondary School.

My first year in Rumbek was not as eventful as I had expected. Unlike Atar, on the banks of the White Nile, Rumbek and large parts of Bahr el Ghazal drew their water from boreholes or shallow hand-dug wells. In the first few months, buckets and ropes were provided for the purpose until the pump fitted to a borehole was fixed, providing water for the whole school. There were a few extra-mural activities to engage the students. The English Department conducted a monthly "Brain Trust" that tested general knowledge and cerebral gymnastics. The department also published a wall-paper titled *Candour*.

Ustaz Isaac Eli, the sports teacher, promoted football and athletics; a cross-country marathon was held at the beginning of the school year. There was the sixth anniversary of seventeenth November, marking the day the military had taken power in 1958. The November event was followed by an occasion at the school on 12 December. It was the day Kenya became independent after a long struggle against settler colonialism. In honour of the struggle of the Kenyan people and in solidarity with the one Kenyan student in the school, the school administration declared the day a holiday. It was marked with a celebration in the evening, at which student leaders made speeches commemorating leaders and freedom fighters like Jomo Kenyatta, Oginga Odinga, Achieng Oneko, and many others who were tried by the British colonial government in Kapenguria.

The school closed in March 1964 and we took the usual route back to Malakal from where I went straight to the village. I had hoped to find some employment but as the days went on in the village, I could feel my health failing. I felt a general fatigue, muscle and chest pains, and had a slight cough. My mother encouraged me to go to a sorcerer to see if I had been bewitched. Instead, I went to the hospital in Malakal. The medical assistant sent me to have my sputum tested for tuberculosis. It was positive. With tuberculosis, admission into the TB ward was obligatory.

Thus, I spent the school holidays in Malakal Hospital receiving daily injections of streptomycin. Many nurses who knew me would come to the ward to cheer me up and keep me company. The young doctor who treated me, on learning that I was a student, was sympathetic and would spend time with me when he came to visit the ward. At the end of three months, my sputum tested negative for TB. Nevertheless, the doctor advised that I should continue taking oral drugs against TB, and that I should eat food rich in protein and fat. I was released from hospital with a letter to the medical authorities at the Rumbek Hospital.

Sometimes fate brings together people who might never have met. A former colleague and classmate in Dolieb, Martin Buywomo Aney, was working as a trainee nurse at the hospital. One day, together with another senior nurse, Nehemiah Cagai Matet Gum, he came to visit me in the ward. I asked him how he had ended up being a nurse and he said he had not made it the previous year, having failed his exams. The good news was that he and a colleague who hailed from Yirol had re-sat the examination as private candidates and been accepted at Rumbek Secondary School. I congratulated them and inquired about Cagai Matet's story. As he told me, Cagai was one of the students who had been dismissed from Tonj Intermediate School after the 1960 Sunday strike. We immediately became friends.

My friend Cagai Matet epitomised the many southern Sudanese pupils and students who fought their way onto the education ladder despite myriad problems, some of them political and economic, inconveniences erected on their path by the oppressive political system. The year 1964 was by no means quiet and was not conducive to learning. The insurgency in the southern provinces got more violent and neared the urban centres. The military regime became more repressive and political resistance in the north was gaining strength through strikes by workers and students. It was clear that the regime would not celebrate its seventh anniversary of taking power in a coup in 1958. The schools closed and students were sent homes.

I met Cagai Matet again in Khartoum in July 1966; he had gone to Kassala where schools were open, while I was coming back from the Anya-nya. We went to the University of Khartoum together, pursuing different professional fields. Later on, we met again in the SPLM/A, during the war of national liberation. Cagai Matet died in 2013 of natural causes. He was a dear friend. May his soul rest in peace.

My second year in Rumbek was different from the previous year in that we were introduced to elements of political education. It was not easy to grasp certain political ideas dispensed in an atmosphere of fear and tension. The messengers themselves were not well grounded in the messages they carried. I believe that knowledge of anything must begin from its basics. An upstart was bound to miss a lot. More often than not, this poor start becomes a fetter to further learning. This occurred with the clandestine circulation of Marxist literature and the small pamphlet entitled "The Dilemma of Southern Intelligentsia: Is it justified?" by Joseph Ukel Garang. Although the intention was to raise our awareness, the material was a difficult read for many of us, in terms of its ideas. Instead of being efficacious, the content blocked our understanding, rendering us unreceptive to these ideas. In fact, many of us were seeing for the first time the picture of Karl Marx, suggesting that the education we had received over the previous ten years had done nothing to make us aware of the world.

Some of the Rumbek students who spent their holidays in northern Sudan came back with experiences and political ideas that were completely alien to southern Sudan. These helped stimulate some intellectual discussions about what was going on in the country. The insurgency in the southern provinces had been stepped up, closing certain routes. In northern Sudanese towns, political opposition to the military dictatorship was expressed in the form of strikes, sit-ins, and demonstrations. The situation was by no means either calm or conducive to learning.

The mood was captured in Alan Paton's *Cry the Beloved Country* when he wrote: "In cold and deserted harbour, waves run endlessly against the stone walls; in dark forest there is a leaf that falls;

behind the panelling white ants eat away the wood. Nothing is ever quiet except for a fool." Nothing was quiet; the school was awash with plainclothes police and informers, some of them weak-kneed students. Fourth-year students, presumed to be the ringleaders, were arrested and detained at the military barracks in Malou, thirteen kilometres south of Rumbek. The police action instilled fear in many of us.

Police action against presumed opposition to the government and Anya-nya sympathisers was carried out throughout the southern provinces. Information filtering of Upper Nile indicated that many schoolteachers, government officials, and workers had been arrested and detained in Kodok. This included my cousin Ustaz Othwonh Bwogo Kir, who had been transferred from Obel to Kuajok Intermediate School as headteacher. Our teacher in Dolieb Hill, Andrew Amum Nyiker, died under torture while Philip Lomodong, a clerk in the provincial headquarters in Malakal, was lucky to survive. This information and the arrest of our colleagues triggered agitation and unrest in the school. Fliers with such slogans as "Freedom for the students," "Only dead Arabs are good," and "We want separation" started appearing in the dormitories, ostensibly to mobilise for action. In Khartoum, opposition to the military regime intensified, forcing Gen. Ibrahim Abboud to dissolve the Military Council and step down from power on 21 October. A new political situation had been created by the popular uprising. Rumbek Secondary School was closed indefinitely, and the students were dispersed to their homes.

When we first came to Juba in July 1963, Sir el Khatim el Khalifa addressed us as the director of education for the southern provinces. He was now the prime minister of the popular uprising government. Sudan was in a transition to multi-party-political dispensation. While in Juba waiting for the steamer to Malakal, we witnessed intense political activities. The Southern Front (SF) was hurriedly formed to select southern politicians for positions in the transitional government. Luigi Adwok Bong was elected to represent southern Sudan in the five-man Supreme Council of the State; Clement Mboro was confirmed as the minister of interior, the first time a southern Sudanese held that portfolio; Ezboni Mundiri became the minister of communication; and Hilary Paul Logali was named minister of works. In fact, before leaving Rumbek, we had gone to listen to Clement Mboro. As minister of Interior, Mboro toured the southern provinces to report back on the atrocities that had been committed by the army and other security forces. In Yei, he was met by people carrying the bones of people who had been massacred by the army.

The events in Rumbek and Juba were a huge dose of political awakening, which I believe my mind could not absorb easily. It required a different type of learning. Many of us were completely ignorant of the history of the Sudan. It had been deliberately denied to us as the knowledge would have provoked in us certain emotions and sensibilities. This was why it was difficult for many of us to connect the dots. Secondary school students in northern Sudan were far more politically conscious than many of us in southern Sudan, including those educated in the southern pattern school system. I must confess that these events did nothing but dampen my interest in political events.

On arrival in Malakal a day after Christmas, we found a very tense military situation. The Anya-nya had engaged the army in a fierce battle in Odwar village, about forty-eight kilometres east of Malakal. Southerners arriving by boat from northern Sudan, having experienced the Sunday events, talked only about the war with the north. It was around the time leading up to the Round Table Conference on the Problem of Southern provinces. Southerners arriving from the north, particularly the youth, went straight to join the Anya-nya in the bush. It meant they had reached the limit of tolerance.

And yet a conflict, no matter its severity, can only be resolved by political means, suggesting that one must be fully armed with political tools in order to argue one's case. I came to understand much later those political tools were acquired through political education, organisation, and action. This requires the cultivation of a political culture that allows people to rely on cerebral rather than muscular energy, and people inculcate this culture in the struggle for their social, economic, civic and political rights, and freedoms. It presupposes a life of civility usually developed in urban centres. Urbanisation and its attendant culture came to southern Sudan rather late in the twentieth century and evolved around the *zaribas*, which essentially were slave markets, and therefore centres of violent relations between the slaves and the slavers. It was not out of the blue that people in the southern provinces resorted to violence: they had not internalised the arts of politics, and therefore failed to articulate politically their grievances. In this respect, violence becomes a political culture.

If Atar Intermediate School had changed me, exposing me to other nationalities besides the Chollo in Upper Nile, then the two years in Rumbek transformed my personal perceptions and prejudices and made me a South Sudanese patriot. This sense of being a southern patriot began during my interactions with northerners at the Melut agricultural scheme, where I experienced social discrimination on the basis of religion and language. These were life lessons, and I am grateful that I had the opportunity to learn and unlearn.

Chapter 5

A Stint With the Anya-nya & the Journey to Congo

We arrived in Malakal on Christmas Day 1964. While still on the boat, we learned the news of a battle that had just taken place in Odwar, east of Malakal. We disembarked from the boat with the knowledge that something was afoot. Some of us knew some of those who had been martyred in the battle. The stories of the fighting in Upper Nile Province engaged much of our first few days in Malakal town. The Anya-nya contingent in Upper Nile had four leaders, the four Pauls as they were known: Paul Adung (Chollo), Paul Awel (Dinka), Paul Nyingori (Anywaa), and Paul Ruot (Nuer).

Ethnic politics and power struggles had split them, leading to separate ethnic Anya-nya contingents. It was mindboggling how, fighting as separate groups and without proper military logistics or a central command, they could defeat a standing professional army. It was like a joke. Paul Adung had been killed in battle earlier in Akoka, and Daniel Chwogo took command of the Chollo contingent. Daniel Chwogo was policeman who had escaped from detention after the police car he was driving struck some people in Malakal. This was in early 1963 and soon, in a planned move, he took over the Atar (Ardieb) Police Station with six other Chollo policemen, together with their weapons including a Bren machine gun. The SAF recovered the Bren machine gun in the Odwar battle.

Many of us came from villages outside Malakal and, according to the arrangement in Rumbek, a letter had been written to the effect that the provincial administration would transport each and every one of us to our villages. However, the security situation in the province was unpredictable. The government was reluctant to send us to our villages as they feared that many of us would enlist with the Anya-nya. Because of this, they preferred to keep us in the town on a subsistence allowance of ten piastres a day. This arrangement was unsustainable and after two months they stopped the subsistence allowance on the pretext that we could take temporary employment with government departments. It was part of the policy to keep us in town.

The overthrow of the military regime had created a changed situation. For the first time, political parties were allowed to openly organise activities. Southern Front was the only southern political party in Malakal, alongside the northern-based Umma, NUP, and the Communist Party. Most of the students and youth joined the Southern Front on the grounds that it was struggling for the right of southerners. Its political ideology was that southern Sudan had a right to self-determination. Since independence, there had never been a time in Malakal when a registered southern political party could engage in open party activity.

The Southern Front convened its convention in Malakal just before the holding of the Round Table Conference on the Problem of Southern Provinces. Delegates came from Juba, Wau, and Khartoum to draft the party's positions and elect its delegation to the conference in Khartoum. Shortly after, in May, the founding conference of the Students Union of Southern Sudan (SUSS) was also convened in Malakal. The relatively safe security situation in Malakal made it a hub of southern political activity, unlike in Juba and Wau where the army was on the loose. It was a learning process as some of these activities made a deep impression on me.

When the Round Table Conference was in session a contingent of the Anya-nya, under the command of Daniel Chwogo, engaged the Sudan Armed Forces (SAF) in Ditang, just across the White Nile and opposite the Malakal Airport. The SAF were on a steamer that limited their military manoeuvrability but they had better weapons than the Anya-nya contingent and managed to dock under the cover of SAF artillery positioned outside Malakal town. The Anya-nya were exponentially outgunned by the SAF but they fought heroically before withdrawing, leaving two casualties on the battleground. It was a dangerous adventure on the part of Commander Daniel Chwogo, as he had not warned the civilian population of Ditang to vacate their hamlets. It was sheer luck that stands of Dolieb trees gave them sufficient cover.

Just as the Anya-nya withdrew from Ditang, and before retiring to Adhikong, Daniel Chwogo is said to have ordered the execution of Edward Amum's three brothers: Obany, Arop and Abwol. No credible reason was given for such a grave decision save that Edward Amum had earlier double-crossed Daniel Chwogo and also because he had gone to attend the Round Table Conference as part of the other opinion group. These were not sufficient reasons to take the lives of three brothers. Despite this, the presence of Anya-nya in the area interested me. I wanted to know from my cousin William Kak if I could join him. He warned me about the jaundice showing in my eyes and advised me to go back to the town. I was lucky to leave in time, because the next day the Sudanese Army attacked and dispersed them. Some of the prisoners they took managed to escape, creating a serious security concern for many Anya-nya sympathisers in the town.

A few days after the dispersal of the Anya-nya, the paramount chief of Watajwok, Otong Agook, was arrested and detained in connection with the murder of Edward Amum's three brothers. It was a serious crime even by Chollo standards, and someone had to be held responsible; unfortunately, it fell on an innocent person. The criminal case quickly transformed into a political contest between Edward Amum and Anya-nya sympathisers, who filled the court room. The Southern Front in Malakal summoned its secretary-general, Maulana Abel Alier, to defend the chief in court. In fact, the prosecution presented a shoddy case. All the facts of the case presented by the prosecution were dismissed by the court as hearsay. In fact, the police did not retrieve the corpses to be examined by the government pathologist. There was no evidence presented that Chief Otong Agook was an officer in the Anya-nya. The court dismissed the case and acquitted the chief. Failing to win the legal battle against Otong Agok, Edward Amum shifted his case to the government army on account of the Anya-nya connection. Later, he had the chief murdered in cold blood alongside two other men: Awook and Jago was Ajang, all from Watajwok.

Driven by the urge to avenge the murder of his brothers, Edward Amum became the commander of the National Guard contingent under the Sudan Army. This was a paramilitary outfit that fought the Anya-nya alongside the army. This paramilitary body closed routes through which the Anya-nya got their provisions from sympathisers in the town. This included ammunition bought from the army or police and smuggled out to them. It was no wonder that the government suspected all southerners of being rebels or rebel supporters, irrespective of their dispositions. The military intelligence and the police could arrest, torture, and kill without warrant. In Bentiu that April a northern policeman shot and killed his commanding officer, a southerner and police captain named Joel Akech, triggering a strike in Malakal. The culprit was just transferred to northern Sudan.

The Round Table Conference on the problem of southern

provinces held in March 1965 ended without much progress in achieving an acceptable and sustainable solution to the civil war raging in the country. In the words of Ustaz Beshir Mohammed Said, it was a mountain that give birth to a dead rat. The traditional theocratic northern political parties—the Umma Party and the National Unionist Party (NUP)—were not ready for power-sharing with the southern political elite. The last time these politicians had engaged in some sort of political relations between the north and south was just before the military stepped into politics in November 1958. These traditional political parties, together with their theocratic mentors, agreed on the definition of Sudan as Arab and Islamic, with the Sudanese nationality being a transition towards full integration into the Umma el Arabiya. It was a contest and struggle of identities, the roots of which continue to impact the recent and contemporary history of the Sudan.

On the southern side, the following parties attended the conference: Sudan African National Union (SANU), Southern Front (SF), and the so-called Other Shades of Opinion, a group of southerners sponsored by the northern establishment. SANU, represented by its president, Aggrey Jaden, was uncompromisingly secessionist, while the Southern Front supported the right of self-determination to be exercised through a plebiscite. The conference ended with a number of resolutions and a twelve-man committee to oversee the implementation of those resolutions and recommendations. In fact, the committee never met; it was not the mandate of the transitional government to implement the conference's outcome, and everything was left to the elected government.

The split of SANU, with one faction returning to play politics in the country, complicated southern politics in regard to their northern counterparts. Southern provinces were still under the state of emergency imposed in 1955. The Southern Front, the sole representative of southern Sudan, pressed for a compromise that would allow the transitional government to conduct parliamentary elections only in the northern constituencies. Little did Southern

Front leaders know of the tricks National Unionist Party (NUP), the social base of which was made up of the merchants and business groups trading in southern Sudan. Behind the compromise not to conduct elections in southern provinces, the NUP nominated its members in twenty-one constituencies in the south; these were later declared to have won unopposed.

The transition from military rule to parliamentary democracy took only eight months. In fact, the transition was only to prepare the country for elections, although the southern provinces were still under a state of emergency. As the government prepared for parliamentary elections, the security situation in southern Sudan continued to deteriorate, to the extent that many southerners relocated to northern Sudan, where it was relatively safe. The army and the police had the power to kill; only northern political parties were allowed to operate. It was an environment that prompted the Southern Front, which was still part of the transitional government, to ask for a postponement of elections in the southern provinces. This request was granted.

However, in a clever move, the NUP nominated candidates in twenty-one geographic constituencies, which the Election Commission declared as having passed "unopposed"; these candidates technically became members of the Constituent Assembly. Nevertheless, the Umma Party won the most seats and therefore its secretary-general, Mohammed Ahmed Mahgoub, became the prime minister of the partially democratic government of the second republic.

In an address to the Constituent Assembly on 15 June 1965, Prime Minister Mahgoub blasted the rebels in the southern provinces and those who supported them. He gave them an ultimatum: surrender within two weeks, by 30 June, or the army would be ordered to crush them. In Malakal, the situation remained tense. The army and police, assisted by the so-called national guards, combed the town looking for Anya-nya sympathisers. Most of the national guards and their leaders were using their government agency to seek personal vengeance, which made the whole affair so complex.

On 9 July, the army rounded up and murdered in cold blood seventy-six civilians in Wau, the capital of Bahr el Ghazal Province. The dead were mostly government officials who had been attending a wedding party. It was an unprovoked crime. On 11 July, in a clear demonstration of war against southerners, the army in Juba went on rampage for a whole day: more than two thousand people, mostly civilians, were killed. Southern Sudan had been turned into a war zone. This forced many people to relocate to the countryside to avoid harassment by the army and police. The Anya-nya controlled areas far from the communication routes— rivers and main roads—which were inaccessible during the rainy season.

The government decided to clear a security zone around Malakal, ostensibly to prevent Anya-nya infiltration. In reality, it was to prevent essential commodities from leaving the market by any means. Thus, anyone leaving Malakal—whether on foot, boat, or car—was thoroughly searched. Any forbidden items found were confiscated and sometimes there were arrests. I decided to relocate to Watajwok. But after only a few days I realised that it was dangerous to stay there. My father advised me to go stay with my aunt in Dolieb. Many of my colleagues lived in the surrounding villages of Palo, Pathworo, Adhidhiang, and Pajur, so I accepted the plan.

It was a rather difficult year. The rainy season started very late; by the end of July the road to Dolieb was passable only by heavy cars. On 30 July an Anya-nya patrol stumbled upon a river steamer that had come to collect fuel wood from Tufakiyia. Most of the rebels in the patrol were drunk and could not clearly see that there was police or army with the sailors. Nevertheless, they formed into a battle formation and fired on the steamer. The experienced sailors quickly sped off on the steamer, leaving behind a barge, which the Anya-nya scavenged for anything they could find. The rebels' operation saw just one casualty, the result of friendly fire.

The incident in Tufakiyia played out as a tragedy for the people of Watajwok and the nearby villages of Adodo. On the morning of 1 August, a brigade-sized army contingent started an operation, presumably against the Anya-nya. The soldiers collected 126 male inhabitants and shot them in front of their wives and children, burned down all the homesteads, and proceeded southwards towards Dolieb. The people living in the villages along the way had fled with their livestock to the west bank or into the nearby bush, but their homesteads were not spared the inferno. The news of the Watajwok massacre reached me when I was in the village of Adhidhiang. My family and immediate relatives had survived the massacre because our village was on higher ground and completely apart from the rest; the floods the year before had forced my people to leave our original homestead.

Dolieb remained the students' priority. Our meetings revolved around whether or not to go back to the town and wait for the schools to reopen or join the Anya-nya and participate in the struggle. Our go-betweens informed us that Daniel Chwogo wanted us to continue with our studies so that we could build the country when it became independent. Then one day the army arrived and razed to the ground the entire village of Dolieb, including the schools and the missionary premises.

An initial plan was for us to travel to the east, towards Ethiopia. However, insecurity on the way to Gambella created by some lawless tribes complicated matters, and the plan was completely dropped. Then the idea of East Africa popped up. Somebody remembered that a group of Chollo intellectuals had been sent to Juba in March to purchase weapons from European mercenaries fighting the Congolese revolutionaries. But travelling by boat or aeroplane, as that group had done, was out of question as it would involve going back to Malakal, which for the Anya-nya was now out of bounds.

We would have to walk all the way to Congo, taking routes that kept us well away from government-held towns. On the appointed day we assembled in Wunikir village, the most distant Chollo village on Ko-oluth (Khor Falus). The commander of the Anya-nya force that was to accompany the thirty-five students bound for the Congo had been briefed and the journey was about to start when an incident occurred. The commander, Capt. Simon Agenyang Odan, got into a fistfight with Joseph Twong Nyinyal, the student leader.

I knew both men; Simon Agenyang had been two classes ahead of Joseph Twong at both Dolieb and Atar but had not managed to go to Rumbek as Twong had. This could have been the source of the friction between the two men. To resolve the situation, Daniel Chwogo made a wise decision to replace Simon Agenyang with Capt. Isaac Awow Aban as commander of the Congo expedition force.

It was difficult to imagine or conceptualise the journey to the Congo, a distance of about a thousand kilometres, all of it to be covered on foot. Yes, I had travelled to Rumbek, an equally distant place from home, but that was by a combination of steamer and trucks and it took eight to ten days on average. This journey— moving on foot, carrying my belongings on my back, not knowing what we would feed on—was something new and frightening, to say the least. The threat of the government troops tracking the Anya-nya outbalanced the uncertainty on the way and became the driving force of the journey.

This was entirely a Chollo entourage, comprising eighty-eight souls made up of Anya-nya officers and men and thirty-five former secondary and intermediate school students, travelling southwards to the Sudanese border with Congo. It would be of interest to divide the journey into legs in order to capture the different episodes on the way. After the dramatic fist fight, we departed in the heat of a midday summer sun, and no sooner did the clouds that were shielding us from the burning sun send a thunderous downpour of rain that sent us running for shelter in the Dinka cattle byres (*luaks*). The Dinka were the immediate neighbours of the Chollo to the south, but their territory did not extend far before we set foot on the lands of the Gawaar Nuer of Ayod, a subdistrict of Fangak.

The Dinka Padang (Upper Nile) and the Nuer, unlike their Nilotic cousins the Chollo, up to this point in time live in dispersed, solitary settlements. This dispersion had a serious effect on our ability to acquire provisions. We were now a large group of people, the Congo-bound Chollo expedition force consisting of both rebel soldiers and civilians. The Anya-nya had an unwritten rule that the people, through their chiefs and headmen, must provide food for any Anya-nya contingent that moved through their territory, whatever the contingent's size or mission. This arrangement worked well in areas where people were settled in closed proximity to each other, as in the Chollo Kingdom. In areas of dispersed solitary settlements, as in Luach and Gawaar, it was really a challenge. Nevertheless, the group experienced no problems until it crossed the White Nile to the west. This was partly because we had taken some bulls with us when we first set off from Wunikir.

In Pul Deng, somewhere in the middle of the journey between Ayod and Duk Padiet in the south, a Nuer gentleman stopped the group and led us to his hamlet. He was the son of the famous Gawaar Paramount Chief Dual Diu. In a show of Nuer hospitality and generosity, the gentleman swore that this Chollo group would leave his *lwak* only after two days. So we spent our time resting and feasting on the bulls he provided. We had travelled for five days since leaving the Chollo Kingdom, and some of us were suffering from swollen feet.

But as we made our way southwards—through the forests, swamps, floodplains, and stony roads—individual and personal hospitality became rarer and rare, until it completely disappeared. The institutionalised order put in place by the Anya-nya to regulate relations between civilians and elements of its rebel army moving from place to place had become the norm. This included crossing the White Nile River to the west. It was incumbent on the Monythany in Malek, who had canoes, to transport Anya-nya across the river.

But when we arrived at the riverside, a steamer was passing, en route to Juba. We rushed back into the bush. Whether it was to terrorise the local people in Malek or a SAF sentry had seen some commotion, the soldiers let loose a volley of bullets, which luckily hit no target either among the Chollo rebel contingent or the local fishermen. Once the steamer was out of sight, we climbed into the canoes to cross to the other bank. John Opech and I were placed so close to each other that our efforts to regain our balance led to the canoe overturning. In a matter of only seconds, we were all in the water, trying to save ourselves and swimming to the shore.

The current was very swift but we managed to reach the shore. John Opech was injured; he had hit his shoulder blade against the side of the canoe. I had lost my bag and so all my clothes, blanket, and mosquito net were gone. The soldier who carried our only rifle had forgotten to take it, thinking only of saving himself. Luckily, the Monythany fishermen were used to this kind of problem. They quickly rushed downstream to retrieve the canoe. The rifle had remained in the belly of the canoe, but my bag and all other items were gone.

It took about six hours to cross to the western bank of the White Nile. It was tiring and painful to sit on one's knees for six hours without being able to straighten the limbs. This was exacerbated by the lack of anything to eat except filling one's stomach with water. When we finally set foot on dry land there was the most dramatic scene. Those who had arrived before us were cooking fish given to them by the Aliab fishermen. I had never seen such a thing as people fighting to grab food from each other.

All along our journey, since we had left Wunikir, nourishment had never been a problem for the eighty-eight individuals that constituted the Congo expedition. We were fed either the meat of a bull or food collected by the different homesteads on our way. Yes, there was an incident in the Bor area when the whole entourage became constipated because of the food we had been served. In Aliab, which was a fishing village, we were offered both fresh and partly decomposed fish. The dearth of cooking utensils meant that they cooked the two types in the same utensils. Some of us were not used to this kind of feeding and preferred to forgo it.

Arriving on the west bank of the White Nile posed a serious problem for me as I had lost all my belongings, including my shoes. My biggest problem now was walking barefoot on the rocky ground that was Equatoria. The whistle blew for our departure. It was about five in the evening and soon we were in the territory of the Mundari. The movement of Anya-nya groups through Mundari land was an uncommon event. In fact, the Dinka Bor would be the only people plying this corridor. Due to the mutual hostility between the Dinka Bor and the Mundari, however, the Bor contingents preferred to travel to the Congo through Moro and Mundu areas. Thus, it was possible to find kiosks and small shops along the way, particularly those collecting and storing agriculture produce like sesame, groundnuts, sorghum, skins, and hides.

One and half day's walk from the riverbank we came to what looked like a small market. A group of us stopped by a trader, a young man, who was buying groundnuts from the Mundari peasants to transport to the markets in Terekeka or Juba to fetch profits. We asked him to give us some groundnuts. He voluntarily filled out hands, but as the group increased, he started to complain that people were finishing his stocks. As soon as the commander arrived, he raised a complaint that some of us had robbed him of his groundnuts. To my surprise, the trader pointed at me. Of course, it was easy to notice a tall and thin barefoot person like myself. The others protested that he was lying. Nonetheless, the commander gave him five piastres to settle the matter.

Two days later, we arrived at Rokon, a small town one hundred and twenty kilometres from Juba. Rokon was under Anya-nya administration. In an insurgency, the enemy weakens if it stretches to occupy all territory in the country. The government must have deliberately abandoned Rokon in order to concentrate its forces in important areas like Yei and Mundri. It was also expensive for the government to maintain road connections between Juba,

Mundri, and Maridi, which passed through Rokon. After the July massacres in Juba, Wau, Watajwok, and other towns, southerners took to the bush and established Anya-nya units that cut the road connections. In Rokon, we met our Rumbek colleagues Olympio Nyampuk and Emmanuel Ijja. They introduced our group to the local Anya-nya commander who, with the help of the local chief, provided accommodation and feeding. With a group of students, I strolled the streets of Rokon and ran into Ustaz Thomas Lado, the brother-in-law of my cousin, Joseph Omoli Nyikango, a medical assistant, whom I had met years before in Malakal.

Ustaz Thomas couldn't believe his eyes, seeing me and such a large group of Chollo in Rokon. This encounter was why the entourage spent another day in Rokon; Ustaz Thomas wouldn't allow us to leave without enjoying the Nyangwara hospitality of meat and sorghum beer. That night, as we prepared to leave in the morning, a group of students led by Samuel Oweti Ajangdit decided to abandon the journey to Congo. They wanted instead to travel to Juba, one hundred and twenty kilometres to the east. In the morning, the commander, Capt. Isaac, allowed them to break off and wished them good luck.

It is worth giving a brief background to this desertion. After travelling so far, the reason for their leaving must have been something more serious than simple fatigue. Going to Juba at that particular time was dangerous so the decision was driven by some serious considerations. In fact, relations between the students and the soldiers had not been harmonious since we left Wunikir. We had not had military training and staying together with soldiers generated friction, especially when the students refused to undertake certain tasks. This marred the relations, prompting Capt. Isaac to adopt stern measures, like a military dictator. On one occasion, he said he was going to apply jungle laws on anyone who did not respect his orders. Rokon provided an opportunity for Samuel Oweti, Samuel Tekijwok, Peter Gwang Akich, and two other guys to leave this brutish leader.

The Congo expedition, its numbers now down by five, climbed aboard two tractors and their trailers which the Anya-nya commander in Rokon provided to transport us to a point on the Lianya–Mundri road where a huge mahogany tree had been felled and placed across the road to prevent vehicles from passing. From this point a narrow winding footpath led to the Anya-nya camp. It was about three hours to the camp through a thick bamboo forest. Upon arriving, the commander, Capt. Isaac Awow, was given a full military guard of honour. The high level of organisation, discipline, and security in the camp was discernible throughout, suggesting that the camp commander, Maj. David Dada, was a professional soldier. The presence of female soldiers in the camp was something that was marvelled at by most of the Chollo soldiers.

The hospitality in the Pojulu camp lasted three days. This gave us enough time to rest our bodies. The military guards led our group out of the camp for a few kilometres in a manner I had never seen before in Upper Nile. The Anya-nya in Equatoria was a real guerrilla army and had complete knowledge of what they were doing. In Upper Nile it was something between a guerrilla army and a traditional Chollo village army. After a day's walk we came to the Yei River, a small stream that was only metres wide but with a treacherous current. A rope tied to a tree on the other side of the stream guided us.

The crossing instructions were to never let one's hands off the rope, no matter what happened. In fact, a bee-like fly with a bitter sting tortured us throughout the time we were in water. Never, under any circumstance, should one raise one's foot from the rocky riverbed. It took almost one hour to reach the other side. One soldier who was careless was swept away by the current; it took quite an effort to save his life. I had never seen how the fear of death could push one's eyes out of their sockets as we tried to pull the soldier out of the surging current. It seemed we were lucky to have crossed when we did because immediately the river started to swell and the current became faster and more deadly. A man we met at the crossing said it would take another three days before the waters calmed down as it had rained heavily in the catchment areas.

Moving further southwest, we encountered many human footpaths crisscrossing in different directions, suggesting that there was a great deal of movement of people in the area surrounding the watershed that marked the Sudan–Congo boundary. The local inhabitants were visibly poor. The heavy movement of the Anyanya soldiers had so impoverished the people that many of them had left their villages, as could be gleaned from the vacant huts and hamlets. The peasants had repeatedly emptied their gardens, planted with cassava tubers and sweet potatoes, to feed their guests. We arrived at a homestead and saw that everyone was visibly tired and hungry. Despite his apparent impoverishment, the owner from nowhere brought a goat as his contribution to quench our hunger. Capt. Isaac Awow thanked the man for his generosity but declined to accept the goat; it was so small that even one person alone could consume it. This left the man shocked but grateful that he had been spared his goat.

As we continued to push westwards, we passed through a tobacco-growing area, suggesting that we were not far from Yei town. Yei River District was well known as a tobacco-producing area. Most of the tobacco farms belonged to Haggar, who set up a cigarette factory in Juba. As we moved through the farms, lots of tobacco still remained in their ovens, a clear indication that the war had disrupted not only communications between Yei and Juba but also discouraged the farmers, some of who must have joined the Anyanya. Many of us, soldiers and students, helped ourselves to the tobacco on the false assumption that smoking would help to stave off our hunger, which indeed was getting worse and worse. Many were no longer able to walk.

There was nothing the commander could do except to divide us into small groups to roam the villages for whatever could be eaten. It proved a good idea because it was easier for the villagers to manage small groups. In those days it was common to survive on a handful of boiled maize or cooked cassava flour, on which one drank litres of water to keep one's balance. In such a situation of physical weakness, it was preferable to keep walking and to never sit down to rest. If you did sit down, when you later stood up you had to stand with your eyes closed for a few minutes, to stabilise yourself before you started to walk again, otherwise you lost balance and fell to the ground.

The hunger forced me to experiment with cannabis leaves, as it was said the cannabis would take away the feeling of hunger. I found it hilarious. First, we did not have paper to roll the cannabis; instead, one had to wrap it in maize cob leaves. And because the maize cob leaves were harder and resistant to burning, the fire quickly tore through the cannabis leaves and took the smoker by surprise when it burned his mouth. I tried it twice but never experienced any quenching of hunger or thirst. Out of fear of its long-term effects, I decided to discontinue with it.

One day, as we walked towards where our colleagues were, we heard volleys of bullets from an automatic rifle. The expedition only had an old Italian, WWI-type rifle. We didn't even have ammunition and carried it only for show, in the hopes that the sight of it would ward off any potential aggressor. We did not think of an enemy and knew that if there was danger those who were in front would run back to inform us. So, we continued walking. Three Chollo Anya-nya soldiers—Venansio Twong, Pius Yukwan Deng, and David Edward Odhok— had been sent from home in March. They had managed to acquire whatever they could and were now heading back to Upper Nile Province. They had armed themselves with a Belgian FN, three Chinese AKM rifles, a German G3, and a rocket-propelled grenade (RPG) gun, together with ammunition and rockets.

It was a great joy for the Chollo expedition to Congo to meet up with them, and Capt. Isaac ordered a parade to review the situation. Commander Daniel Chwogo must have briefed him about the group. In fact, one of them, Ustaz James Ogilo Agoor, had to return to Malakal. He was accidentally wounded in an army shoot out on the steamer just before Mangalla. Since then, nothing had been heard of Matthew Obur Ayang and his entourage. It was sheer luck that our paths had crossed and we were able to meet. The spot where we encountered the group was a Kakwa village of about five families, lying about eight kilometres northwest of Laso and eleven kilometres from Abba in the Congo. They called it Gha-bat.

The commander of the expedition decided to make camp in the village and instructed the student leader and the students to get ready to travel to Abba. I requested to meet the commander and informed him that I would not be travelling with the students to the Congo. I had decided to join the Anya-nya. He was pleased with the decision and accepted that I remain and, indeed, attached me to a squad. In fact, in the village I had gathered some intelligence and heard terrifying stories from two schoolgirls who had travelled to Aru on the border of Uganda. They had to return to the village because life in the refugee camp was unbearably dangerous. This was so, in particular, if one did not speak Lingala or French; on the Ugandan side, the government was hostile to Southern Sudanese. So, I opted to remain in the camp when my colleagues left the following morning.

It was about the middle of October 1965. What would be counted as fresh news reaching us in Gha-bat came from Abba and could be weeks or even months old. We learned there had been a change of government in Kinshasa, and that Mobutu had overthrown Kasivuba; that the white mercenaries helping the government were getting an upper hand in their war against the Simba rebels—the Congolese revolutionaries, whose leader Patrick Lumumba was assassinated in 1960. Without an international friend to assist, the Anya-nya bought their weapons from the white mercenaries, who had taken them from the Congolese revolutionaries.

The Anya-nya did not have a clear political or ideological direction, and this made them natural allies of Mobutu. Most of the Chinese weapons passed through Sudan to the Congolese insurgents.

Being an ally of imperialism, Gen. Ibrahim Abboud impounded these weapons on orders from the US government. However, the popular-uprising government lifted the embargo on these weapons in early 1965 and sent the arms to the Congolese revolutionaries; most of their leaders were then in Juba.

The Anya-nya was a highly tribalised, regionalised, and apolitical guerrilla army. This highly decentralised configuration affected its acquisition of military logistics. Each ethnic group had to fend and struggle independently to secure its own logistics. They also organised battles independent of other neighbouring commands, which inadvertently affected their communication channels and strategy against the enemy. But the worst failing was the propensity of some Anya-nya to attack other Anya-nya units in order to acquire weapons to use against the common enemy. This was a determinant factor in the evolution of a unified political front. The confusion in the rebel bases echoed the confusion among the politicians in the capitals of East Africa. It was for this reason that the small Chollo group was lucky that they met the larger Chollo Congo expedition. If they hadn't, they could have been robbed or even liquidated on the way.

The expedition had brought some money to purchase weapons, but the leadership of the expedition faced the problem of exchanging the Sudanese money, mostly coins, into Congolese francs or Ugandan shillings. Those who were entrusted to conduct the exchange played tricks that reduced the amount so much. Moreover, a large amount went into purchasing food. A team was sent to Caramba Park to poach wildlife for both trophies and meat. This was not successful.

Then one day, nearly four weeks after they had left our camp, the group of students that had left without me for the Congo arrived. Their stories corroborated what the village girls had told me about the situation in Uganda. The condition of the Sudanese refugees and some of our former colleagues in Rumbek and Juba they found in the camp was so appalling that they decided it was better to return home. They also arrived with some provisions, which improved our diet for a few days; one could sleep on a full stomach. This meant that the East African project had failed. There was no reason to continue staying in Gha-bat, and a decision was sought for the entourage to depart for home.

Capt. Isaac ordered Sgt Jago Nyagany to remain in Gha-bat with a number of soldiers and await orders from the general headquarters. The students, three officers, and a number of soldiers were to travel back to Upper Nile. After almost four months of hardship, we were now sent back as porters to carry the ammunition and RPG shells. It was now about the middle of November. The rains had completely stopped and so the journey back was much faster. In four days, we covered the distance to the point at the White Nile River where the notorious crossing awaited us. Because it was the beginning of the dry season, the crossing had shifted southwards from Malek to Pariak. As the last groups were wading out of water, a steamer sailed by on the White Nile. This time, an enthusiastic soldier fired a volley of tracer bullets over the steamer. The soldiers on the steamer did not fire back so the group melted into the nearby villages to spend the night.

The government's military intelligence in Bor and Juba must have concluded that an Anya-nya contingent had crossed and was heading eastwards. There were no mobile or cell phones then to conclude that a spy was tracking us. But as soon as we left Kolnyang village, two Sudan Air Force fighter planes appeared overhead, dropping bombs that scattered us in different directions. It was a very dangerous experience for all of us, running about in the open without knowledge of military tactics or manoeuvres.

Our soldiers, including the commander, were not trained to know that during an air raid one should take cover in a bunker to avoid being hit by flying shrapnel. We were lucky because the area was not rocky so most of the bombs sank into ground without doing much damage. It was only late in the afternoon and at Anyidi village that we managed to collect ourselves. There had been no casualties, although some of us had dropped or lost bullets, something for which they were rebuked.

Walking through the now dry areas of Bor, Kongor, Duk, Ayod, and the Luach, we reached the Chollo Kingdom in only six days. The idea was to catch up with the Christmas celebrations. Capt. Isaac was instructed to camp in Obay Nyitho village, where we were treated to the hospitality of the people of Obay. It was a great excitement for many of us to be treated to *athabobo* Chollo (sorghum beer), fish, and traditional dishes after nearly six months in the bush. The commander-in-chief of the Chollo Anya-nya division, Daniel Chwogo, arrived the next day in the midst of a huge celebration. Capt. Isaac reported on the mission and the encounter with the group headed by 1st Lt. Venansio Twong Deng. After the parade, the people were informed to keep to one side as weapons would be tested. The RPG was the only new weapon. It was tested by firing it at a lalob tree: the rocket pierced the tree, suggesting it was a powerful weapon. One deaf spectator said he had felt the strength of the RPG.

After the celebrations, Gen. Daniel Chwogo addressed the students and a group of civilians. He thanked Capt. Isaac and 1st Lt. Venansio Twong for their leadership. He said that he regretted that the students had not found education in East Africa, but added, "You can go to Malakal and find a way to Khartoum. I heard that some of you who left on the way are already studying in northern Sudan." He gave permission to all the students to leave the camp while the soldiers were to wait for further orders.

When the people dispersed, I went to meet my cousin and mentor, Lt. William Kak, who was at the headquarters. It was almost four months since we had parted in Wunikir. He informed me of the developments and how the survivors of Watajwok village, mostly women and children, had been taken and resettled in the Dangershopi suburb of Malakal. He was not happy that we had returned. He wanted me, in particular, to continue with my studies. I told him all that had happened to me, including the canoe incident in Malek, saying that I was lucky to have survived, although I had lost all my property. I disclosed my intention to remain as a soldier in the Anya-nya. Lt. William kept quiet for a while, then suddenly stood up and left. I was the only student remaining in the camp, and this did not please him at all.

Three days later the forces were ordered to vacate the camp and marched in different directions, according to operational plan. It was the week before Christmas. Lt. William must have spoken with the commander-in-chief, telling him that I should be assigned to the headquarters under the command of Maj. Matthew Pagan Nyilek. I knew these men quite well, particularly Maj. Matthew Pagan. He had been three years ahead of me at Atar Intermediate School in 1959, but instead of Rumbek he had been accepted at Juba Commercial Secondary School. I had not met him since then. Maj. Pagan was so happy to see that I had grown into a young man. The headquarters was then located in the midst of a dense lalob forest in a place called Agaak, a Dinka Paweny territory on the east bank of the tapering end of Atar River. On the western bank were the hamlets of Pakwar village.

Following military tradition, the day after our arrival in Agaak, Maj. Matthew Pagan ordered a general parade where every officer and soldier was present. Along with other soldiers, I was commissioned as a sergeant in the headquarters' company under Capt. Raphael Odwel, who was then on a mission. My duty was to keep the financial records of all the taxes (both in cash and kind, usually bulls, sheep, goats, and sorghum) brought in from different parts of the Chollo Kingdom, including Malakal. I had a platoon of men under my command. Some of them carried the bags of coin money. For reasons I could not understand, the Anya-nya would not accept paper money. Other soldiers kept watch over the animals and the food stocks.

I took on the job with enthusiasm and saw to it that the soldiers did exactly what was required of them. For instance, I would at any time during the day call for inspection of all the money bags to make sure that everything was in its place. Sometimes there were reports that someone had lost a coin of five piastres and I would record the loss. A week later, Capt. Raphael arrived to take over the command of the headquarters' company. As he was my immediate boss, I regularly reported and took orders from him. He preferred that I gave my weekly report on Mondays. It consisted of an accounting ledger: in one column, I listed what in kind had been received; a second column showed what in kind had been spent; and the third column was the remainder in stock, or balance. This was very simple, and he deeply appreciated the format of the reporting.

We were in the middle of January 1966. It was really boring in Agaak. There were no activities, apart from the morning and evening parades, thus we spent most of the day following the shade of lalob trees, sleeping or playing with wet mud on the ground. On the third Monday I went to report in the usual manner, but with one change: this time there was a column of money reported lost by the soldiers. The commander was satisfied and was about to dismiss me when I told him I wanted to say something. He nodded, suggesting that I could say whatever I wanted.

I told him that I had recorded which days soldiers reported a loss of cash. These days, I realised, coincided with days when there was sorghum beer available in the village. These soldiers, unlike their other colleagues, didn't have the leisure to go far looking for their relatives or friends. I believed they feigned the loss of the coins on the weak bags in which they carried the coins. The amount that had been lost through this cunning was about thirty-five piastres. I suggested that the commander approve an amount of twenty-five piastres a week for the purchase of sorghum beer. Capt. Raphael looked at me from foot to head and said, "That seems a brilliant idea, but do you think that will resolve the issue of leaking bags?" I told him it would be an experiment, and after a week we would review the situation and he could decide what was to be done. We never had any more losses and the soldiers were happy.

Life in the headquarters approximated the stay in Gha-bat, save for the accounting functions I undertook. I never took part in the drinking of sorghum beer, which seemed the alternative occupation of everybody in the camp. In fact, life there was boring, to say the least. We spent the whole day chasing shade and sleeping as there were no books or newspapers to read. On one very hot day I was awoken by a rowdy commotion in the camp. I was soon to learn that one of the soldiers, while having a nap, had his money bag abruptly removed from under his head. The thief ran towards a swamp next to the camp. We quickly organised and searched the place.

In due course, we met Gwang Nyikango coming out of the swamp with mud on both of his hands. He looked nervous and this increased our suspicion. We followed his footprints and immediately found where he had hidden the money bag. I ordered the soldier to count the money. It was intact, suggesting that the thief had had no time to take anything from the bag. I reported the matter to the commander and a parade was called. The thief was summarily sentenced to fifty lashes of the whip and dismissed from the Anya-nya.

It was such an embarrassing thing for me. The soldier was my relative, in fact, one of my uncles, for he was my father's first cousin. He was my age-mate and we had been initiated into adulthood together three years earlier. What Gwang did was a disgrace and a shame to our clan of Ajak wad Lathnyal. I still remember how tears ran down my cheeks in sympathy as I saw him agonising under the cruel Anya-nya lashing. It took me days to recover from witnessing his humiliation.

The situation of boredom in Agaak showed the difference of attitudes between an enlightened and an ignorant person. In the absence of intellectual entertainment, like news and music, I suffered internally, sometimes to the level of questioning what had impelled me to join the Anya-nya. There was no comparison between the Pojulu camp near Lianya in Equatoria and our camp in Agaak, in terms of military activities and social entertainment. It was also depressing that, except for our commander and myself, the rest of our colleagues were illiterate. Any kind of innovative initiative to enlighten them on political matters hardly penetrated their ossified traditionalism. But there was more discomfort to come.

As time went by, a rash began to spread over my body. I was covered with itchy pimples, particularly on my hands, ankles, and buttocks. They told me it was scabies – skin disease brought into the Chollo Kingdom by elements of the Anya-nya returning from Ethiopia. There was no medical treatment and the only advice was to keep clean and frequently wash the body with carbolic soap. Scabies is a stigmatising ailment because it is contagious and therefore one must keep a distance from others. The story was that the Anya-nya had brought this disease from Ethiopia, where it was common but relatively mild in cold and hygienic conditions.

On the plains and in hot conditions, however, scabies is excruciating. The open pimples attracted flies and made me embarrassed. Life became not only very uncomfortable, but I also started to have second thoughts about continuing in the Anya-nya. The tapering end of Atar River started to dry up and it became difficult to find water to bathe. This increased the intensity of the scabies.

A group of officers arrived to the camp and I recognised from my resting place my cousin William Kak and Pious Yukwan. Capt. Raphael summoned me to the officers' mess and ordered me to make a parade of the platoon and collect all the money in one place. As I was leaving, William called to greet me but was taken aback when he saw that I was moving with flies. He told me that an expedition to the Congo had been ordered to take the cash and purchase weapons, adding that this time I would have to go to school. I was excited about the opportunity availed by this new Congo expedition and thought I should not forego it. The commander of the expedition, Capt. Peter Awol Aleijok, was a certified nurse. He was a very humble man whom I had known before, when I spent three months in the Malakal Hospital being treated for tuberculosis in 1964.

The marching orders were issued for the expedition to begin its journey. It was the first week of February, the middle of the dry season, and it would be extremely difficult to get water on the way as the seasonal streams and water points had dried up. The expedition needed to make haste and reach the crossing place in Bor before it was too late. This also meant that we had to travel by night, making use of the bright moonlight. After six days we reached the Anya-nya camp at Anyidi, east of Bor town. The reception in the camp was rather lukewarm. It was as if the Chollo commander had not heard of the problems of finding food and water on the way to the Congo.

Not long after we had rested, we were told that only a small group, not more than twenty men, would be allowed to travel further. The rest were to return to where we had come from in Agaak. It was depressing news. I had the feeling that I would not be part of this small group travelling further to the border with the Congo, and I was right. An officer read out the names of those who were to return, and my name was among them. We were to start our journey back immediately. The issue of the disappearing water points bothered everybody. I was also going to miss the penicillin injection Capt. Peter Awol regularly administered to me. While it was not a treatment for scabies, it minimised infections and inflammation of the skin.

Having not bathed for a few days and with my body covered in scabies sores was the worst nightmare of all my days in the Anya-nya. Because of the excruciating pain the scabies caused my body, I preferred to keep walking. This created friction and tension with the other soldiers, who preferred to sit and rest after every twenty kilometres of walking. We reached Magog after two days and found the seasonal stream completely dry. We had to dig a few centimetres into the sand to get water enough to boil the sorghum grains we had taken from the Nuer grain stores.

After our evening meal of boiled sorghum, I went to the officer and suggested that we continue to walk, making use of the cool weather and the moonlight. He rejected the suggestion on the grounds that the soldiers needed rest and that we would start moving at about four o'clock in the morning. I was so disappointed that I told my friend Othaj that I would not partake in the sentry duty and would not leave the place before sunrise. And then I went to sleep. The duty sergeant came to me at about ten o'clock to tell me that it was my turn at the sentry. I told him I was sick and would not perform the duty. At about three-thirty they woke everyone for the parade and started moving. I refused to get out of the *lwak*, saying that I would only get out when I saw the sun. I could hear them arguing about what to do with me, but I soon fell asleep once more. I awoke when the sharp sunlight hit my eyes and I realised that I must leave quickly. The fear of travelling alone so gripped me that I no longer felt the pain of the scabies. I searched for foot-prints and followed them. In fact, the footpath was narrow and surrounded by high grass that was taller than me. This increased my fear. I had run for about one hour when I came face to face with a huge and fierce eland with very sharp horns. I had heard stories about eland and how they attack humans, so I decided to push on without changing my speed. Luckily, the eland jumped into the grass and abandoned the footpath.

I had no weapon of any sort that I could use to defend myself; only my legs would save me from any wild animal. Then suddenly there appeared in front of me an open grassless space, the dimen-sions of which were larger than four football pitches put together. In the middle of this open space was a pond where a number of hyenas were fishing. I thought to myself that it would be dangerous to stop running. If the hyenas tried to attack me, I decided I would try to reach the trees on the other side of the open space. In the meantime, I thought I should frighten the hyenas. I gathered some strength and shouted at the top of my voice. The hyenas, caught off guard, ran out of the water and into the grass as I continued running, still trying to catch up with my colleagues. At about ten o'clock, just as the temperature was getting hotter, I caught up with the group. They were resting under some trees just by the footpath.

My friend, John Othaj, was definitely worried about me and

had expected me to appear at any time. He was the first to see me coming. With tears of joy running down his cheeks he embraced me and thanked providence that I was alive. When we were alone, he confided to me that the officer had decided to shoot me and leave me for dead in Magog. But the rifle failed to shoot and that is how luck was on my side. One and half days later we arrived in Agaak and for the first time in five days I was able to bathe and wash thoroughly. When I came out of the water the wounds from the scabies were bleeding profusely.

I spent three days thinking and planning what to do after all my efforts to go to East Africa had failed. By the end of February 1966, I would have completed eight months in the Anya-nya. It was an experience full of episodes that were interesting, but sometimes life-threatening. With nostalgia, I remembered the swamps and mosquitoes in Bor, the narrow escape from drowning when our Monythany canoe flipped, the hazardous crossing of Yei River, and my experiment with cannabis. The pain and itching of my hands, ankles, elbows, and buttocks interrupted my thoughts, and in the midst of all these recollections I decided to ask for leave to go to my village.

"Which village do you mean, Adwok?" asked my commander, Capt. Raphael Odwel. I told him about my village, Watajwok, on the west bank of the White Nile. He gave me three months' leave, an allowance of fifty piastres, and a departure order. I thanked the commander, saluted him, and went to bid my colleagues goodbye. In my heart of hearts, I knew I was never contemplate coming back to the camp.

The Chollo Anya-nya contingent was not, in the strictest sense, a guerrilla army. Nor was it going to evolve into one, given its poor armaments, the quality of its training, and the command structure. It was something between a civilian formation and a militia outfit. None of its leaders was a professional army officer or soldier, and only a few of them were policemen. Some of them were formerly primary schoolteachers, office workers (clerks and bookkeepers) or paramedics. None of them had received training in military strategy, tactics, armament, or command. However, Abraham Nyodho Odhok, who hailed from Watajwok and worked for the American Mission in Malakal before joining the Anya-nya; he was an ingenious artisan who repaired rifles, sometimes innovatively created means of fitting the G3 ammunitions to fire from Mark V rifles. The lack of professionalism in the force inadvertently affected the way they managed themselves and their soldiers. I was happy to leave.

The journey to Watajwok involved a fifteen-kilometre walk to Obay Abujook to catch a canoe to the west bank. The fresh wounds and scars on my body betrayed me as an Anya-nya soldier, or at least someone coming from their camp. I had to tread with care as the area was infested with informers and elements of the national guard sent from Malakal. The scabies was indicative of where I was coming from. I crossed the White Nile, arriving on the west bank at Owechi village. For security reasons, I stayed on the riverbank, waiting for the sun to set and pretending to bathe in the river, and deliberately arrived at the village under the cover of the night. I was aware that despite the massacre that had occurred in the hamlets on the east bank, Watajwok had two notorious national guard leaders. I stayed for five days in the house of my cousin, Obur Ador-Nyawello, coming out only in the evening.

The fact of my stay in the village became known only much later, after I had already departed. The Chollo in the villages could be meticulous in keeping secrets and this is an important aspect of their feudal legacy. Although the government had recruited spies or *haras watan,* to report the movement of the Anya-nya in every Chollo village, it was difficult for them to get correct information. These spies were usually frowned upon and completely isolated from society. This explains how the Anya-nya managed to get their supplies and even imposed taxes without much political work amongst the masses.

Looking back at those Anya-nya days, especially at this advanced age and comparing the time with my experience in the SPLM/A, I believe there is something I must say about these two experiences. I joined the Anya-nya when I was politically inexperienced and culturally backward, while I enlisted in the SPLM/A when I was politically mature and had been to many areas outside my home in Watajwok. The Anya-nya were sometimes brutal, particularly in dealing with those who challenged the rebel group's system. Although not driven by any political ideology, the Anya-nya were nevertheless genuine about their objective to separate southern Sudan from the rest of the Sudan. While the Anya-nya had organised the civilian population in a manner that made it easy for its contingents to move from one location to another, the SPLA, on the other hand, brutalised, dehumanised, and terrorised the civilian population, sometimes forcing them to join the enemy.

The SPLM/A started off as a socialist movement struggling for a united secular Sudan. This ensnared many other marginalised African nationalities in northern Sudan to join the rank and file of the liberation movement. But after twenty-one years the SPLM/A had to make a political compromise for South Sudan, leaving the Nuba and Funj in the jaws of the atavistic Islamic fundamental regime. In South Sudan the SPLM/A has instituted an oppressive totalitarian dictatorship modelled on the NCP system. It is no surprise that the NCP operatives soon took over the SPLM and its government.

Chapter 6

Scabies & my Return to School

*I*t was a great risk to stay in Watajwok. The chances of government spies finding me were so many. That none of my family members came to visit me could only point to two possible reasons: either the information had not reached them or they were afraid to come to Watajwok lest it expose the secret. Most probably, the national guards were keeping a close surveillance on them. I discussed with Obur in detail the danger I had exposed him and his family to. I told him I would leave that evening, without mentioning where I would be going.

I went to stay in Kwogo, at the home of my sister Piero. The place was familiar to me and was more secure than Watajwok. In my calculation, my sister had more interest in protecting me than my sister-in-law, the spouse of Obur Ador. Any slight disagreement between the two for whatever reason could easily spill the beans. The following day my sister left the house with the express warning to her children not to tell anyone that I was in the house. She went to my parents in Dangershopi. In the evening, Piero and my mother arrived. It was a sorrowful reunion as my mother could not control her sobs. They had been led to believe that I had died. The other students had returned but none could give my family any concrete information about my fate. I told the two my whole story, assuring them that I was well, only that I was suffering from scabies.

My father wanted to know my plans. I told my mother that I wanted to heal and after that I would decide. "Do you want to go back to become an Anya-nya?" asked my mother in such a desperate voice. In the dim light of a burning piece of wood, I could see the tears rolling down her face. This made me feel so sorry that I had put her in such anguish. I remembered how proud she was when I returned from Melut with some gifts. I believe both she and my father wanted me to go and complete my education. This would give some respite to their dire economic situation. They had lost everything they had in the 1965 army attack that saw all of the male population of Watajwok massacred. I apologised to my mother, saying I was sorry for all the troubles I had brought on them. I wanted my father to know this. I told my mother that I wanted to go back to school. Both my mum and sister were delighted. We went to bed happy with each other.

It was apparent that the government had scaled down its belligerency and hostility towards southerners suspected of being Anya-nya sympathisers. This shift in counterinsurgency tactics coincided with the presence of Abbas Fagiri as the chief provincial administrator of Upper Nile Province. So successful was this shift that Fagiri nearly succeeded in disbanding the Anya-nya in the Chollo area. He was said to be an anti-war activist: those who had deserted from Anya-nya and returned to the town were not apprehended or punished. In fact, due to harsh dry season conditions, the Anya-nya forces had moved far away to the *toich,* where they could fish and hunt for their feeding.

Although the situation seemed favourable to go to Malakal, I did not want to take any chances. My mother, Piero, and I agreed that I would travel by the next boat, which was five days from then. My mother returned to Malakal to raise the necessary funds for the ticket and pocket money. The arrangement was such that my mother would bring the money and *damuriya* cloth, which would serve on the way as a blanket, on Tuesday evening. My cousin, who worked in the hospital, would purchase the ticket on Wednesday, and I would leave the village in the late afternoon and sneak into the town in a canoe as the sun was setting.

It all played out as planned. The Kosti-bound steamer was already in the quay and was scheduled to leave by eight o'clock. I left the village and walked leisurely to the riverbank where I climbed into the canoe that was waiting for me. The canoe dropped me away from the lights, where I met my cousin who had been assigned to purchase the ticket. He gave me the ticket, some pocket money, and the cloth and left quickly. The operation had not taken much time and so I wasn't in a hurry as I walked to the quay and boarded the barge. Once on board I looked for a dimly lit place to avoid being recognised. By eight-thirty the steamer was out of the dock.

The journey to Kosti was three days and nights, with brief stops in Kodok, Melut, Kaka, Renk, and Jebelein. I did not know when the boat stopped, for instance, in Kodok or Melut: I was fast asleep. I woke up as the boat was leaving the quay in Kaka, at about seven o'clock the next morning. Between Kaka and Renk, close to Jebel Agha, which Chollo people call Kit Thwor Gwang, we passed the wreckage of a recently destroyed steamer. All that was left was the engine boat. I turned around to ask the man sitting next to me what had happened. In a low voice he told me the boat had been hit by Nyikango. He was astonished that, as a fellow Chollo, I did not know about what had happened to this boat.

I discovered common social and political ground between the man and myself and without reservation we entered into a personal conversation. Like me, he was a deserter. I told him about my journey to the Congo, and perhaps that would explain why I had not heard about the boat. He then went on to relate how some time during the previous year, in 1965, government soldiers had burned down Nyikango's shrines in Akorwa, not far from Kaka. The man graphically described the incident to me.

Immediately after the government soldiers razed the village and the shrines, they hurried back to the boat and started to sail northwards. Nyikango then came in a small cloud and struck the boat with a bolt of lightning, disabling it and making it partially sink. The man even sang for me the song later composed to tell the story of how it all happened. It was not possible for me to argue against the metaphysical interpretation of this coincidence: the burning of the holiest of Nyikango's shrines in Akorwa and the lightning that struck the boat carrying the soldiers who had caused the inferno. In this context, Nyikango is the spiritual existence, separate and apart from the Chollo sovereign, who is an incarnation of Nyikango.

The boat passed Renk and Jebelein by night, while we were asleep, and arrived at Rabak Bridge at about eleven o'clock in the morning. The bridge over the White Nile carried both vehicles and trains; there was also a footpath for people and animals moving across the bridge. In fact, it was the only bridge in central and western Sudan. I was amazed to see such a structure over the river. A place in the middle of the bridge opened to allow boats to pass, momentarily stopping the movement of cars, trains, people, and animals to the other side of the river. No sooner had the railway workers arrived to open the bridge the boat was already on the other side of the bridge heading to Kosti, where a train awaited the Khartoum-bound passengers.

Travellers to Gezira and Khartoum rushed to book seats in third class; of course those travelling in second- and/or first-class would have already been reserved. To my great disappointment, indeed intense anger, I discovered that the ticket my family had bought for me in Malakal would only take me to Kosti. It did not include the final leg by train to Khartoum. This meant that I needed another ticket to board the train to Khartoum. I did not have extra money to buy a ticket; the little money I had was just enough for buying snacks on the way. I asked the Chollo man whom I had met on the boat but he himself was ignorant of the regulations and procedures. Somebody who saw me looking depressed and desperate advised me to climb aboard the train because sometimes the inspection for tickets was not very thorough. The last whistle went off and the locomotive started to move. I jumped into one of the third-class carriages, taking a window seat.

There were four train stops before Sennar Junction. The ticket inspectors began moving through the train only after the locomotive had left Rabak. As the train was approaching the second stop, Jebel Moyia, the inspector reached my car. I told him I was a student of Rumbek Secondary School, that I had come by boat from Malakal, and that my ticket got lost as I boarded the train. The inspector did not believe my story and said I would be arrested if I did not produce the equivalent in money plus a twenty-five-piastre fine. He must have come across such cases before and assumed that I was trying to cheat. As I didn't have the money, I was taken to a police cell on the train, where I found another man who did not strike me as a typical prisoner. I told him of my predicament, which did not seem to impress him. He told me that I should just be calm because they would throw me off the train at Sennar Junction.

The train arrived at Sennar Junction at about four o'clock. Here they replaced the steam locomotive with a modern diesel engine, which travelled faster. The railway police came to take me out of the train with a stern warning: if I ever returned without a ticket and was found in the course of inspection, it would be considered a crime and I would be sent to prison. This was rather a different game from the one we used to play with ticket inspectors on the steamers plying between Atar and Malakal. On the steamers, there would be many of us and the sailors were not very strict with students from Atar. The sailors appreciated that the students would sell vegetables to them for a small price.

I watched the train roll out of the station and had no idea what

I should do. It was a completely different environment. There were no familiar faces and people were rushing about, catching lorries and buses. It really was a junction. I put on a stern face in an attempt to not look like a stranger. I had heard stories from my colleagues in Atar and Rumbek who used to travel to northern Sudan of robberies and murders at this particular spot. Sennar Junction was the meeting point of the railway lines from Khartoum, Gederef, and Damazine. It was very close to Sennar Dam on the Blue Nile River, draining the Ethiopian highlands. The dam stored water for the Gezira Scheme, which we had studied in our Sudan Geography class at school. The junction was a busy spot, with people and goods coming and going in all directions. I did not know what to do or where to go.

I went to what appeared to be a tea shop and restaurant. It was a spot for travellers, providing *angareb* (beds) for those intending to spent the night. It was still early in the evening so I could not ask for one, but I pretended to be very tired and in need of lying down to rest. The long sleeves I wore hid the scabies so no one noticed my suffering. After consuming some food, I ordered a glass of tea and stretched out on the *angareb*. I covered myself with the *lawo*, and no sooner was I asleep. Notwithstanding the severe pain in nearly every part of my body, I slept soundly, waking up only with the morning *azan,* the Muslim call to prayer.

Unlike most of southern Sudan, the electricity generated by the dam brightened the place like it was day. I could now clearly see one of the canals that carried the irrigation water to the Gezira and Manaqil extension. I walked up to the canal and climbed to the apex to see if I could find where to enter the water to wash myself. I looked to my right and left and could see people already bathing; this assured me that I was doing nothing wrong. I waited at the edge of the water until it was sufficiently warm before I headed towards the town.

I walked towards a group of people who appeared to be southern Sudanese. As I came closer, I could hear them speaking in the

Chollo language. This raised my spirits, particularly when one of them recognised me and shouted out my name. I told them my story of how I had ended up in Sennar Junction. I could clearly see that they sympathised with my situation. One of them, Henry Otuk (Hassan) Dak, though much younger than me, seemed to have intimate knowledge of me; he suggested that I go to the dispensary to get some treatment for my scabies. Later, I came to know his village and, indeed, his cousin, Samuel Oweti, was one of us in the Congo expedition but deserted us in Rokon. Like many youths in southern Sudan, Hassan had come north to look for education but ended up working as a labourer on construction sites. When the intermediate schools were reopened in Juba, he returned to the south.

Henry Otuk and his group generously put together a small sum of money to enable me to take a lorry to Wad Medani, the capital city of Blue Nile Province and headquarters of the Gezira Scheme. They accompanied me to the lorry park and left only after I had climbed onto one of lorries leaving for Wad Medani. It was a rough ride through the cotton fields. It was all dirt roads, and in many places indented by irrigation water. The lorry arrived at the parking yard of Wad Medani at about five in the afternoon to a frightening episode. For the first time, I witnessed a person being stabbed with a knife. The police came and immediately arrested the two men and restored order. The two men appeared to be Dar Furi; in fact, the Dar Furi tribes have a penchant for using knives in their fights, unlike the Chollo and other Nilotic people who prefer and enjoy fighting with sticks.

The commotion in the parking yard had attracted spectators, which turned out to be good luck for me. As I stood there, unable to decide what to do or where to go, someone came up to me and introduced himself as the nephew of my stepmother. He asked what I was up to. I told him I had just arrived from Sennar and was on my way to Khartoum. I asked if he knew my stepsister Achol, who had eloped from home with a certain Macpilo Achien, a man from Palo. He answered in the affirmative but said that would be for the next day. I stayed with his family for the night. I spent the whole evening relating to him the situation at home and my time with the Anya-nya, including the trip to the Congo and how I caught scabies, which was the principal reason I had left the Anya-nya. I could sense from his responses that he was scared of scabies, particularly since it was a contagious disease and could easily be transmitted to his children.

The first thing he did in the morning, immediately after taking tea, was to take me to the house of my sister. She couldn't believe her eyes. She wept in a manner that made me think that perhaps she had not wanted me to know her whereabouts. She had reason to be worried about my presence: she had eloped with Macpilo, even though she was already married to another man who had paid part of the dowry. A girl who respects her parents and other siblings would not do such a thing. I got so annoyed that I told her I was not in Medani because of her. I was on my way to Khartoum and if she continued crying, I would just abandon her and leave. She wiped her tears and began to ask about my journey and the people at home. I told her about the tragedies that had befallen the people of Watajwok, about those who had died, including our niece, Nyathow, the daughter of her elder sister Nyakoth.

I stayed in Medani for another three days, during which I made my own research about the school. I found out that my friend and schoolmate Andrew Arop Amon was working with the Irrigation Department. I found him and he gave me more information: almost all of the students who managed to come to northern Sudan in 1965 had been taken to Kassala; those who were in senior classes were accommodated in Khartoum. Now that the schools were on holiday, they had been brought to Khartoum and were accommodated at Khartoum Secondary School.

I booked a seat on the Express Bus service to Khartoum; it was the most secure and fastest travel to Khartoum. The road to Khartoum, the first highway in the Sudan, was a single-carriage tarmac road constructed with American aid. The bus left at six-thirty in the morning. I sat at the window to watch the cotton fields and the canals that criss-crossed the fields. I marvelled at the hydroelectric power transmission line that I had been seeing ever since leaving Sennar Junction and asked the man sitting next to me about it. He explained that while the Sennar Dam stored water for irrigation, it also produced hydroelectric power that provided electricity to industries in Gezira and Khartoum.

The bus arrived at about three o'clock in the afternoon and I took a taxi to Khartoum Secondary School. As I got out of the taxi, I was excited to reconnect with my colleagues from Bahr el Ghazal and Equatoria, and fellow Chollo, some of whom had travelled with me to the Congo. Many of them kept their distance from me, knowing about my scabies. It was a development that made me so uncomfortable. I was shown where I would sleep and where to keep my belongings. It was a Thursday and the next day would be a day off so nothing could be done for me until Saturday.

A Chollo man working at the school informed me of the whereabouts of some of my relatives who were living and working in Khartoum. Thomas Othom Bol, who worked at Bata, stayed in Omdurman. I remember vividly how his uncle, Akoch Awaker, the commander of the Ngu warriors of Watajwok, had asked me to write a letter to Othom. It was in 1957, when I was an elementary school pupil. After a few days, Othom obliged and sent his uncle money. My cousin, Amos Ajak Adung, was living in the Mizad suburb of Khartoum North. At my request, this worker agreed to take me to Mizad. There I found nearly all the relatives I was looking for. I believe they had even had a come-together ceremony. They were pleased to see me. Every one of them asked me to visit them in their places so I could be assisted with clothes. It was true that I appeared shabby in my long-sleeved shirt with a Chollo *lawo* on top, part of my effort to try to hide my scabies.

On Saturday, the student prefect accompanied me to the Ministry of Education. The clerk asked what form I had been in when the school closed in 1964. I told him I was in form 2C and in a short time he retrieved my name. It took only two days to complete the registration process. Now I had my identity card, confirming my status as a third-year student at Rumbek Secondary School. It was around the beginning of May, the hottest time of the year in Khartoum. In addition to the heat, there were occasional dust storms, which made life very uncomfortable.

One day, in the midst of a dust storm, I asked my colleague whether there was really anything compelling one to stay in Khartoum, apart from the insecurity in southern Sudan. He told me there was nothing, and indeed many of the students of Upper Nile had travelled back to the south to return to Khartoum in July when the school was to reopen. The next day I went back to the Ministry of Education and told the official responsible for Rumbek Secondary School that I wanted to travel to Malakal. He was in friendly mood. As there were two months before the schools would reopen, I could come the next day to collect the warrants and three weeks of subsistence allowance.

On the way back to the dormitory, I thought about how this time I would be returning to Malakal from Khartoum as a Rumbek Secondary School student, rather than as an Anya-nya rebel returning from Agaak. My health had improved considerably in the three weeks I was in Khartoum. Most of the scabies wounds had healed but there were scars on my hands and legs. I was not as skinny as I had been when I first arrived; more nutritious food had played an important part in this improvement. The people of southern Sudan, under the circumstances they existed in and the constant struggle for their rights of identity and civic freedoms, were by all accounts like a semi-colonised people. And because of this, I believe they could be justified for behaving in the manner I categorise as socio-political duplicity, characterised by pretence and double-talking when dealing with northern Sudanese.

When a person hides his real feelings, he shows that he does not expect to be taken seriously by the other side. No southerner would ever admit that he or she was a separatist in the company of his or her northern colleagues. In Khartoum, only southerners would know who among them was or was not with the Anya-nya. In Malakal, I could easily deny any association with the rebels. It was necessary to build that defensive psychology. My decision to return to Malakal was essentially driven by the urge to escape the heat and *haboob* or dust storms.

I also wanted to clear myself of any possible charges and become an ordinary (loyal) citizen: a loyal citizen of a country whose ruling elite denied my Sudanese nationality except as a transition into Sudan's full integration into Arab nationhood! That definition troubled many southerners psychologically, although for personal convenience no one questioned it. We pretended to go along as unionists. At this material point, my perception of the time I spent with the Anya-nya registered as my patriotic contribution to the national cause of the people of southern Sudan, and therefore I would never under any circumstances apologise for it. Therefore, the thought of self-redemption was not out of remorse for having committed treason against the state but was to place myself in a position to deny any charges. It would only be after many years of political enlightenment and consciousness that I was able to explain politically my stint with the Anya-nya, and to define it as an act of duty, rights, and honour.

On boarding the Kosti-bound train at the Khartoum central railway station, deep anxiety lingered in mind. Some part of me did not want to return to southern Sudan. I was worried about one guy who had travelled with me on the trip to the Congo: on returning home, he had immediately enrolled in the *haras el watan*, the national guards. However, on second thought, and despite this potential danger, something defiantly told me, "You were not the only one who joined the Anya-nya, and so what? Many of these former student-cum rebels were already in Malakal."

I believe the guy, Aywok, who hailed from Watajwok, had actually been blackmailed into joining the *haras el watan* to save his own neck. He was found unawares in the village before I returned from the second trip, which ended at Bor. As someone told me later, those *haras el watan*, as government spies, acted subjectively and selectively. In many instances they were not completely obliged to expose everything or everybody they knew because they were never paid regular salaries. However, they used their positions to intimidate and blackmail others and to extort money. It was really a dangerous gamble. I decided to put everything to the back of my mind.

My stint with the Anya-nya and the short stay in Khartoum had combined to raise my political sensibility to at least above that of a village teenager. On the boat travelling from Kosti to Malakal I was fearful of every person I met; indeed, I didn't talk freely even with Chollo people I encountered on the journey. On arrival at the Malakal quay, the reality I saw was quite different from what I had expected. The tense political situation that characterised Malakal in 1965, which forced many of us into the countryside, had dissipated and some degree of normalcy had been restored.

The northern police, army, and their southern paramilitary surrogates, the *haras al watan,* looked like normal mortals. The impunity with which they harassed and mistreated people, particularly southerners arriving from elsewhere and suspected of being rebels, had considerably eased. Southerners went about their daily business in the town as though peace had completely returned to the country. It required careful study of the situation to gauge that there was still a state of emergency in this part of the country.

I went to stay with my cousin Philip Acuil Kulang in Mudiria suburb, the area where government officials lived. He was working as a junior extension agriculturalist with the Department of Agriculture. In the southern provinces, areas of towns carrying the names Mudiria, Malakiya, and Jellaba characteristically connoted quarters for government officials, civilian or "de-tribalised" people, and the merchant class. During the war years it was safer for southerners to stay in Mudiria. As a government quarter it was not subjected to frequent searches like in Malakiya or other informal settlements like Dangershopi. In fact, the return to Malakal gave me the chance to visit my parents, who had settled in Dangershopi after the massacre of 126 male adults in the Watajwok hamlets in August 1965. The scorched-earth counterinsurgency policy, which the Sudanese army conducted in what was called the security periphery of Malakal, resulted in a mass influx into Malakal, creating informal settlements that later became part of the municipality.

My parents were happy that I had made the decision to stay in Mudiria; they were not certain of my security in Dangershopi. In fact, they would have preferred that I had not come back to Malakal. The Misseriya Arabs who had been our neighbours in the village were resettled in Baam, not far from Dangershopi, and were now enemies of the people of Watajwok in particular. They were always pursuing the sons of Watajwok to avenge the killing of their people by the Anya-nya in 1965.

In Mudiria, southerners socialised and had close friendships with northern colleagues who were in charge of provincial policy and decisions. In a way, Mudiria gave them some degree of security and made arbitrary arrest and harassment less likely. However, this socialisation between southerners and northerners obscured an apartheid-type relation that existed throughout the southern provinces between northerners and southerners even ten years into Sudan's independence, reflecting the colonial legacy of uneven development and the repression of southerners.

Northern government officials generally enjoyed a considerable advantage over their southern colleagues in remunerations, allowances, and other perks. Consequent to such disparity in socio-economic conditions, the northerners in southern Sudan fared better than their southern colleagues at the same level, which in a way reinforced the inferiority complex of southerners, instilled by the substandard education provided by the Christian missionaries. This differential treatment applied to southern graduates of southern pattern schools. Those who had a fluent command of

Arabic had an edge over their fellow southerners who could neither speak nor write Arabic. These monetary advantages, categorised as a "southern allowance" for northerners working in southern provinces, were intended to reinforce the psychological image of northerners always being richer when compared to their southern counterparts.

In distressful social, economic, and political situations people, as I said above, tend to behave in a manner that seems to negate their reality. One pretends that things are good when in fact they may be horribly bad. If you asked a person burying a close relative, perhaps murdered by the security forces, how he was he would never show his pain but calmly tell you there was nothing wrong, or that it was the will of God. In the same vein, as if to cover their agony, as I saw in the few weeks, I spent in Malakal in May and June 1966, southerners would throw dancing and drinking parties every weekend. They danced to East African music, doing the rumba, twist, and chachacha, with their wives, sisters, and daughters.

They would invite northerners: government officials, army, and police officers. The socialisation strengthened acquaintances between southerners and northerners and gave southerners a reprieve from wanton arrests and murders. It's no wonder that people behaved this way: they needed to protect themselves. Such situations occur across the board, throughout the subregion, when people are trapped and are unable to join an insurgency because of personal or family responsibilities.

The visit to Malakal was also an opportunity for me to reconnect with some of my colleagues from the Congo expedition. It was great to meet them again. We would spend time, over sorghum beer or other local drinks, reminiscing about those days on the way, particularly when days without food prompted some of us to smoke marijuana. They were curious to know what had impelled me to remain in the Anya-nya camp. It was also time to socialise, to date and court schoolgirls with the intention of finding a girl-friend or potential future spouse. Of course, in those days to have a girlfriend or someone with whom you exchanged love letters was highly prized. A certain young man exaggerated his zeal for girlfriends and discretely courted three; it was a disaster for him because in the end the girls discovered each other and all agreed to desert him.

I was completely reserved about this girlfriend business. Although I was already initiated into adulthood and was eligible to marry, I did not countenance this until I had completed my education, which I believed must end with a university degree. In 1965, during the month I was in Malakal, I had an affair which did not last because the girl wanted marriage immediately and I was not ready for it. So I did not want to repeat this experience. During one of my visits to my parents in Dangershopi, my father raised the issue of marriage. It was two years since I had been initiated into adulthood, he said, and some of my age-mates had already married.

Someone had tipped me off earlier that my father had in mind the daughter of his brother-in-law, the younger sibling of my step-mother. Chollo tradition permits relationships with in-laws. It would have meant suspending my education to find a job in order to support a family. But I was not disposed to marriage at that time; moreover, the girl was illiterate. I politely told my father that marriage before completing my education was something for which I wasn't psychologically prepared. I tried my best to discourage the idea, citing the dire economic conditions under which we lived. The kind of job I could find before sitting the school certificate would be low paying, and I resented government employees augmenting their incomes by allowing their spouses to brew and trade in alcoholic drinks. It would be better if I completed secondary school and then I could start the courting for marriage. We left the matter at that.

With all the socialising and enjoyment in Malakal, time flew by very fast, and soon we were expected to leave for Khartoum. I was filled with motivation and an urge to go back to Khartoum. There were more than a hundred students returning to their schools in northern Sudan. It was like a great party. Parents, relatives, girlfriends, and well-wishers thronged the Malakal quay, to a capacity unprecedented before, to bid farewell to their loved ones. Mothers, sisters, and girlfriends were shedding tears, some ululating, others happily embracing and enjoying themselves. I won't forget that evening. A few of us sat on the deck singing Harry Belafonte's "Jamaica Farewell" as the steamer sailed past Malakal Airport, approached Ditang village, and cruised northwards.

In retrospect, I believe it had been a good idea to come back home after two years of unpredictability. My parents, particularly my mother, were extremely relieved that I was still alive. There had been so many wild rumours after I left the hamlet. A sorcerer my mother contacted even told her that I had drowned in the White Nile. I was therefore satisfied that I had achieved the objectives for which I had returned to Malakal. Now I was going back to Khartoum as a bona fide student and a law-abiding citizen.

Chapter 7

The Slow Evolution of Political Consciousness

*I*t became a practice that every time political tension heightened, or violence erupted in the southern provinces, education at all levels was suspended and the schools closed. In my lifetime, this phenomenon occurred twice: first in the aftermath of "disturbances in the southern provinces" in 1955, and ten years later, in 1965. What remains an important footnote is the fact that southerners already in the school system or who had enrolled in school in 1955 lagged at least by a factor of one year behind their counterparts in the rest of the Sudan. This couldn't have been more of a general punishment meted out against every southern Sudanese.

In fact, in the wake of the October 1964 popular uprising, schools in southern Sudan closed and did not reopen until July 1966. The government had managed to reopen routes hitherto blocked or closed by the Anya-nya. The security situation had improved in many places and intermediate school pupils from Upper Nile and Equatoria gathered in Juba. The two secondary schools were transferred to Khartoum. We had not even cleared second year when the school closed in November 1964; we would have to wait to sit the exams for promotion to third year until March 1965. But this did not happen and many of the students were either loitering in the towns and villages or were in the Anya-nya camps. When we came to Khartoum in 1966, we were asked to join the third year, together with others who had been in first year when we were in Rumbek. Khartoum Secondary School did not have boarding accommodation, so space was found for us; hostels vacated by the Italian engineering company that built the Shambat bridge were reserved for our accommodation. This meant that we shuttled daily to and from classes in Khartoum.

There was a marked difference between Khartoum and any town or city in the southern provinces in terms of the personal, physical, and psychological security of southern Sudanese students. In the southern provinces, because of the civil war, the army and police were let loose on southerners, including government officials. They were perpetually harassing, arresting, and beating, even raping, killing, and murdering southerners with impunity. In Khartoum, southerners exercised their rights and enjoyed civic and political freedoms like any other Sudanese. Furthermore, in Khartoum, southern-based political parties—the Southern Front; Sudan African National Union (SANU), a breakaway faction the SANU in exile; and the Sudan Unity Party (SUP)—operated freely and frequently mobilised their constituencies.

Speaking about civil and political freedoms, it was evident that our northern Sudanese colleagues in school were far more advanced than we were in articulating some of the issues we were all facing. My mother used to tell me that the white and red men were predestined to be above the Black man, and I tended to unconsciously accept this as a fact. I realised much later that the determinant factors in the exercise of rights or enjoyment of civic and political freedoms are social awareness and political consciousness. In many instances, the freedom to organise, associate, and speak freely are earned or won through relentless struggle. During the military dictatorship those rights and freedoms were proscribed, but the people won them back by overthrowing the military regime.

We in the southern provinces came indeed from a different world of oppression, repression, and violence. It was a world antithetical to freedoms, whether human, civic, or political. It was a world that only suppresses awareness and consciousness. That's where the difference came from: it was not predetermined as my mother, a village woman, used to tell me. In retrospect, looking at the situation then and the constitutional provisions in respect of citizenship, it was as if southern and northern Sudan were different countries. While we southerners exhibited a culture of timidity and servile obedience to authority, the northern students oozed a certain level of political readiness to display the freedom they enjoyed. This freedom helped them gain skills at organisation, to articulate their thoughts rationally, and to speak truth to power. Back in Rumbek, such a level of political awareness and activity among the students did not exist. Indeed, for many of us, coming from a background of political repression at the hands of security forces, this level of student activity was unimaginable.

It was also a legacy of the Christian missionary education in southern Sudan. It is worth saying something about the Christian missionaries and the education they offered in the southern provinces, and to a lesser extent in the Nuba Mountains and southern Blue Nile, as part of the colonial policy of Closed Districts. I was part of that education system and indeed internalised much of it. This led to belief in a Christian God and an undivided loyalty and subservience to power and authority, with its corollary of suppressed awareness and apoliticism. It was an education that did not allow a person to question beyond what was taught, all of which we banked as the gospel truth.

This loyalty to authority, deep-rooted among the Christian missionary-educated southern Sudanese intelligentsia, was reflected in the tradition of not clearly defining their interests and goals, and even giving neutral names to their social and political organisations. This subculture loathed or avoided open confrontation with power, and would prefer to exhibit duplicity. A culture rooted in personal obedience to and fear of authority by day and rebellion and sorcery by night is nothing but hypocrisy. It did not permit political learning, organisation, and action against the oppressive reality. I remember some teachers in Dolieb who, instead of confronting the headteacher, would go search for a sorcerer. It was an education which resonated with Chollo traditions and culture that forbade a child to look in the face of an elder while speaking, or a Chollo man to speak to the *rath* while looking him in the eye. It was no surprise that many of my colleagues remained conservative or even apolitical.

The school administration would not permit any piece of knowledge that could in any way raise the self-awareness of students, or acquire a correct perception of political reality in the country. Thus, in the southern pattern schools, the history of the Sudan was taught only in the fourth year of secondary school, and was one of the optional subjects in the Sudan School Examination. In Rumbek, the nearest we came to engaging in social awareness activities was contributing to the English wall-paper *Candour*, published bi-weekly by the students but edited by the English Department.

It was social and cultural in content, and the school administration saw to it that issues of a political nature did not appear, although sometimes such ideas would be smuggled in as parables or satirical prose or poems, as if emulating George Orwell's *Animal Farm*. The objective of *Candour*, established by the English Department, was to train the students in the art of English writing, and to criticise and correct some antisocial attitudes and behaviours that didn't resonate with school discipline. Rumbek was a typical conservative–liberal environment that was designed to conform with the colonial metropolitan society.

It was thus a very sharp learning curve for many of us when we came to Khartoum, where our northern colleagues managed wall-papers that were political in content. Many of us from conservative tribal backgrounds found it difficult to cope. The Chollo society from which I hail is a conservative society at the pinnacle of which is a hereditary royalty—a feudal monarchy system frozen at a primaeval stage of development; at a stage in which the state had not fully evolved with its bureaucracy, standing army, and an economy controlled by European colonialism since the first quarter of the nineteenth century.

This sociocultural background, coupled with a Christian education, produced in us the most apolitical and reactionary character. In order to avoid sociocultural and political discussions with our colleagues we opted to spend out leisure time attending the extra Bible study classes at All Saints' Cathedral. For my first one and half years in Khartoum, this retreat into the teachings of the church almost turned me into some sort of a Christian fundamentalist.

The weak culture of organised political action amongst us played out in our attitudes towards politics in general, and our interaction with political parties. Most of us were right-wing in our thoughts and reactionary in action. We found ourselves enlisting in the youth wing of the Southern Front (SF), which had a wide following in the three towns (Khartoum, Khartoum North, and Omdurman), although it seldom conducted political rallies to inform their constituency. It was an elitist party and everything in it occurred at the top echelons. The Sudan African National Union (SANU) was populist and appealed to Dinka ethnic sensibilities and sentimentality.

Both parties were right wing and their political thoughts were bound up with "the problem of southern Sudan." Whether in SANU or in the SF, the articulation of what they called "the problem of southern Sudan" didn't go beyond the raging war in southern provinces. They made no effort, whether in print or oral, to explain in plain terms the elements of the problem. The SF and SANU, notwithstanding their respective policy statements, twinned with northern Sudan's Democratic Unionist Party (DUP) and Umma Party respectively as their financial and political patrons. I never experienced a meeting at which SF leaders came to address their followers at the school.

With SANU, it was different. It was a grassroots party and conducted grassroots mobilisation. On a Friday afternoon, a SANU delegation led by its president, Sayyed William Deng Nhial, came to us in Shambat. There were about sixty of us from different nationalities in South Sudan. Hugo Dhol Acuil rose and spoke in English to introduce Sayyed William Deng Nhial, who greeted his audience in the Dinka language. He appeared upbeat: it was an opportunity to speak to an enlightened audience—the students of Rumbek Secondary School. He spoke gently and in a voice that was filled with complete confidence and a command of the subject matter. Somebody politely told him that many of people in the audience did not speak Dinka. But he continued speaking in Dinka, prompting the non-Dinka audience to stand up and leave the room.

This experience left me extremely shocked. Back in May 1965 I had witnessed Sayyed William Deng Nhial hold a political rally in the Malakal Cinema. He spoke eloquently in English, rebutting some of the allegations hurled at him by members of the Southern Front for betraying the people of southern Sudan after breaking away from his colleagues in SANU. He was in the company of Philip Obang Ojway, Samuel Aru Bol, and Ezekiel Machuei Kodi, among others. The audience in Malakal was rather hostile but he and his entourage remained composed. In hindsight, I believe we must have completely misunderstood Sayyed William Deng. Addressing an audience in their mother tongue, or at least in a language that they have command of, was important. It was better to address a group of students, whose knowledge and skills of politics was still rudimentary, in their mother tongue.

A political party like SANU or SF could have also been a school for politics, where its leaders, cadres, and bona fide members learned or unlearned ideas. Without question, it is always better to start learning a subject in the language that a person knows best. Sayyed William Deng Nhial was a seasoned politician and definitely knew what he was doing. But the multi-ethnic character of southern Sudanese society dictated that he deliver his message in a language that everyone could understand at the same time. His mistake stemmed from his false belief that the Dinka were the majority in southern Sudan and, therefore, southern Sudanese must be addressed in Dinka. This produced an outright negative reaction from the non-Dinka and also entrenched the Dinka ethnic character of SANU, which later played to the sentiments of Dinka people in Bahr el Ghazal (including the districts of Rumbek, Tonj, Gogrial and Aweil).

The traditional conservative and liberal politics that the southern politicians in the SF and in SANU played did much damage to, and even prevented, a scientific understanding of "the problem of southern Sudan" among those of us who were the younger generation of southern intelligentsia. Nor were we educated in the political skills of organising. At Khartoum Secondary School, we witnessed northern students engaging in national politics, including discourses on the war then raging and the so-called problem of southern Sudan. Instead of taking part, some of us chose instead to go to the Khartoum suburbs to socialise. The idea was to concentrate on our studies, as some of our elders and politicians had advised, in order to secure government employment. Thus, many of us became bookworms and went on to become career bureaucrats. This explains why I only discovered politics and progressive politics when I was in my third year at the University of Khartoum.

In July 1968, together with some of my classmates at Rumbek Secondary School, I was accepted to the Faculty of Sciences (Biology). It was the first time a large number of southerners had been admitted to the University of Khartoum. On a personal level, this was a paradigm shift in my life. I was past my teens and entering adulthood, although I would have been something like five years behind my age-mates in the school system. I wanted to study agriculture after clearing the first year in the Faculty of Science. The University of Khartoum was the hub of student politics. The Khartoum University Students' Union (KUSU) was the centre of student extramural activities and all the student political parties. Social and cultural organisations registered with KUSU and had offices in the Students' Club.

Southern students at the university were organised under the aegis of the Students' Welfare Front (SWF), which had kept a registry of southern Sudanese students admitted to the University of Khartoum since 1956. SWF represented all southerners in the KUSU, although its membership had been suspended since 1961 on account of an incident in which a southern student removed a painting that negatively depicted the people of southern Sudan from a cultural exhibition. In 1968, however, not only did the executive committee of the SWF negotiate its readmission into the KUSU, it also spearheaded a change of the name from SWF to the African Nationalist Front (ANF), ostensibly to give it political and ideological content. The ANF was neither politically nor ideologically monolithic: that its members hailed from the southern Sudan only underpinned its organizational unity.

Other than its yearly general assembly to elect the executive committee, the ANF did not engage in political activities. If the southern students were not in lecture theatres or the library, they would go to the student club, but only to play cards and engage in conversation. Otherwise, they would be partying somewhere in the suburbs of Khartoum. One day at the club I met a northern student at the cafeteria. We had both gone to buy tea and began a friendly conversation. After a brief introduction, he started to share ideas that I was completely unfamiliar with, yet I could guess he was talking about the politics of the country. Pretending to be in agreement with what he said, I continued listening until one of his colleagues came to pull him away.

That encounter disturbed me a lot for the simple reason that I did not really understand what he was saying and could not respond appropriately to the political ideas embedded in our conversation. I began reading social science books, hoping to stumble onto some of the things we had discussed that afternoon. It is said that luck occurs when opportunity meets necessity. The university had closed for the holidays and I had taken a temporary employment with the Department of Rural Development. I was on the post-boat returning to Malakal from Bor, where I had travelled to conduct data collection.

The boat had just cleared Tonga station when a physically challenged boy fell into the river and disappeared. Under normal circumstances, the boat would search for four hours to find the body of the victim before it continued on its journey. A certain white man who had seen me agitating against the decision of the captain to proceed without recovering the body came to meet me in my second-class room. He was an American by the name of William E. Smith, a journalist, then the *Times* magazine correspondent based in Dar es Salaam, Tanzania. "Call me Bill," he said, offering a handshake. I told him my name and what I did and thirty minutes of cordial encounter ensued. It centred on the situation in southern Sudan. There were suspicious persons moving around us and I felt I had to warn him. He left me with a book whose Swahili title was *Ujamaa na Kazi*, which translated to "Socialism and Work," a collection of speeches by Mwalimu Julius K. Nyerere, the president of the United Republic of Tanzania. I must confess that this was the first political literature I ever owned.

Bill Smith must have concluded that as a university student I would be interested in reading Nyerere. Living in Dar es Salaam, he was familiar with the lively discourse surrounding left-wing politics among students and faculty then in the University of Dar es Salaam. This was at the height of opposition to the Vietnam war and protests by the civil rights movement in the United States. Smith couldn't have known that I was not interested in politics, leave alone left-wing political activities.

While the civil war raged in the southern provinces, tensions were simmering in Khartoum over promulgation of the Islamic Constitution, the draft text of which was being debated in the Constituent Assembly. The Communist Party of Sudan had been outlawed in 1965 and the political left was completely ostracised and excluded from participation in the political life of the country, including promulgation of the constitution. Southerners were resolutely opposed to the Islamic Constitution, but because of their numbers in the Constituent Assembly, their voices were muted. Only the leftist putsch saved the country from a recoil into the sixth century's era.

On Wednesday, 21 May, I arrived in Malakal after my journey to Bor. On Sunday, 25 May, we woke up to the news that the Umma Party government had been overthrown in a military coup. Most southern Sudanese people were cautious about commenting on the news and waited to know the attitude of the new rulers towards the southern provinces. It soon became clear that the Umma Party had fallen to a left-wing coup led by the Free Officers Organisation in the Sudan Armed Forces.

Since independence in 1956, Sudan has been pulled apart by two opposing political–ideological trends. On the political right are the traditional theocratic family dynasties: the Ansar and the Khatimiya, which control their respective conservative–liberal secular political parties, the Umma Party and the Democratic Unionist Party. On the political left are the Communist Party of the Sudan, Arab Baath Party, Nasserites, and an assortment of small leftist groups. The political left is numerically small and has its base in the modern forces, mainly the workers' trade unions, famers, and students. In a country where the majority of the people are poor, ignorant, illiterate and superstitious, it was always a field day for traditional and theocratic politics. The political space for the political left had shrunk even further in 1965, when the Communist Party was outlawed, and its elected members were removed from parliament.

The May 1969 coup was an attempt by the left to regain its space after the retreat of the mass movement that toppled the first military regime. Unlike the governments of the Umma and DUP, the country's traditional theocratic political parties, the new regime recognised, in what became known as June 9th Declaration, the historical social and cultural differences between the people of southern Sudan and their compatriots in the north. It also announced that the solution to the problem of southern Sudan lay in regional self-rule: southerners would manage their own social and economic development. But this turn to self-government would depend on the emergence of democratic forces in the southern provinces and their assumption of power.

Except for the top leadership of the southern Sudan political parties, some of whom had been detained by the revolutionary government, many southern Sudan intelligentsia tried to adjust to and accommodate themselves with the new regime, socialist sloganeering notwithstanding. The regime called for the youth to support the revolution and to enrol in the Sudan Youth Union and the Sudan Women's Union, both under the leadership of the Communist Party. I was then still new to politics and therefore had little enthusiasm for taking part in leftist political activities, even though I had begun to develop some left-wing ideas through my reading. I was not fully converted, and indeed sometimes took very reactionary positions on certain matters that concerned southern Sudan.

Barely two years after it usurped power, the May Regime ran into its own hurdles, and the internal fissures deepened and widened. The Communist Party, the ideological leader of the left, split into two factions: at issue was whether or not it should dissolve itself into the amorphous thing called the May Revolution, or maintain its independent existence while cooperating with other leftist groups to implement the national democratic revolution programme. This precipitated a rift in the revolutionary camp and the Communists lost out. The pan-Arabists, with the support of Libyan leader Col.

Muammar Gaddafi. carried the day. The political and ideological struggle was pronounced at the University of Khartoum: The Democratic Front, led by Communists aligned to Abdel Khaliq Mahgoub, took over the KUSU under the guise of the Alliance of Progressive Forces. This triggered a clash with the regime on 11 March 1971, leading to a six-month suspension of classes in the university.

From a political perspective, this long closure of the university was a blessing in disguise. It was an opportunity to educate myself politically and ideologically away from the academic duties. It allowed me to study and investigate certain social phenomena, albeit superficially. Othwonh Dak, a close relative and friend, had returned home from exile in Uganda, and was then a senior bureaucrat in the Ministry for Southern Affairs, established ostensibly to implement the June 9th Declaration. Although a Chollo prince, Othwonh Dak was leftist in political and ideological orientation; in fact, he was my mentor and encouraged me to study and undertake scientific investigation of issues. I started reading *The Communist Manifesto* by Karl Marx and Friedrich Engels, and Engels' *Anti-Dühring*. I found them difficult to digest without a knowledgeable guide. I found reading Nyerere's *Ujamaa na Kazi* and Franz Fanon's '*The wretched of the earth*' and '*Black Skins White Masks*' closer home and more palatable. It was easy to follow the logic of collectivism that underlay the philosophy of *ujamaa* ("familyhood" or "villagisation"). However, these reading did not satisfy me curiosity I felt needed a knowledge of dialectics to further my investigative endeavour to understand social and political processes. This could obtain only under the tutelage of Marxist party.

That the university remained closed for six months meant staying in Malakal where I could receive coaching from some advanced Marxists. In July, the left wing of the Free Officers Organisation pulled a coup and overthrew Nimeri, under the guise of the movement seeking to rectify mistakes. The coup was dismissed as pro-Moscow and drew the wrath of pro-imperialist forces in the region and far afield. Meanwhile, Col. Gaddafi forced down a British Airways plane en route from London to Khartoum at Benghazi: aboard the plane was the leader of the revolution, Lt. Col. Babiker el Nur.

In Khartoum, Nimeri supporters launched a counterattack and reversed the revolutionary wave that had taken over the country. In the ensuing mayhem, the military leaders of the revolution—Lt. Col. Babiker el Nur, Maj. Hashim el Atta, Maj. Mohammed El Zein, and Maj. Farouk Hamdalla—were executed by firing squad, while the leaders of the Communist Party—Abdel Khaliq Mahgoub, Shafie Ahmed el Sheikh, and Joseph Ukel Garang—were hanged. It was a tragic moment for the political left. In the aftermath many leaders, cadres, and members throughout the Sudan were thrown in jail. Many of them were my colleagues from the university's Democratic Front.

The events of July 1971 had a profound impact on me, particularly the execution of civilians linked to the coup attempt. The sentiments and sensibilities emanating from those events thereafter became the determinant factor in my political thoughts and actions. A close friend couldn't believe this shift in my views as, throughout the revolutionary surge, I had purposely presented myself as a benign liberal, unlike the many outspoken and rowdy Communists who found themselves serving as regime apologists during the July events.

He once told me, "Peter, you think with your heart rather than with your mind." We laughed at this because it resonated with Sir Winston Churchill's words that if in your teens you are not a Communist, you have no heart; but if by thirty-five you are still a Communist, then you have no mind. It seemed that I was on my way to becoming a Communist. Back on campus, I socialised and kept company with progressive students with the aim of acquiring a deeper understanding of politics.

Nimeri was now in the middle of the political wilderness. The civil war in the southern provinces still raged. In 1970 he had bitterly fought against the National Front and now, in 1971, against the Communists, alienating himself from the political left that had brought him to power while still claiming to be a socialist. Nimeri had only one option left to retain power: he had to make peace with the southerners carrying arms in the bush. The agreement to end the war and grant local autonomy to the south was undertaken through the auspices of the World Council of Churches (WCC), under the patronage of Emperor Haile Selassie. The Addis Ababa Agreement (AAA) of 1972 ended the civil war and provided for the establishment of the High Executive Council (HEC) and a People's Regional Assembly in Juba.

Southerners came out in support of the AAA and Nimeri was now the hero of peace. The African Nationalist Front (ANF) hosted a political seminar to analyse the AAA; the majority of the members were in support of it. Among the minority who did not support the agreement was a small group made up of Edward Lino Abyei, Atakdit Mawien Yal, Bol Kolok Manjing, George Maker Benjamin, Karlo Kiir Deng, and me. While we recognised that the AAA had stopped the war, it had not addressed the fundamental contradictions of socioeconomic underdevelopment and the cultural backwardness of the people of southern Sudan.

We asserted that the AAA was a distorted version of the 9th June 1969 Declaration. This uncompromising position eventually led to our resignation from the ANF and the establishment of an independent forum called "The Southern Progressives." We even produced our own wall-paper, *The Alternative: Voice of Southern Progressives*, which published well-researched articles about the situation in the Southern Region, including the many financial scandals involving ministers and senior bureaucrats.

I was the virtual editor in chief of *The Alternative*. I had the liberty to use the reading room in the Department of Geology, where we wrote the pages before hanging them in the "standing club," popularly known as Nashath (an Arabic word referring to "student activities"). In our editorials, we exposed the close relationship between the ANF leadership and the Sudan Socialist Union (SSU). The ANF was now more than just a student group: its leadership had become an appendage of the Sudan Socialist Union in Juba and Khartoum. They now acted as the regime's spies on campus, reporting on those among their colleagues who were opposed to the May satellite regime in the Southern Region.

Writing and editing *The Alternative* was indeed an education in political activism, as was day-to-day life on the university campus. I discovered that the campus was not only a place for acquiring academic knowledge and credentials: it was also a place for all-out social, cultural, and political development of the students, and prepared them for leadership. I realised that in my four years at the University of Khartoum there had been remarkable change, in fact an improvement, in my attitude, perception of reality, and political thoughts. The campus and the student club were the hub of anti-regime politics that drew in political parties from outside the campus.

As a result of these anti-regime political activities, the university was frequently closed and academic functions suspended. One such closure came at a critical time in February 1974, just two weeks before I was to sit my final written examination. It was my year of graduation. Instead of travelling as usual to Malakal, my home-town, I opted to fly to Juba with the rest of students from Equatoria on a flight chartered by the regional government. Sighting me on the plane, some students who knew I was anti-government started to agitate against me enjoying the flight to Juba, which they claimed was the fruit of supporting the regional government.

As I was a finalist in geological science, I obtained provisional employment with the Department of Rural Water Development. Here, I could apply my knowledge of geology and hydrogeology in the water drilling section. Two weeks into my employment, the ANF convened a student conference, ostensibly to drum up support for the regional government. Because it was an SSU-sponsored activity, those of us who were part of the Southern Progressives intended to disrupt their plans. We linked up with the local branch of the CPS to strategise. It was agreed that we would prepare anti-government posters and slogans to be hung on the eve of the conference day. We divided up Juba town and assigned cadres to specific areas of the city, including residential, business, and government offices. On Sunday evening we carried our posters to the area assigned to us, which was Juba Town. At the provincial headquarters we encountered a police patrol that wanted to know what we were doing. We told them about the conference the next day and to our surprise they helped us hang the posters and nail them to the trees. They were illiterate and unable to read the offensive language we had used on our posters.

On Monday 18 March, Juba woke up to a rude shock. For the first time in the history of Juba, anti-government posters were hanging from the trees and slogans had been painted on walls, even on those of the Malakiya Police Station. The security forces knew the easy targets—the local Communists, whom they immediately rounded up and sent to Juba Central Prison. My colleague, George Maker Benjamin, was among the first batch of suspects collected from his sister's house in the neighbourhood of Hai Malakal. My name was also on the list of suspects, but the police did not know where I was staying. The following day, on Tuesday, two police officers came to my workplace. They asked me to come with them to where I was staying in Hai Jellaba.

Off we went to the house of my relative, Edward Nyawello Amum, where I had been staying. I showed them my bed and suitcase. I had unfortunately left in my suitcase objects like nails, paints, and brushes, which easily could have implicated me as having participated in the writing of the posters and slogans. To my relief, however, their attention was drawn elsewhere: they picked up two pamphlets, one was on "democracy and self-determination" and the other on the war in Vietnam. They drove me to the Central Police Station where I was searched and relieved of my watch, some money, and a pen. I was then led to the Central Prison, a few steps from the police station. I was taken to what was known as the Special Treatment Ward. This was where they usually held senior political detainees.

There were eleven of us. I knew only Ustaz Ismael Suleiman Sayed, the CPS branch political commissar, and George Maker Benjamin. The others I came to know over the course of our imprisonment. We were not criminals, per se, but were being held under the preventive detention law. Ustaz Ismael was a frequent tenant of the Special Treatment Ward. He said he was honoured to welcome me and the others. As he had prior experience of how imprisonment affects a person, he warned us against nursing any thoughts that could trigger depression or stress. Maker had been arrested and detained in 1971 so he also had prison experience. As evening fell, the ward door and the perimeter gate were securely closed and the warden left. My thoughts flashed back to the search. Weren't the two police officers meticulous enough to know that I was a student, and therefore there wouldn't be a chance to find nails, paints, and brushes in my suitcase? Or did they have no plans of gathering evidence against me? I was flabbergasted why the police had not linked the presence of those items to the anti-government posters and slogans.

Prison is a place where people come to know each other very quickly, particularly if they find themselves sharing the same ideas and political thoughts. We became close in a short time, and found out that some of us were completely innocent. They had no part in the action against the state. They were not part of any political group and had even never heard of the Communist Party of the Sudan, though they knew Ismael personally as a teacher at Buluk Intermediate School. Their understanding of politics was completely rudimentary, leave alone anything about a political left or right. For instance, two relatives of Ustaz Ismail were arrested simply because they were found in the house, in a case of what they call guilt by association.

At the beginning, being arrested and detained in prison spurred a feeling of heroism. But as time passed by, first in days and then in weeks, there were other feelings: guilt, anger, and apathy, especially amongst first timers like myself. Prison rules stipulated that we were completely insulated from the world outside. It was impossible to get news about what was going on outside the prison walls. Anything coming to prisoners from the outside, including even food, was thoroughly searched at the gate.

In the prison, time moved very slowly. The routine was that the guards would open the ward's door, locked from the outside, at five o'clock each morning and close it at four o'clock in the afternoon. This meant that we spent twelve hours locked inside the ward and twelve hours moving freely, chasing the shade cast by the prison's perimeter wall during the day. To rid ourselves of boredom, anxiety, and depression, we started a series of lectures, sang revolutionary songs, and told stories and jokes. This would last until everyone was asleep. The ward had one electric bulb that was switched on and off from outside the ward. The guard would switch it off at eight o'clock as he left for the night, and switch it on at five in the morning, when they came to check on us. We negotiated an agreement whereby we could leave the light on and turn it off ourselves by loosening the bulb.

It was impossible to receive information, outside the official propaganda, except with the cooperation of the prison wardens and guards, sometimes at a cost. The CPS cell, with the cooperation of our families, knew well how to gain cooperation with the prison staff. They were able to sneak in information about the social and political developments outside the prison. These were usually coded messages written under the food containers brought to us. The prison wardens would open the lid of the containers, shake up the contents, and then replace the lids before bringing the food to be brought to the ward.

Ustaz Ismael would decipher these messages and read them to us. In this way, we managed to learn that there were more than three thousand students, including both those at university and secondary school, being held in different prisons throughout the Sudan.

George Maker Benjamin was registered in the police records as a student while I was recorded as an official with the Department of Rural Water Development. Mohammed Ismael, although a student of law at the Khartoum Branch of Cairo University, was not recorded as a student. This became a problem later, when President Nimeri ordered the release of all students.

In one of the evening discussions, as we reached the sixty-day mark in prison, a question about our political future imposed itself. Up to this point in time only Ustaz Ismael was a bona fide CPS member. We were in prison on accusation that we were members or affiliates of the CPS. The CPS did not consider us members but counted Maker and me as democrats or friends of the party. We engaged in serious discussion about this issue but to no satisfactory conclusion. There were issues brought up in the discussion that could not be resolved. Then Ustaz Ismael joined the discussion, and said, "Once you get soaked, you'd better swim," suggesting that the only option in front of us was to join the CPS, with all the prospects for detention and even spending life in prison. It was too frightening an option for nearly all of us. No one could accept permanent state surveillance.

May 25 was the fifth anniversary of the May Revolution which had catapulted Gaafar Mohammed Nimeri to power as president of the republic. At the celebration of the anniversary in Khartoum, Nimeri decreed the release of all political detainees throughout the country. The news was brought to us in the ward on the next day by the prison officer, who read out the list. He asked Maker to fold his "number" (bed) and follow him to the prison office: he had been released. Two days later, a Boeing 707 flew into Juba to transport the university students to Khartoum. I was released two weeks later, in good part due to pressure on the government from my colleagues and the KUSU. Outside the prison, I saw that *Masa el Khair*, the organ of the Democratic Front, had published a bold headline in red: "Release Peter Adwok who is still detained in Juba Prison."

Spending more than two months in prison was a good induction into politics—anti-establishment or activist politics, for that matter. It had personal and impersonal ramifications. On hearing that I had been arrested and detained because the government suspected I was a Communist, the reaction of my family was that of fear and anxiety. My mother took the book collection I had in Malakal and threw it into the White Nile River. She did not know which of the books were political, but she worried that the books might implicate the family.

On being released, I went to the Department of Rural Water Development to collect my salary, but the director-general refused to pay my two-month salary. I noticed that many of my friends and acquaintances now treated me with disdain. It was like a danger-ous thing to be a Communist in southern Sudan. However, for me, the die was cast. I decided that whatever the struggle, I would always be an activist on the side of the people. I learned later that the difference between a political activist and a politician is their respective attitude: the activist struggles for change while the poli-tician struggles for power.

Looking back over my shoulders at my slow but steady evolu-tion from an innocent rural boy in 1954 to a full-blown urban intellectual political activist, notwithstanding the stint as minister in government, at the advanced age of seventy-six years in 2021, I am amazed but not overwhelmed by this development. However, what shocks and puzzles me still is the political context of South Sudan which suggests that we are still rural in everything we do. It is apparent that the war of national liberation was fought with-out knowledge and a clear understanding of state formation and nation-building processes.

The SPLM/A political and military elite took control of what was part of a modern state. In all their actions, however, they are attempting to reduce it to perhaps what it was in the seventeenth century. The policies and actions of this elite run against the concept and practice of liberation. This would be a matter of criticism and self-criticism, particularly for the revolutionary democrats who joined the ranks of the SPLM/A.

Chapter 8

Red Sea Hills Project

Invitation to Join the Communist Party

After graduation I could have returned to my work with the Ministry of Cooperatives and Rural Development in Juba. My experience with "preventive detention" in Juba Prison was not the only thing that discouraged my return to Juba. I had trained as a geologist, specialising in petrology and geochemistry. This was a speciality I never had the opportunity to apply in the Southern Region. I was afraid I would lose my theoretical knowledge because the Southern Regional Government did not have opportunities for undertaking serious geological research; it had neither laboratories nor funds for undertaking meaningful research work.

I therefore decided to place my application for employment with the Geological and Mineral Resources Department of the Ministry

of Industry and Mining in the central government. The employment process took a relatively short time. After three weeks of
waiting, three of us—Eltahir Osman Idris, Ahmed Hussein Ahmed,
and I—were given our employment letters. Eltahir had trained as a
geophysicist and was sent to a water project at an Eritrean refugee
camp in Shoak, Gederef area. Ahmed Hussein and I were sent to
a Soviet Union-funded geological survey and mineral prospecting
project in the Red Sea Hills.

It was in the first week of December 1974. The Red Sea Hills,
unlike the rest of the Sudan, enjoys a Mediterranean type of climate.
It is cold and rainy between December and April, that most suitable
season for geological field expeditions. After a few days of administrative orientation to acquaint us with how to deal with the workers
and general administration of the project, Ahmed Hussein and I
were asked to choose the part of the project in which each of us
would be comfortable working. I chose to engage with geological
surveying and mineral prospecting. I believed it was more challenging as the work required a command of theoretical and practical
knowledge, an understanding of geological formations, and knowledge of mineralisation processes.

The area known as South Sinkat was a vast area lying south of
Sinkat railway station and extends southwards into the Butana
region. It is a highly rugged topographic configuration comprising
deep valleys and dry, sandy riverbeds. I believe it was the indications
of gold and copper mineralisations and the ubiquitous occurrences
of skarns [late magmatic hydrothermal effect on limestone forma-
tion], which prompted the decision to focus on the exploration of
this area more than anywhere else in the Red Sea Hills. The expedition comprised twelve geologists, of whom eight were Sudanese and
four were Russian, and thirty workers: drivers, cooks and porters.
There were also three Russian interpreters, as the Russian geologists rarely spoke or understood English. I was the only trainee
geologist fresh from university. All of our field equipment: tents,
mattresses, sleeping bags, vehicles, generators, water tankers, field

radios, geological hammers, uniforms and boots had been shipped in from the Soviet Union.

Divided into four teams, we would start off early in the morning, carrying our food rations and water, and return to base late in the afternoon or sometimes at night depending on the distance we had traversed. After dinner we would meet for about one hour to debrief and determine the next day's programme. With the help of topographical maps and aerial photographs or their mosaics, the teams' objectives were to map the rocky outcroppings and measure their inclination (if any); collect samples of rock, residual soil, and plants for biogeochemical investigation; and reveal any prominent geologic structures that may indicate regional or continental dimension or trend. It was great learning for a fresh graduate, and indeed I felt that I was enjoying my work, not only gaining insights acquiring a correct understanding of the geology of the area but also putting my theoretical knowledge to practice.

Then one day the leader of the team received a radio message from Port Sudan, the project headquarters: the Sudanese manager of the project, Adli Abdel Mageed, wanted me to come back to Port Sudan and told our team leader that he should put me on the fuel tanker that was returning to Port Sudan to collect fuel for the expedition. These were bureaucratic matters not meant from discussion: I was only to oblige, and therefore had to prepare myself. We left the camp early the next day on the six-hour trip to Port Sudan. In the geologist' mess, I received a letter instructing me to be ready at seven o'clock the next morning; a vehicle was coming to take me on a trip to Serakoit, some three hundred kilometres northwest of Port Sudan. It meant that I was to catch up with Adli Abdel Mageed, Akasha Ali, Ahmed Yassin, and a senior geologist who had arrived from Khartoum and already left for the gold exploration project in Serakoit.

I arrived at Serakoit at about eight o'clock in the evening, and was rushed into a meeting that had already started. It was decided that I was to remain in Serakoit as acting camp manager, to continue with the drilling work already in progress, and to undertake all scientific and administrative functions in the camp. I tried to put up an argument against the decision but it was apparent there was some unspoken matters between the project manager and the senior geologists attached to the project in Serakoit and the authorities in Khartoum. This would only become fully understood later, after the end of the field season. However, I noted the final words of the project manager as he bid me farewell. "*Inta id waratah,*" he said in Arabic, meaning "You have trapped yourself."

Serakoit was a place in the middle of nowhere. In the nearest Beja (Hadendawa section) village, a sheikh called Shariff Ahmed ran an Islamic school (*Kalwah*) with the assistance of the Saudi government. The village was located on the banks of a dry riverbed that flowed for only a few days once a year. The geology camp got its water supply from the village well at a cost of some litres of diesel, which were used to run both the water pump and the village's only grinding mill. When the sheikh heard there was a southern Sudanese manager of the camp, he visited the camp with a few rams as gifts. It was a gesture that ensured cooperation over the next few months.

The drilling was intended to strike the gold-bearing quartz veins in an area that had been surveyed and explored for gold thousands of years before the time of Christ. They had been drilling for two months and there was no showing of quartz veins or mineralisation. The Russian advisor, a Mr. Sergei who barely spoke English, could not convince me why he had advised the drilling. It was a futile exercise; it was obvious the Pharaohs were better exploration workers than our modern days geologists; for they had removed all the gold bearing veins we were now drilling for. In fact, I really wondered why he kept on with this challenging task in such a hot place as Serakoit. The temperatures sometimes hit fifty degrees Celsius in the middle of the day and the Russian tents we lived in turned into ovens. The generator brought from Siberia produced more heat than electricity. Out of humanitarian consideration, I sent the Russian back to Port Sudan.

Serakoit was the most wasteful project I ever witnessed. I spent two weeks conducting a geological survey of the area. The only gold-bearing quartz veins in the area of 250 square kilometres had already been mined by the pharaohs and they had refilled the mine with the tailings. I ordered the workers to remove the tailings to investigate the shape of the mine. We discovered that the mine shaft tapered with depth, suggesting that the pharaohs had reached the end of the quartz veins. I wanted to end the season but that was the prerogative of the director general in Khartoum. We had to remain under the conditions of extreme heat in Serakoit for the next nine weeks. The only incentive for braving such terrible conditions was our field allowances, the monetary value of which was greater than our monthly salary.

Back in Port Sudan at the end of the field season, I raised a complaint with the project manager, Adli Abdel Mageed, about the way I had been treated: a new graduate, I had been left alone in the field while the senior geologist, whose experience I should have benefited from, was in Port Sudan. This became a topic of discussion among my colleagues in Port Sudan, forcing the project manager to report the matter to Khartoum. As I said earlier, there were matters of which I wasn't party to. In the end, as a means to silence me and because we were entering the dead season, I was given air tickets to take my leave in Malakal. I could not resist what I thought was a bonus as I was not yet entitled to annual leave.

The month of June was the beginning of the hot season in Port Sudan and many people were leaving the Red Sea port city for cooler parts of the country. This made it difficult to book a seat on the Sudan Airways Fokker aircraft, which had two flights daily to Khartoum. The only reservation I could get was five weeks away. One day a certain Bukhari came to see me in the office. He worked as a technician with the Geophysical Department of the Red Sea Hills project. He wanted to discuss something important so, after some courtesies, we decided to go out to a place where we could have some privacy.

"I was sent by the Communist Party of the Sudan to convey to you the following message: You are welcome to Port Sudan and the branch will be happy to receive in your own handwriting an application to join the party," he said. I thanked the party for recognising me and told him that I would immediately write the application but that I was virtually on leave, only that I was waiting for my flight to Khartoum. We agreed that I would hand in the application, but all the formalities would only be completed after I had returned from leave.

The Communist Party of Sudan had been banned, and its eight members of the Constituent Assembly unseated in 1965 through a conspiracy hatched by the Muslim Brotherhood, the Islamic Chartered Front (ICF). The Umma government of Sadiq el Mahdi had refused to execute the order of the Supreme Court overturning the legislation. After the events of July 1971, the party could only operate with utmost secrecy. At that time, it was a serious risk to one's life to be known as a Communist. Many of the party's staunchest members, sympathisers, and friends had either deserted it or become apologists of the Sudan Socialist Union (SSU), which now established a totalitarian dictatorship in the country.

My arrival in Malakal in the second week of August 1975 coincided with student upheavals linked to protests against the Jonglei Canal Project and I had to cut short my stay. When I informed my eldest sister, Piero Nyaba, that I was returning to Port Sudan, she was extremely disappointed: this meant that I couldn't start the process towards a marriage project. I hurried back to Port Sudan to formalise and complete the process of party membership. It was by no means simple; I met people I did not know beforehand who grilled and subjected me to tough questions about myself. I was to learn later that the process necessarily had to be tough to weed out infiltrators, spies, and weak elements who would not endure the brutality of the police or security and might jump ship at critical times.

The interview gave me the opportunity to change my mind if I wanted to. I knew perfectly well that I was entering a red zone of danger. There was the risk of being arrested, tortured, imprisoned, and even executed like the three martyrs—Abdel Khaliq Mahgoub, the party secretary-general, Shafie Ahmed el Sheikh, and Joseph Ukel Garang. In addition to these men, many Communist cadres and members were killed in the wake of July coup and counter-coup. The membership of the CPS registered as an honour, a duty, and a right. It was a place for sacrifice not of privilege. I was not able to define what drove my determination to become a member of the CPS.

I became aware of my motivation much later in the course of the struggle. But I believe the events of July 1971, in which govern-ment agents and religious fanatics hunted down the Communists and their supporters, had a major impact on me for by that time I had started reading Marxist literature. In 1970 I undertook, as part of a geological sciences course in palaeontology, the study of old forms of life found in rock formations and came into contact with Darwin's theory of evolution. The two pieces of knowledge shook my faith in the Christian religion. I did not feel the same again about going to church and started to look at people and their actions differently, and always took the side of the underdogs.

Therefore, my decision to join the CPS was the outcome of my personal conversion and belief in people's ability to transform their reality. I did not suffer any qualms or regrets. After the first and second "cadre schools" in the party, the global picture in my mind started to clear up and things crystallised in their different perspectives. In retrospect, I would rewind my memory to 1974 in the Special Ward of Juba Central Prison. My level of social aware-ness and political consciousness could not then enable a correct understanding and scientific analysis of the situation. One and half years after my release, however, I had learned not only how to analyse the genesis and elements of the contradiction, but also to work hard to resolve it.

I was a member of the CPS for twelve years and had to resign from it in 1986 to enable me join the SPLM/A. During this period, I abandoned the project in Port Sudan to take a teaching job in the University of Juba. Abuk and I established our small family. After the birth of Keni, our first daughter, we went to the People's Republic of Hungary, where I pursued postgraduate studies towards a PhD in petrology and geochemistry. I was involved in the Sudanese as well as African and Arab student politics in Hungary. The party's general guidelines for students, whether graduates or undergraduates, was academic excellence and a return to the homeland. I served for one year as the branch political commissar; my functions were to handle relations with the Hungarian Workers' Socialist Party, its youth wing, and the World Federation of Democratic Youth.

As a state employee, given that University of Juba was a parastatal institution, it was a precarious balance of loyalties to the Sudanese state and to the CPS. The state security apparatus was still not fully developed enough to cover anti-government activities in the diaspora. The only Sudanese embassy in central Europe was in Prague. As post-graduate students we had direct relations with the cultural attaché at the embassy but I am not sure if the embassy wrote security reports about our activities.

After the birth in Budapest of Pito and Kut, our small family had grown to five members. We returned to Juba in October 1982. This was a period of internal political upheavals in the Southern Region, but there was nothing to indicate that the state security organisation had any case against me on account of my political activities in Budapest. I settled down to combine teaching with trade union work as secretary for external affairs in the Juba University Staff Association (JUSA). My connection to the party had been relayed from Budapest to Khartoum and from there to Juba, in accordance with party procedures. It is worth mentioning that the party activities, including communication between the centre and the branches, was conducted under strict security considerations.

The politics of decentralisation (*kokora* or redivision), pushed largely by elements from Equatoria and Upper Nile, dominated the political situation in the Southern Region when I arrived back to the country. The *kokora* was a bait Nimeri introduced into the political foray to quell political opposition to his totalitarian regime. The Equatoria Branch of the CPS, under the illusion that *kokora* was a democratic demand of the people of Equatoria, threw its support behind Nimeri's pet project of *kokora*. This triggered bitter internal debate within the party's cell at the university, with almost all of my northern colleagues taking the false argument. In hindsight, state security's search of my house, which occurred sometime in April 1983, must have been connected to the attitude of my colleagues in the party and their links to the university administration.

Nearly all of these northern colleagues were recruited as deans and heads of departments in the university colleges, in a pattern that smacked of selective favouritism of northerners and discrimination against southerners. To hold on to their privilege, including administrative perks, they had to support Nimeri's political programme in southern Sudan. They viewed the issue through an Arab–Islamic lens rather than a Marxist or working-class lens. It was like pretending to be struggling against Nimeri's totalitarianism in the country while supporting his policies against the people of southern Sudan. But this duplicity soon came to an end. Another hot debate erupted within the cell, questioning why at a JUSA meeting I had not put up a fight against their removal from their administrative positions. They called me names for maintaining the principled position that JUSA would defend their right to continue teaching but would not support their continued privileges as college deans and department heads.

The CPS always warned against petty bourgeoisie attitudes and the liberalism of the intelligentsia within working-class movements and parties. These are the kind of attitudes that vigorously defend one's own privileges and view privilege as an entitlement on account of class, race, or religion. It is the kind of attitude that led to the breakup of the Second Communist International just before World

War II. As such, the CPS encouraged party cadres and functionaries to engage in relentless ideological struggle against liberalism, both inside and outside the party precincts. Being ideological in nature, its essence outside the party was to distinguish between real and false friends of the revolution; to disseminate correct ideas; and to strengthen and enlarge the revolutionary camp by winning to it more friends. Internally, within the party, it reinforced the political, organisational, and ideological unity and effectiveness; identified its weak points; purged the rank and file of false ideas; and strengthened party unity on the basis of principles, which become clear and precise in the cause of the ideological struggle.

I envisioned this ideological struggle against totalitarian rule in the form of heightened trade union activity, in collaboration with other trade union organisations in Juba, and as far afield as Khartoum. If need be, the struggle also entailed taking up arms. The uneven socio-economic development of different parts of the Sudan had left an indelible mark in southern Sudan, in the form of social and cultural backwardness of its people which was characterised by the lack of a culture of political organisation and action. As a consequence, it was easier to mobilise southern Sudanese to take up arms for war than for picketing, strikes, processions, and demonstrations to support demands for political rights.

It must be admitted that by 1983 Nimeri's totalitarian regime was at the height of acute social, economic, and political crisis. The Southern Region had, since 1976, been the regime's only base of support. But Nimeri's repeated interference in the region's democratic right to choose its leaders had sufficiently alienated its leaders. The region had become restive, especially after the discovery of petroleum reserves in Western Upper Nile (later renamed Unity) Province and the decision to locate the oil refinery in Kosti instead of Bentiu. By 1980 it was clear that Nimeri had lost the south. The two parties of the National Front, namely the Umma Party (UP) and the Democratic Unionist Party (DUP), withdrew from the government, leaving the Islamic Chartered Front (ICF), the agenda of which was to take over the government and to promulgate an Islamic constitution for the country.

The incompatibility of the Southern Region with an Islamic constitution was a complicating factor in Nimeri's power calculus. Indeed, defining Sudan along the parameters of Islam and Arabism, as well as considering the Sudanese nationality in transition to full integration into the *umma el Arabiya,* triggered the Southern provinces' demand for federation in 1958. Although the Addis Ababa Agreement of 1972 restored the hope for unity of the Sudan based on freedom, justice, and fraternity, the lack of social and economic development in the Southern Region led to the rebellion of units of Anya-nya that had been absorbed into the Sudan Armed Forces (SAF). Anya-nya II was soon engaging the army in a low-key insurgency in the south.

Nimeri's stratagem was to dismantle the Southern Region by dividing southerners along ethnic and provincial lines; relations between peoples were already strained because of the poor performance of the High Executive Council (HEC). This pitted the Equatorian political elite against elites from Bahr el Ghazal and Upper Nile in what was known as *kokora* or redivision of the Southern Region into its constituent subregions. The sharp divisions which Nimeri encouraged among the southern political leadership set the scene for him to abrogate the Addis Ababa Agreement and dismantle the Southern Region.

On 16 May 1983, the army command in Juba attacked Battalion 104 in Bor, heralding the formation of the Sudan People's Liberation Movement/Sudan People's Liberation Army (SPLM/A) and the beginning of the second civil war. On 1 June, Nimeri decreed the redivision of the Southern Region into the subregions of Bahr el Ghazal, Equatoria, and Upper Nile. In September, Nimeri decreed the Islamic sharia laws (September Laws), making the Sudan a de facto Islamic country.

The SPLM/A and its leadership were something new in the Sudanese political theatre. However, its manifesto suggested it was part of the forces of the national democratic revolution in the Sudan. Even in the Southern Region, people did not know anything about Dr. John Garang de Mabior. Nimeri's information minister, Khogali Salihieen, committed a political blunder when he announced, incorrectly, that John Garang was the late Joseph Garang's brother and that he was a Communist. With logistical support from the Derg, the SPLM/A quickly captured regional and international newspaper headlines; the BBC's correspondent in the Sudan, Carol Berger, captured and reported every SPLA military action. The SPLM/A was a force to reckon with. *Al-Midan* (The Square), the clandestinely published official newsletter of the CPS, directed its cadres and functionaries to support the SPLM/A as one of the pillars of resistance to Nimeri and his totalitarian regime.

The war in southern Sudan intensified and escalated from eastern Upper Nile into Equatoria and Bahr el Ghazal, and the Nuba Mountains and Blue Nile in northern Sudan. Nimeri's wholesale implementation of the World Bank/IMF structural adjustment program (SAP) triggered a severe social, economic, and political crisis in the country. The famine in Dar Fur and eastern Sudan, and the cost of war in the southern Sudan exacerbated the situation, triggering anti-regime demonstrations in Khartoum and culminating in a popular uprising. On 6 April 1985, Field Marshall Gaafar Mohamed Nimeri was overthrown.

The fall of Nimeri was no panacea for solving Sudan's plethora of social, economic, and political contradictions; the mass movement that had led to Nimeri's fall retreated in the face of right-wing betrayal even before the regime's political establishment had been dismantled. Instead of continuing the intifada to transform it into the national democratic revolution, the CPS acquiesced to a political compromise, similar to that of October 1964, and joined with the traditional sectarian and theocratic political forces to support the holding of parliamentary elections in April 1986. This was the first sign of the mass movement's retreat and the stealing of the revolution by the political right. The attitude of the CPS leadership towards the SPLM/A moved sharply away from its initial support of the movement. This was reflected in internal and external party communications and publications that echoed sentiments of the northern Sudanese left that saw the SPLM/A as nothing but a southern Sudanese Trojan Horse.

The document of the fourth party congress in 1967, entitled "Marxism and the Issues of the Sudanese Revolution," stated clearly that Sudan was in the stage of national democratic revolution and that this stage required the unity of all patriotic social and political forces under the leadership of the workers' party. This analysis came after the retreat of the mass movement that overthrew the first military government in 1964. It was a serious error of judgement that the party was repeating the same mistake for which it had criticised itself in 1967. In a country like the Sudan—where the vast majority of the population live in poverty, illiteracy, ignorance, and superstition—liberal democratic elections will invariably favour the sectarian theocratic and traditional political elite. I was then of the opinion that liberal democratic processes at a time when the country was in a revolutionary situation of war would smother the revolutionary zeal of the masses.

In Juba, where public opinion among the elite was anti-SPLA, the May Regime's symbols remained powerful in both government and society. The workers and other trade unions that appeared overnight, some of them unregistered and whose agendas were more local than national, made it difficult for the popular uprising forces (PUFs) to chart a course to further the gains of the popular uprising. The individual we had delegated to go to Khartoum forgot about his assignment and, instead, lobbied for a political position in the Equatoria State government.

It could be said with some confidence that the CPS political line ran contrary to the expectations of many of its cadres and functionaries, particularly those of us from the peripheral Sudan. Many of us favoured dovetailing the popular uprising with the war of national liberation which the SPLM/A had spearheaded. However, party internal order did not countenance any unilateral action; any action must be through and sanctioned by the party. The party cell at the university appeared to have died. We rarely held formal meetings and members had broken into like-minded groups that engaged in private discussion of party matters. As secretary for external affairs, I represented JUSA in the trade unions and at meetings of the PUFs in Khartoum. When the university administration refused to release JUSA funds to cover my travel costs to attend meetings, I had to risk taking flights on cargo planes.

At the end of November 1985, seven months into the popular uprising regime, the DUP sponsored a PUF conference in Wad Medani. I had to attend, hoping that I would have an opportunity to meet the CPS leadership there. The conference enabled the social and political forces of the peripheral Sudan (mainly from southern Sudan, Dar Fur, Nuba Mountains, Beja, and northernmost Sudan)—actually, the politically excluded, economically marginalised, and socially discriminated Sudan—to meet and agree to form the Sudan Rural Solidarity (SRS). The declaration was broadcast the next day on SPLA Radio, to the chagrin of the Arab-dominated northern political establishment. I also made use of my presence in Wad Medani to arrange for a meeting with Secretary-General Ustaz Ibrahim Nuqud. I wanted to discuss the SPLM/A and what stand southern Sudanese members of the party should adopt.

The meeting started off cordially but soon degenerated into something I never could have imagined. The party position was that Garang was a stooge of Ethiopia's President Mengistu Haile Mariam, who himself was an agent of imperialism, and that the CPS was a proletariat party and had never entertained adventurism—meaning military action—over the course of its long history. I came out of the meeting completely depressed, wishing that I had not requested the encounter, particularly after the secretary-general coolly rejected my request to resign from the party on the grounds that it should be discussed at the party branch level in Juba. On my way back to the hotel, I decided that I should leave immediately for Khartoum and then proceed to Juba.

The decision to join the SPLM/A was cooking in my mind but I would not execute it before April 1986, when I would have completed my teaching and fieldwork. I was then head of the Geology and Earth Sciences Unit at the College of Natural Resources and Environmental Studies, University of Juba. Besides me, the unit had another geologist, a geomorphologist, and a teaching assistant. I was obliged to stay on until the academic session ended. I also had family problems to be addressed. My father and younger sibling Paul Otuk, as well as my father-in-law Payiti Ayik, had passed on the year before. My children were still quite young and it was obvious my wife wouldn't countenance me joining the SPLM/A.

In the first week of January 1986, I took the students for four weeks of geology field studies in Khartoum and parts of the Northern Province, where geological studies had been previously conducted. Outcrops of sedimentary, igneous, and metamorphic formations were present there and provided students with valuable field experience. By the middle of February, the students had completed their fieldwork, so I took them back to Juba for their final examination. I did not want to leave my family in Juba, so I took them to Khartoum and rented a house on Tuti Island. On 2 April I cast my vote for the Graduate Constituency and on 4 April I left for Addis Ababa to join the SPLM/A.

Khogali Ali Khogali, a colleague in the U of J party cell, later told me that the party's Equatoria Branch summoned the cell to investigate the reasons for my defection to the SPLM/A. He and I had first met in Nairobi in 1990, when he was doing his postgraduate studies on a DAAD scholarship. The party rejected the reasons given by the cell, claiming that I, Peter Adwok Nyaba, was an opportunist and this was why I had defected to the SPLM/A. The decision of the party branch, however, was that I had left out of frustration over the lack of political activities. For that reason, the U of J party cell was disbanded, and its members distributed to other cells in Juba.

I terminated my membership of the CPS on my own volition. It was not that I had renounced Marxism as a guiding political philosophy: I wanted to change the means of struggle from passive politics to revolutionary armed struggle. What then was the CPS? This question came to me in a natural way. I don't know if others had the same experience as I had. When I finished the first cadre school my first impression was that the CPS was a school to learn both Marxist theory and practice, as well as being a programmatic platform on which to apply theory and practice of socioeconomic and political development of Sudanese polity and society. In this respect, it would be appropriate to reflect on the following words of Fidel Castro, the great Cuban revolutionary, in order to put into context my decision to abandon the CPS, twelve years after joining it, for the SPLM/A in 1986:

In the complexity of the present-day world, where circumstances are so diverse and countries are in such different situations and at such varying levels of material, cultural and technological development, it is impossible to hope to conceive of Marxism as a kind of a church, some kind of religious doctrine with its Rome, its pope and its ecumenical council. Marxism is a revolutionary and dialectical doctrine; not a religious one. To endeavour to contain Marxism in some species of catechism is anti-Marxist. The diversity of situations must inevitably lead to an infinity of interpretations. Those who give correct interpretation and apply them logically will triumph. Those who are wrong or who do not follow the logic of revolutionary thinking will fail; they will be overturned and supplanted, for Marxism is not a private property inscribed in a land register. It is a doctrine of revolutionaries written by one revolutionary and developed by other revolutionaries for revolutionaries (Granma, English weekly edition, 12 March 1987).

I entertain no negative feelings about anyone whom I interacted with in the CPS. I certainly did not join the SPLM/A out of bitterness with the CPS; nor do I believe that joining the SPLM/A was an act of opportunism or ambition for power, not at all. I had, however, in the context of study and the pursuit of revolutionary knowledge come to realise that only the revolutionised peasants, and not the industrial proletariat, would uplift the masses of the Sudanese people from the centuries-old condition of socioeconomic underdevelopment and sociocultural backwardness. The bulk of the masses constituting the SPLM/A were sedentary agrarian and agropastoral communities in southern, western, central, eastern, and northern Sudan. They were like train carriages that needed a diesel engine to pull the train to its destination: that diesel engine, in my opinion, was the CPS. That was my idea when I went to meet Ustaz Nuqud.

The failure of the CPS to provide the ideological and organisational assistance the SPLM/A desperately needed, on account of the class origin of its leadership, resulted in the failure of the SPLM/A to evolve into a genuine national liberation movement. It also denied the agrarian proletariat the revolutionary role they could have played in their own liberation and the larger development of the Sudanese revolution. It is worth mentioning that peasants and cattle herders constitute the vast majority of the Sudanese people. The party missed an opportunity to stamp its ideological mark on the mass movement in Southern Sudan, Nuba Mountains, and Blue Nile. This would have been an opportunity to reverse the trend set by the British colonial administration with its Closed Districts Ordinance.

When the time came for the party to take up arms in 1995 against the Islamic fundamentalist regime, it was not a fundamental change in its political strategy but, in the context of the National Democratic Alliance (NDA), a kind of political coordination with the traditional and theocratic parties. A wall of resentment and suspicion had already been erected between its contingent of fighters and its would-be natural allies, the New Sudan Brigade or SPLA in Eastern Sudan. This did not create the required synergy with the political left in the armed struggle, made up of former CPA cadres and functionaries, as well as other democrats who had joined the rank and file of the SPLM/A.

As I write these lines, I can still recall every episode in the revolutionary struggle I consciously decided to thrust into my life and that of my small family. I am no longer a member of the SPLM/A, having resigned in 2014 in the wake of the civil war that erupted in 2013, barely three years into the independence of South Sudan. I joined Riek Machar's second rebellion but, as you will read in the coming pages, I also later resigned from the Sudan People's Liberation Movement/Army–In Opposition (SPLM/A–IO). I am now just a political lone ranger, unfettered by or unhinged to any political artefact.

I would like to discuss this apparent political nomadism— moving from one political standpoint to another—in the context of a few points in a long quote from one of Fidel Castro's speeches. It is noteworthy to mention that some party cadres and functionaries I knew at the University of Khartoum, by virtue of our connection in the Democratic Front (DF), were staunch Communists but had left the party. I knew that Khatim Adlan, a member of the Central Committee, had left the party to establish Haq, a civil society– political party outfit, with some other Communists and democrats. Dr. El Shafie Khidir, who contested for the position of the party's secretary-general following the demise of Ustaz Nuqud in 2013, also left, possibly because he was dismissed from the party.

I mention these instances not to try to justify my actions but to underline the importance of personal conviction and the internal political environment that allows thorough discussion of decisions. I believed adherence to democratic principles and a tradition of continuous learning and unlearning could save the party from splits and bitter frictions, particularly as we were still struggling to capture state power. There were great lessons to learn from the collapse of the Soviet Union, the historical model for many Marxists and workers' parties, and the shift in the world order. As Fidel Castro said, Marxism is not a private property inscribed in a land register, suggesting that no one has a monopoly on the truth. Different societies will definitely arrive at socialism via different routes, as determined by their objective reality.

The fact that I abandoned the CPS to join the SPLM/A was not intended as a repudiation or criticism of the principles and fundamental tenets on which the party stood. No, on the contrary, I had not abandoned Marxist solutions to the problems of socio-economic underdevelopment and sociocultural backwardness of the vast majority of South Sudanese. By joining the armed struggle, I transformed my means of struggle qualitatively in response to the prevailing reality: the mass movement was in retreat after the traditional theocratic political parties had hijacked and stolen the popular uprising that overthrew the May Regime.

Chapter 9

Education Tourism in Europe

A Marriage Project & Employment at Juba University

The advantage of employment as a geologist with the Sudan government, unlike being in the private sector, was the early opportunity to receive a government or foreign scholarship which would allow one to obtain either a master's or doctorate in the discipline of speciality. Geological sciences are essentially based on research, meaning that a specialist requires more than a bachelor's degree.

After successfully completing my second field season I was entitled to receive a government scholarship for any university in the United States; the cost of such scholarships would then be part of the corporate social responsibility Chevron Oil Company paid exploring for oil in the Red Sea and in southern Sudan. The management of the Red Sea Hills project instead nominated me to attend a UNESCO-sponsored international course called "Mineral Prospecting and Mining in Developing Countries" in Leoben, Austria.

Travelling to Europe was something every young Sudanese desired, and was an opportunity he or she would catch with both hands. I was so happy, filled with the feeling that I was lucky. Many Sudanese come back with fancy stories from travels to Europe, America, and other parts of the world. I thought this was my turn to make a trip outside the Sudan. However, I soon realised what I was being offered was only an eight-month-long non-certificate course. My nomination for the Austrian course suggested that the administration was playing a trick on me, robbing me of an opportunity to complete a master's degree.

The project manager had not forgiven me for the embarrassment I caused him when I exposed the corruption scandal the year before. I had questioned why they were receiving field allowances when they were not in the field but staying in Port Sudan. He did not want me on the project but had no power to dismiss or transfer me to another project. I did not want to reject the offer and give him an excuse to label me as difficult. I accepted the advice of my colleague, Gaafar Abdel Mageed, who had just returned from the same course. He encouraged me to take it because it would give me an opportunity to discover Europe.

I was working on my field report when news of the nomination reached me. Khartoum had already sent the clearance for travel, which made me suspicious that someone did not want me in Port Sudan. Just before I started my journey, the National Front, on 6 July 1976, stormed Khartoum with a huge military force numbering ten of thousands of fighters, of mixed nationalities: Sudanese [mainly Dar Furi], Chadians, and other West African nationals. The force originated from Libya, suggesting Gaddafi's connivance. His relationship with Nimeri had floundered and he was now supporting the National Front's invasion and Nimeri's removal from power in the Sudan. The Sudanese disparagingly referred to it as *gazwa el ajnebi* or foreign invasion.

By their very appearance, poor knowledge of the geography of the three towns that constituted Khartoum, as well as the locations of the important political figures they were meant to eliminate, these invading forces were conspicuously not Sudanese, or if they were, like the Dar Furi, they had never been to Khartoum. It was really a meaningless adventure. Although they managed to take over the Armoured Division in Shagara, Khartoum South, they were unable to start the tanks. They captured Radio Omdurman but could not broadcast their political message; Radio Juba, in the south of the country, became the alternative transmitter of government information and propaganda. In just two days, the Sudanese Army rooted these forces out of Khartoum, returning the country to normalcy, although Khartoum remained under curfew from ten at night until five in the morning.

I managed to arrive in time to attend the required interview at the Austrian Embassy. I still had four months until the course's scheduled start time in November. I had the option of returning to Port Sudan or request my annual leave, which entitled me to air tickets to Malakal. I stayed with an old friend, James Amum, in his family residence in the Shagara suburb of Khartoum. He had received a telephone call from a mutual friend, Joseph Bol Chan, who was studying in Budapest, Hungary, and had just come on holidays. We had a good time remembering our younger days. Joseph informed us that he was on a mission to conduct his marriage. We both knew his fiancé and future wife, Ruth Aba, the daughter of the school overseer at Dolieb Hill and sister of my colleague Samuel Akwoch Aba. When he asked me to join his team, I obliged.

Together we flew to Malakal and accompanied him to his home village in Agodo to arrange for the dowry (cows) to be driven to Pathworo to finalise the Chollo traditional marriage rituals. Over a period of two weeks, we completed Joseph Bol's marriage process and bade the couple farewell as they set off for their honeymoon in Khartoum and Budapest. I now had time to look after my own affairs. Marriage and forming a family can be a contagious social virus. Once a friend has completed his marriage, others start to think immediately about their own affairs. Chollo society is very particular about family and a person continuously faces the question from friends and relatives: "When are you going to marry, or are you going to remain a bachelor for the rest of your life?"

I had been for a long time under enormous pressure from my parents to marry. As a matter of fact, I did have a relationship, but my arrest in Juba 1974 had caused some turbulence. My fiancé's uncle challenged the relationship and wanted her to marry another man. I was lucky that my prospective father-in-law stood with me. Abuk would recall years later her father's response to his brother, "I want her to marry that Communist if that is what she wants." This assured the success of our affair. When I went to inform them of the acceptance of my proposal and that I had everything ready, this was a piece of news that my parents were happy to hear.

Of course, I had started planning as soon as I was employed, sending money to my nephew and close friend, Prince Kwongo Dak, who was then working at the Juba Commercial Bank in Malakal. He was to use the money to purchase heifers towards my dowry collection. It was important that I completed the marriage arrangements before I left for Khartoum. I directed my sibling, Paulo Otuk, who worked in Khartoum, to go to Malakal to finalise the traditional Chollo rituals in my place.

My fiancé, Abuk Payiti, had travelled to Juba before we sealed our final arrangements. She had been accepted at Juba Commercial Secondary School. This meant I had to travel to meet her in Juba. We agreed that a church ceremony was completely unnecessary: the traditional ceremony would be enough to legitimise our marriage. We needed only marriage rings. I gave our measurements to my uncle, Okony Onwar, who was travelling to Khartoum, where the rings were crafted. While still in Juba I visited the Department of Cooperative and Rural Development and presented my case to receive my unpaid two months of salary from 1974. I was lucky:

the new minister, Ezekiel Machuei Kodi, understood the claim and agreed to pay the money, which boosted my budget.

Back in Khartoum I started the process of acquiring a passport. It was a daily tussle with public transport to reach the Immigration Department only to be told to come the next day. This went on for nearly two weeks. As soon as I got the passport, I started the process of acquiring an exit visa. This was another nightmare. It was good that I had started the application early. There was a deliberate policy by the security organs to frustrate individuals identified as anti-government. It took me almost a month before I met the security officer who had taken possession of my passport.

He had information about my political activities while at the university and my arrest and detention in Juba. He questioned me about El Khatim Adlan, Sidgi Kabelo, Edward Lino, and others. I told him they were my contemporaries at the university. At the end, he told me to go the Immigration Department the following day. It was just in the immediate aftermath of the foreign invasion episode and, therefore, the attention of the security agencies was focused more on the Dar Furi and members of the Umma Party in general. They seemed to lack interest in southerners, which would explain why the questioning wasn't that severe or insightful.

As I was preparing to travel, after the day's errands in the city centre and before we hit the road to Shagara, James Amum and I, first drove to the residence of our political mentor, Prince Othwonh Dak, in Mugrhan. I wanted to get his advice before leaving to Europe. We spent a good part of the early evening on the lawn, enjoying chilled beers or a glass or two of Johnny Walker. My flight to Rome the next morning was very early, so James Amum and I left Othwonh Dak early in order to have enough time to sleep. It was my first ever trip to Europe, and didn't have the slightest idea in terms of clothes, suitcase etc. I assumed it was like travelling in the Sudan. I purchased a travelling bag, the type travellers on rural bus journeys usually carried their belongings in. On checking-on, I presented the bag, and it weighed less than ten kilos, which meant that I could have carried it on me to the cabin. This was my first cultural shock, as fellow passengers came in with sophisticated suitcases.

I was to stay overnight in Rome before continuing next day the travel to Vienna in Austria. They advised us to collect our luggage at the conveyor belt. I could not find my travel bag. At the reporting desk the clerks couldn't find anything on their luggage guide that matched or resembled my bag; mine was locally produced and was completely different. The Sudan Airways representative told me not to worry. It would be brought back when the plane returned from London. "Come earlier to have time before your flight to Vienna," the man advised me.

I climbed onto the shuttle bus to the hotel, which was not very far from the airport. I wished someone had offered some orientation because I was going to suffer another cultural shock. After settling into the room, I thought I needed toothpaste and a toothbrush. I went down to the gift shop to purchase the two, together with a few postcards I wanted to send home to announce my arrival in Italy. The price was in thousands of Italian liras. I told the shop attendant to keep the items because I did not have that money. The man just laughed and told me to show him the money I had; he picked out two two-dollar notes and gave me a balance in lira. Back in the hotel room, I picked up the telephone to call room service. I told the waiter at the end of the phone that I wanted some cold water and ice cubes. He paused and said, "Sir, for cold water, you can get from the tap, but I will bring the ice cubes soon." In fact, I did not have to purchase the toothbrush and paste as the hotel provided them for free. It was towards the end of October and the weather was getting cold in Europe. Indeed, I really did not need the ice cubes—a second and third cultural shock. In the morning I took the first bus to the Airport, collected my travel bag, and waited for the Alitalia flight to Vienna. I arrived there in the afternoon and managed to get a hotel reservation.

It was interesting to visit the different historical sites in Vienna, triggering memories of my history of Europe lessons at secondary school. After two days in Vienna, I boarded a train for the three-hour trip to Leoben. The travel to Leoben was not as complicated as I had feared. A travel plan was available on each seat and indicated that I had to change trains in Bruck/Moor to take a local train to the central station at Leoben. The mining high school, Montanehochschule, its name in the German language, was situated in a village populated predominantly by mineworkers who laboured in the iron and lead/zinc mines in the surrounding hills.

It was indeed an international course. Apart from its academic programme which included excursions to mines in Yugoslavia and Italy, there were eleven participants from ten so-called third-world or developing countries: two from Afghanistan, and one each from Bolivia, Ghana, Nepal, Pakistan, Panama (a female student who went on to marry an Austrian in Leoben), Sudan, Tanzania, Thailand and Uganda. At the hostel I shared a room with a Nepalese student, a quiet and humble man.

Three weeks into the course the eleven international postgraduate students took part in a miners' ritual called *ledersfprung*. We dressed in mining attire, drank a pint of beer, and one by one jumped over a leather belt, shouting whatever slogan came to mind for the occasion. The course subjects, except for metallurgy and mining, were topics I had already studied in my undergraduate classes. In fact, had my predecessor in the course, Gaafar Abdel Mageed, told me this I would have declined to attend course. It actually suited people like Gaafar, who did only a general degree course in geology at an Egyptian university. I was so disappointed that I almost decided to come back to the Sudan. But I remembered Gaafar's advice that I should travel and discover Europe. Didn't Speke, David Livingstone, and other European explorers and travellers claim to have discovered parts of Africa, places that had been populated by Africans for more than a hundred thousand years before these foreigners set foot on the continent? The feebleness of the academic course prompted me to search out and discover where the discos and red-light districts were in Leoben, and to travel to Graz, Vienna, and Munich in Bavaria, Federal Republic of Germany.

In the München Hauptbahnhof I ran into a tall Black man whom I guessed correctly was a Sudanese. Kiir Manchol hailed from Kongor, in the part of Upper Nile Province since renamed Jonglei. He had studied Islamic philosophy in Egypt. After the leftist coup in Sudan in May 1969, he sought political asylum in the Federal Republic of Germany. He was happy to meet me and always welcomed me whenever I came to Munich from Austria. I learned a lot from his wide knowledge of the situation in Germany. I visited him every other weekend during the winter months, except the Christmas season, which was spent in Budapest with Joseph Bol Chan and his young wife.

A book on Kiir's bookshelves caught my attention. It was the name of the author rather than the title that attracted me. I still vividly remembered meeting William E. Smith on the steamer in May 1969, when I was returning to Malakal from Bor. He was coming from Dar es Salaam and was just passing through the Sudan, perhaps to discover it. *We Must Run While They Walk* was a profile of Julius K Nyerere, then president of the United Republic of Tanzania. Kiir and I spent a whole evening speaking about the book, Nyerere, and the author. I did not meet Kiir again until 1986, when we trained together in the SPLM/A and renewed our friendship, updating it to comradeship. Sadly, Kiir was martyred at the hands of a Toposa militia, together with a female comrade, Lt. Naomi Philip, a Moro from Mundri, when SAF recaptured the garrisoned town of Kapoeta from the SPLA in April 1992. She and I had trained together as officers.

In this profile, Mwalimu Nyerere couldn't have been more on the point. Given the wide gap between the African people and their former colonisers in socioeconomic, technological, and cultural development, it requires double efforts on the side of the Africans to catch up with the western world. The onus, therefore, falls on the educated ones among the Africans. Mwalimu Nyerere put it succinctly when he said, "Many of us who acquired education did it at the expense of our people. In our context, you are like a young man in a hungry village to whom the people gather the little food they had to give you enough energy to bring resources from a distant village. If you eat the food and fail to bring back resources, you will have betrayed the people." The essence therefore of coming to Europe was to go back with knowledge to contribute to uplifting our people from poverty and ignorance. I took the book home, and ever since those words have influenced my thinking.

The main reason for my displeasure with Leoben was the problem of language. They spoke a German dialect that was difficult for an *ausländer* and, since it was a workers' town, very few people spoke English. The foreign students, mostly from Iran, Algeria, and Morocco, were there on Austrian scholarships and had to behave themselves, bordering on instantaneous obedience to the school authorities and absolute respect for Austrians, in order to keep their scholarships. They had to endure all kinds of humiliations and racist slurs on the campus and in the town. Of all the landers, or provinces, in Austria, the people in Styr were the most openly racist and culturally backward. In the restaurants, bars, and discos we had most of the time to keep together in groups of two or three to avoid attacks by the rowdy youths. They hated foreigners and, in particular, the Africans. Upon seeing us walking down the street, they would shout at the top of their voices: "*Niger, niger, gehest bezucht zum heimat!*" (Nigger, nigger, go back home!)

This forced me and my African colleagues to not frequent social places. It was unnecessarily inconvenient and sometimes dangerous. One Sunday out of boredom in the hostel, my Thai colleague and I went to the only swimming pool in the town. As we were returning to the hostel, a group of Austrian youths started to harass us, targeting me in particular. We tried our best to ignore their insults until one of them hit Kamol Tantitanananta. It was his command of the martial arts that saved us. But when the police arrived at the spot, without even listening to our version of the events, they accused us of starting the problem. At least in the Sudan the police, who do not have to make judgemental decision, would listen to both sides in order to build their case. Was it racism or were we more advanced in upholding and protecting our rights? In fact, the course manager, Dr. Polegeg, himself being a Jew was a victim of racist discrimination, later on told us point-blank that it was a problem that occurred to every course attendant, especially those from Africa to the point that the institute was negotiating with the Ministry of Education to end the course.

A few days before Christmas I paid a visit to Joseph Bol in Budapest, Hungary. This visit completely transformed my perception of Europe. Notwithstanding the difference in the political systems, I found the Hungarian people sociable and knowledgeable about different parts of the world. An ordinary Hungarian worker would be informed of the Sudan, at least know who its president was and how he had come to power. The impact of the Hungarian Workers' Party, a coalition of revolutionary democrats (Communists) and social democrats, on society was visible in terms of how they treated themselves and visiting foreigners. János Kadar's philosophy that "not all those not with us are against us" went a long way to minimise social fissures, tensions, and conflicts, although political contradictions are deeply rooted and sometimes erupt violently.

The Russian occupation after WWII, and resistance to socialist collectivisation triggered the Hungarian counterrevolutionary uprising in 1956. The Hungarians had neither forgotten nor forgiven Tsarist Russia for helping the Austrian Hapsburg empire defeat the Hungarian nationalist rebellion in 1848. Hungarians resented the presence of the Red Army in their country and the staging of its annual 4 April military parade on the streets of Budapest. The joke told in the Hungarian wine shops went like this: "A Russian asked a Turk how they managed to rule Hungary for nearly five hundred years. The Turk replied, "We did not do anything to remind them we were here.""

After the war, Hungary was a peasant country, therefore, collecti-visation helped the Hungarian state to industrialise and modernise. By the time of my visit, collectivisation had ceased to be a bone of contention between the political or ideological groups in the country. With Joseph Bol interpreting, a Hungarian pensioner told me that in the past Hungarians were passionate about cattle; they did not know that livestock was an agent of backwardness. Now you can walk a cow down the street with a million forints tied to its tail and no one will ever stop to take it. This was a clear indication of how industrialisation and modernity had shaped Hungarian society.

The rapid industrialisation of Hungary led to cultural trans-formation, which impacted people's attitudes and behaviours. Statistics revealed that Hungary had the highest rate of divorce and suicide in central Europe. They say the Hungarians could establish a friendship or marry in the morning, and by the night of the same day they would be enemies or divorcees. This behaviour, according to sociologists, was attributed to the rapid change of lifestyle.

The day before I flew out of Khartoum, I met a certain Hussein, a Palestinian refugee who I knew as a student of geology at the University of Khartoum. He had heard from a mutual friend that I was travelling to Austria and wanted me to post two packets of photo slides to someone in Budapest. I took the packets but refused to take the fifty-dollar banknote he tried to give me to cover the postal charges. In the course of him offering me the money and me refusing to accept it, he forgot to give me the name and address of the person in Budapest. I realised this mistake only when I reached Leoben.

Joseph Bol and I were discussing what to do about the slides, when someone by the name of Beirzansky Szilard called. They talked at length and my name would pop up in their conversation. When they had finished, Bol told me that Beirzansky was with a certain Dr. Fenyö, an American of Hungarian origin. He was asking if Bol by chance knew a Sudanese geologist who had come to Austria to attend a course. Bol said yes and indeed that Sudanese was with him in Budapest and, in fact, we had been talking about the slides when Beirzansky called. Hussein had written to this Dr. Fenyö about the slides and how he forgot to give me the address. The problem that had bothered him for weeks was now resolved.

What luck! It was difficult to explain such a coincidence. Out of excitement that the slides had been found, Dr. Fenyö took a taxi to Bol's apartment, and we spent a good part of the evening drinking together. The man was so happy to have the slides. He was on sabbatical from the Hungarian Academy of Sciences. He encouraged me to benefit from Hungarian–Sudanese cultural exchange programme to pursue postgraduate studies towards a PhD. This increased my interest in Hungary, and I promised to start working on that project as soon as I returned to the Sudan. During the spring holidays, I planned to travel to Czechoslovakia, DDR, and Poland to complete building a picture of life in the socialist countries. The strategic political objective of the CPS was to build socialism in the Sudan.

My modest short experience in Hungary, and notwithstanding the relatively low level of their material development compared to Austria, convinced me that the socialist system was a more humane system compared to the capitalist west, in terms of human rights, dignity, and solidarity/fraternity amongst the peoples of the world. That the state owned all the means of social production, which meant that labour was a human right, to the effect that nobody could live without their own labour, had a big impact on me.

It was not easy to get a visa to the DDR, so I settled for a visit to Prague in Czechoslovakia, Warsaw and Kraków in Poland. It was appropriate to travel during the spring leave because the student hostels, arranged through the World University Service (WUS) would be cheaper and ready to receive visitors. In Prague I had the opportunity to visit the Sudanese Embassy, the only one responsible for Central Europe; the embassy in Bonn catered for western Europe, including Austria. At the embassy, the reception was astonishing: from behaviour of the Sudanese diplomats, I felt as if I had entered an office in Khartoum. No one seemed to care or pay attention to my enquiries as I was a Sudanese postgraduate student in Austria. It did not fall under their jurisdiction of the Embassy in Prague and therefore they didn't oblige. The fact that I was a southerner, only added to their disinterest. The official was more interested in speaking to my Algerian colleague whom they thought was closer to them racially and culturally than a South Sudanese. The official, who was as black as me, was shocked that the Algerian did not speak Arabic: he spoke French and German.

The express train to Warsaw left on schedule from the Prague Central Station at eleven in the evening. Unfortunately, we failed to get seat reservations. In all my train travel in Austria and Hungary, I had not seen carriages so packed with people. It was almost impossible to get a space to stretch and sleep. Unlike the Austrians, Germans, and Hungarians, the Poles travelled a lot. I thought this must have something to do with labour laws in Poland, which permitted unemployment for a relatively longer period than in Hungary. I was completely exhausted and only wanted a place to get some sleep. The Algerian had been to Poland before and he thought it was better we took a train to Bydgoszcz, a city on the line to Kraków. When he came back from the ticket office, a Polish girl had hooked herself onto him and now we became three in the group. She said she was travelling to Kraków. In Bydgoszcz, we booked ourselves into a pension. I was surprised she was still with us and I warned the Algerian to be careful.

I had not completely fallen asleep when somebody knocked hard on my door. It was the Algerian. "What is wrong, Jody? I am so tired and want to sleep," I told him. "That girl disappeared with my small bag where I had all my money and passports," Jody said, his voice shaking. I told him to calm down. "No, I cannot rest until I get my passport," insisted Jody. I felt I was in a deep dilemma between going with him to the police or continuing my sleep. "Do you know her name?" I asked him, to which he replied in the negative. I told him it was a hopeless situation since we did not have her coordinates: name, city, workplace. I advised him to rest, after which he could think rationally about what to do next.

The next day, Jody and I agreed to separate as he had to return to Warsaw to address the question of his passport with the Algerian Embassy, while I would proceed to Kraków. We would meet later in Leoben. I took the slow train to Kraków to enable me get a glimpse of the area it passed through. It was also full of passengers, just like the Warsaw-bound train we had taken the previous night. I sat at the window in the buffet and ordered a beer. To my surprise, the waiter refused to serve me. I was still thinking of what to do when a drunkard came and started speaking to me in a manner that suggested he was aggressive and insulting. I looked around and saw that the only sympathetic face belonged to the bartender.

I went to him and, luckily, he spoke English. He informed me that the man was bad but there was nothing even the police could do. I was very angry but decided I would defend my dignity. I ordered two pints of beer and returned to the seat at the window. I held a pint in my left hand as I watched the drunkard come back. He not only repeated the same insults but also came so close that I decided to throw the beer in his face. Shocked by my reaction to his misbehaviour, the man, and all those whom he had tried to amuse, turned around and left the buffet, leaving me alone with the bartender, who raised his thumb as if in a salute of solidarity.

It was a situation that filled me with such a rage that I decided I should proceed back to Austria. However, I still had to get to Kraków and that was enough time to cool down. There might be some interesting episodes along the way to make me change my mind. Indeed, in the student hostel I met a Sudanese who wholeheartedly welcomed me. On learning that I was a geologist on a course in Austria, he took me to meet a colleague, Allam el Huda Abdelbagi, who was working for Chevron Oil at its Red Sea concession. He had come to visit his family and was planning to stay on to work on his PhD thesis at the University of Kraków. Abdelbagi seemed familiar with the attitude and behaviour of the

Poles towards Black people; he advised me to take it easy and forget about everything that had happened to me.

Back in Leoben, I faced another problem of anti-Communist sentiment. In Kraków I bought a T-shirt with Cuba's national emblem, which I wore under an American army jacket. No sooner had I removed the jacket to sit down to lunch with my course mates than an Austrian shouted at me, "You black monkey, and also a Communist!" It was a horrible scene because the waiters also did not want to serve me. This was around the time of intense media coverage, bordering on xenophobia, that the Ugandan dictator Idi Amin was rumoured to have disappeared somewhere in Europe on his way to Britain. This heightened racist sentiments and made any Black person the target of abuse and humiliation. It was also around this time I received a letter from my brother Paulo Otuk; as earlier arranged, he would soon travel to Malakal to conduct my traditional marriage ceremony.

I did not have to wait for the last day in the course. I also did not need the piece of paper which affirmed my attendance. I decided to spend the last two weeks in June in Hungary. It was the beginning of summer and the weather was quite favourable. People now wore light summer clothes and it was beautiful. Ruth had just delivered a baby boy, Donato, and it was fun helping out, changing and washing his nappies, while Bol went to university. He was in his semi-final year and had a lot of academic work to do. One of Bol's friends, Szép Zoltan, would come and spend time with me. He didn't speak English and the German I had learned in Austria was not enough for a proper conversation; moreover, he was blind and that made things more difficult. He was really interested in keeping me entertained in Hungary and proposed to Bol that he take me to Lake Balaton, where we spent the weekend with his family. His wife drove the Trabant. That was one of my best times in Hungary. Back in Budapest, I took the first bus the next day to Vienna to catch my flight to Khartoum via Rome.

I arrived in Khartoum on the last day of June; James Amum and

Ms. Abuk were at the Airport to receive me. According to Chollo tradition, Abuk and I were now formally wife and husband. We spent a few days in Khartoum, during which I wrote my report about the course and submitted a request for my annual leave. We flew to Malakal and because the schools had reopened, we spent a few days before Abuk had to travel to Juba. In Malakal, I had the opportunity to meet Prof. Samani Abdalla Yagoub, the vice chancellor of the newly opened university in southern Sudan. I had known him in the Faculty of Science at the University of Khartoum. He was seriously searching for southerners to be recruited as teaching assistants (TAs) for the different colleges of the yet to be inaugurated University of Juba. He asked me to meet him in Juba.

It is worth mentioning that establishing a university in southern Sudan was a political demand of the southern political elite and one of the resolutions of the Round Table Conference on the Problem of Southern Sudan held in March 1965. I thought joining the University of Juba as a TA would give me the opportunity to return to Hungary to pursue my PhD studies. After a few days in Malakal, I flew to Juba. Unfortunately, Prof. Samani had travelled overseas but the secretary-general, Dr. Abdelrahman Abu Zayd, seemed to have discussed me with Dr. Samani. He offered me a provisional appointment in the College of Natural Resources and Environmental Studies, pending acceptance of my resignation from the Geological and Mineral Resources Department (GMRD), Ministry of Industry and Mining.

The contract I signed before travelling to Austria obliged me to work with GMRD for at least seven years. "Since you are joining a government institution, you don't have to resign," said the director general, Sayed Yousif Suleiman. "We will issue you a letter stating that GMRD has no objection releasing you to the University of Juba." The letter and my confidential and open files were sent to the Juba University Centre in Khartoum. In a matter of a week, I received the letter of appointment which specified the terms of my employment at the College of Natural Resources and

Environmental Studies. There were also instructions, in bold type, to "report to the Atlabara Campus of the University of Juba by 1 September 1977."

By the time I arrived to report, the university's academic staff and workers had all become manual labourers in the process of converting into a university environment what originally was a girls' secondary school. From very early in the morning until late in the afternoon all of us were involved in one of the manual assignments, transforming classrooms meant for forty students into a lecture hall to seat one hundred and turning the dormitories into hostels. The first intake of students was expected to reach six hundred. The inauguration date was set and Prof. Samani, as though to further enthuse his colleagues to create a university environment, swore he would eat his shoes if the inauguration date was not met.

The University of Juba was inaugurated as scheduled on 25 October 1977. There were displays of southern Sudanese culture at the ceremony but the event lacked political symbolism. Dr. Joseph Awad Morgan, the first director of the University of Juba project (1974), was only there as a member of staff. President of the Republic Field Marshall Gaafar Mohammed Nimeri graced the ceremony and formally declared the University of Juba open. With "excellence and relevance" as its motto, the University of Juba started with three colleges, namely Natural Resources and Environmental Studies (CNRES), Social and Economic Studies (CSES), and Adult Education and Rural Development (AERD). At the end of the ceremony and after all the guests had left, Prof. Samani sighed with relief. "It would have been a serious embarrassment," he said. "None of the dignitaries who accompanied the president requested the service of a washroom." It was an unexplainable oversight; the entire campus did not have a functioning toilet. In all the rush to complete the renovation work no one had thought to erect at least one or two toilets.

The University of Juba was meant to serve human resource requirements for the Southern Region. Its curriculum was tailored to that objective and therefore was different from the that of the University of Khartoum. According to the plan, the students would first study towards a diploma course, undertake a two- to three-year practical experience in the community, then return to complete their bachelor's degrees. This arrangement, however, was not reflected in the admissions policy, which was centralised, in accordance with that of University of Khartoum. The 1977–78 batch was admitted on the basis of having a bachelor's degree; there was no way it could have been changed midway. The university programme soon ran into serious problems, however, and the students went on strike to force a change.

Transforming from a diploma to bachelor programme was not an easy task, especially for some of us—the TA—who did not have senior lecturers or professors heading their department or units to design the syllabus. In the CNRES, I designed the syllabus for geomorphology and mineral resources of the Sudan as part of the Sudan Foundation Course (SFC), which together with Communications Skills were common courses for all the colleges. The syllabus was designed in support of the university motto of excellence and relevance. The TAs were the foundation of this new university. The college deans, as well as most of the senior Sudanese staff, came from the University of Khartoum or other universities in East Africa; a few had come over from the civil service. The four professors and a librarian were all from the United Kingdom. Sayed Hilary Paul Logali, a minister in the High Executive Council, was chairman of the University Council. This relationship ensured smooth collaboration with the government of the Southern Region.

The vice president of the republic and president of the High Executive Council of the Southern Region, Sayed Abel Alier, did his best to assist the newly established university. In fact, many southern intellectuals considered the university as their own equivalent of the University of Khartoum. The regional government, therefore, obliged to offer the university three residences in the Yugoslavian-built ministerial quarters in Hai Amarat. The university staff club became an intellectual centre where ministers, legislators, and senior bureaucrats gathered to socialise and engage in social and political discussions.

The job with the University of Juba had brought me back to the Southern Region, which I had left in 1974, hoping not to come back under any circumstances. However, it seemed my attitude and behaviour had polluted my work environment and relations in the Red Sea Hills project in Khartoum and Port Sudan. First, I had irritated the project management on the question of them receiving field allowances while staying in Port Sudan. I believed I would be in serious problem if I went back. The second was my colleagues' concern about the recommendation I had made in respect of the Austrian course. The graduates of the University of Khartoum were particularly incensed that I had said the course was appropriate only for graduates of Egyptian universities. Nevertheless, even without all these reasons I would have preferred employment with the University of Juba. I had just married and therefore did not want to be separated from my wife by fieldwork in the mountains.

In Juba, I stayed with my relative Edward Nyawello Amum, who was also from Watajwok village. Edward was a senior bureaucrat with the parastatal Equatoria Trading Corporation. Although Abuk and I were formally a married couple, we still lived in separate places. Abuk was still attending Juba Commercial School and lived in the dormitory. I was waiting to find a house and purchase pieces of furniture before shifting my residence. It was not going to be long though; one day returning from the university, I found Abuk had come to where I stayed in Edward's house; she was feverish, nause-ating, and vomiting. Laboratory tests indicated early pregnancy. It was like a sledgehammer had hit my head. After consultation with Edward and my uncle Okony Onwar, they dismissed the idea of Abuk returning to Malakal; instead, she should relocate to Ben Otwel's house for the time being while I looked for accommodation.

Of the servant quarters of the two ministerial residences the government offered the university, I was allocated one. The other was allocated to Mrs. Vera, the Czech widow of engineer Pech, who was now working with the university. It was a two-roomed, self-contained structure convenient for a small family. I managed to secure a fifty-pound kit-loan from the Ministry of Finance to purchase furniture and kitchen utensils. In a matter of a week, Abuk and I settled into our small residence, which had now been enclosed in a bamboo fence. I now started to behave like a family man, usually returning home to be with Abuk at the earliest possible time. We were both excited and happy about how things had turned out. I sent the news to my mother in Malakal to conduct the necessary Chollo rituals since I had kept Abuk in Juba and would only return to her family after delivery sometime in April 1978.

As the year 1977 closed on humanity, the political mood in the Southern Region was rather uneasy and unpredictable. Nimeri had signed the Port Sudan agreement with the National Front, whose intention was to return southern Sudan to the pre-Addis Ababa Agreement relationship. Dr. Hassan Abdalla el Turabi, the Muslim brotherhood ideologue, started to occupy centre stage in the Sudan Socialist Union (SSU), the ruling political party. The term of Sayed Abel Alier as president of the HEC was coming to an end, and elections for the second People's Regional Assembly (PRA) were due. Beneath the canopy of the SSU and the totalitarian dictatorship in the country, a popular discontent quietly simmered against Abel Alier's politics of submission to the northern political will. This discontent echoed the power politics within southern political elite. However, instead of the traditional Southern Front (SF) and Sudan African National Union (SANU) dichotomy, the drivers of this discontent were such that they smacked of a split at the SSU power pinnacle in Southern Sudan.

A radical, highly educated group had emerged among the southern political elite; its politics were a little bit left of the centre. It was completely different from the old-school southern politicians. Names like Akuot Atem, Benjamin Bol Akok, Matthew Obur Ayang, William Ajal Deng, Malath Joseph, and others appeared on the political stage. While playing the game within the SSU, they christened the movement the "wind of change," suggesting that as southerners they wanted to pull harder on the political strings to achieve social and economic development of the Southern Region. The Southern Region could not play its political role in the politics of the Sudan as long as it was economically dependent on the central government in Khartoum. To allay Nimeri's fears, the group nominated Maj. Gen. Joseph Lagu, formerly the chairman of the Southern Sudan Liberation Movement (SSLM) and commander-in-chief of the Anya-nya, for the presidency of the HEC. The CPS, meanwhile, instructed its members, friends, and sympathisers to boycott and not to support any faction in the elections, which were marred by massive corruption and rigging of votes. I went to check and found that someone had cast my vote for the graduates' constituency contested at the level of Southern Region.

The results of the People's Regional Assembly elections of 1978 circumvented all the plans to maintain Sayed Abel Alier as president of the HEC. All his big political shots, including Hilary Paulo Logali, were trounced. The amorphous group won the majority in the People's Regional Assembly and elected Maj. Gen. Joseph Lagu president of the HEC. Dr. Zachariah Bol Deng was appointed minister in the HEC to provide a voice for the Abyei area and its people. It is worth mentioning that the Addis Ababa Agreement provided for a referendum to determine whether the Dinka Ngok of Abyei (Kordofan) and Uduk (Blue Nile) would join the Southern Region or remain in northern Sudan. The HEC under Abel Alier had failed to provide the leadership needed to deliver the referendum. The radical but amorphous political group was determined to restore the trust and confidence of the people of southern Sudan in their leaders. However, the group's amorphous nature and lack of defined political ideology was its weakness and source of internal fissures.

Within a short period of time after the changes in the HEC, the University of Juba lost its vice chancellor. Prof. Samani Abdalla

Yagoub was killed in a tragic plane crash in Malakal while travelling to Khartoum. Prof. Abdelrahman Abu Zayd succeeded him as vice chancellor, while Moses Machar became the secretary-general. The university did not have its own Act and based its organisational system on the University of Khartoum Act. It appeared that the university was managed on the strength of personal relations rather than on clear management principles and rules. This engendered serious contradictions. The administration had failed to complete certain amenities to enable a timely inauguration; these became serious contradictions that led to a strike by the students and industrial actions on the part of the workers and academic staff. Neither Abu Zayd nor Machar had experience with university administration, and this exacerbated the crisis.

The strike gave me time to stay with Abuk, who was now approaching the expected time of delivery. As she could not travel to Malakal, I asked my mother-in-law to come to Juba. Chollo customs do not permit close association between mother-in-law and son-in-law, particularly in such amenities as washrooms. I was not used to the strict Chollo customary mores, so I would spend time at the university and come home late in the afternoon. On the morning of Saturday 22 April, I noticed that Abuk was behaving oddly, treating her mother with unusual rudeness. I decided to walk her to the hospital to meet the gynaecologist. "This is the expected date of delivery; she is in labour," the doctor said. He sent me to buy some medicine to assist with the labour. My mother-in-law camped outside the ward, just to follow up on how her daughter was doing. I also did not see any reason to leave the hospital; every time I went to the maternity ward to see, I could feel the pain that Abuk was experiencing. Our beautiful, tiny little girl arrived at nine o'clock in the evening after a whole day of labour. It was a great relief for all of us, including the gynaecologist who delivered her.

There can't be anything more exciting than becoming a father. I received hundreds of congratulatory messages from relatives, friends, and colleagues at the university. Our small house now teemed with visiting friends and colleagues of Abuk. We also received gifts from our neighbour Sayed Alexander Nageb, which thoughtfully included a huge candle; it helped Abuk during the night as power was switched off at ten o'clock. My relative supplied us with three names from which to choose. Abuk and I agreed that our first child would be called Keni to symbolise the care we needed to carry ourselves through life. After exactly one month, Abuk, Keni, and my mother-in-law took the Sudan Airways flight to Malakal. Eight months into familyhood I was again alone. It was a very difficult time because I had become used to Abuk and the little Keni. I took a week off to visit them in Malakal.

It had been a while since I had last attended to Communist Party functions in Port Sudan. The trip to Europe had virtually cut my relations with the party. My return to Juba without first passing through my base in Port Sudan exacerbated my estrangement from the party obligations and its connections in Juba and Port Sudan. The rules of access to party organs are undertaken formally in organised meetings where minutes are taken. But no matter how long it took, I knew I would reconnect with the party. I knew some members of the party in Juba but because of the strict rules guiding the clandestine work of the party, I couldn't try to inquire about my status.

While the student strike raged and the university appeared bogged down by issues of physical infrastructure development, I started the process of applying for a Hungarian scholarship. It took me almost two months to receive the acceptance to my application. It would have remained lying in the Khartoum office of the University of Juba if I had not asked a colleague to check. The scholarship was in accordance with the cultural cooperation agreement between the People's Republic of Hungary and the Democratic Republic of the Sudan. It was managed by the Hungarian Academy of Science. It stated clearly that I would be working at the E tv s Loránd University in Budapest under Prof. Kubovics Imre, with effect from 15 September 1978. According to the agreement, the Sudanese partner would provide only travel to and from Budapest. This scholarship was a relief for the University of Juba, which had an obligation to fund my postgraduate studies. The contract agreement for me to proceed to Hungary was duly signed by the vice chancellor, the secretary-general, and myself. I made the necessary arrangements to travel to Malakal and from there to Khartoum with my family.

In the second week of September, Abuk, Keni, and I arrived in Khartoum from Malakal. We still had time before the flight to Budapest. On my checklist of things to do was health card for Keni. Abuk and I already had our international vaccination cards; for Keni, it was a different matter. According to procedures followed in Khartoum Province, a child health card is provided, together with the birth certificate, by the area health visitor. The Primary Health Care Centre in Shagara could not provide the document until the day of our departure on account that Keni had been born in Juba. Later on, in Budapest, the paediatrician who attended to Keni viewed this omission as irresponsible on the part of the medical officer who delivered her, and without qualms started the process of her vaccinations, which was necessary for Keni to be admitted to day-care centre.

From Khartoum, we took the Sudan Airways flight to Frankfurt in West Germany. It was an eight-hour bumpy flight that worried nearly everybody on board. The captain could be heard reciting Quranic verses, suggesting it was a really difficult journey. It was about time I remembered and worried about life then and after. We missed our Lufthansa flight and had to wait six hours at the departure terminal before boarding a Málev Hungarian Airlines flight to Budapest. Frankfurt was a busy airport. Abuk couldn't believe her eyes, seeing planes landing every other minute. I explained that Frankfurt was one of the largest airports in Europe, receiving flights from different parts of the world.

Our flight to Budapest was just under one hour. The passengers disembarked into a large arrival terminal, and everybody rushed to be first in the queue at passport control. I motioned Abuk to wait until all the others had finished before we took our turn at the passport control desk. To our surprise, before any of the passengers had been processed, the passport officer closed the gate and came out picked Abuk by the hand and asked me to follow to the desk; there she quickly processed our papers. Joseph Bol later explained to us; it was procedural to process parents with babies and children. Because of Keni, therefore, Abuk had priority over everyone else. Outside the arrivals' terminal, Joseph Bol and his Hungarian friend waited to welcome us. It was chilly autumn weather and we had to rush to the city in order to keep the tiny Keni warm. She had already become an attraction, particularly for the elderly Hungarian women.

It is rather a baffling experience that human knowledge of other human groups, whether they are African or European, starts and ends with their respective adults and somehow fails to recognise their young ones. The Chollo were used to seeing white adults but marvelled in astonishment when the Americans came with toddlers to Dolieb Hill in 1902. "Look, they also have small ones," the Chollo would whisper amongst themselves. At the sight of my daughter, whether in the tram or while walking down the street, I had similar experiences with Hungarians. "Oh my, God is great that I met a black angel before I died," the old women would say. Not only that but they would offer our infant daughter chocolates and sweets. Sometimes it really became a nuisance.

In a matter of a week, we were able to complete all formalities and settled down so I could start my studies. With the good connections of Joseph Bol, Abuk was awarded a scholarship by TESCO, the Hungarian side of UNESCO, which provides technical training for third-world students. This was starting from the very beginning of the education ladder; Abuk wanted to study laboratory science. She had previously been a student of commerce and had not studied science. We also found a day-care for Keni, though it was quite a distance away from where we resided, requiring two trams to reach. The secretariat of the Academy of Sciences concluded an arrangement with the Faculty of Arts that a professor of Hungarian language would coach me twice a week so I could speak and interact in society. Since the Hungarian language required time to master and would enable me write my geology thesis, I chose to undertake research rather than course work with the other postgraduate students.

The Hungarian Academy of Sciences determined that I should spend only four years doing my research, taking into consideration the five years I had spent at the undergraduate BSc (Hon.) level, three years of geological research work completed in the Red Sea Hills, and eight months at the Austrian course. The Expert Committee of Mining, Geological, Geodetical, and Geophysical Sciences approved my thesis proposal to conduct a petrological and geochemical investigation of Velence Hills in central Hungary. This investigation involved fieldwork to survey the area and collect rock, soil, and plant samples for petrological, mineralogical, and biogeochemical analysis. The objective of the investigation was to prove the occurrence of gold mineralisation in Velence Mountains and nearby areas.

An earlier PhD student had studied the geological configuration of the same area and concluded that there was gold in some of his rock samples. This meant that my task over the coming four years was to prove to myself and my examiners that the quartz veins and rocks in the area were auriferous or gold-bearing. The task proved daunting, to the point that I had to use an electron microscope to prove that there was no gold mineralisation. On 15 June 1982, the examiners accepted my argument and awarded me a PhD, pending confirmation by the Expert Committee of the Hungarian Committee of Scientific Qualifications of the Hungarian Academy of Sciences.

My academic tourism in Europe had begun as a youthful joke and turned into the serious business of building a family and gaining employment at a university. The turn of events was humbling.

I had started a journey in Austria and ended up completing my post-graduate studies in Hungary. When my family of five landed in Khartoum in September 1982 to await our onward flight to Juba, the writing of things to come was already on the wall.

Chapter 10

The Crisis of May Regime & My Decision to Join the SPLM/A

I returned to the Sudan in September 1982 at the end of my post-graduate scholarship in Budapest, Hungary. I had submitted and defended my thesis the previous June and spent the intervening time waiting for the air tickets. Repeated telegrams to the Juba University Centre in Khartoum could not move the officials there to act on the travel arrangements for me and the family. I had to make a short trip to Khartoum to push the process of the return tickets and the shipment of personal belongings to Juba through the Kenyan port of Mombasa; it was nearer to Juba than Port Sudan.

This trip demonstrated how in less than one year, since December 1981 when we were on holiday in the country, the social, economic, and political symptoms of a regime in crisis had become obvious at every point of engagement. The first manifestation of this which struck me immediately upon arrival in Khartoum was the melt down in the bureaucracy; no one attended to their duties and that explained why my repeated telegrams were not responded to. And it was only getting worse: there was near complete breakdown of communication and transportation between Khartoum and Juba, reflecting the growing political unrest. There was virtually no direct Sudan Airways flights to Juba except through Nairobi in Kenya; meaning that to fly to Juba one had to fly to Nairobi and return on the same plane to Juba on its way to Khartoum. The Sudan Airways blamed it on the lack of aviation fuel in Juba.

I did not have time to spend in Khartoum. I managed to secure the return tickets from Budapest to Khartoum through Rome. There was even a problem with this route, the Hungarian carriers had outstanding debts with the Sudan Airways and therefore did not want to cover the Budapest-Rome trip. It was after the intervention of the Hungarian government that we were allowed to fly. The University of Juba Office in Khartoum could not provide money for the shipment of my personal belongings; I had to take a loan from a friend. It enabled me return to Budapest. On the 26th of September1982, we finally arrived Khartoum. I thought it was going to be a short transit wait before we flew to Juba. I was kidding. Gaafar Nimeri was engineering something in the Southern Region.

The Southern Region was the weakest link in Nimeri's totalitarian dictatorship along which political contradictions erupted violently. Although the elections in January had produced a pro-re-division High Executive Council, and the Equatorian Eng. James Joseph Tombura was now president, ethnic politics and the alliance between Southern Front and SANU had cooled down the process in the interest of a united Southern Region. Nimeri pursued division politics, manipulating small groups and isolated politicians. Some politicians were in jail and there was gunrunning all over the Southern Region. Nimeri responded by cutting air transport between Khartoum and Juba, Malakal and Wau; it was not possible to fly from Juba to Malakal or Wau. The political situation was tense, just waiting for a spark to explode.

When a political system is about to collapse, it creates unbelievable scenarios. Many of the ministers of the High Executive Council were in Khartoum, staying at the Araak Hotel and unable to travel to Juba. If the ministers couldn't travel, it meant the fate of the ordinary people would be unimaginable. This was how we consoled ourselves every time I visited my mentor and friend, Minister of Finance and Planning Othwonh Dak, at the hotel. One day, back in the guesthouse in Khartoum Two, where I stayed with my family, I got a note from the University of Juba Centre, telling us to be ready to travel to Juba the following morning. I was excited and told my family to prepare for the journey.

To our dismay, however, there was just one seat. The new vice chancellor, Prof. Abdel Aal, had found me a seat on a small aircraft chartered by the Islamic Call Organisation. I turned it down on the grounds that I could not leave my family in Khartoum. But my wife intervened to say that I should travel to prepare accommodation for them in Juba. It was a three-hour flight to Juba. The family joined me five weeks later. It was a terribly bad beginning after four good years in Hungary. Keni and Pito spoke only Hungarian, making communication difficult with other children, while Kut was still a toddler.

The social environment in Juba, and the Southern Region for that matter, was tense with politics of division (re-division or *kokora*) and also the politics unity for this self-governing region of the Sudan. I witnessed part of this terrible situation when I came on holiday in December 1981. In less than a year the situation had visibly deteriorated. After four years in Hungary, I had acquired, besides my academic qualifications, analytical political tools, scientific understanding of and the ability to explain, political developments. I had also risen to the position of CPS branch political commissar. It took me sometime before the party's central committee connected me with the party branch in Juba, and with the cell at the university. This was a time of intense political activity concerning ethnic and provincial sensibilities. The struggle pitted supporters of the Equatoria Central Committee (ECC) against supporters of the Council for Unity of Southern Sudan (CUSS): all of them were members of the Sudan Socialist Union (SSU), with Nimeri managing the conflict from behind the scenes.

Ever since the 1972 Addis Ababa Agreement, the Southern Region had been the bulwark of Nimeri's support base against the political opposition in Khartoum. By 1980, however, as a consequence of Nimeri's repeated interference in the political and democratic processes in the self-governing region, he eroded this support base, and the bulk of south's political elite had turned against him without necessarily challenging the SSU or its totalitarian dictatorship. It will be recalled that Chevron, the American oil company, had struck rich oil finds in western Upper Nile, which Nimeri quickly renamed "Unity Province" to underline the importance of the country's unity. Acquiescing to the desire of Chevron to profit from its US$1 billion investment, Nimeri decided to place the oil refinery in Kosti instead of Bentiu, depriving the people of Bentiu and the Southern Region at large of the economic benefits of the oil.

This triggered serious disagreements between Nimeri and his northern elite on one hand, and the southern political elite on other hand, who were then unified in their resolve to bring social and economic development to Southern Region through the development and exploitation of the oil reserves found in the Southern Region. Conscious that a break with the southern political elite would spell his political downfall, Nimeri embarked on a policy to destroy the unity between southern politicians in SANU, Southern Front, and Equatoria Central Committee, who in 1978 supported the candidature of Gen. Joseph Lagu Yanga to the presidency of High Executive Council. The redivision of the Southern Region was supported by some honourable and progressive southern politicians. But the decision should be viewed as a project designed by

Gaafar Nimeri and Hassan Abdalla el Turabi, leader of the Islamic Charter Front, to weaken and destroy genuinely strong political leaders in the Southern Region, and to promote weak-kneed and chicken-hearted politicians. It was meant to achieve two strategic political objectives: abrogate the Addis Ababa Agreement and dismantle the Southern Region; and impose *sharia* Islamic laws and transform the Sudan into an Islamic republic modelled on Iran.

In Juba, the ECC operatives agitated for redivision in a way that appeared to challenge the regime. The party branch, ostensibly in the hope of fuelling the regime's contradictions, supported the ECC versus CUSS on account that redivision was the demand of the people of Equatoria. I couldn't understand how the party branch and the university cell had failed to discover Nimeri's hands behind what they believed was the demand of the people. I took a different and independent opinion. I believed redivision was not a political demand of the people but a deliberate attempt by the regime to divert attention away from its socioeconomic and political crisis.

It took quite some time after I had arrived in Juba before I was formally connected to the Communist Party and invited to take part in party functions. But even without having been connected, state security stalked me everywhere I went. One day, I believe it was in April 1983, two guys appeared in front of my residence on campus. They introduced themselves and wanted to carry out a search. When I asked to see the search warrant, they said they were members of the national security organisation and did not require a warrant. So I asked to search them lest they carried some implicating materials and they agreed. They finished the search of my residence after about forty-five minutes and declared they had found nothing, for which I thanked them.

To my surprise, I later learned that the national security guys had also searched the residence of Prof. Arop Yor Ayik, who was the dean of students. Although we both hailed from Chollo ethnicity, Prof. Arop Yor was a right-wing politician with close ties to the Umma Party. I failed to understand why the national security would be interested in only the two Chollo academics. It turned out later that the search of my residence was a smokescreen for the search of Prof. Arop's residence. The Islamic fundamentalists wanted to Islamise the administrative positions at the university. They knew Prof. Arop well and wanted to replace him with a Muslim fundamentalist.

Field Marshall Gaafar Mohammed Nimeri achieved his two objectives. On 1 June 1983, he abrogated the Addis Ababa Agreement and dismantled the Southern Region into the three subregions of Bahr el Ghazal, Equatoria, and Upper Nile. On 1 September, Nimeri decreed the imposition of Islamic *sharia* laws, including *hudud* punishments—the amputation of limbs. This was against the backdrop of an insurrection in Bor that led to the formation of the SPLM/A. In February 1984, in an operation that witnessed the death of foreign workers and the capture of others as hostages, the SPLA closed down Chevron's operations in Unity Province and the digging of the Jonglei Canal in Upper Nile. Buttressed ideologically by the Islamic Charter Front, the May Regime had become a full-blown totalitarian dictatorship. At the same time, the regime was implementing the structural adjustment programs (SAPs) dictated by the Bretton Woods Institutions (World Bank/International Monetary Fund, IMF), which targeted the social services sector of the economy. This implementation of the SAPs made the economic crisis in the country even more acute. The suspension of oil production and withdrawal of Chevron from the Sudan, coupled with the increasing intensity of SPLA military operations, created the conditions for a popular uprising against the regime.

In April 1985, the May Regime was overthrown in a pattern similar to October 1964. In 1985, however, the army top brass was already infiltrated by Islamic fundamentalism. This meant that the military were able to intervene to prevent the radicalisation of the popular uprising. There was no change for it to transform into a revolution or link up with the armed insurgency in the Southern

Region. The popular March–April 1985 uprising led only to a change of guards at the Republican Palace: was the uprising nothing more than a farcical replica, or was it a drama re-enacting the scene of the October 1964 revolution?

Abboud's military dictatorship did not create a political party; it was therefore easy for the uprising to uproot the whole establishment. The May Regime was an established political system with institutions that could influence or distort the dynamics and outcome of the popular uprising. The popular uprising therefore was not a clean break with the past; a large part of the system remained to resist or compete with the forces of the revolution. The Islamic Chartered Front (ICF), more organised and institutionalised than the traditional and theocratic parties in the National Front (NF), had since 1977 captured the ruling Sudan Socialist Union (SSU). Sheikh Hassan Abdalla el Turabi became its chief ideologue and architect of the Islamic sharia (September 1983) laws. The regime's power remained intact and fiercely resisted the revolution on the grounds that no Muslim, whatsoever, could go against Islam and its tenets. Thus, the change of guards at the Republican Palace was a mere cosmetic façade meant to provide a smokescreen for reorganising state power in favour of the traditional and theocratic political parties. The compromise to hold elections after one year was a clear indication that the social and political forces that triggered the popular uprising, essentially the left-wing political forces, had lost the end game, just as they had in October 1964. The popular uprising did not last long enough to transform the Islamic character of the regime and the destructive changes it had wrought to the state and society. The situation remained the same in the peripheral Sudan, particularly in the southern states where the SPLM/A waged its revolutionary armed struggle. Its leadership had rejected the idea of participation in the transitional government.

In Equatoria, political forces linked to the May Regime continued in a position of authority. The ECC, now reorganised as the People's Progressive Party (PPP) and made up of agitators for redivision (*kokora*) of the Southern Region, resisted the reunification of the southern subregions and conspired with the Military Council to prevent Gen. James Loro from returning to Juba as chairman of the Southern Coordination Council. At the University of Juba, members of academic and support staff originating from other regions of southern Sudan suffered harassment, humiliation, and sometimes physical threats from the agents of EEC now in power in Juba.

In fact, there were attempts to divide the university into three as a means of getting rid of some of us. The threat grew in intensity, exacerbated by the SPLA's incursion into parts of Equatoria. In December 1984, a contingent of the SPLA's Zendaya Battalion, comprised of mainly Bor Dinka, traditional rivals of the Mundari, made an incursion into Terekeka. After enjoying the hospitality of the Mundari, the SPLA soldiers went on a raping and looting spree, not even sparing children and old women. This infuriated everyone and turned the people against the SPLA. Insecurity made many of us vulnerable. There was a blanket suspicion by the security forces that people from Upper Nile and Bar el Ghazal were generally sympathetic to the SPLA. These were external threats that required personal tact in dealing with them.

At the university, I faced threats or challenges from some members of the executive committee of the Juba University Staff Association (JUSA). This emanated from a lack of clear understanding and distinction between JUSA as a trade union organisation and the execution of its functions and mandate in relation with the university administration. Some colleagues in the executive committee, ostensibly to avoid any confrontation with the administration over trade union matters, believed that JUSA was an extension of, and therefore should be collaborating with, rather than struggling against, the university's administration. This created serious friction that almost destroyed the association.

The most serious challenge came from my colleagues in the university cell. This stemmed from a superficial understanding by two colleagues of my membership in the party and the role I had played as a member of the JUSA executive before being formally connected to the university cell. The general assembly of the staff association had been convened before I was formally linked to the cell. Although my left-leaning ideas were known at the university, the cell's political commissar did not want me to have anything to do with the cell. In such a case, I should have been treated as a friend of the party, or a democrat entitled to receive certain party literature to keep abreast of developments and only certain internal communications would be denied. I was elected to the executive committee of JUSA as secretary for external affairs. Most of my colleagues in the cell were northern Sudanese and occupied admin-istrative positions at the university and in the colleges. This was done under the administration of Prof. Abdelrahman Abu Zayed, a pan-Arabist, who went to Khartoum to recruit Communists because he had no alternative. The problem with my colleagues arose when the university had a new vice chancellor, Prof. Abdel Aal Abdalla, an Islamic fundamentalist. Prof. Abdel Aal changed the college deans, removing my two colleagues in the cell. They had wanted me to take up their cases to remain deans of colleges in the university. It became a problem when I told them that JUSA would fight for their right to work as university professors or lecturers but not their right to be appointed deans. My colleagues would not listen or accept this reality. This spoiled our personal relations and, in turn, made it difficult to carry out political work in the cell.

During those days in Juba, life was extremely precarious, like treading on a thin thread hanging over a huge fireball. I would say that the danger I faced both inside and outside the univer-sity precipitated my decision to join the insurgency. It was worst outside the campus from the government of Equatoria Region and the political parties which agitated for the region. As secretary for external relations, I used to attend the meetings of the coordinating committee of the uprising forces. At one such meeting I disagreed with another member of the committee over our respective analysis of political developments in the country. As if Equatoria Region had become a separate country, he addressed me like a foreigner who was interfering in their affairs, further telling me to go back to Upper Nile Region. In fact, SPLA operations in parts of Equatoria had raised to boiling point anger against anyone perceived to be an SPLA sympathiser. I was afraid that this attitude could easily link up with the counterinsurgency operations of SAF in Juba and pose an existential threat to me and my family.

As someone once lectured us in the staff club, resentment is an emotional response to different kinds of failures and often involves a sense of defeat, of failure to achieve or fulfil personal aspirations. Prof. Ambrose Ahang Beny, I, and a few friends were sitting under the canopy in the staff club chatting about the bad situation the SPLA had created in Terekeka, and saying that the headquarters should be informed of such breaches. We had ignored, out of anger, the news from the Juba suburb of Hai Jellaba: an Arab merchant was said to have shot and killed a boy who refused to be sodomised. Then a former colleague at the University of Khartoum came to our table, fuming with anger at the SPLA over the Terekeka incident. We told him that it was despicable and must be condemned. But he insisted on the topic, until one of us reminded him of the incident in Hai Jellaba and suddenly our friend hurried away. It seems he had come from there and was running away from the women who were wailing and condemning those cowards who had refused to pick up the gun.

Six months after the fall of the May Regime, the strongest voices for the post-May political dispensation came from the traditional and theocratic political establishments. It was a clear indication that the mass movement was on the retreat after overthrowing the dictatorship. In November, the Democratic Unionist Party (DUP) hosted, in Wad Medani, a conference of the social and political forces of the popular uprising. Being JUSA's secretary for external relations, I travelled to Wad Medani to represent the staff association; it was also an opportunity to meet and coordinate with other political forces from the peripheral Sudan. In fact, on the side-lines of this conference, the Sudan Rural Solidarity (SRS) was formed to represent the uprising forces, the political voices of rural Sudan.

I had the opportunity to meet the general secretary of the Communist Party of the Sudan, Ustaz Ibrahim Nuqud, to discuss the situation in southern Sudan in view of the socialist claims made by the SPLM/A. It was my first time to meet Nuqud, who had been in a clandestine situation since the July 1971 countercoup. He was a very composed individual and modest in his presentation. I disagreed with his view that the SPLM/A was counterrevolutionary and in the service of imperialism. I asked Ustaz Nuqud why the party considered the SPLM/A part of the opposition to the regime during the struggle against the May totalitarian dictatorship, but now that the regime had been overthrown the party despised the SPLM/A. I was not convinced by his answer, and in the end told him I was submitting my resignation, to which he replied coolly, "Go back to your branch and discuss it there."

Dr. Walter K. Kunijwok and I were arriving at the function of signing of the conference's final communique. Kunijwok was then president of the Sudan African Congress (SAC) and a professor of politics in the Faculty of Social and Economic Studies at the University of Khartoum. As all the northern delegates were dressed in white *jellabeyas* and white turbans, it was almost impossible to recognise even familiar colleagues. The few southern Sudanese, standing alone as if by design, were dressed casually and looked completely different. As if thinking along the same lines, Kunijwok and I remarked simultaneously that these northerners were indeed one people and working with them would lead nowhere. The only way out of the political impasse was to join the armed struggle. This was the same feeling I had had when I left my meeting with Ustaz Nuqud.

Back in Juba, I opened a discussion with Abuk about going into exile to participate in the revolutionary struggle to transform the country. It was indeed a difficult time for both our families. My father and younger sibling had passed on in August 1984, with only two days between their deaths. Abuk had lost her father in June 1985, just six months earlier. We had not performed the traditional rituals, or funeral rites. Therefore, her negative attitude towards me joining the insurgency was understandable, even given the dangers that the situation in Juba posed for all of us. The security situation deteriorated further and most of the staff were relocating their families to Khartoum. But Abuk and I could not agree on a plan.

I made up my mind to leave the family in northern Sudan; it was safer than any place in southern Sudan. I was convinced that the war would engulf the whole region sooner than later. I found them a convenient house on Tuti Island and paid the rent for six months, in the hope that after half a year she would make up her mind to follow me with the children. And this is how my plan eventually worked out. In December 1986 Abuk, her sister Nyabedi-jwok, and the children flew out of Khartoum to Nairobi, Kenya. But this was only after the forceful intervention of my mother-in-law.

From a political perspective, it was a right, honour, and duty to join the SPLM/A to participate in the war of national liberation. It was clear to me that the mass movement was in retreat, and that the traditional sectarian parties, the Umma Party and Democratic Unionist Party, would ascend to power. They continue to build on their traditional alliance, established since 1965. This conjured up the memories of 1965, when government forces had massacred southerners in the towns and villages. This time, it would be even more vicious. Having experienced the bitterness and resentment among southerners during the political fallout of the dismantling of the Southern Region, southerners would massacre themselves, as exemplified by the actions of the SPLA in Mundari.

The time for my final departure was still far off. I had academic functions to undertake, including taking my students for fieldwork in northern Sudan, setting their examination, correcting the papers, and handing the results over to the dean of the College of Natural Resources and Environmental Studies. I managed to complete everything by the third week of March and returned to Khartoum to spend leave with my family. With the cooperation of the SPLA's clandestine cell in Khartoum, I arranged for my Ethiopian visa, which I got in good time. I was scheduled to depart Khartoum on 4 April at six o'clock in the morning. It would be difficult to leave from Tuti Island as the ferry stopped at midnight. I decided to take my suitcase to the university campus and leave from there at an appropriate time. I bid my family goodbye. Only Abuk knew I was on a journey of perhaps no return. We had settled that dispute amicably.

The country was still bogged down with the general elections. I arrived at the airport and quickly cleared the departure arrangements and climbed to the departure lounge. The Ethiopian Airways flight, unlike those of Sudan Airways, was to take-off as scheduled. I was a bit nervous due to the uncertainties in front of me. I had never been to Ethiopia before, and indeed was worried what I would do if things didn't work out. The final minutes before passengers were asked to board the plane were tense and stressful. A security officer came around and took my passport. He looked through all the pages, perhaps to know the places I had visited, then returned it to me and left. He came back once more, and once more looked at my passport and stared into my face, as if to tell me that he knew I was off to join the insurgency.

It was only through the intervention of a man of God that the security operative was convinced that I was indeed travelling to attend a conference on geology at Addis Ababa University. Rev. Canon Clement Janda was booked on the same flight to Addis Ababa, where he would take a connecting flight to Zurich, Switzerland. He was a political friend through his connection with Matthew Obur Ayang and Othwonh Dak Padiet. Given his close links with the clandestine cell in Khartoum, the reverend would definitely have known what I was up to.

Addis Ababa Bole International Airport was under major rehabilitation and our flight was diverted to Debre Zeyit, fifty kilometres to the south. This sudden and unexpected change meant that Rev. Janda could not spend time in Addis Ababa to meet some of the people he had planned to see. Before disembarking, he quickly handed over to me items he had brought from contacts in Khartoum for Cdr. William Nyuon Bany, a member of the SPLM/A's Political–Military High Command. We were taken by bus from Debre Zeyit to Bole International Airport and, after passing through immigration, went to the city.

I booked myself into the Ras Hotel, near the central railway station, and immediately called the SPLA office. The man on the other end of the telephone line asked if I knew anybody in the movement. It was rather a stupid question. I told him that I knew some officers, especially those in Radio SPLA, and I was coming to join the liberation movement. I also informed him that I had some materials I had brought along for Cdr. William Nyuon Bany. "You will be attended to as soon as possible," he said, and hung up the phone.

It was about forty-eight hours later that I received my first visit from agents of the SPLM/A office. In a way, it reminded me of the workings in the CPS cells and branches. Because of security considerations and due to the clandestine nature of the party's work, things moved quite slowly. The SPLM/A's office in Addis Ababa and its activities in Ethiopia, however, were no secret. Perhaps the SPLM/A needed to receive some intelligence on me before taking the required action. At least, this is what I assumed. I discovered later that the delay to come to me and receive the things I had brought was a case of organisational ineptitude. This is the same ineptitude that haunts the SPLM and its institutions to this day. Some members of the movement's top leadership were in Addis Ababa and their presence had thrown the office into a confusion preventing its normal function of welcoming new members. The man who answered my phone call either did not care; it was not his duty, or perhaps he forgot to share the information about my presence in Addis. On the third day, when they knew of my presence,

I was invited for dinner in a posh restaurant to mark my formal welcome into the SPLM/A.

This was officiated by Cdr. Arok Thon Arok, a member of the Political–Military High Command, whom I had known in Juba. Maj. Arok Thon Arok then was in military intelligence. Between 1973–78 he had represented the army in the People's Regional Assembly in Juba. I found it puzzling that he now held this high position in a revolutionary movement, the SPLM/A. The movement's chief political ideologue, Cdr. Alfred Lado Gore, later told me that Cdr. Arok had congratulated, saying that "one of leftist hardliners" had come to join the SPLM/A.

I was then transferred to the Marabeti Hotel, on the northern outskirts of the city. It was only then that I was able to meet some members of the SPLM/A whom I had known in Juba and Khartoum. While I was not yet a member of the movement, during the almost twenty-five days I spent in Addis Ababa, I was in the company of, or socialised with, senior members of the movement. I could only become a *bona fide* member after I had met Dr. John Garang or have graduated from the military training centre.

Chapter 11

Inside the SPLM/A Insurgency

It was at the Marabeti Hotel that I met Cdr. Pagan Amum. I did not remember having met him before, although I knew his parents and close relatives. In fact, I attended the wedding of his parents at the Presbyterian Church in Dolieb Hill in 1956. I was surprised to meet him in Addis Ababa; all I knew was that he was the deputy commander of the SPLA's Rhino Battalion then deployed in Bahr el Ghazal. He was in Addis Ababa to receive medical treatment for piles and guinea worm and accompanied by his young spouse. He impressed me as someone who could provide leadership.

I took my time to learn about the inner workings of the liberation movement. This was a rather tricky endeavour. There was a certain kind of secrecy in the liberation movement, which seemed to underline two traits shared by its leaders, cadres, and foot soldiers: a desire to keep people ignorant, and the idea that the possession of information—whatever it might be—was power, suggesting that the more one was informed, the more one wanted people to remain ignorant such that one oozed importance in the liberation movement and in society. My colleague and comrade in the Southern Progressives at the University of Khartoum, Capt. George Maker Benjamin, was very frank when he told me that for all practical purposes, real membership of the SPLM/A began only after one had graduated from the military training centre and been commissioned by the chairman and commander-in-chief. This meant that I was in Addis Ababa only awaiting my orders to travel to Gambella and the Itang refugee camp. In regards to political work, Maker was blunt: he told me that I should not expect any kind of political meetings or discussions, and warned me not to talk about important matters with anyone.

In addition to the SPLA officers accommodated at the Marabeti Hotel, Ethiopian security was also hosting a group of Ugandan intellectuals. They seemed to belong to a rebel group. Our evenings were spent together, sitting around having a drink, socialising, and engaging in some kind of political discussions. I came to know that they were members of the Uganda People's Congress (UPC), led by President Milton Obote, who was overthrown in a military coup in July 1985 by Tito Lutwa Okello and Bazilio Olara-Okello. Among them was the late Dr. David Anyoti, whom I came to know was a minister in the Obote government. They wanted to start an armed insurrection against the National Resistance Movement/Army (NRM/A), led by Yoweri Museveni; The NRM/A stormed and captured Kampala, overthrowing the two Okellos just months after they took power. In my conversation with him, Dr. Anyoti strongly believed the NRM/A created the political conditions for the military coup that overthrew their government, and therefore, was their principal enemy.

Dr. Anyoti and his colleagues struck me as progressives. However, in our discussions I would wonder out loud why, instead of fighting Museveni, they didn't join him in an alliance. This did not go down well with them. In fact, they believed the coup by the Okellos was a ploy to weaken the Ugandan army and enable Museveni to easily capture power in Kampala. I would meet some of these guys in the SPLA training camp in Bonga eight months later. Mengistu must have asked Dr. Garang to train them together with the SPLA. They were known in the training centre as "Equatorians".

I met Dr. David Anyoti again in Nairobi in 2014, and he was still on the path of fighting Museveni. However, most of his officers and men had returned to Uganda, responding to a general amnesty. I was saddened, indeed shocked, when a mutual friend, Prof. Eduard Oyugi, called to inform me one day that David had passed on. I had started to build a working relation with him and other Kenyan civil society activists like Oyugi and Koigi wa Wamwere through the Venezuelan and Cuban embassies in Kenya. The mysterious relationship between the Ugandans and the SPLA would later be a source of friction between the two friends, President Yoweri Museveni and Dr. John Garang.

After the three weeks in Addis Ababa, what someone jokingly referred to as hospitality time, had expired, we were put on a bus bound for Gambella, a journey that took three days. A young graduate lawyer, Deng Biong, and I were the only recruits on the bus. The rest were trained SPLA officers and men who spoke with an air of power and authority. They had been in Addis Ababa for a variety of reasons, ranging from personal issues to medical concerns. The bus travelled only during the day-time and it gave me a glimpse of rural Ethiopia as we drove past the green coffee and tea estates. It was high altitude in some places, like in Gore, and really cold for people like us coming from hot lowlands. As we descended to the plains of Illababur, it started to get warm and warmer. In fact, in terms of temperature, Gambella was just like Malakal or Juba at that time of the year.

We arrived in Gambella on the morning of 1 May. It was a holiday in Ethiopia, and everything was closed. The bus required a special pass to travel to Itang, so we had to wait for nearly six hours before departing to the camp, arriving there at about four o'clock.

The camp was alive with traditional Nuer and Anywaa dances, apparently for different reasons. The Anywaa, mostly Ethiopians, were celebrating Workers' Day. It turned out later that the Nuer were celebrating the Anya-nya II victory and capture of Bukteng earlier that morning. The area commander, Amon Mon Wantok, took me to his house. Apparently, he had instructions to watch my activities and report back to the leadership.

In terms of the population living there, the house was like a miniature camp. There were more than five families and other hangers-on in the compound so one could not speak of privacy. I found it difficult to cope. At the same time, I was not allowed to be with the recruits. Luckily, I got a place near the house of my nephew, John Diwad Adwok, who had interrupted his medical studies at the College of Medicine at the University of Juba. He and his young wife had survived the Anya-nya II attack on Bukteng and taken refuge in Itang. I designed a double tukul, joined together by a spacious veranda and compound. Here I could manage my life without much difficulty. It was then about two months since I had left Khartoum and the issue of my family started to trouble me. It was a situation of deep uncertainty: they did not know where or how I was, and I had no inkling of their condition without me.

Comrade Amon Mon Wantok, a very committed revolutionary, assigned me to teach Marxist philosophy to the former senior civil servants who were awaiting military training. This was indeed a daunting task. Although a former member of the Communist Party, teaching Marxist philosophy was not an easy task; moreover, any recruit into the SPLM/A needed not Marxist philosophy as would be taught in a political science class, but an introduction to the recent and contemporary history of the Sudan, a clear and scientific understanding of the SPLM's *Manifesto*, and knowledge of revolutionary and national liberation movements the world over. This would widen their scope and help absorb the socio-political dynamics of national liberation they were part of.

I took it up as a serious assignment for about a month until it was stopped by an order 'from above'. This unexplained lack of consistency puzzled me. It was by mere accident that I got a glimpse of what may have been behind the order. A friend who accompanied Dr. Garang on his trip to Itang told me that in a conversation about the current situation. My name came up in connection with Itang and the political work I was engaged in. "I was taken aback, he said, when Dr. Garang quipped, 'So Adwok has not yet taken cover.'" "It took me time to reflect on this statement. Comrade Amon could offer no help to decipher this coded message. I am sure this was to be subject of my midnight interview with Dr. Garang at the training centre. It was only in this year of 2021, while writing these lines, that I got a satisfactory explanation for the coded message. In the early days of the movement, sometime in 1984–85, the leftists had formed a ring of confidantes around Dr. Garang, ostensibly to protect the revolution. According to Dr. Chol Deng Alaak, this discussion group included colleagues at different levels of ideological training and experience, which conditioned their understanding of issues, and action in the movement. It wasn't long before the group, under continuous attack by reactionary forces in the movement, disbanded. In hindsight, Garang's words then suggested that my teaching of Marxism in Itang was like courting trouble, and this would explain his order to stop the class and the organisational activities with the women in the camp.

I had wanted to meet the chairman but was informed that he had tight schedule. After his departure, two days later Comrade Amon informed me that I was now the secretary of the Committee for Agitation, and that our mandate was to work with the Women's Association. The committee chairman was to be comrade Amon himself. I asked about the other members of the committee but Amon would not divulge any names. It turned out to be a trap laid by a member of the High Command, Cdr. Arok Thon, with the aim of identifying former Communists and socialists in the Sudan, now categorised as enemies of the 'revolution', to expose and defeat Garang and the left in the power struggle simmering in the High Command. Cdr. Arok Thon used his position in the High Command to bully comrade Amon and the leftists into executing his orders. Thus, Amon established the Committee for Agitation without getting its terms of reference from Arok.

Instead of pestering Amon, I carefully brought together a group of five former party members and trade unionists. I knew this type of assignment was a trap, but convinced my colleagues that it was necessary to raise the social awareness of women, as this would enable them to contribute effectively to the struggle by taking good care of their families. We agreed to perform the task to the satisfaction of the movement's leadership. At the same time, we formed ourselves into a cell to discuss and analyse ideological matters in the movement. This was exactly what Cdr. Arok Thon had wanted. Itang refugee camp was divided into seven administrative areas (*tellul*) in which the women's organisation functioned. They were at different levels of organisation and enlightenment. To my surprise, I found the less enlightened rural women more cooperative and more enthusiastic for knowledge than the urbanised women, who were dismissive of our efforts to enlighten them. We decided to concentrate our efforts on these rural women.

In the course of this assignment, it became clear to me that two of our committee members: Lueth Garang and Atem Garang (not relatives), who hailed from Cdr. Arok Thon's home turf were constantly reporting to him some very private ideological discussions. One such report they rendered was about our analysis of the objective situation in the SPLM/A and whether or not the cell could function independent of the movement's structure, the High Command, while still executing its orders and directives. A report of this kind to Arok Thon was the intelligence product for which he ordered the formation of the Committee for Agitation in order to trap and eliminate the radical elements still embedded in the movement. It was going to be a repeat of the action against the progressive elements around Garang, and the blow to the politicians in 1984–85. Comrade Mangar Aping was an experienced political activist and had the advantage of being a Dinka himself. We quietly conspired to raise at our next meeting the idea of dissolving or disbanding the cell. The idea was to deny Cdr. Arok Thon the intelligence he was collecting freely from our discussions. In what would be our last meeting as the Committee for Agitation, Lueth and Atem tried to resist the dissolution of our small cell, but Mangar and I defeated their arguments and bid ourselves goodbye.

As I said above, the simpler a person the easier it is to deal with him, or her. This was my experience working with the Women's Association in the Itang refugee camp. It was possible to differentiate and distinguish the peasant and pastoralist women, who were ready to learn and acquire knowledge from the urban lumpen who knew nothing and did not want to learn. I found it hard to deal with the spouses of senior officers or members of the High Command. It was as if they carried with them the ranks of their husbands; some of them even had bodyguards who had the audacity to rough up some of my colleagues. I concluded from this experience that the SPLM/A was replicating, albeit in a different way, the oppressive reality of the Sudan. It was a repeat of history.

After five months in Itang, recruits were organised to go for military training. Between Itang and Bonga was a distance of ninety kilometres. I was on the committee organising the youth for the journey to Bonga. There were eight thousand recruits. The ninety kilometres to Bonga would take fifteen hours, moving under the cover of darkness to ensure secrecy of the operation. It was not possible. We managed to pass Gambella town (fifty-four kilometres) around three o'clock in the morning, but the final leg to Bonga could only be completed the following night; by sunrise, the recruits had to disappear into the nearest forest to rest and get some sleep. We started again in the late afternoon and at about ten o'clock we were met by some SPLA instructors who with whips mercilessly started beating us until one guy quipped, "Maybe we have fallen into an ambush of Anya-nya II. Are these really SPLA comrades?"

The Bonga SPLA training camp was a huge centre which

accommodated up to fifteen thousand recruits formed into battalions. The Zalzal (Earthquake) Division, as it was named, comprised six battalions of which the sixth battalion was that of the Red Army. These were very young boys aged between eight and twelve years. The idea of recruiting them had to do with Garang's political strategies. These children would grow up knowing no other leader in the movement except Dr. Garang. They were indoctrinated to memorise that fact.

Each SPLA battalion under training comprised one thousand four hundred and forty recruits. This was a brigade-sized in the conventional military formation; in fact, the SPLA was a conventional rather than a guerrilla army *sensu strictu*. I was appointed the regimental sergeant major (Sole) of Sonke Battalion. My function was to manage the battalion's exact parade which reported daily to the headquarters in the form of present, absent, or sick; the reasons for absence were also recorded. This was a routine I managed so well that battalion's commissioned officer, Lt. William Padhour, treated me exceptionally well, which was not the case with my colleague Dhol Acuil Aleu in Magnun Battalion. Some battalion commanders in the camp had unwritten orders 'from above' to make the training exceptionally difficult for certain named individuals among the recruits; in particular, former politicians and senior bureaucrats by without explanation subjecting them to extra drills and other punishments. Comrade Dhol Acuil Aleu was the vice president of the High Executive Council of the defunct Southern Region. He joined the SPLM/A in late 1984 or early 1985. Instead of sending him for training, Dr. Garang appointed him representative of the SPLM/A in Kenya, under the rubrics of the humanitarian wing of the SPLM/A, the Sudan Relief and Rehabilitation Association (SRRA). Dhol, myself, and a few others were under security surveillance during our training. It was around midnight when a car was sent to pick me up from the battalion. It was a worrying development. It was on the order of Chairman Garang. Arriving at his headquarters, I was led to his room.

I was standing at full attention when he raised his eyes to see my face. He nodded and looked back into the huge notebook in front of him. "You were agitating negatively against the movement when you were in Itang," he said. I told him that it was not true but he insisted that it was, saying that his security officers had informed him. I told him that they must have lied to him because what I and others did was enlighten the people and explain to them the SPLM's *Manifesto*, and this could not amount to negative agitation.

Dr. Garang began to lecture me about the Ethiopian revolution, telling me that Mengistu and his colleagues had spent about ten years before launching the Ethiopian Workers' Party. He accused the leftists in the SPLM/A of impatience, of wanting to achieve everything in one day. After about forty-five minutes of the lecture, Dr. Garang asked if I had anything to say. I told him that Ethiopia and the Sudan were two different experiences. While the Ethiopian revolution was top down, it was necessary to take an even longer period for the revolutionary forces to transform themselves into a political party, particularly given the feudal character of the state and society.

This required first the liberation of land, the most important means of production, from the feudal lords and redistribution of it to the peasants. The other important task was enlightenment and literacy to enable the people to read and write, and Ethiopia had reached eighty-five per cent literacy. These actions required time and that was why the Derg was now establishing the party. In the case of the Sudan, it was a bottom-up process which required clarity and transparency to permit the people to know what we are doing and the objectives of the movement which required explanation. And this was what we had been involved in in Itang. "I will call you again," said Dr. Garang. And then he dismissed me. He never called me again.

The SPLA training, whether general or officers' training, was severely brutal, harsh, dehumanising, and de-revolutionising. Apart for gaining military and combat skills, the real objective was to instil instantaneous obedience and loyalty to the SPLA leader. The morale songs, which we sang almost all the time, were only in praise of Dr. John Garang de Mabior, Kerubino Kuanyin Bol, William Nyuon Bany, Salva Kiir Mayardit, and Arok Thon Arok—in that order— instead of the revolution and the country. The South Sudanese instructors overzealously enforced the inculcation of Garang's cult of personality. So much so that at the end of training, graduating troops had only the knowledge and memory of the instructors and Dr. John Garang de Mabior. Garang purposely stamped his image on the recruits by personally handing over to each and every soldier his uniform and the AK–47 rifle. No wonder that the unarmed civilians became the first victims of the SPLA's brutality and dehumanisation: the soldiers were trying to psychologically regain their manhood, which they had lost to the instructors at the Bonga training centre.

Some of the experiences in Bonga were deeply scarring and dehumanising. Being the regimental sergeant major of Sonke did not protect me from the brutalisation meted by the instructors to the other recruits. The instructors would try to prove their worth by being menacing, particularly to respected citizens, former bureaucrats, and politicians. To circumvent and avoid their wrath, generated by their feelings of social inferiority, I had to humble myself and obey their orders. Sometimes their behaviour pricked their own consciences and they were embarrassed. One day, without any rational explanation, a certain instructor visited his own frustration on me. He ordered me to attention and said that I was behaving as if I were the chairman of the movement. He began to beat me and told me to lie down and roll on the ground. I did it without complaint. Then he ordered me to stand up and dance. I hesitated, and suddenly he shouted, "You think you have PhD. It has no use here in Bonga. You better use it to roll tobacco." I became so angry that I forgot I was just a recruit and told him that the PhD was not a piece of paper but knowledge in my head. This infuriated him and he started beating me once more. I retaliated with a force that sent him to the ground in serious pain. This triggered a terrible situation which brought on eleven instructors, some coming from the neighbouring battalion of Maaban. In the end, I had to be carried to my hut; I could not walk by myself.

For two days I refused to attend the morning and evening parades, registering as a sick person. The sergeant major of the first company replaced me in managing the parade. Unfortunately, he did it so poorly that the parade was not accepted at the head-quarters, to the chagrin of the battalion commander, Lt. William. On the third day, Lt. William was again sent back to redo his parade. As he walked away from the headquarters, the commander of the training camp, Lt. Col. Mawien, shouted and signalled Lt. William to see him. "I have observed in the last two days that you were sent back to your battalion. What happened to that RSM who used to prepare the parade?" "He has fallen sick," responded Lt. William. "No, he is not sick. I don't want to hear that he is sick tomorrow," said the commander.

Lt. William Padhour hailed from Fangak and was a primary schoolteacher before joining the SPLM/A. He had a human touch that had not been completely eroded by the SPLA's militaristic culture. After being rebuked by the camp commander, William resolved my problem in a manner unthinkable in the SPLA. He visited me in my tukul, carrying something that stirred up trouble, particularly given the rules in the training camp. He apologised for what the instructors had done to me and asked me to forgive them. I thought I would not disappoint him for this gentle and civil behaviour and so I promised him that I would resume my duties as the battalion RSM in the morning. Yunis Dumi, the logistics RSM with whom I shared the tukul, was so impressed by what Lt. William did.

The training lasted three months. It was mainly about military drills, tactics, fire and manoeuvre, armaments, reconnaissance, and sentry, which allows an individual to engage in contact with the enemy at the tactical level. They started deploying some of the troops. At about the beginning of December the chairman and commander-in-chief arrived and the process of selecting for officers' training began. The Revolutionary War Studies College, as it was called, was walking distance from the general training centre. The training was led by Ethiopian officers and offered more theory than practice; they empathised militarism in relations between officers and their men, and the need for discipline and total obedience.

One day during the training, I was called by the college commander, Maj. Chol Deng Alaak. "I have been instructed to inform you that your family has arrived and proceeded to Itang. Is that clear?" he said. "It is clear, sir," I replied. "Fall out," he ordered. As if he knew what was on my mind, he told me not to ask for permission to go to see my family because it would never be given. Regardless, my family's arrival in Itang was the best news I had received in eight months. It raised my morale.

In the second week in the college, I was made the senior under officer (SUO), equivalent to the RSM in general training but a much easier task given that all the cadets were either officers in the police, prisons, or wildlife, or had received military training before. My administration coincided with the committing of an act that was strictly forbidden in Ethiopia—killing wildlife. Some SPLA soldiers attached to the college had gone to Baro River and killed a hippo. This was a criminal act punishable by death in Ethiopia. The order therefore was that the cadets must bring the meat of the slaughtered hippo to the camp and leave no traces at the riverbank. It was to be cooked and consumed under the cover of darkness lest the Ethiopians discovered what had happened. As the SUO, the task of cover-up fell to me and my colleagues. I supervised the orderly execution of this order, seeing to it that the cooking was done in the deep dry riverbeds. By sunrise, the cadets had consumed all of the meat, the bones had been buried, and the whole area cleaned up. The week ended without a serious crisis and I handed over to the new SUO.

After my arrival in Bonga in September, never did I even for one day stray into the Anywaa village near the training centre. But one Saturday a fellow cadet invited two of us to come the village to relax away the training fatigue, and immediately after the evening parade we left. We had a nice time there, drinking *araki* and eating meat. Behind us in the college something happened. One cadet had sneaked into an Ethiopian village near the college and bought a bottle of *araki*. Instead of consuming it there and then, the cadet took off with the bottle. The owner ran after him, shouting at him to return the empty bottle. The row alerted the Ethiopian police who stopped the cadet and brought him to the college. It was about eleven o'clock and the cadets were called to parade.

When we arrived at the college, the cadets were still in drill but were released immediately after it was realised that the three of us who had been missing had arrived. At four o'clock they sounded the whistle for the parade; my body was aching all over. Luckily, because it was Sunday, they did not keep us for long. I went straight to sleep, even forgoing the breakfast served at six thirty. At ten o'clock, when it had started to heat up, the six of us were called to the administration. The punishment was obvious, only that instead of sending us into the stream to be soaked in water, it was three hours of extra drill—jumping, rolling, frog-jumping, standing upright at attention— which was really horrible for a hangover. That was the day I promised myself that I would never drink alcohol again.

The worst part was the verbal batting from Comrade Prof. Bari Wanji, who was one of our Sudanese instructors. Prof. Bari Wanji was many years my senior, in fact, he graduated with honours in Economics from University of Khartoum in 1965, when I had just cleared second year in Rumbek Secondary School. He was a revolutionary and a strict disciplinarian. We were ideologically very close, and he had not expected me, as a fellow revolutionary, to behave in the manner I had. I apologised to him personally, while at the same time performing the rituals of self-criticism.

At the end of February 1987, we were passed out and I was

commissioned as a captain in the SPLA. Many of my colleagues were deployed but eight of us remained in the college; Cdr. Maj. Col Deng Alaak would not say anything except that he was not allowed to deploy any of the eight of us; nor was he able to give me permission to go to see my family in Itang. It was really depressing. One day I wandered over to the headquarters and ran into Cdr. James Wani Igga, the alternate member of the High Command. After saluting him, he asked me about my family; I told him I had not seen them. He said he felt sorry for that, pulled out a paper and wrote to the commander of the college, ordering him to give me seven days' leave to visit my family in Itang. Although Maj. Chol Deng did not seem to like the idea, he reluctantly issued me with a departure order. He refused to give me ten birr for transport, and only relented when I told him he was practicing discrimination because I knew he had allowed his cousin to travel to Itang.

I arrived at Itang as the sun was going down but was able to clearly see my children, their mother, and Aunt Nyabedi-jwok. Almost a year had passed since I had left them in Khartoum. I was so happy to see them. Abuk was so delighted but was in tears. We spent the night conversing and reflecting on their situation. In the morning, when Abuk saw me in daylight, she thought I was a moving skeleton. Indeed, six months of military training with a poor diet had left my bones showing. She told me that it was good I had built the double tukul, otherwise it was going to be difficult to build a house. She had already sold most of the valuables she had brought from the Sudan in order to feed the children. This, according to her, was because the UN food rations were not reaching the refugees; the SPLA administration in Itang sold the food intended for the refugees.

She was preparing to welcome me when I received orders to report to Zinc; an officer in the mobile headquarters of Dr. Garang was sent to pick seven of us in Itang. I told Abuk that I had not expected that joining the SPLM/A would turn out this way. I was sorry that she had to follow me. However, I had to carry out my orders and would try to get permission to come back to be with them. I wished her and the children good health. I left the house to catch the car taking us to Zinc, an Ethiopian army camp seven kilometres outside Gambella. There we were issued with personal weapons—an AK–47 and a pistol—but no ammunition. We were rushed to the airport in Gambella without being informed of where we were travelling to. We boarded the helicopter and after about one hour in the air we landed in Pochalla.

It was about four o'clock in the afternoon when we landed. Lt. Col Majur Nhial immediately escorted eight of us to Cdr. Salva Kiir Mayardit, member of the High Command and deputy chief of staff for operations, in order to report ourselves. He was aware of our journey, welcomed us, and asked us to sit down. I had never seen Cdr. Salva Kiir so close, and had never seen him talking. He was soft spoken and appeared to be a simple man. Over the days he remained in Pochalla, Kiir would ask us to join him during meal times. This treatment of junior officers by Salva Kiir was not emulated by the other members of the High Command, including the chairman and commander-in-chief, who passed through Pochalla while we were still there.

When Cdr. Salva Kiir left for another location, we remained under a situation in which the area commander was a junior officer who had no authority over us. Things came to a head the day that Capt. Dhol Acuil attempted to board an Ethiopian military helicopter bound for Gambella. The area commander quickly mobilised his troops to stop Capt. Dhol from boarding the plane; there had been no prior arrangement and no orders had come from above for him to leave. That day Cdr. Dr. Lam Akol, alternate member of the High Command, arrived at Pochalla with a large number of troops, mainly Chollo and Dinka from northern Upper Nile. Dr. Garang arrived the following day and Pochalla became the centre of activities, with troops arriving and troops leaving. In the month of April, Pochalla and its environs were the migration route of the white-eared cop. The idea was that troops transiting through

Pochalla would be able to improve their health by consuming the meat provided by these animals.

The need to improve the health of soldiers through better feeding underpinned the decision for the troops to take a long detour from Bilpam (where they had been trained) to Pochalla, Pibor, and back through Akobo to the Nasir area. This was the route Cdr. Dr. Lam Akol and his troops followed to reach northern Upper Nile. Instead of returning to his station in Nairobi, Capt. Dhol Acuil was ordered to join the forces bound for northern Upper Nile. I could see the anguish in Dhol's face: he thought Garang had set him up for the worst. When all the troops had left Pochalla, the level of activities subsided. To while away the time, we returned to our hunting in the nearby bush and fishing in the Akobo River. I began to question the wisdom behind why I was not allowed to stay with my family and instead was bored and idle in Pochalla.

A few days after the departure of the chairman and commander-in-chief, Capt. Prof. Bari Wanji arrived in Pochalla. According to him, Dr. Garang had promised to give him troops to take him to western Bahr el Ghazal. Bari Wanji was so upbeat about taking the revolution to his home turf. In his lectures in the college, it had been Bari Wanji's dream. We spent a good deal of time speaking about revolutionary theory and practice in view of Cabral's paper on "The Weapon of Theory," delivered in Havana in 1966. Prof. Bari Wanji had named one of his sons Cabral after the Guinean revolutionary. It was a topic dear to his heart. Bari Wanji and I also spent some time with Nyie Agada Akwai Cham, the undisputed king of the Anywaa people, both in Sudan and Ethiopia.

Pochalla is a small village of about two hundred inhabitants, if the SPLA troops are not counted. Its history is closely linked to the struggle of people in southern Sudan against regimes in Khartoum. It is strategic, lying on the Ethiopian–Sudanese border, which is marked by the Akobo River. The Anya-nya captured it in 1962 at the height of the guerrilla activities in Upper Nile Province. I was in Pochalla in April 1987, one year after the SPLA had captured (liberated) it from the enemy. Land mines were still molesting people, including SPLA soldiers. That August I had the opportunity to meet Maj. Francis Jago Nyibong, who commanded operations for the liberation of Pochalla, in Itang. I had known Francis Jago from my days with the Anya-nya in the Chollo contingent led by Daniel Chwogo in 1964–65. It was a wonderful reunion.

It was clear that we were not going to remain in Pochalla for long. One morning the area commander came to inform us that a helicopter was arriving at two o'clock in the afternoon to pick us up. I was surprised that Capt. Prof. Bari Wanji was with us in the plane. He had been ordered to relocate to Gambella; he remained on the plane when we landed and disembarked in Magok on the Baro River. It was obvious to me that we were being readied for the battle of Jekau, a border post still occupied by the Sudanese army from where they directed their friendly forces, Anya-nya II and Gaajak militia, against the SPLA. It was here that two task forces—the Daniel Chwogo Task Force under my command, and Shamis Task Force under the command of Capt. Ashiek Anot—were formed, commissioned, and ordered to move to frontline positions in Nyaplou and Jekau respectively.

Nyaplou was an abandoned Gaajak settlement. It had been deserted partly as a result of a series of battles between the SPLA and a civilian force commanded by Chuol Bileu, who was killed in battle with Cdr. William Nyuon Bany that year. It was about eight kilometres from Jekau. We struck to camp there, organised the forces into their segmentary formations with their commands, and waited for further orders. It was a rich area in terms of wildlife and fish in the Baro River. The soldiers, fresh from the training centre, now had enough to eat and their health improved. After a week, they were able to drill and practice engagement tactics without difficulty. The morale was very high. Dr. John Garang, the c-in-c arrived two weeks later, and we started the process of enemy appreciation and modelling on sand the operations against the enemy in Jekau.

Several SPLA tasks forces and allied Ethiopian forces had

gathered in the area and were poised to attack the enemy. Cdr. William Nyuon had forces on the northern side of Jekau, while the allied Ethiopian force and Shamis Task Force was on the east bank, directly opposite the enemy's position in the west. The tactical command headquarters, from where Garang commanded and directed the operations were moved from Nyeplou to Nyang, half-way to Jerusalem, a part of Jekau. At about nine o'clock in the evening I was ordered to move to Nyang with Daniel Chwogo Task Force's 1st and 2nd companies, together with my second in command 1st Lt. Majok were combat ready. The two companies formed a protection force for the commander-in-chief in case of any unforeseen developments. From my position in that deployment, I could hear Dr. John Garang issuing orders and commands to all the forces. There was a point in time that the commander of Shamis Task Force disappeared from communication; he had closed his radio. I could hear Dr. John shouting to raise him but to no avail. I asked Dr. John to allow my force to advance since Capt. Ashiek Anot had disappeared. He refused and said he knew when to call me.

The call came at about four-thirty in the morning. "Captain Peter, you have forty-five minutes to reach the enemy lines. Forward march!" came the orders from the commander-in-chief. In only a short time, my forces were on the march to the battle-field. Somewhere in the middle of the road, indeed in what was the market, I got orders to wait there until further orders. There was another SPLA force in front of my force; they cleared only at sunrise. The enemy force, from its vantage point, could see clearly in daylight. With a 12.7–mm heavy machine gun they pinned us down at the gap between the riverbank and the water. The first to be shot was my bodyguard and he was quickly hurried to the rear. I was the only one remaining in the front as we were still proceeding in single file. It was a dangerous spot; many of my men, including my second in command 1st Lt. Majok, were either killed or wounded there.

I ordered those who remained to withdraw to where the river

curved as it was a safe place to stay. I was already wounded in my left leg and was bleeding heavily but because it was a sandy spot, I dug myself deep into the sand into a position that I could feel the 12.7–mm bullets passing a few centimetres away above my head. The enemy continued shooting long after our guns had ceased firing that it became difficult to evacuate me. When I realised that all my forces now behind me could not advance to where I was, I decided to jump into the water and with one leg pushed myself into the river bend. They got me out of the water and carried me to a dilapidated brick building that had been a shop during the good old days of Jekau. The commander-in-chief had already been informed and ordered me to be driven to Nyang and from there to Nyaplou, where I received first-aid from a former gynaecologist, Dr. Justin Yaac Arop.

Our attempt to attack and capture Jekau was a damning failure on many counts. We had not only underestimated the enemy's strength, there were serious flaws in the planning based on poor appreciation and wrong intelligence. Although, the enemy was only a one-company-strong force, it was dug down in bunkers over a small area. The information the combat intelligence offi-cers provided was completely wrong and at variance with facts on the ground. It was not wise to attack the enemy while it was in a defensive position. Thus, even after several similar attempts, the SPLA could not dislodge the enemy from its positions. The SAF forces had to withdraw on 31 May under the cover of night, when the army command in either Malakal or Khartoum failed to send reinforcements. Thereafter, the SPLA started boasting about the liberation of Jekau, whose ground has been severely polluted by gunpowder. SPLA victories—wherever they occurred—were invariably pyrrhic. As were the battles for the capture of Jekau, which went against the basic law of war: preserve one's forces but destroy the enemy.

The first-aid Dr. Justin Yaac Arop provided at the rear base was to be the cause of amputation of my limb. I had lost so much blood that there were moments when I fell unconscious and was not aware of what was going on. To my surprise, I discovered, upon waking, that he had plastered my whole leg, from the foot to the thigh. Although I was evacuated in good time to Gambella Hospital, and because as it appeared, I had already been attended to, time elapsed and by the time they removed the gypsum, my leg was already gangrenous and too late to save my limb, hence the decision to amputate. It was a traumatising moment for my wife when they informed her that I had been wounded and brought to Gambella. Initially, I resisted the idea of amputation. Prof. Bari Wanji and many other comrades came to convince me that it was better to lose one's leg than losing life. Abuk told me that it was my presence alive that was more important to her and our children. She then signed the consent form on my behalf for the Cuban doctors to amputate my leg.

Gambella Hospital was busy due to the ongoing military operations in southern Sudan. In order to leave space for others wounded in action, I was released from the hospital fifteen days after the operation and was accommodated on the SPLA compound in Gambella. It was there that the SPLA's commander-in-chief, Dr. Garang, came to visit me, ostensibly to raise my morale and to inform me that I would be travelling to Cuba to receive a prosthesis. He gave me a copy of Mao Zedong's *On Guerrilla Warfare*. I found a discrepancy, indeed a contradiction between Garang's strategy in Jekau and Zedong's wars of national liberation. Instead of attacking a small force like the enemy force in Jekau, I believe Mao would have just besieged the town, following classical guerrilla warfare.

During my recovery, I was able to get the enemy's side of the battle for Jekau. As mentioned, earlier, the enemy force of about two platoons withdrew from Jekau under the cover of night. The SPLA got wind of where they were and stormed the place, capturing them and their commander, Lt. Col. Suleiman Sayed. The SPLA treated them honourably and brought them to Dr. Garang, who welcomed them with respect. Impressed by this treatment, which he had not expected, Lt. Col. Sayed told Garang that if there was anything he could do to harm Prime Minister Sadiq el Mahdi's government, he would do it immediately. Garang took up the offer, and asked Lt. Col. Sayed to request that an SAF helicopter be sent from Malakal. Lt. Col Sayed drafted and coded the message, asking for a helicopter to evacuate them to Nasir or Malakal.

What follows looks like straight from a Hollywood film. This talk between Garang and the prisoner of war immediately established communication between the SPLA unit tasked with the operation on behalf of Lt. Col. Sayed and the SAF command in Malakal. On the first day, the helicopter flew overhead what was supposed to be the rendezvous but could not locate the SPLA force, now masquerading as SAF. The following day they repeated the trick and helicopter indeed landed but, unfortunately, aboard the helicopter was a Gaajak Nuer who immediately recognised his own brother coming to the helicopter and pretending to be wounded SAF soldier. As the pilot tried to take off, the SPLA shot it down with an RPG. The command in Malakal now realised that they had SPLA duped them and called off any operation to rescue Col. Sayed and his men.

June 1987 was a dramatic month. The euphoria and dust raised by the capture of Jekau had hardly settled down when the liberation was rocked by a serious political crisis leading to the arrest and detention of Cdr. Kerubino Kuanyin Bol, the movement's deputy chairman and deputy commander-in-chief. This operation to arrest Kerubino took place in Addis Ababa with the assistance of the Ethiopian intelligence and security agencies. In the Itang refugee camp, where I had relocated from Gambella to stay with my family, no one talked openly about the incident. But many officers with relatives and friends in the signal corps knew what had gone wrong.

Cdr. Kerubino had serious disagreements with Dr. Garang, and had indeed revolted. He planned to relocate from Blue Nile Province to northern Bahr el Ghazal, then devastated by the *murahalieen*, Baggara Arab nomads of Kordofan and Dar Fur. Cdr. Kerubino would have succeeded had he not accepted Garang's trick that lured him to Addis Ababa. There he met with Prof. Bari Wanji, who convinced him against making the revolt a Dinka or a Bahr el Ghazal issue, insisting that the problem was structural within the movement. Kerubino was arrested and taken to an SPLA prison in Blue Nile Province. Capt. Prof. Wanji, however, resisted arrest and found asylum in the Cuban Embassy.

A small group of officers led by Francis Jago, Michael Miakol, and others—calling themselves "non-progressive SPLA officers"—at the behest of Cdr. Arok Thon Arok, started to stir up trouble in the movement. They demanded the arrest and execution of the so-called progressive officers. The political situation was really tense. Cdr. William Nyuon and Cdr. Arok Thon Arok were in the "non-progressives" group. In fact, Cdr. Arok was in mourning for his wife. She had died only a few days earlier and her body was brought from Addis Ababa to be buried in Itang. It was clear that apart from the funeral, which nearly every officer in Itang attended, something sinister was afoot.

I remember how Cdr. Arok insisted that I not leave the funeral early. It had started to rain and I wanted to leave to avoid being stuck in the mud with my crutches. One of his relatives had to intercede on my behalf, arguing that I should be allowed to leave on account that I was disabled. Cdr. Arok had an ideological axe to grind with the leftists. It was indeed a paradox of history that Nimeri's intelligence and security officers — who zealously prosecuted the Communists, socialists, and democrats for Nimeri— were now leaders in the national liberation and playing the same role of prosecuting progressive southern Sudanese.

The next day, Cdr. William Nyuon sent me a vehicle to make sure that I left Itang for Gambella, from where I would take a plane to Addis Ababa. He knew my name was on the list of the officers who were to be arrested. To his credit, he did not want the embarrassment of arresting a wounded soldier who was still recuperating. William Nyuon wanted me to leave Itang before they started to execute the order to arrest the SPLA officers. Two days after I left Itang, twenty-six SPLA officers were arrested and sent to Bilpam from where they were later transferred to the SPLA's central prison in Boma. Most of those arrested came from Bahr el Ghazal and were led by Lt. Col. Amon Mon Wantok, the former area commander of Itang refugee camp.

It was a very complex political and military situation that represented the prevailing crosscurrents in the SPLM/A. The progressive officers were just a scapegoat in this highly personified power struggle, which played out along regional lines. In this interplay of power and regionalism, the arrest of Kerubino and the Bahr el Ghazal officers marked the summit of the power struggle between the Bahr el Ghazal and Bor elites and the bitterness that followed the assassination of veteran politician Benjamin Bol Akok. Both Garang and Arok believed that leadership of southern Sudan must be centred in Bor.

Arok Thon, however, on account of clan hubris, never recognised Garang's leadership. He even had the audacity to openly challenge Garang's authority when he was ordered to arrest and detain all of the so-called progressive SPLA officers. It was the schism between the two that later led to the arrest and detention of Cdr. Arok Thon, as payback for his condescending attitude towards Garang. It was not at all because of any ideological differences.

I must count myself lucky to have had William Nyuon on my side to avoid being arrested together with my colleagues. My runner and I left Gambella on an Ethiopian Airline flight to Addis Ababa arranged by the SPLA office in Gambella. The flight to Addis Ababa took much longer than usual because the plane had to pick up passengers at three more airstrips on the way to Bole International Airport. In Addis Ababa, I was accommodated with full board at the Dama Hotel, where several officers and men working for Radio SPLA stayed. Now aware of the situation in the SPLA, particularly the manner that the combat intelligence officers and men had framed comrades to put them in a bad light with the leadership, I kept a low profile, only talking to people I knew well. I waited for two weeks before taking my flight to Havana.

Chapter 12

Visits to Revolutionary Cuba

First as a Medical Tourist, & then as a Government Minister

On a sunny 8 October 1987, I was led up the ladder steps of an Ethiopian Boeing 767 plane, limping on my wooden crutches. I was at Bole International Airport in Addis Ababa and the plane was about to take off for Luanda, Angola. We had been waiting in the shade of a hanger for this was not a normal commercial flight. There were no tickets, no check-ins, and of course no passports. My journey for treatment in Cuba was about to begin. A young man, Monybuny, and I were the only Sudanese on the plane. Monybuny, whom I had never met before coming to the airport, was then a soldier in Dr. Garang's mobile headquarters.

His injury had occurred in a road accident between Rahad and Boma. He was so bitter when he related the road accident because the officer who caused the accident was not a driver; he took over the vehicle just to demonstrate his power. Several of his colleagues had been killed. Luckily, he survived but his right leg had been amputated above the knee. Mine was the left leg above the knee. The rest of the passengers were Cubans returning home, presumably for rest and recreation holidays after duty in Ethiopia, of which the Cuban mission with the SPLA was an integral part. This was the material expression made by Mengistu, that Ethiopian people would share the same *dábo* (bread) with their Sudanese counterpart in the SPLA.

On the flight to Luanda, my thoughts carried me to places near and far, then suddenly my memory took me back to the scene in Leoben, Austria, in 1977, when a group of youths attacked me for wearing a T-shirt bearing the Cuban flag and coat of arms. That I was now travelling to Cuba felt surreal. We arrived in Luanda at about five o'clock in the evening. It was a busy airport, with mostly military transport planes landing and taking off. The passengers, including me, were hurried into a waiting large Russian plane. After only a few minutes, we were cleared for take-off, flying westward over the waters of the Atlantic Ocean. I was seated at the window and as the plane turned to the north, I could see the sun setting. It was a beautiful sight, but it soon became dark outside. This was the most unusual flight I ever took, in terms of lack of information about time schedules and destination. All I knew was that we were chasing the night towards the northwest.

In the middle of the night, I awoke to the sound of people talking on the ground. At first, I thought I was dreaming but then realised that our plane was actually on the ground; it was being refuelled and some passengers were embarking. I asked the guy next to me where we were. He told me that we were in Cape Verde, off the West African coast of the Atlantic Ocean. I immediately remembered Amilcar Cabral and the PAIGC (Partido Africano para a Independência da Guiné e Cabo Verde; African Party for the Independence of Guinea and Cape Verde). I remembered the night in October 1987, Edward Lino and I arranged a protest rally in the students' square against his assassination at the hands of Portuguese imperialist. I only wished that it was daytime so I could get a glimpse of the island's beauty. The plane soon took off once more and turned westwards over the Atlantic Ocean.

At about three o'clock in the morning we landed at José Martí International Airport, Havana. Our guide, who only spoke Spanish, recognised Monybuny and me and immediately whisked us off to what we later came to know was a quarantine: a medical facility where visitors from Africa and the Middle East were kept for at least three days to undertake a thorough medical check, specifically for malaria and HIV/AIDS. We were informed that the Cubans had completely eradicated malaria, and although there were mosquitoes in the island, they did not cause malaria. I had slept on the plane, but I was still very tired when we reached the quarantine. After my samples were taken, I immediately fell into a deep sleep, a kind of jet lag that must have lasted for forty-eight hours. The SPLM/A's representative to Cuba, Comrade Gabriel Acwoth Deng, a former member of the CPS, had come to see us, but found me asleep. He did not have much to do with us, as we were firmly under the care of the Cubans. Once the results of our tests were ready, Monybuny and I were transferred to the Frank Pais Hospital, a really modern orthopaedic hospital, where we were to remain until February 1988.

The reason for this long journey to Cuba was to acquire prosthetic limbs. I remembered that when he came to see me in Gambella, immediately after my release from hospital, Dr. Garang had told me, "You will travel to Cuba to get one of the best artificial limbs in the world to compensate your leg." At the time I did not take his words seriously; he had spoken to me as if he was talking to a child. But this was somehow normal in the SPLM/A. I had observed this as soon as I joined the movement. Without guilt or embarrassment, someone would say things that he or she knew were not true or bordered on a white lie, the aim being to make someone else happy or as they used to say, raise the morale. This is a sociocultural trait shared by the Dinka and the Nuer. Dr. Garang knew very well that Cuba was technologically speaking a third world country and the best prosthetic limbs in the world could not come from there.

In all honesty, the decision to send us to spend five months in Havana at the expense of the Cuban people for a treatment that we could have acquired cheaply in Addis Ababa, Ethiopia, was like a deliberate and malicious squandering of a friend's resources. Cuba was a friend indeed, but she was heavily overburdened by her inter-nationalist obligations, on account of solidarity with liberation movements in Africa and the Middle East: Frelimo (Mozambique), MPLA (Angola), PAIGC (Guinea Bissau and Cape Verde), Ethiopia, Yemen, SWAPO, ANC, and SPLM/A, all of which had schools in the Isle of Youth. If this matter had been discussed before I left Itang, the benefit of gaining Cuban experience notwithstanding, I would have suggested to the leadership that the opportunity to travel for treatment in Havana be used for more serious cases that required specialised medical or orthopaedic attention.

Frank Pais Hospital was a highly specialised orthopaedic centre. It was part of Cuba's medical tourism centres. People from different parts of Latin America came for specialised medical treatment, including plastic surgery. Monybuny's case was outright acquisition of a prosthetic limb, and so the hospital for him was just a matter of accommodation and board as we waited for the prosthetic limbs. In my case, however, the doctor wanted to perform a surgical oper-ation to remove five inches off the stump for a more comfortable fit onto an above-the-knee prosthesis. Every Wednesday and Sunday, the hospital provided its patients with some recreation, showing recent American films. We rolled our wheelchairs into the theatre so we could watch the movies. In this manner we punctuated with pleasant American English comedies the boredom in the hospital accentuated by our lack of knowledge of Spanish language.

The standard procedure was for us to remain in the hospital until we were taken back to Ethiopia. But it was a new experience for the Cubans when the SPLM/A's representative insisted that the hospital release Monybuny and me to stay at his residence for the rest of our time before we were to return to Addis Ababa. The Cubans acquiesced and we were released to his residence, from where we would return to the hospital every morning for physiotherapy. This was a typical Sudanese sociocultural attitude. It was decided that Monybuny would stay with Mama Nyandeng, Dr. Garang's wife, while I stayed with Comrade Gabriel Acwoth and his family. Mama Akuch was a very kind and sensitive woman. Like a real Nilotic woman, she took good care of me with pride and humility of a mother. The talkative toddler Chol, Gabriel's last born, was such an interesting being who would entertain us with his jokes about politics. When we met again thirty years later in their house in Juba, Chol had evolved into a quiet listener who like his father Gabriel spoke less. He would shake his head in negation when asked if he still remembered what he used to say when we were in Havana.

Havana vividly spurred my memories of the small booklet "Cuba, the Island I loved" by Dr. Yousif Bashara, which I had read while a student at the University of Khartoum. I wanted to experience its magic. Dr. Yousif and Sheikh Ali Abdelrahman had travelled to Cuba on invitation to attend the First Tricontinental Conference of the peoples of Asia, Africa, and Latin America, held in Havana in January 1966. Sudan had just emerged from a military dictatorship and the right-wing traditional political forces had stolen the revolution; Mohammed Ahmed Mahgoub was the prime minister of an Umma–NUP coalition government, to the chagrin of all progressive Sudanese social and political forces. In fact, in 1966, in a plot cooked up by the two coalition partners, the Constituent Assembly outlawed the Communist Party of the Sudan.

The Cuban revolution inspired many oppressed people the world over, and was an example for many leftist parties and liberation movements in Latin America, Africa, and Asia. During the time that I was recuperating in Havana, Cuba's international solidarity with the revolution in Angola defeated the South African army. This historic defeat opened the way for Namibia's independence and the eventual collapse of the apartheid regime in South Africa.

It was also a new era in the Soviet Union, where Mikhail Gorbachev, the Soviet leader, was experimenting with his twin ideas of *perestroika* and *glasnost*. It was a phenomenal ideological shift that would have resounding ramifications on the world stage. Gorbachev had convened a meeting of Socialist countries in Moscow to discuss perestroika and glasnost. I remember watching on Cuban television as Fidel Castro openly disagreed with Gorbachev over the applicability of perestroika and glasnost, especially in Cuba, given its proximity to the leading imperialist country in the world—the United States. Of course, later political developments vindicated Castro and those who had opposed Gorbachev, at least from the perspective of those who sought to continue the Soviet model. In 1990 the German Democratic Republic (DDR) regime collapsed, and the two German republics reunited. The socialist regimes in Poland, Czechoslovakia, Hungary, Bulgaria, Romania, and Yugoslavia were no more and, eventually, in 1991, the Soviet Union disintegrated.

These events leading to the collapse of the Soviet Union impacted on the regimes that depended much on the Cold War's political and ideological rivalry between the East and the West. In February 1991, the regime of Mohamed Siad Barré in Somalia fell, and in June, the Derg in Ethiopia was forced out of power as the EPRDF and the Eritrean People's Liberation Front (EPLF) shot themselves into power in Addis Ababa and Asmara respectively, ending the thirty-year war in Ethiopia. These events also impacted on the SPLM/A, leading to an ideological shift to the right. The bi-polar world disappeared with the emergence of the United States as the sole world power.

In Cuba, I spent my time reading books, periodicals, and the weekly English edition of *Granma*, the mouthpiece of the Communist Party of Cuba. It showed how high-level political and ideological consciousness and alertness had enabled the Cuban Communists to fight back against American propaganda and disinformation in the information warfare between the United States and Cuba. In fact, the Cuban government and party spent lots of resources to thwart the falsehoods peddled internationally by the American press and the CIA. One interesting story I came across while in Havana was about the Cuban dissident Armando Valladares, whom the CIA claimed was being held in a Cuban jail despite him being confined to a wheelchair. The Cuban government had tried to ward off this US propaganda by showing pictures of Valladares exercising in his cell. The authorities had placed a spy camera in his cell—something Fidel Castro, in an interview with Regis Debray, condemned as illegal. Debray had been sent by French President François Mitterrand to meet with President Castro to press for the release of Valladares on humanitarian grounds. In this interview, Fidel told Regis that Valladares was healthy and the issue of him being permanently on a wheelchair was just a hoax.

In the end, Fidel gave into the demand and released Valladares. On his arrival at Charles de Gaulle International Airport in Paris, diplomats and journalists crowded around the plane. To their surprise, Valladares stepped out of the plane, walking without assistance and flashing a victory sign. Fidel had been right, but the strength and concerted efforts of CIA propaganda not only enlisted the support of the French president but also made Valladares leader of US mission to the United Nations Human Rights Commission in Geneva, where perpetual battles fought on ideological lines raged over human rights in the world.

Havana and its people made me feel as if I were in any of the cities in the Sudan. On several occasions in the street, I ran into people whom I was sure were Sudanese on account of their skin colour, only to realise that they were Cuban and spoke only Spanish. Because of the American embargo, nearly everything was rationed in the shops and canteens in the neighbourhoods, in accordance with socialist government policy. This policy discouraged conspic-uous consumption; you could only buy extras at exuberant prices from special shops. In fact, these shops were meant for foreigners who had access to foreign exchange. Even in restaurants, a diner could only have two bottles of beer for each dish of food ordered. I found it very difficult to cope with this reality. In Addis Ababa, and even Khartoum before the sharia laws in 1983, or Addis Ababa, where in a restaurant served as many bottles of beer as you wanted.

Before our medical tourism ended in the last week of March 1988, the veteran southern politician Joseph Oduho came to Havana for medical treatment. As a very senior person in the movement, Oduho was accommodated at Havana Libre, a five-star hotel in the centre of Havana. He had only a short time in Cuba. Uncle Joseph was not a fan of Communist ideology but he liked the progress the Cubans had made in spite of the American economic embargo. During his stay in Havana, he often invited me to share ideas, as well as his rations at the delicious Havana Club. He had his operation and was released to leave for Africa via Europe.

In the intervening days before we left Cuba, students attending the Nico López Political School—Pagan Amum Okiech, Nhial Deng Nhial, Peter Pernyang Daniel, and many others—came to visit me and we discussed the serious problems afflicting the movement. In these discussions, I always found myself at odds with them. Sister Cecilia, the wife of Comrade Edward Otomi, who was a colleague at the University of Juba, also came from the Isle de Juventus to Havana to visit me. She had heard that I had lost my leg and was really upset by the news. Sister Cecilia had come to Cuba as a teacher at the SPLA school on the Isle of Youth.

If not because of language, Cuba would have been a good place to stay. However, as they say, east or west, home is always best. I started to feel homesick, especially when Uncle Joseph Oduho came and then left us. On 28 March we started our journey back to Africa. I don't know what happened but the flight was not well coordinated. We had to spend six days in Luanda waiting for the flight to Addis Ababa. It was a very difficult time as Monybuny, and I could not speak Portuguese. The workers in the small pension where we stayed did not speak English and, being physically challenged, we could not move far from the pension. At last we left Luanda on the morning of 4 April.

We arrived in Addis Ababa to get the news that Cdr. Arok Thon Arok, had been arrested. When we left Addis Ababa in October, it was a few months after the arrest and detention of the second man in command, Cdr. Kerubino Kuanyin Bol, and a number of officers whom Cdr. Arok had categorised as progressive officers. Now it was his turn to face the music. We also learned that Uncle Joseph Oduho, who had left me in Cuba, had returned to Ethiopia from Italy and been arrested by the SPLA and sent to the SPLA jail in Boma. This was a serious and worrying political development in the movement. I requested permission from Cdr. William Nyuon Bany, who was then in Addis Ababa, to proceed to Itang.

My second trip to Cuba came many years later, after the peace agreement with the NCP government of Sudan ended the war. This came in February 2010 as an invitation to attend the fourth bi-yearly conference on higher education, which was attended by ministers, academics, and scientists from many third world countries. I was then minister of higher education and scientific research in the Sudan's post-war Government of National Unity. I had planned to travel with the vice chancellors of three universities (Khartoum, Juba, and Gezira), the ministry's secretary-general, and the executive director in the office of the minister.

To my great dismay, just a day before the journey to Havana, the executive director said that only I would travel; the Ministry of Finance had vetoed travel by the others on account of financial insolvency. In Juba, I briefed the president of the Government of Southern Sudan (GoSS), who doubled as SPLM chairman. Although the trip to Havana was a national government affair, the SPLM chairman was expected to be interested on account of the historical relations between the SPLM/A and the Cuban government. Surprisingly, neither Salva Kiir nor the SPLM secretary-general appeared to have any idea that the trip was an opportunity to renew contacts with the Cubans, particularly after the Comprehensive

Peace Agreement (CPA) which made the SPLM/A the second major partner in the government of the Sudan. But it was too late to correct the situation; I had to travel alone to Havana. I knew the Islamic fundamentalists would not be interested in sending a delegation to Communist Cuba, although Sudan had strong diplomatic, economic, military, and cultural ties with Communist China.

At the José Martí International Airport in Havana, a fleet of three limousines arrived to transport the Sudanese delegation. The embassy, it seems, had not been informed that the Sudanese had only asked for one visa. On the way to the city, the protocol officer asked if I had a programme I would attend to besides the conference. I told him I wanted to meet the Communist Party of Cuba. At the conference, apart from the different scientific sessions, I had a statement I intended to make at the plenary to be held in solidarity with the "Cuban five" imprisoned in the United States; a session with the minister of education; and another with the minister of foreign affairs.

I was informed that at the party's central committee, I would meet the director of the Africa and Middle East desk, Comrade Pinto Ferro, a veteran of the war in the Congo and the companion of Ernesto Che Guevara. It was, in fact, a very cordial meeting. "Who killed Garang?" Ferro asked me. It was the CIA, I told him, to which he replied, "Everything is always blamed on the CIA." We both laughed. I informed him that before I had started my journey to Havana, I had stopped in Juba. Salva Kiir and members of the SPLM/A leadership were all aware of the cordial relations between the SPLM/A and the Cuban government and its people. It was time for a high-level delegation to go to Havana to rekindle the relations. It goes without saying that the Cubans had kept the SPLM/A in high esteem, on account of its armed resistance to the regime in Khartoum. The country had provided unconditional political and military support, as well as a school for the SPLA children on the Isle of Youth. The SPLM/A's leadership, for its part, seemed to have abandoned the Cubans at the most difficult of times, when the Soviet Union cut off its much-needed aid.

The collapse of the Derg, with the corresponding ascension to power in Addis Ababa by the EPRDF, forced a sudden unorganised withdrawal of the SPLM/A into liberated areas in southern Sudan. It also ordered back to Africa its representative, Cdr. Pagan Amum, who was resident with his family in Havana. Years later, the teachers and youth on the island, some of whom had been trained as medical doctors, engineers, and other professions, were allowed to seek political asylum in Canada. The hard feelings the Cubans harboured towards the South Sudanese were evident in Comrade Pinto Ferro's question to me, "Why did you abandon us?" I had no ready answer for him. Whatever the case, the party was pleased that members of the SPLM/A still remembered the former solidarity.

Back in the Sudan, I travelled to Juba to submit a report to the SPLM leadership about the visit and my observations in Havana. I recommended that the SPLM leadership consider re-establishing relations with Cuba. I was particularly concerned that in a few months the people of Southern Sudan would exercise their right to self-determination in a referendum and, given that a large majority of the people would vote for secession and independence, there was a need to start sounding out and mobilising former friends who had assisted in the liberation process.

On 9 July 2011, the Republic of South Sudan was born. The Cuban government sent a high-level delegation, led by the vice president of the Council of State, to the independence celebration. Their attendance was ostensibly to underline the importance the Cubans attached to the young Republic of South Sudan and its relations with the SPLM/A. It was a matter of pride that the South Sudanese Cuba alumni of the Isle of Youth and other institutions in Cuba, rather than SPLM or the government, played the important role of entertaining the Cuban delegation. I was appointed minister of higher education, science, and technology in the first government of independent South Sudan. Since South Sudan had not established diplomatic relations at embassy or consular levels, I believed that through the contacts I had established during my last visit to Cuba I could encourage further cooperation in the fields of education, medicine, science, and technology. It was in this context that I accepted an invitation to attend the fifth bi-annual conference on education in Havana in February 2012. This time the invitation came through the embassy of Cuba in Addis Ababa.

The president approved my request to attend and to travel to Havana with a few of my colleagues from the public universities. It was an opportunity to introduce them and their institutions to the Cuban education system. My entourage to Havana included three vice chancellors, a legislator from Upper Nile State, and an administrator in the ministry. I agreed to the request of my daughter, Agyedho, to join us on the condition that she financed herself, which she did. The journey to Havana took us through Madrid, Spain. Since we were paying our own expenses, we stayed at the conference centre. I encouraged my colleagues to attend the conference's scientific programme while I made political contacts.

I did not need to meet the party because we were already an independent state and it was preferable to have government-to-government meetings. The SPLM had not authorised me to contact the party; this was different from 2010, when I had volunteered to meet the central committee of the CPC. I insisted on having a one-on-one meeting with the conference convener, Minister of Education Miguel Díaz-Canel, a youthful leader whom I understood was being groomed to take over from President Raúl Castro. I received a verbal commitment that Cuba would offer South Sudan some scholarships for medical studies for 2012, with the option of additional space for South Sudanese students who wanted to study in Cuba at their own expense. It was cheaper to study medicine and other science-based specialities in Cuba than any other country, including South Sudan. Comrade Pinto Ferro was already retired but he came to the conference centre to visit our delegation. It was nice of him and, indeed, we had a good conversation.

In early 2013, I was called to go to a Cuba–Africa solidarity

meeting in Addis Ababa. This was a meeting attended by delegations of former liberation movements, political parties, and youth
groups in the context of Cuban internationalism. It was held in
commemoration of the Cuban internationalists and martyrs of the
war between Ethiopia and Somalia in 1978. It was definitely one
way of expressing solidarity with the Cubans. I was not surprised to
meet in Addis Ababa the SPLM's secretary-general, Comrade Pagan
Okiech, the minister for security in the Office of the President, Gen.
Oyay Deng Ajak, and the minister for postal service and telecom-
munications, Gier Chuong Aluong, each coming separately from
Juba to attend the event. It tells volumes how the SPLM as a party
organises itself and its participation in international events. I met
some youths from Kenya who introduced themselves as members of
the Communist Party of Kenya. I told Benedict Wachira, the head
of their delegation, that he must be kidding: to introduce oneself
as a Communist in Kenya was like committing suicide. Having
lived in Kenya for fifteen years, between 1990 and 2005, I knew the
Kenyan political dynamics. Later, I found out they were members
of the then-emerging Social Democratic Party of Kenya, led by
Mwandawiro Mghanga, whom I had met at Prof. Dani Nabudare's
institute in Mbali, eastern Uganda.

The SPLM's participation in such events could have been more
profound given the large number of South Sudanese who were
enthusiastic about Cuba and the revolution. In fact, as far as Cuba
was concerned, the leaders of the SPLM behaved almost the same
as the Islamic fundamentalists in the NCP, who tried to sabotage
my trip to Havana in 2010, and I found that really baffling. The
people of South Sudan stood to benefit from relations with Cuba
in terms of its advances in medicine, animal husbandry, agriculture,
and the experience of literacy and adult education. The SPLM leadership, including even those who spent time studying or training in
Cuba during the war of national liberation, unfortunately did not
seem to value that aspect of relations with Cuba. I can say with
confidence that, essentially, part of the problem was the SPLM/A's

ideological shift that occurred in the 1990s; it was obvious that the leaders did not want to be reminded of their supposedly socialist pasts. In the dying days of the war of national liberation, as the rebels engaged in serious peace talks with the government of the Sudan (between 2002 and 2005), the SPLM/A's political leaders and military top brass evolved into an elitist class that was completely alienated from the masses.

This elite class preoccupied itself with the primitive accumulation of wealth through the extraction and plunder of natural resources like livestock, minerals, timber, wildlife and cultural trophies. Some of these elites roamed western Equatoria in search of priceless decorated traditional grave markers of important personalities made from hard woods; this they sold to Europeans, Congolese, and Nigerians, who then roamed the liberated areas. As a result of its exercise of state power in the interim period (2005–2011) and thereafter, this elitist social formation transformed itself into the parasitic capitalist class now at the helm of South Sudan's political and economic power. It is parasitic by virtue of the reality that it controls no means of production. Its main source of wealth is from its connections to the South Sudan state as ministers, legislators, senior army, police and security chiefs, judges, and senior bureaucrats. This elitist class embarked on implementing liberal economic policies dictated by the Bretton Woods Institutions that encouraged the extraction and plunder of natural resources, especially oil deposits in western and northern Upper Nile. It jettisoned social and economic development of South Sudan that could lead to transformation and improve the quality of life of the people. In this manner, the SPLM-led GoSS failed to provide social services, education, or health care; they purchased these services in the neighbouring countries for their own children and relatives. No wonder that this ruling elite did not want to hear of the Cuban experience; to many of them, socialism was anathema.

Chapter 13

Couldn't Avoid the SPLA Detention Camp

An Academic Opportunity in Asmara & FR Germany

The stories about the liberation movements even the objectively written accost hardly speak to the manner the combatants treated themselves. In the SPLA, they were not the reactionaries one would meet in the detention camps, prisons, but the revolutionaries. In 1987, a group of leftist officers were rounded up and send to Boma detention camps. I fancied that wounding in action and amputation of my limb had saved me from joining the comrades. I was kidding myself.

Upon my return from medical treatment in Cuba, I was full of energy and revolutionary zeal. I wanted to continue the liberation struggle, but by political means. I had hoped to find the chairman and commander-in-chief in Addis Ababa, at least to report back. Although I was now physically challenged, there was much to be undertaken in the social, economic, and political domains, whether in the refugee camps or in the areas captured from the enemy. Dr. Garang was the only authority in the movement to deploy SPLA officers and men, in whatever capacity. Unfortunately, Dr. Garang was not in Addis Ababa when we arrived. Instead, I found Cdr. William Nyuon, who could only provide me transport to Gambella and Itang.

Itang was an opportunity to reconnect with my family after a long period of time away. I hadn't seen them since April 1986, when I left them in Khartoum. Exactly two years had passed and I was really very happy to see them again. The children had grown: Keni was now ten years old, Pito was nine, Kut was seven, and Agyedho was three. The real concern for Abuk and me, the most literate parents in the camp, was that there was no functioning school in Itang. It was a confused situation as there seemed to be no efforts to convince the UNHCR to establish schools for the Sudanese. The movement had undertaken mass recruitment into the army, resulting in the mass movement of people away from their villages to the refugee camps in western Ethiopia. In this, the SPLM/A failed to factor the education of children and adults into the process. Thus, children were growing up in the camps without basic literacy skills. This situation disturbed Abuk and me as our boys, Pito and Kut, were already chanting SPLA morale songs and, like the other children, calling themselves "comrades". The worst was that they had started to forget the little education they received in Juba and Khartoum. It seemed their fate was bound up with becoming combatants in the SPLA. It was a prospect none of us could accept.

I spent the month of May in Itang, doing nothing of importance. There were few friends to engage with in any kind of intellectual discourse. Life couldn't be more boring, especially when we consider that a liberation process involves more that shooting at the enemy or forcing it to withdraw from garrisoned towns. It was now a year since the SPLA had liberated Jekau, but no one had returned to do any development work or to resettle the Gaajak Nuer people of the area who had been displaced by the fighting. They were all in Itang being fed by the international community through the UNHCR. It was very depressing to realise that the movement had no social, economic, or political plans for transforming the sociocultural backwardness of the people of South Sudan.

The SPLA was only carrying out military actions against the enemy. It was no accident that civilian populations in areas that came under the SPLA administration abandoned their villages and flocked to the refugee camps in western Ethiopia. In some areas especially in Jonglei, people including children and elderly were encouraged or coerced into leaving their homes for the refugee camps; it was a strategy for attracting resources for the SPLA. This completely contradicted the basic tenets and underlying principles of war of national liberation or revolutionary guerrilla warfare. While in Havana, I had envisaged my task as helping to implement the SPLM/A's political programme in the social, economic, and political spheres, turning the liberated areas into effective SPLA rear bases. The concept of the rear base is congenial to a guerrilla war of national liberation. A large guerrilla rear base suggests that the rebels held sway of the country, and the enemy's movements were restricted to small areas and, therefore, the guerrilla army and its political commissars engaged in constructing its state with its own political and administrative instruments, in which a counter-society emerged, different from the one under the enemy in terms of ethics and morality, and built on the basis of freedom, justice, fraternity, self-reliance, and self-sufficiency. In the absence of this political thinking, Itang and other refugee camps became centres where people came to depend on the international community as they waited for the SPLA to liberate the country.

While we were in Itang, Abuk and I completed the marriage process of her youngest sister, Nyabedi-jwok, who had helped us with the children since 1982, when we returned from Hungary.

She married Biel Torkiech; an SPLA officer related to our in-law Ustaz Peter Lam Ngouth. It was a tricky affair because of ethnic sensibilities and prejudices. Many Chollo men did not approve of Nyabedi-jwok marrying a Nuer suitor on account of nothing else but ethnicity. If we rejected the Nuer suitor, however, Abuk and I ran the risk of being branded tribalist or ethnic chauvinists in the national liberation movement. This would be the worst insult for me.

The weather in the region was now gearing towards the rainy season. It had started to rain, turning the Itang refugee camp into a muddy lake. I had been there at about the same time in 1986. The rains made it difficult, if not impossible, for people in the camp to move around. Physically challenged people and those disabled by war injuries, who moved only with the assistance of crutches, found life in Itang terribly depressing. They spent their time indoors, without any form of recreation. I started to experience serious difficulties with the prosthetic limb I had brought from Cuba. It was built and fitted at a time I had gained body weight but which after only two months in Itang had dissipated that the stump no longer fit comfortably into the prosthetic limb. I had to resort to the use of crutches in order to move from place to place within the refugee village. Indeed, I needed another prosthetic limb that fitted me comfortably to be able to walk.

The UNHCR office in Itang provided limited medical service for the refugees; sometimes this included artificial limbs for former combatants. A Sudanese medical officer working in collaboration with the Ethiopian medical authorities would identify cases for referral to either Gambella or further afield to Addis Ababa, where an NGO associated with the church handled the referred cases. Dr. Stephen Anyak assessed my condition and decided that I needed a completely new prosthetic limb. I started the process for travelling to Addis Ababa, which first required permission from the SPLA authorities. My referral to Addis Ababa was also an opportunity to receive medical help for my son Kut, who needed an operation for a sinus problem. We had been waiting for someone to accompany him since his mother could not leave me alone in Itang; reduced to an invalid, I constantly needed her presence. This meant that Abuk, Kut, Agyedho, and I had to travel together to Addis at the expense of UNHCR, leaving Keni and Pito with a relative in the refugee camp; Nyabedi-Jwok had already shifted home to her husband's.

In Addis Ababa, I went through the same process as in Havana to build the prosthetic limb. It took three months of waiting. Kut was operated on successfully for the sinus problem and healed. The completion of the limb and its fitting came around the end of October. By that time the rains had stopped and conditions in Itang would be more suitable for residence. As I prepared to travel back to Itang, I thought I should meet the chairman before I left Addis Ababa. I learned that he was in town to meet Mohammed Osman Mirghani, the leader of the Democratic Unionist Party (DUP), the junior partner in the ruling coalition government in Khartoum led by Sayed Sadiq el Mahdi. I asked Maj. Deng Alor Kuol, Chairman Garang's officer manager, to arrange a meeting with Garang and it was fixed for 11 November. I thought this meeting would determine what my status in the camp was to be. When the day came, Comrade Deng Alor escorted me in to meet Dr. Garang.

After some brief courtesies, Dr. Garang informed me that SPLM/A discussions with Mirghani had led to Sudan's agreement to suspend implementation of the *hudud* (Islamic punishments including amputation of limbs for theft, flogging, and lashing). I congratulated him for the breakthrough, informed him of my situation, and told him that I was ready for any assignment. To my surprise, disgust, and anger, Dr. Garang told me point-blank that he had no assignment for me and said that I should settle in the refugee camp and take care of my family. Nothing could be as depressing as the insinuation that the SPLM/A considered me no longer of value after having lost my limb. In spite of my intense anger, I composed myself, thanked him for his time and left without making any noise. Given what I now knew of Garang's attitude, I would have to conduct myself with caution if my family and I were to survive in Ethiopia.

Who would dare cross swords with Dr. Garang or anyone in a position of power and authority in the SPLM/SPLA? No one, I guess. The SPLM/A's power and authority covered every place in Ethiopia. No SPLA officer or soldier could act independently or outside of the SPLA's authority. Prof. Bari Wanji was lucky because he took refuge in the Cuban Embassy and managed to negotiate the safe return of himself and his family to Tanzania. Not everyone was that fortunate whom the SPLM/A had targeted. Lt. Young Paul, an SPLA deserter originally from Bentiu, was shot and bundled into a waiting car by SPLA officers in broad daylight in the neighbourhood of Arat Kilo, just next to Mengistu's office, at the very time that Mengistu was meeting Dr. Garang. Ethiopian security retrieved him from the SPLA on the way to Debri Zeyit and gave him medical treatment. Paul was allowed to return to Sudan, but his family remained in the Itang refugee camp in Ethiopia. Two years later, in 1989, he returned to Addis Ababa and was lured to Itang by an SPLA intelligence officer, a certain Peter Nyieth. It was there, in Itang, that William Nyuon executed Young Paul, ostensibly for the crime of desertion.

Abuk and I discussed thoroughly the steps we needed to take in Ethiopia to avoid friction with the SPLM/A authority. We toyed with the idea of relocating to another country through the UNHCR, but this would require the UNHCR to first recognise us as urban refugees and that process must start in Itang. It was risky because it involved declaring to the protection officer, an Ethiopian, that one's life was in danger. Given the cooperation between the SPLA and the Ethiopian security system, this would be suicide. We decided I would travel to Itang to look for resources, while Abuk, now heavily pregnant, would remain in Debre Zeyit to help Catherine, Uncle Joseph Oduho's wife, who was in the final days of her pregnancy. Immediately after his return from Havana in March, Uncle Joseph Oduho had been re-arrested by the SPLA and sent to the prison in Boma.

On my arrival in Itang, I found that Nyabedi-jwok had gone to the Dimma refugee camp, taking Keni and Pito with her. Her brother-in-law, Cdr. James Hoth Mai, was the area commander and wanted her to be near him in Dimma because her husband was in an SPLA jail. Nyabedi-jwok cared for her niece and nephew as if they were her own children so I was not worried about my children. Since the massive arrests and detentions of SPLA officers that occurred the year before, things were really different in Itang. There were very few people with whom to socialise. Moreover, I had to tread carefully lest I fall into the usual SPLA traps, whereby a small mistake could translate into flimsy charges, serious accusations, and a possible detention.

One day, as I was walking to the SPLA administration office, I met a friend who informed me that Capt. George Maker Benjamin was being held in the Military Intelligence jail. I decided I would visit him, although with the SPLA's poor record of observing human rights, even that was risky. I knew the officer in charge and he allowed me to see and speak with Maker. He was asthmatic and had been brought back from Bilpam because of his condition. I continued going to see Maker in jail until one day he told me to stop coming: it was jeopardising his presence in Itang, where he had privileges to see his family. I was completely taken aback, but I respected his words. Indeed, two days later Capt. George Maker was returned to Bilpam under heavy military police escort, and from there he and his family were flown to Boma.

Barely two days later, they sent an agent provocateur to my house. He was a Sudanese prisoner of war let loose by the SPLA authorities to roam in the refugee camp. There was a scuffle, a gun was fired, and someone was wounded but not fatally. Three days later I received a radio message, purportedly from Cdr. William Nyuon, the SPLA's chief of staff, ordering me to report to prison in Bilpam. There were no charges quoted in the message but the Military Intelligence officer who came to arrest me had already prepared a speedboat and armed escort to take me to Bilpam. This was the usual SPLA method of dealing with its officers and men who were considered dissidents; one could be arrested and detained for some mistake committed months or even years before. My arrest should have been made in July 1987 but had been put off then because of my physical condition; it was now triggered by the skirmishes in my house. So it was that as of 28 December 1988, I was in SPLA detention.

In Bilpam, Capt. Bol Agany was the acting area commander and responsible for the prison. He looked completely unhappy about the jailing of an SPLA wounded hero. He ordered that I be placed in the officers' mess instead of the main prison, three kilometres away. In fact, it was a sub-prison where they kept officers on lesser criminal or disciplinary charges. With me at this sub-prison were eight officers, three mentally deranged soldiers, six men, and two Chollo women who were considered prisoners of war. The six men had survived an ambush on their commercial vehicle as they travelled from Juba to Maridi, while the women had come from Malakal to the Sobat area to purchase sorghum. The SPLA considered them spies and had forced them to walk all the way to Bilpam.

The sub-prison was a compound with five tukuls, all of which was surrounded by a thorn fence. The prisoners or detainees would spend the day, usually from four o'clock in the morning to five in the evening, in the compound. At night, we would be locked inside our tukuls. Conditions here were considered much better than in the main prison, which was a massive hole in the ground holding more than thirty officers and men who had been arrested with Cdr. Kerubino Kuanyin Bol a year earlier. Regarding my own case, it was impossible to ask about my charges or the conditions of my detention as there were no case papers. The only thing the prison officers could say was, "Wait for the leadership to send us a message." This thing of the 'leadership' could have been a senior officer that ordered the arrest for some trivial affair and could have forgotten it leaving the victim to remain in detention for a very long time since there was no judicial review of cases.

I knew none of my fellow inmates but was aware that the SPLA's Military Intelligence sometimes planted its agents in the detention centres to gather information, which was then used as evidence against the accused officer during the military tribunal. More often than not, however, the detainees were released without court hearings. As time went by, with most of our days spent playing cards, I came to know Capt. Deng Akuot, 1st Lt. Deng Kidit, Capt. Akot Deng Akot, and Capt. Deng Lual. They were prisoners who had been held for the longest time at the sub-prison. The guards kept bringing new prisoners and releasing others, sometimes after a span of a few days or even only hours. The arrest of myself and the other officers was said to have been on the order of Cdr. William Nyuon, and therefore no one could interfere with our cases. There were times when our numbers would rise to thirty and some of us had to sleep outside the tukuls in the compound. One day they brought in Capt. Kuac Kang, who would spend the day with us in our prison but return to his village in the evening. I believe he did not have serious problem with the SPLA, and this was why he received special treatment. Kuac's brief stay with us was a blessing because I was allowed to go with him to his village, which was a much-needed change to my physical and psychological environment.

The sub-prison, unlike the main prison, received visitor at all times of the day. The way that the SPLA commander and his senior officers treated themselves and those below them smacked of people who were enemies of each other. The jealousy and cruelty suggested a lack of underlying ideological unity. One evening, around eleven o'clock, an SPLA officer was brought under tight security. I had never witnessed such cruelty against a person one would call a comrade. It was 1st Lt. Malik Agar, then an officer serving at Cdr. William Nyuon's headquarters. He was tied to a tree and mercilessly and severely tortured. I believe had he not had such a huge body; Malik would have been a corpse. Throughout his ordeal, the other prisoners were not allowed to go near him or to speak with him.

In the morning, I untied him from the Dolieb tree and brought him inside my tukul to rest in my bed. I also gave him four tetracy-cline capsules, to help his body resist infection from the wounds he had received in the beating. It did not take long before they came to take him away. Surprisingly, after all this humiliation and dehu-manisation, Malik Agar survived to become a commander in the SPLA, the governor of Blue Nile State under the SPLA, third vice chairman of the SPLM, minister in the Government of National Unity in Khartoum after the Comprehensive Peace Agreement, and later governor of Blue Nile State.

It was to speak about this kind of cruelty in the SPLA that 2nd Lt. Deng Kidit and I would meet, alone and in private. I was trying to learn as much as possible about things that had occurred in the SPLM/A. Deng Kidit had been a private in SAF Battalion 104, which rebelled in Ayod on 5 June 1983 under the command of Maj. William Nyuon Bany. I asked Deng Kidit about a rumour I had heard regarding Capt. Sebastian Thuch and his mysterious disappearance from the sub-prison. Capt. Sebastian Thuch and I had trained together in the Shield Four officers' course at Bonga. He had deployed in February, leaving me in the college. I met him briefly again in Mangok, a few days before we were deployed to attack Jekau. According to Deng Kidit, Capt. Sebastian had been blamed for the desertion of troops hailing from Bahr el Ghazal. Desertion and escape to one's home area was not uncommon in the SPLA. Regardless, Cdr. William Nyuon ordered the arrest and detention of Capt. Thuch. One evening, William Nyuon's hench-men came and took Capt. Thuch from prison and that was the end of the story.

Captain Sebastian Thuch's disappearance was part of the systemic cruelty routinely witnessed within the SPLA. I corrobo-rated the story of 2nd Lt. Deng Kidit with Capt. Dhol Acuil Aleu much later, in 1996 in Nairobi, Kenya. The bodyguards of Cdr. William Nyuon had tortured Capt. Sebastian to death in Maker, a small village on the Baro River. The bodyguards put the body in a sack and dumped it into the middle of the river, leaving it to float downstream as their speedboat travelled upstream towards Itang. But unbeknownst to William Nyuon's bodyguards, according to Comrade Dhol Acuil Aleu, the sack bearing Sebastian's remains had hooked itself onto the speedboat: they had towed his body all the way to Itang under the cover of night. In the morning, people who came to fetch water from the river found the sack floating beside the boat. This exposed the evil work done to eliminate Sebastian Thuch. In my conversation with him, Capt. Dhol Acuil believed the order to kill Sebastian couldn't have been from William Nyuon but from Dr. Garang, who had an axe to grind with Sebastian. The grudge was said to go back to their days at Tonj Intermediate School. It was Sebastian Thuch, so went the story, who protected John Garang from the other Dinka boys who bullied him at school. Such cowardly elimination of comrades was common in the SPLM/A.

In prison, days turned into weeks and months. Indeed, I gave up expecting to be released. Finally, on 31 August the Military Intelligence officer responsible for the detainees strode into the middle of the compound and called out, "Capt. Peter Adwok!" I responded, "Yes!" He turned to where I was seated and said, "Take all your things and follow me to the office. You have been released." There were shouts of "*Mabruk! Mabruk!*" from the other prisoners. I thanked them and said I hoped they too would be released soon, and followed the officer. I had been in the SPLA jail for exactly eight months and fourteen days. At the Military Intelligence office, I received a clearance letter and departure order. As I was leaving, the officer handed me a radio message that had been received eight months earlier. The message said me that I was the father of a baby boy. Abuk had delivered and wanted me to send a name. I shook my head in disbelief. The withholding of the news was a petty and heartless act.

Two soldiers were assigned to paddle the canoe that would take me to Itang. We waded through the swamp between Bilpam and Maker on the Baro River. In some places, they had to carry me because of the difficulty of walking through the deep water with my prosthetic limb. The Baro was quite high, swollen by the heavy rain upland in the Ethiopian hills, and the current was very strong. It took us nine hours to reach Itang. I arrived at the refugee camp at night, which allowed me to avoid people's inquisitiveness. In the morning, I quickly debriefed Abuk's relative, who was taking care of the house. Abuk was in Addis Ababa. She had come back to the camp but only to collect some of her valuable belongings before returning to Addis Ababa. It was the middle of the rainy season, and I wouldn't survive in Itang without her so I prepared to travel to Addis Ababa.

Since this was not a medical referral case, I had to procure the necessary SPLA permit and some money for transport and upkeep. I sent a radio message to Cdr. William Nyuon, thanking him for releasing me and requesting his indulgence to allow me to go and see my family in Addis Ababa. I was lucky: the response came in only a few days. The SPLA was then mourning the tragic demise of Senator Mickey Leyland in a light aircraft crash as he was visiting the refugee camps in Itang and in Piny udo, recently established to accommodate the refugees.

As soon as I received the departure order and some money from the SPLA administration in Itang, I left by bus for Addis Ababa. I travelled in the company of another Chollo officer, 1st Lt. Acwanyo Arop, whose foot had been blown off by a landmine in the attack and capture of Nasir. We arrived in Addis Ababa after three days. It was a happy moment to be reunited with my family. Abuk had named the baby boy Maulana. He was already crawling. From the moment he saw me, he wanted to be near to me, as if he knew that I was his father. Abuk told me about the day Sayed Jonathon Malual, who was visiting from Khartoum, told a group of women who had come to greet him that Maulana must be the child of Peter Adwok, and they all said yes, pointing at Abuk adding that she was my wife.

I was relieved to have survived the imprisonment. I did not want to hold any grudges or recrimination against Cdr. William Nyuon, given his prompt response to bail me out of Itang I swallowed my anger and tried to think strategically about the future of my family. All the fancy ideas I had about my role in the process of national liberation had evaporated. I was now, as Dr. Garang had advised me the year before, concerned only about taking care of my family. It was not easy to stay in a city like Addis Ababa without secured economic income. I tried to find temporary employment with the Department of Geology at Addis Ababa University. I had known Dr. Gitana Assefa, the department head, ever since we had worked together at a 1975 meeting of the African Geological Society in Khartoum. Our last meeting had been in August 1984, during the proceedings of the Fourth International Geological Congress in Moscow, USSR.

But he was not very keen about employing me; perhaps he feared my physical condition and my high profile as a rebel. Nevertheless, I kept returning to his office to keep myself up to date with advances in geological knowledge. As a result, I even wrote and submitted to the SPLM/A's leadership a project proposal on how to exploit the gold showings in Kapoeta area, which had then fallen under the SPLA administration. But Dr. Garang was not enthusiastic about it. According to Maj. Deng Alor, Garang dismissed the proposal as "theoretical" or even "theatrical"; I did not fully confirm from Comrade Deng what Garang really meant.

In the theory of knowledge—epistemology—everything starts as an idea, a simple idea out of which emerges a theory, and through practice and application the theory is transformed into material things. I trained as a geologist and indeed practised theory in the prospection of minerals in the Red Sea Hills. Comrade Deng Alor seemed to not grasp my point. I could glean from his attitude that my continued presence in Addis Ababa was completely unwanted as it constituted a precedence. According to SPLA regulations, any SPLA officer who received medical treatment in Addis was required to return to the SPLA-controlled Itang refugee camp after his treatment was completed. Perhaps, Dr. Garang would only accept me remaining in Itang, to waste away there as a refugee.

It was about the end of November, almost two months since my return to Addis Ababa. While lingering in the streets, I ran into a former colleague from the University of Juba, Dr. Andrew Malek Madut. It was way back in 1982 that Malek and I had parted ways at the University of Juba Guest House in Khartoum. He was then on his way to the UK for postgraduate studies, while my family and I had just returned from Hungary and were waiting to travel to Juba. While in Britain, Dr. Madut had been following the political developments back home. He had heard of my joining the SPLM/A, the war injury leading to the amputation of my limb, and indeed was well informed about what was going on in the liberation movement. Madut was sincerely sorry for me and wanted to assist me by all means, particularly after I told him about Garang's attitude. He asked if I would accept a position of assistant professor as he knew there was a vacancy for a geologist in the Faculty of Sciences. It was impossible to turn it down. I gave him my application and curriculum vitae.

After some time, I received a letter appointing me assistant professor in the Department of Geology in the Faculty of Physical Sciences at the University of Asmara. I was to start at the beginning of the second semester in February 1990. I was booked to travel to Asmara on 11 February 1990, a day that coincided with the release from prison of the African revolutionary Nelson Mandela. I thought I shouldn't miss watching live on TV such an important international event. Rather than miss the television coverage, I paid a penalty to reschedule my flight for the following day. Moreover, I had scheduled a meeting with Prof. Kwesi Prah, a former colleague at the University of Juba, who was in Addis Ababa and wanted to have a discussion after we had watched and listened to Nelson Mandela.

Prof. Andrew Malek Madut was at the airport to receive me. Asmara was a small and clean city with streets and buildings modelled on Italian architecture. I was given a villa in a neigh-bourhood called Tiravolo, which was close to a former American base and a distance away from the university. My neighbours were an Indian professor called Rao, who would be my colleague in the department, and an American professor, Margaret Lacuna, whose villa was the mirror image of mine. The Ethiopian province of Eritrea had been a war zone ever since Emperor Haile Selassie abolished Eritrea's federation with Ethiopia in 1952, annexing the territory. Eritrea had remained outside the Ethiopian empire since 1895, when Menelik II defeated the Italians in the Battle of Adwa. An Ethiopian friend told me that Menelik had not wanted to press on following his victory and liberate Eritrea because he was afraid of uniting the Tigrayan nationality living on both sides of the border.

The Eritrean war of liberation was first led by the Eritrean Liberation Front (ELF). Later, the Eritrean People's Liberation Front (EPLF) or *shaabia* became dominant. It was a leftist organisation. In fact, I witnessed some aspects of this war when I was part of an iron-ore exploration project in Garora, on the border with Eritrea, in 1975. I had arrived in Asmara at the height of the war: the EPLF had liberated the Port of Massawa, cutting off the country from international trade and commerce on the Red Sea. Its forces had encircled Karen and Asmara, which showed all the signs of being a city under siege. The Ethiopian military was deployed at every corner of the city and the people in Asmara were living through a social and economic crisis. The government ordered the rationing of consumer goods, especially food items, but kept prices stable.

I was entering my third week in Asmara and was beginning to settle in, and also gaining a more concrete perception of my new environment in its social, economic, and cultural dimensions. I made a few friends, both at the university and in the residential neighbourhood. The Eritreans are, by and large, similar to the northern Sudanese, particularly those who claim semitic heritage. The difference was that the Eritreans are industrious and hardworking people. They were hospitable and kind and, to some extent, easy-going. Then suddenly, without warning, rockets and missiles started raining down on suburbs of Asmara that were close to the airport. With this bombing of Asmara, I felt as if I'd jumped from the fire into the frying pan, or vice versa.

Like a supporter of the SPLA in Juba or any town in southern Sudan, I believed that many Eritreans were happy with the bombs falling on Asmara as it reflected the military prowess of the *shaabia*. It reminded me of the feelings I had in Juba whenever we learned of the SPLA military successes. There was always jubilation. The bulk of Asmara's population were clandestine supporters of the *shaabia*. I remember very vividly how my house-help, Saba, after becoming confident that I was not a sympathiser of Ethiopia, would lecture me about the insurgents and say that everyone in Eritrea supported the *shaabia*. One day I told her that I lost my limb. From that day, I found myself receiving almost daily visits from Saba's relatives and friends, who stopped by to enjoy the coffee ceremony with me.

The situation got worst, particularly for the many unemployed people. But even for those working and receiving regular pay, it was getting difficult to procure certain commodities; rationed items became scarce or were no longer even available. Essential commodities like bread, cheese, and sugar became so scarce that we decided to forgo tea or drank it without sugar. By the end of June, the university closed for the holidays, which was a relief. I decided to spend the holidays in Debre Zeyit.

It was while I was in Asmara, I believe, that it was brought to the attention of Dr. John Garang that I had found a job at the University of Asmara. My acceptance of the position made it clearer than ever that I was on the verge of breaking myself loose from the SPLM/A. Garang ordered Maj. Deng Alor to bring me to meet with him. While he knew there was no way I could accept living as a refugee in Itang, he still wanted to contain me within the boundary of his authority. Garang congratulated me and asked me what the movement could do to assist me. I told him that I needed a passport, whether a UN travel document or an Ethiopian national passport, it had to be done through the Ethiopian security agency. Maj. Deng Alor was then instructed to procure one for me because I wanted to travel to Kenya. I knew that the job with the University of Asmara would open up more opportunities for me and my family but the situation in Eritrea was unstable. I thanked Dr. John Garang and left.

My family stayed in Debre Zeyit as members of the SPLM/A, even though I was working and being paid as an expatriate. I was able to obtain foreign exchange of US$120 every month, which I sent to the account of a South Sudanese colleague in Nairobi. As soon as I got my passport, I arranged to travel to Nairobi. I stayed with a former colleague at the University of Juba, Khogali Ali Khogali, who was then studying for a PhD in mathematics at the University of Nairobi on a German government scholarship. In a conversation one day, Khogali suggested that we visited the DAAD office. It was possible that I could get a three-month sabbatical sponsorship. I found the idea very interesting and agreed to make a try. Dr. Patrick Legge, a mutual friend and fellow South Sudanese who had studied in Germany, was supportive.

At the DAAD office in Westlands, Nairobi, we had a conversation with the director and the idea of a possible sponsorship came up. He asked what relationship I had with DAAD. I told him that back in 1984 I had acted as the academic secretary and written letters to the DAAD office in Nairobi in support of colleagues who were sponsored by DAAD at the University of Nairobi. He stood up and went to look for some files in a cabinet. He came back and said, "Yes, you are Peter Adwok. I will give you a three-month sponsorship for July 1991." It was quite simple and straightforward. I went back to Addis Ababa. With the deteriorating situation in Asmara, the university administration had decided to temporarily relocate the university to Addis Ababa.

Prof. Rao, I, and two other geologist colleagues joined the Department of Geology on the Arat Kilo Campus of Addis Ababa University, where we shared lecture halls, laboratories, and seminar rooms. This relocation of the university was convenient. I stayed in

Debre Zeyit and shuttled daily to Addis Ababa. As the war in the regions raged, it was also important for my personal security and that of my family to maintain close links to the movement's system in the capital. The war's impact was already being felt in Addis Ababa. The Ethiopian new year was celebrated in a rather gloomy mood, echoing the general public's discontent with the regime. It was clear that Mengistu Haile Mariam was losing the war and it was only a matter of time before the regime fell. Meanwhile, in neighbouring Somalia, President Siad Barré was forced out of power.

Inside the SPLM/A, things had begun to unravel and bad blood started to flow within the leadership. It was not a surprise. There had never been any effort to benefit from the mistakes and internal contradictions since 1983. The movement had grown into a huge animal, and its head was too small to manage its body. When I studied palaeontology, we used to say that the dinosaur grew so large that its small mouth could not feed it, and this was why the dinosaur became extinct. Similarly, Dr. Garang could no longer alone manage the SPLM/A by himself. But no internal democratic structures, institutions, or instruments of governance and public authority had been created. By the end of 1990, Dr. Lam Akol circulated a document titled "Why Garang Must Go Now," in which he outlined the systemic failures in the movement. I remember going to Itang in early 1991 and discussing the matter with him. We agreed on the need to democratise the SPLM and build political structures and institutions.

On 21 May, President Mengistu Haile Mariam left Addis Ababa on a light aircraft bound for Nairobi, Kenya. It was an open secret that the Derg had indeed fallen. The Ethiopian army stopped fighting the *wayene*, as the EPRDF forces were called, and surrendered in large numbers. Why fight for someone who had escaped, was the rationale behind the desertions. It was a smooth takeover of power in the capital. I remember coming upon a column of *wayene* while I was going to collect my salary from an office at the University of Asmara; they were calm and disciplined, unlike the SPLA.

The leaders of the SPLM/A were slow on understanding and preparing themselves politically for the turn of events in Ethiopia leading to the fall of Derg. I believe too much dependence on external resources including ideas, does not allow critical thinking and independent appreciation of events; the leadership remained waiting for someone to make the decision. While divisions and brigades of Ethiopia army were deserting or putting down their arms refusing to fight the rebels, the SPLA was sending re-enforce-ments to battle the Oromo Liberation Front and Gambella People's Liberation Movement in Wallega in which many lives were lost. It could have been time to open up negotiations with the EPRDF over the future of the Sudanese refugees in western Ethiopia. However, under the pressure of being defeated an unorganised withdrawal into the Sudan was ordered with enormous loss of life and property.

It is worth relating the sad story of a Libyan air-force pilot, who on a bombing errand in Jonglei and eastern Upper Nile ran out of fuel but managed to safe-land in an open space not far from an SPLA camp. The Libyan was of course arrested, but because the SPLA leadership wanted to exchange the Libyan officer for some financial ransom, he was brought to Addis Ababa. 1st. Lt. Hugo Luigi Adwok and 1st Lt. Chau Mawien were attached to the Libyan as his guards. In Addis Ababa, the only place to accommodate a group of this social-legal-diplomatic configuration was the prison. Permission was obtained from the security for Chau and the Libyan to be in the prison, while Hugo stayed outside, where I met him.

When the Derg regime finally collapsed, Chau and the Libyan were in still prison because the negotiations for the exchange had not begun; The Libyan worked for the Sudan Government, and Garang was out of Addis Ababa and nobody could make a deci-sion. Moreover, there was no clear documentation about the case. However, the Ethiopian authorities released both and allowed them to go wherever they wanted. For the Libyan it was very simple, he had to look for the Libyan embassy Unfortunately for Chau, the SPLA office in Addis Ababa had been closed and the remaining few officials were now housed in the Kenyan embassy; he had now to rely on his former Libyan prisoner for his security and sustenance until he finally connected up with Deng Alor in the Kenyan embassy.

Chapter 14

Seeking Political Asylum in Kenya

The wind of change that in 1990 blew through and broke down the pillars of the socialist system in eastern Europe did not spare other parts of the world. It also had serious ramifications in the Horn of Africa, leading to change in the regional balance of forces. The Somali dictator Siad Barré was deposed in Mogadishu, followed by Ethiopia's Mengistu Haile Mariam when the joint forces of EPLF and EPRDF shot themselves into power in both Asmara and Addis Ababa in May 1991. This dramatic turn of events forced the SPLM/A to order the evacuation of its bases in western Ethiopia.

This evacuation included anyone with links to the SPLM/A caught up in Addis Ababa; ten vehicles were made ready to transport them to Kenya. This included the SPLM representative in Kenya, Dr. Justin Yaac Arop, officers and guards stationed at Chairman Garang's Addis Ababa headquarters, SPLA hangers-on, and a Sudanese diplomat who had defected to the Umma Party in exile. The SPLA's withdrawal from Ethiopia not only marked the termination of relations with the Derg but heralded an ideological shift within the SPLM/A. The shift was complete by 1990, when Dr. Garang offered to send five hundred SPLA combatants to fight on the side of the western alliance in the first Gulf war.

As a professor at the University of Asmara, I and my family could have stayed on but there was the fear of uncertainty. It was rumoured that elements of the Sudanese military had accompanied the EPRDF into Addis Ababa to clear out the SPLA. This rumour was strengthened by the mistake the SPLA committed when it engaged in combat against the EPRDF in western Ethiopia, particularly in Assossa and Gambella, even after the Ethiopia army had already surrendered. It was therefore possible that the EPRDF would avenge their losses on the SPLA. Out of this fear and uncertainty, Abuk and I decided that we should join the convoy to Kenya. In fact, I already had a plan to travel to the Federal Republic of Germany on DAAD scholarship, and since the journey was to start from Nairobi, it was reasonably appropriate to join the SPLA convoy to Kenya. The three-day journey from Addis Ababa to Moyale, Kenya, went smoothly. The Ethiopian state remained surprisingly intact, without signs of fragmentation, even though the Derg's government had collapsed, and a new government had not yet been installed.

The drama, to say the least, was with the convoy itself, which was characteristic of the unruly nature of the SPLA. The incident occurred as the convoy crossed the bridge marking the border between Ethiopia and Kenya. The way the SPLA soldiers wore their full military attire and brandished their AKM rifles was like a triumphant army invading Kenya. The Kenyan press reported on the unruly scene and this created a big diplomatic row. Obviously, it couldn't have been anything more than an expression of reckless triumphalism, arrogance, and ignorance of relations between states. Kenya's chief diplomat, Bethuel Kiplagat, the permanent under-secretary in Kenya's Ministry of Foreign Affairs and International

Cooperation, seemed to know the mentality of South Sudanese. He intervened to calm down rather than escalate the diplomatic and security upheavals triggered by the incident. Whatever happened to the convoy after this episode was dealt with by professionals within Kenya's security organs.

The convoy crossed at about nine o'clock in the morning. Eight hours later, at five in the afternoon, we were still holed up in the Kenyan Customs compound in Moyale. There was a loud silence and uncertainty about the reason we had to wait this long, what and when would anything happen. Dr. Justin Yaac, the SPLA's representative to Kenya, was in no position to answer questions raised by an officer, senior to him in the SPLM/A's hierarchy, which made relations amongst ourselves even more awkward. At about five-thirty a number of paramilitary vehicles arrived and parked just outside the compound. Everybody was asked to board the vehicles: we were going to travel by night to avoid the embarrassing episode of the morning. The convoy started off at eight in the evening.

The journey from the border town of Moyale in northeast Kenya to Nairobi was the most difficult I ever experienced, in terms of travelling under the cover of night and not having enough space to rest during the daytime. I believe we were paying for the poor conduct of the SPLA soldiers in Moyale. In Ethiopia, partly because of cultural backwardness and ignorance, the SPLA officers and soldiers invariably misread and abused the hospitality afforded them by the Ethiopian people, sometimes even biting the hands that fed them or, in a more vulgar way, shitting into the plate out of which one ate, because the Ethiopian people had high respect for their country and state. The Kenyan security forces had no time for complacency and carried out their orders professionally.

They ordered the SPLA soldiers to hide their weapons, change into civilian clothes, and to never be seen again in military attire. All the vehicles were to move in an order set by the officer commanding the Kenyan paramilitary forces (General Service Unit and Police) accompanying us, and the vehicles would move only at night. Since none of us had been given Kenyan visas at the border, no one, including the Sudanese diplomat in the convoy, was allowed to leave the convoy until it reached the Kenya–Sudan border at Lokichogio.

The difference between the professionalism of the Kenyans and the lack of discipline among the SPLA was apparent. In Ethiopia, the army and security forces were under strict instructions not to mistreat or abuse the Sudanese combatants, and invariably the Ethiopian army and security officers treated SPLA officers and soldier as comrades as soon as they uttered the SPLA's secret pass-code "007". Indeed, most of the SPLA soldiers were from a rural background and did not know urban and civil etiquette. The sudden imposition of order by the Kenyans was a shock even for Dr. Justin Yaac, the SPLM representative in Kenya. He had wanted to leave the convoy in order to travel to Nairobi to undertake diplomatic work for the SPLM/A. He tried to use the different passports he held, including a Kenyan diplomatic passport, but to no avail. The convoy had to proceed as directed by the junior Kenyan officer escorting us.

The sun rose as we were approaching Marsabit, not far from Moyale. The SPLA vehicles, busted due to the lack of maintenance, could not gain speed or accelerate above fifty kilometres per hour. The convoy was diverted into dry riverbeds a few hundred metres off the road. Under the hot sun of north-eastern Kenya, we waited for nightfall before restarting our journey. The whole day was spent following the shade made by the few trees and shrubs. It was a really hard time for the children, who were unfamiliar with the rural environment. On the second night, the convoy started at about eight-thirty; there seemed to be heavy traffic between Marsabit and Isiolo, which caused the convoy to stop for long intervals. We managed to reach Bahati at about three o'clock in the morning. This was a heavily populated area in central Kenya. The convoy had to stop for the day at the police station; at least there were many trees to provide shade and so we rested.

On the third evening, the convoy managed to reach the main

highway at Nakuru. We were now about six hundred kilometres away from Lokichogio. The convoy managed to reach Kapenguria, West Pokot County, at about eight in the morning and parked at the District Commissioner's compound to spend the day. It was here, in Kapenguria, that negotiations began with the district administration to give permission to those who wanted to travel back to Nairobi. Dr. Justin Yaac, by virtue of being the individual recognised by the Kenyan government, led the negotiations. He was successful in the task and permission was given to some of us in the convoy to drive back to Nairobi. However, we had to part with some of our belongings, including money to elements of the security escorts. I gave my small radio to a soldier who had been asking for it since the first day he saw me with it at Marsabit.

In Nairobi, we did not have the money to stay in a hotel, so we opted to put up with my niece, Deborah Dak Othwonh Bwogo, and her family at the Magiwa Estate in the Kenyatta area. Although I had stayed for almost a month in Nairobi in 1990, I was still not familiar with many areas. I was in a race with time to complete a few important things before I left for Germany. This required that I reside somewhere near the city's business district and Magiwa was an ideal location for this. I began to appreciate the wisdom of having saved part of my salary in foreign exchange and remitting it to a former colleague at the University of Juba, Dr. George Tombe Lako, who worked at the International Centre of Insect Physiology and Ecology (ICIPE) outside of Nairobi. My first task was to get the money needed to rent a flat for the family until I returned from Germany. The second assignment was to finalise our application for asylum in Kenya. It would be tricky to leave my family in Kenya without first determining their status, and indeed, it was not easy. There was no government policy in respect to Sudanese refugees, particularly those who had come to Nairobi. It became still more complicated when it was known that I was travelling on a UN travel document issued by the Ethiopian government. Every time I went to meet the principal immigration officer, he would warn me not to continue disorganising myself by insisting on the idea of travelling to Germany without my family.

While waiting for my departure to Germany, I managed to secure a two-roomed accommodation in a secured estate at Rongai, outside Nairobi, for my family. The issue of personal security was a major determinant of where to reside in Nairobi. The presence of three Sudanese families in the estate provided mutual security and gave me a sense of confidence in the place. After the day's hassle in the city centre, we would congregate in cordial conversation in one of the flats. We also followed the news of refugees who were flocking back into liberated areas and finding virtually no food to sustain them; many then went straight to the government-controlled towns.

In the last week of June, I secured the visa and air tickets and was ready to leave Kenya for Germany, though we had yet to secure refugee status for my family. I had not realised that determining the status of my family in Kenya was going to be a difficult problem. I had become used to the way things were solved in Ethiopia. I departed Nairobi on 30 June 1991 on a seven-hour flight. I fell asleep immediately after take-off and did not wake up until the plane was landing in Frankfurt. After passing through immigration, I went straight to catch the Rhine LH Express to Dusseldorf and from there to Aachen.

At Aachen University, Prof. Klagenberg had arranged that I would start my sabbatical at his Department of Geophysics two weeks before I went to the Technical University and Free University of Berlin. I had to design what I really wanted to undertake at the academic and technical facilities available at these institutions over the course of three months. The sabbatical scholarship was planned around the idea that I would do something of academic value. At the same time, I was saving some money from the scholarship to purchase a new prosthetic limb. Aachen lies in the west, on the border with the Netherlands, while Berlin lies in the east. After spending two weeks in Aachen, and before reaching Berlin,

I visited Dr. Peter Nyot Kok, a law professor at the University of Khartoum who was on sabbatical at the Max Planck Law Institute in Hamburg. Dr. Kok was with his family in Hamburg, so I stopped over the weekend. Dr. Peter Nyot Kok was one of the three, along with Dr. Lam Akol and Edward Lino Abyei, who ran the SPLA clandestine cell in Khartoum between 1983 and 1989 before it was discovered. I had wanted to spend the weekend with him to discuss the situation in the movement after the fall of the Derg in Ethiopia. Unfortunately, Peter was occupied; his youngest child was sick and he and Amal spent much of the time in the hospital, leaving me to watch their two other children, Majak and Acuonhdit.

In Berlin, I settled on a plan to digitise the eighteen sheets of the topographic map of southern Sudan. It was a new technique in which information a cartographic map contained was corroborated and aligned with the digital information contained in a Land-Sat imagery in a process of digitisation. Digitising maps that had been created by cartographers was a very tedious procedure: the information contained in them was either incorrect or exaggerated. I had hoped to correct them and come out with an up-to-date map of South Sudan. Little did I know that it was a project that demanded time and resources. It was not possible to complete the job in the time that I had in Germany. The computer was not fast enough to handle the enormous digital data I had generated. After eight weeks I had managed to complete only one topographic sheet and had to stop at that point.

My status remained as that of an SPLA soldier—a rebel—although there was no organic link. This gave me the freedom I needed to do whatever I wanted. When I arrived at the Technical University of Berlin to spend a few days with Prof. Günter Matthias, I met my former colleagues from the Geological and Mineral Resources Department, Abdalla Kodi and Abbas Kirfis. They were part of the German–Sudanese Technical Cooperation exploring the Bayuda Desert and were in Berlin studying towards their PhDs. I remember very well that Dr. Gunter Mattias, who supervised them, was rather unhappy that I pursued previous relations we had in the Sudan; he preferred that my relations with him had nothing to do with the two Sudanese.

I experienced the same attitude with the CEO of Inter-freight, a company operating in East Africa, at the residence of Ambassador Joseph Severio in Bonn. I had come from Berlin to pursue my visa application with the Kenyan embassy but decided to put up with my relative. The Inter-freight CEO accompanied H.E. Martin Malual Arop, a member of the Supreme Military Council of the Sudan, who was visiting Germany. Col. Malual and I were colleagues at Rumbek Secondary School and could joke without restraint. The German turned red when Malual told him I was a rebel with the SPLA. He could not imagine that a member of the Revolutionary Council of the Sudanese state could joke with a rebel in such a manner, going so far as to demand a military salute. He thought Sudanese were strange people; during the Cold War, the West German ambassador would not shake hands with the East Germans. Indeed, the Sudanese and, for that matter, southern Sudanese, *are* strange people. Sometimes, out of decency or to be viewed as a generally good and generous people, they become sarcastic or passive when they find themselves in a serious situation, where they would be expected to act otherwise.

It was towards the end of August, in fact a few weeks before I would return to Kenya, that I started to work on the prosthetic limb. The DAAD scholarship was three thousand DMs, out of which I paid for my accommodation in East Berlin, the former capital of the DDR. The rents there were low, allowing me to remit some of the scholarship money to my family in Kenya. In that tight financial situation, I had to solicit funds. The Sudan Relief and Rehabilitation Association (SRRA) in Britain chipped in a large portion, thanks to Mading Deng. John Joak Deang, a southern Sudanese refugee in Germany, also contributed, and I was able to make the advance payment.

Since Kenya is a tourist destination for Germans, I believed I could obtain a tourist visa. I had only to send my UN travel document and the required fees by registered mail to the embassy of Kenya in Bonn. A few days later I got back the travel document but without a visa, suggesting that I could not go back to Kenya or that I would need to get the visa on entry. At about the same time that I received the response from the Kenyan Embassy, the University of Asmara administration replied to the letter I had sent on my arrival in Germany. The official in Asmara thanked me for the services I had rendered but wrote they did not expect me to return because the Eritreans had come back and, therefore, they no longer needed my services.

It was a very depressing moment for me. I was not certain I would be allowed entry into Kenya, and travelling to Addis Ababa would create more problems because the South Sudanese had left the country. The two letters put me in a serious dilemma. Time was running out. I consulted with friends and the option that came up was to apply for asylum in Germany. Nobody was sure how long it would take to German refugee status; some Sudanese, including a Chollo, a certain William Nyajwok, and his Laotian wife and their son, had come from the Soviet Union and been in Berlin for almost a year. I wanted to reunite with my family by all means and so did not contemplate seeking asylum. I decided that the time had come for me to leave, and so I would board the plane back to Africa.

Newspapers headlines told of the dire humanitarian situation in southern Sudan. The government of the Sudan further worsened the situation of the refugees returning home by bombing their routes and rest stations along the way from western Ethiopia. Then, suddenly, a political development captured the international news headlines. Three SPLA commanders— Dr. Riek Machar, Dr. Lam Akol, and Cdr. Gordon Koang Chol—in Nasir had pulled a coup against the SPLM/A's leader, Dr. John Garang de Mabior. In a statement sent out on 28 August 1991 to all units of the SPLA, the three commanders declared that Dr. John Garang de Mabior, chairman and commander-in-chief of the SPLM/A, had been overthrown. Broadcast of the statement by the BBC on 30 August threw the SPLM/A and the people of southern Sudan into complete confusion. There was both support and condemnation of the Nasir Declaration throughout the world, among Sudanese and non-Sudanese alike. When I heard the news, I thought my dilemma had been resolved.

I immediately threw in my support for the Nasir rebels. I believed the announcement from Nasir was an opportunity to put the movement on a genuine path of national liberation. In this, Dr. Peter Nyot and many other friends disagreed with me. In fact, he did not forward to me a document Dr. Lam had sent to me through him. The document about "the sweeping revolution" was supposed to enlist me in the movement to oust Garang. The atmosphere was polluted with rumours, (mis-) as well as disinformation. However, Abuk in Nairobi kept me abreast of the situation in southern Sudan and in the SPLM/A through daily telephone calls.

I left Berlin as scheduled and arrived at Nairobi's Jomo Kenyatta International Airport at about seven in the morning. It was almost impossible to get entry into Kenya. I stayed in the transit area for six hours, making phone calls to find a way. Emma McCune, Dr. Riek Machar's English wife, worked for a Canadian NGO, War Child Canada. She shared a compound in Dagoretti Corner with a Mr. Christofferson, a Norwegian with wide connections in Kenya. She had asked Christoffersen to help me obtain a Kenya visa as I was coming to join the Nasir team in Nairobi. Christoffersen, through the office of the permanent undersecretary of the Ministry of Foreign Affairs, managed to get permission for me to enter Kenya. He came to pick me up at the airport.

After a day of uncertainty at the airport, I was at last reunited with my family. In my absence, they had remained alone in the compound as the other Sudanese had shifted estates. We had no incentive to stay in Rongai. The decision to leave Rongai further arose because of the lack of good public schools in the area. Keni, Pito, and Kut had been enrolled in a nearby public school but their attendance was not regular due to daily disturbances by the *chokora* (street children), who perhaps wanted to recruit them into their ranks.

A new estate, Nyayo Estate, had just popped up in the vicinity of the Nairobi Dam. It was crowded with many Sudanese families, most of whom were members of the movement. However, with the divisions within the rank and file of the SPLA, association and socialisation could not be as warm and cordial as it had been in Addis Ababa, or even in the refugee camp in Itang. People were reserved but could still speak to each other. But passions flared if conversations turned to politics. My neighbours were Daniel Kodi and his family, who hailed from the Nuba Mountains, and Eli Magok, who was a member of the Nasir group, although he originated from Rumbek. He had married Fatma Kok Malok, the youngest sister of Dr. Peter Nyot Kok. Living with Eli Majok was a relative called Ustaz Moses Majok; he was a staunch supporter of Dr. Garang and usually made it difficult to engage in any discussion near him. Years later during my civic and political activism days, I found Ustaz Major a very interesting character. He was a die-hard supporter of SANU, and his support for Garang and the SPLM/A was out of political conviction and correction perception of issues. He was the man we relied on in Rumbek when we agitated for protection and respect of human rights and civil freedoms.

Our status as refugees in Kenya had not been determined. Nevertheless, humanitarian agencies like the African Committee for the Rehabilitation of Southern Sudan (ACROSS), Lutheran World Relief, Norwegian Church Aid (NCA), and Norwegian People's Aid (NPA) worked to assist the refugees, mainly women and children, in Nairobi, irrespective of the side of the political divide of the SPLM/A they supported. This helped the huge South Sudanese community in Nairobi maintain fellowship with each other, despite the sharp and bitter political differences that emerged following the split in the liberation movement. The International Organisation for Migration (IOM) came to receive applications for resettlement in the United States of America and Canada. Many Sudanese left Kenya on that programme. I was reluctant about filling out the forms, and indeed did not want to go to America. In fact, in January 1986, I turned down a Fulbright scholarship to specialise in remote sensing at the United States Geological Survey in West Virginia. I had already decided to join the armed struggle, and it would appear despicable if I now changed my mind. However, I had to discuss the opportunity thoroughly with my family. I suggested that they could emigrate to America and leave me in Nairobi. Many of my colleagues on both sides of the political divide in the liberation had already allowed their families to emigrate. Abuk couldn't countenance the idea. She refused on the grounds that it was not morally right to leave me alone in the condition I was in: either we all emigrated or we all remained in Kenya.

People for Peace in Africa (PPA) and the National Council of Churches of Kenya (NCCK) co-sponsored the inter-SPLA peace negotiations in Nairobi. This process enabled the Kenyan government to issue me with a UN travel document, which in a way was a kind of recognition of my refugee status. With that document I was able to move within and outside Kenya, between 1991 and 2005, without the usual police obstruction. In 2005, I finally returned to Sudan following the signing of the Comprehensive Peace Agreement (CPA).

My family stayed in Kenya for fifteen good years. There were both good and bad memories, but that is how life treats people. Our last girl child, Ayileew, was born on 25 May 1993. We named her Suzan, in memory of Suzan Khamisa, the wife of Dr. Justin Yaac, who died on the same day. If it were the time of Nimeri's Sudan, Suzan would have received the May Regime's medal for being born on the revolution's day. Sadly, we lost our son Payiti (Maulana), who drowned in the YMCA's swimming pool while celebrating his eleventh birthday on 20 January 2001. It sometimes occurs that happiness ends in tragedy and sadness. In retrospect, Kenya was a better option for asylum than emigrating to the United States. From

Nairobi, I was able to send my children to schools in Kenya and Uganda. But life would never again be as it had been in Ethiopia or in the Sudan, where I had economic security because I had a regular salary from teaching positions at universities.

In Nairobi, it was a daily struggle to make ends meet. I had to fend for everything by engaging in consultancy jobs with humanitarian agencies operating in war-torn southern Sudan under the aegis of the UN's Operation Lifeline Sudan (UN/OLS). More often than not, this required me to travel to the SPLA-administered areas where those agencies operated. A Kenyan friend working for the New Sudan Council of Churches (NSCC) in Nairobi once told me that unless my children changed their names or dropped "Nyaba" from their names, they were not going to receive NSCC scholarships to go to school. How a church organisation whose mandate was to assist Sudanese refugees in Kenya could decide to discriminate my children surprised but did not much worry me. My children were my responsibility and it was my duty to take care of their needs. I would try my very best to educate my children without seeking external support. Through personal efforts and determination, I saw to it that at different times Keni, Agyedho, and Suzan successfully completed their school-leaving certificates in reputable schools in Uganda, and their first degrees, in different disciplines, in the United States International University–Africa, Nairobi Campus.

The boys, Pito and Kut, had the same opportunities as the girls, but unfortunately did not take education seriously. Something, most likely explainable as psychology linked to the war conditions in the country, seemed to have afflicted South Sudanese boys. This is particularly true with children of the SPLM/A's political and military elite who were staying in cities in Kenya. Many of the boys, unlike the girls, did not do well in school. Pito and Kut ended up joining the army, although Abuk and I had tried our best to help them acquire good education up to the university level.

Abuk and I tried our best to improve our social status. She attended extramural studies and courses in Nairobi that enabled her to engage positively and creatively in organising women and involving them in social activities through the Sudanese Women's Association in Nairobi (SWAN), and later as part of the SPLM Peace Desk. She was quite good at building bridges to help reconcile members of the SPLM. This contributed to her appointment to the South Sudan Legislative Assembly after the signing of the CPA. She became one of leading legislators as chairperson of the House Specialised Committee on Gender, Child, and Social Welfare. For Abuk Payiti, this was a historic achievement, which we must owe to the correct decision we all made in 1992 to seek political asylum in Kenya.

At a personal level, the life in Kenya was, in many ways, a great learning curve. It must be admitted that necessity changed me and made me a student of society. As a person with a disability, living in such an aggressively competitive environment as in Kenya, there was no possibility of survival without developing skills of researching and writing legible reports in order to earn money to live in relatively modest comfort. It also would not have been easy without the support of my Dutch friends, Dr. Simonse and Koert Lindyer, and my nephew Prof. John Adwok, who from time to time came to our assistance, especially during my six months' incarceration in Tonga. My Eritrean friend, Yohannes Tecle Drar, at the African Refugees Education Foundation (AREF) mentored many young men and women, provided scholarships, and at times invited me to teach courses. He emigrated with his family to America in 1998. I was so sad to hear about his passing in 2011, especially that because of government functions I could not attend his burial in Asmara.

In view of racial injustice and police brutality against the Black people in the United States that has triggered movements such as Black Lives Matter, I feel vindicated that I refused to emigrate with the family and chose to remain in Kenya. In fact, one of the young men who went to America in 1996, Jameson Nyachol, advised us against sending Pito and Kut to the United States. Many of young men and girls, who were taken to the United States under the rubrics of the so-called lost boys, at the turn of the century ended up in jail because of drug addiction and other crimes; they were raised in a different sociocultural environment and could hardly fit into the system in America.

Chapter 15

The Nasir Declaration

The Illusion of Democratic Transformation of the SPLM/A

As Regis Debray wrote, "Everything that makes a revolutionary organisation a living thing—flesh, nerves, muscles, blood—depends not on what you call it, but on its relationship with the people. It depends on its origin; on whether it has come into being artificially or naturally; whether its vanguard was formed in a laboratory test tube or in warmth of life and society, from the reality of the grassroots class struggle." The preceding lines may constitute a prelude to the formation in 1983 of the Sudan People's Liberation Movement/Sudan People's Liberation Army (SPLM/A).

From its printed and oral literature, it appeared the SPLM/A's leadership parachuted into Southern Sudan body politics from nowhere in South Sudanese experience. Hitherto, there was nothing in the southern Sudanese political lexicon about "liberating" the Sudan. Those of us who had long witnessed the dynamics of southern Sudanese politics recognised that there was always a clear distinction between political parties in the towns and the armed groups fighting in the bush. This was due to security concerns. While those in the towns (politicians) supported those in the bush (rebels), the politicians did not accept responsibility for the rebels. Nor did they admit that there was a direct relationship between those in the towns and those in the bush. This was the reality that existed between the Anya-nya and Southern Front, and later SANU, in the towns and villages in southern Sudan (1964–1972). This was despite the fact that it was these same Southern Front and SANU leaders, organised in the Sudan Socialist Union (SSU), who inherited and exercised power following the Addis Ababa Agreement of 1972 between the Sudan Government and the Southern Sudan Liberation Movement (SSLM), which established the Southern Region.

That the SSLM leadership lost out in the Southern Region perhaps explains why the SPLM/A had to emerge as it did, as "two in one," being political as well as military. At the same time, Garang's contempt for the SSLM and Anya-nya leadership was evident in the SPLM's *Manifesto* of July 1983. In this respect, the SPLM/A evolved and developed like Siamese twins conjoined at the head. This rendered difficult, if not impossible, separation into their respective professional domains and functions. By virtue of their respective modus operandi, the military was bound to dominate the politicians. The SPLA became deliberately more pronounced than the SPLM, and in a way that meant that the movement was not really political and the army was not just the military. This constituted another structural weakness of the liberation movement, being both the trigger as well as the driver of its internal contradiction and conflicts.

The concept and vision of revolutionary armed struggle to construct a "new" Sudan was a political innovation. It required a paradigm shift powerful enough to push it down the throat of every southern Sudanese separatist who now had to engage with this narrative whether or not he or she liked it. This dichotomy, between the people's aspirations and decisions made by the few individuals at the helm, inhibited the promotion of South Sudan's national consciousness. There was a general assumption that the New Sudan vision somehow united southerners with other marginalised groups in northern Sudan. Southerners were now expected to internalise Sudanese national sensibilities. This duplicity was a fundamental structural weakness of the SPLM that appeared in the CPA negotiations, which eventually led to the disaster in Abyei, Nuba Mountains, and Funj. It was this duplicity that prevented Abyei from being placed with the Nuba in Southern Kordofan, instead of negotiating a separate protocol, particularly after the dissolution of Western Kordofan State. The tragic death of Dr. Garang and the ascension of Salva Kiir Mayardit to the helm of SPLM and the government of South Sudan provided the NCP with a reason to renege on implementation of the three areas protocols.

Speaking about triggers and drivers of the SPLM/A's internal contradictions and splits and their relation to the Nasir Declaration 1991 requires a digression to enable a complete and scientific understanding of these dynamics. As with the birth of any child, formation of the SPLM/A was accompanied by anguish, sweat, tears, and blood. There were political divisions within the southern Sudanese political elite, and between them and the northern Sudanese political establishment. The SPLM/A's formation absorbed these contradictions and failed to transform them in the context of state formation and nation-building in South Sudan.

The Addis Ababa Agreement of 1972 had shortcomings and therefore generated rebellions and mutinies among the Anya-nya forces absorbed into the Sudan Armed Forces (SAF). Some of these rebels formed Anya-nya II groups in Abyei and in northern Bahr el Ghazal. The mutiny in Akobo in 1975 led to the formation of Anya-nya II, under the command of Maj. Kerubino Kuanyin Bol, in western Ethiopia; these rebel forces went on to engage in combat with SAF forces in Pochalla. When the mutineers of Bor (16 May 1983) and Ayod (6 June 1983), together with veteran politicians, arrived at Itang they found the Anya-nya II organised under the command of Lt. Vincent Kuany Latjor. The popular idea then was to unite these groups to fight for the secession of Southern Sudan.

This was anathema to the Ethiopian Derg, which led to the Derg's military intervention on behalf of Dr. John Garang de Mabior to ensure his leadership of the nascent liberation movement. This intervention was on account of Garang's academic and military credentials, and his vision of a united socialist Sudan. The intervention led not only to the split and animosity with Anya-nya II, but also inadvertently distorted and prevented the SPLM/A's development into a genuine national liberation movement in which the military wing operates at the behest of the political leadership. Empathise a point I made earlier: in a classical sense, the SPLM was not the political wing of the liberation movement, nor was the SPLA its military wing. The movement/army had no constitution or political programme. It had as its only institution, the Political–Military High Command (PMHC). But, it did not have rule of conduct of its business; in fact the PMHC never met as an institution or an instrument of SPLM power and public authority, becoming the weakest point which the Nasir commanders attached as reason to overthrow Dr. John Garang.

The absence of defined structures and institutions of governance was the SPLM/A's greatest structural weakness that generated serious internal contradictions between the politicians and military. As a political organisation, the SPLM needed to discuss, debate, and reach consensus or resolve democratically its issues. But because it was an army at the same time, it relied on orders and commands. In this respect, disagreements which were essentially political in character were resolved only by military force, resulting in extra-judicial executions and detention without trial in SPLA prisons.

Following the split with the Anya-nya II in July 1983, the

question of the movement's structural organisation and the distinction between its political and military functions inevitably arose.
It was not resolved amicably. In hindsight, this dispute must have
led to the assassination of Benjamin Bol Akok by SPLA agents
in Addis Ababa in September 1984. Bol Akok was the SPLM/A's
representative to the United Kingdom. He had come to Ethiopia to
welcome his constituents from Aweil, who had arrived at the SPLA
training centre. According to sources then present in Addis Ababa,
Benjamin Bol was taken off the plane by Ethiopian security agents
and driven to the SPLM/A's security office in town, where SPLA
officers tortured him to death. The elimination of Bol was linked
to Garang's fear of political leaders, especially those of the Dinka
nationality. Bol's murder caused a huge row internationally. The
following year, in 1985, the SPLA arrested and detained the veteran
politicians Joseph Oduho, Martin Majier, Joseph Malath, and Bol
Ayualnohm. They too were all killed while in SPLA detention.

Many of the accusations against the politicians could not be
independently proven. What was clear is that the arrests were part
of a campaign against the political elite. The claim was that in
pursuit of their "jobbist" ambitions, these individuals were likely
to betray the movement in their efforts to reach an agreement with
the regime in Khartoum. After neutralising or completely removing
the politicians, Garang's campaign turned against his detractors in
the military, beginning with the powerful Kerubino and Arok Thon.

In June 1987, Deputy Chairman Cdr. Kerubino Kuanyin Bol was
arrested and detained with a number of officers and men under
the guise that Kerubino planned to mutiny and relocate to Bahr el
Ghazal. In April 1988, another member of the High Command, Cdr.
Arok Thon Arok, was also arrested and detained; it was said that he
had challenged the leadership of Dr. Garang. Later, Garang would
turn his attentions to Cdr. William Nyuon (1992) and Salva Kiir
(2004). The common denominator in all these cases was personal
conflict between Garang and his immediate lieutenants in the
SPLM/A hierarchy. This echoed the structural weaknesses of the

SPLM/A in terms its structural organisation, and a mismatch in political and ideological orientation. Its leaders and cadres chanted liberation while acting counter to the tenets of liberation.

Agitation for structural reorganisation of the liberation movement started to simmer at the lower levels of the SPLM/A following the arrest and detention of the veteran politicians. In fact, given the low political consciousness obtaining in the movement, any challenge to this system would require political and organisational astuteness. The progressive officers revealed their ambition for power, leading Garang to deal them a deathblow as a group. With a group of former CPS members, I tried in 1986 to organise and build structures in the refugee camp, but before we could realise any results, we were sent to Bonga for military training.

In the aftermath of Kerubino's arrest and detention in 1987, Dr. Garang sought to divert attention away from growing unrest within the movement. Hoping to exploit the knowledge of the then SPLA's freshly graduated commissars from the political school in Zinc, Garang toyed with the idea of establishing the "New Sudan," whatever that really meant, in Itang refugee camp. This was at a time when large areas of southern Sudan, including district headquarters like Pibor and Kapoeta were already "liberated". It must have been just a gimmick; an indirect admission that the SPLM/A lacked a political programme to implement once in the course of fighting towns and villages had been captured from the enemy. Presumably, New Sudan was expected to emerge from the liberated areas not from the refugee camps. This was why the idea fizzled out without a trace. The fresh political commissars must have learnt from their political training that the SPLM/A could only transform the objective reality of rural southern Sudan through a well-studied political programme, and this must have put him at loggerheads with them thus deploying many of them in combat duties than in political enlightenment of the combatants and the masses of the people.

By 1990, the agitation for structural organisation of the SPLM/A was picked up by former political activists in the Sudan, who had now risen to the rank of alternate members of the Military High Command. Dr. Lam Akol Ajawin, the first to be disillusioned by the bogus power structure called the Politico-Military High Command and its minor or junior associated organ, the alternate membership, which essentially was politically vacuous save in the military where an alternate member ranks higher than others. Dr. Lam Akol and Dr. Riek Machar were closer to the centre of power, especially after the arrests of Kerubino and Arok Thon. They wanted the SPLM/A to be formally organised and roles and duties separated. They proposed to Chairman Garang that a meeting of the movement's top leadership organ, the High Command, be convened to discuss political and military developments in the country and the internal situation in the movement after the arrest and detention of two of its members. Rather than agree to the call for such a meeting, Dr. Garang instead gave Dr. Riek and Dr. Lam marching orders to their operational zones in northern Upper Nile ostensibly to deny them opportunity to agitate in Itang but created condition for friction between them. Dr. Lam responded to this by authoring a document titled "Why Garang Must Go Now!", which was circulated clandestinely and eventually became the manifesto of the Nasir group in August 1991.

The Derg regime, the main SPLM/A benefactor collapsed in May 1991 prompting the SPLM/A to beat a sudden and unorganised withdrawal from its bases in western Ethiopia into southern Sudan. With the demise of the Derg, which had chosen Garang to lead the SPLM/A, elements within the rebel army who sought his removal were emboldened. This new reality must have encouraged Lam Akol and Riek Machar to force themselves free of Garang's autocracy and launch their escapade. This would be the brief background to the 'sweeping revolution', as it was called, that began in Nasir, and the broadcast of the Nasir Declaration in a radio message sent to all SPLA units on 28 August 1991. Dr. Garang ordered all SPLA units to neither receive nor circulate the content of the message. Lam and Riek knew that only the chairman and commander-in-chief, and no other officer in the movement, had the power and authority to address "all units" of the SPLA. Faced with this obstacle, the renegade commanders in Nasir made sure that the message reached a wider audience through the reporting of the BBC's Focus on Africa, which carried the news on 31 August.

In the event, the target—Col. John Garang—was not apprehended or eliminated, as in a classic putschist overthrow of a regime, only a few SPLA units responded positively to the message and supported the move to remove Garang from the leadership of the SPLM/A. Many officers, including Dinka officers who, together with the Nasir commanders, were involved in the conspiracy at the planning stage, developed cold feet, chickened out and instead elected to declare their loyalty to Dr. Garang. As they say, blood is thicker than water. The "sweeping revolution," was limited only to Nuer- and Chollo-inhabited areas. There was one exception in the Chollo Kingdom: Capt. Marconi Okuch rejected the Nasir move and attacked the area commander, A/Cdr. Akwoch Jago, with the aim of taking command of his troops. He was defeated and had to withdraw to Pariang, where there were loyal SPLA units.

Rejected by the majority of SPLA forces, the move to overthrow Garang as leader of the SPLM/A failed. He was still issuing orders from his headquarters in Torit. The "sweeping revolution" now moved towards a split within the rank and file along ethnic lines. Given the speed of its spread in the Lou Nuer areas, the split must have been fuelled by bitter memories of the ethnic fighting that accompanied the formation of the SPLM/A in July 1983. The Anya-nya II forces, due to that fighting, had aligned themselves with Nimeri as his "friendly forces" and were the first to pick this fight along ethnic lines. How could we otherwise explain the immediate, spontaneous alignment and incorporation of the Anya-nya II forces at Dolieb Hill into the Nasir faction forces, and their southwards movement to cause devastation in the Dinka-inhabited territories of Kongor and Bor? This social and economic devastation wrought in Kongor and Bor stemmed from the falsehood that these people must pay for Garang's sins involving the destruction in Lou Nuer territory in the aftermath of SPLA murder/assassination of Samuel Gai Tut by the SPLA in 1984.

The split along ethnic lines saw the ensuing internecine conflict between the SPLA factions reach to the community level. This went well beyond what had been intended by the rebellious commanders in Nasir. The split posed an existential threat to the liberation movement as the government in Khartoum stood to exploit to its advantage the internecine fighting between the SPLA forces. Extrajudicial and summary executions of innocent officers and soldiers on account of their ethnicity were carried out by both sides, more often than not on the flimsy charges that they supported the other side. These killings exacerbated and rendered irreconcilable the split. The two sides also engaged in devastating propaganda about their military gains in this tragedy. International supporters of the people of South Sudan feared the costs of the split to the SPLM/A and, rather than speak out about the disaster, were largely silent.

After my return from Germany, I enlisted myself into the information and propaganda function of the SPLM/A–Nasir Faction. Together with Emma McCune and Telar Ring Deng, we made press releases and attended meetings with international humanitarian and relief agencies operating under the UN's Operation Lifeline Sudan (UN/OLS). We sought to secure humanitarian assistance for Nasir and other areas under the control of the faction's forces. We also waited to receive the team that was to attend the Nairobi peace talks between the factions. The Nasir team was led by Dr. Lam Akol and included Taban Deng Gai, Deng Tiel Ayuen, Timothy Tot Chol, Bapiny Tim, and Rebecca Joshua. Prof. Bari Wanji, Telar Deng, and I were to join the delegation at the peace talks.

People for Peace in Africa (PPA), the National Council of Churches of Kenya (NCCK), and New Sudan Council of Churches (NSCC) joined forces to bring peace and reconciliation to the SPLM/A factions then known as the Nasir and Torit factions. But the conference, held in Nairobi over nearly a month, generated bitterness and acrimony, as it focused on the secondary rather than the primary contradictions underlying the split. To the chagrin of many South Sudanese and members of the international community, the conference only confirmed and made permanent the split between the factions. There was no reunification or reconciliation. The only rational thing to come out of the peace talks was the agreement that all political prisoners held in the SPLA jails were to be released.

The peace talks enabled the factions now known as SPLM/A–Torit, or mainstream SPLM/A, and the SPLM/A–Nasir Faction to co-exist in Nairobi and engage in diplomatic, humanitarian, political, and propaganda work. With the benefit of hindsight, this failure, driven more by power ambition than by the morality of the split, is comparable to IGAD's efforts twenty-three years later, in 2014, to resolve the new conflict in the Republic of South Sudan. The civil war was triggered and driven by the same elements – Salva Kiir and Riek Machar - who in 1991 could not consider the lives of the innocent people of South Sudan. The same vainglory continues, to this day, to afflict South Sudanese political leaders.

I want to objectively, though from an insider's viewpoint, discuss the Nasir Declaration and its political ramifications, both internally and externally. The absence of correct and objective reporting in the SPLM/A coupled with the powerful theoretical exposition, credit of Alfred Lado-Gore, beamed out of the SPLM/A radio prevented me to look critically into the SPLM/A as an organisation before I joined it in 1986. My enthusiasm and support for the movement, while still in Juba was subjective to say the least. Reality within the SPLM/A hit me only when I had joined, and it was too late to rescind. That explains I was more than ready to join any move for change in the SPLM/A. I had supported the struggle for democratisation of the liberation movement ever since my arrival in Addis Ababa in April 1986. I threw in my support for the Nasir Declaration while I was still in Germany. And because of this support, I came into conflict with some of my dear southern Sudanese and German friends who admired Garang's leadership. Two of these friends were Peter Anton Von-Armen, a German social worker who helped rehabilitate amputees who had been victims of the *sharia* (September 1983) laws in the Sudan, and Rev. Canon Clement Janda, may his soul rest in eternal peace. Von-Arnhem believed, and rightly so, that the National Islamic Front (NIF) was behind the move in Nasir or was going to exploit it. It's unfortunate that our paths never crossed again, even after I had re-joined the SPLM/A in 1995. My problem with Rev. Clement Janda had to do with the resolution condemning the Nasir move of a meeting of "Concerned Southerners" in Adare, Republic of Ireland, which he and others including Bona Malual, Peter Nyot Kok, David de Chan attended. But it was not long before Clement and I were over that hitch and normalised our relations.

In, *The Politics of Liberation in South Sudan: An Insider's View*, (1997) I criticised myself for having supported the Nasir Declaration. We had just re-joined the mainstream SPLM/A and had enthused about the superficial reforms that had started to occur therein. I criticised the Nasir Declaration, in part, out of bitterness over Dr. Lam Akol's jailing of me for six months in Tonga. I am now writing these lines in September 2020. In between 1997 and 2020, a period of twenty-three years, a lot of political currents have passed under the bridge. Looking back, perhaps the most important event was the infamous Khartoum Peace Agreement (1997) between the NIF regime and the individual movements or splinter groups led by Riek Machar, Lam Akol, Kerubino Kuanyin Bol, Arok Thon Arok, and Kawach Makuei. The agreement was infamous because the NIF government clearly knew it was a hoax, and yet the dissident groups believed that the people of southern Sudan would exercise their inalienable right to self-determination.

The agreement also enabled the NIF government to develop and exploit the petroleum reserves in western Upper Nile, thus securing money to prosecute its war against the SPLM/A. The NIF transformed itself into the National Congress Party (NCP) and absorbed into its system all the different political groups these southern renegades had created. But the NIF did not implement the self-determination clause of the Khartoum Agreement. By 2003, the splinter groups had re-joined the SPLM/A, strengthening the SPLM/A in its peace negotiations with the government of the Sudan.

In 2004, a crisis similar to the Nasir Declaration arose in Yei in Central Equatoria. Categorised falsely as a conflict between Chairman Dr. Garang and his deputy commander, Salva Kiir, this crisis was instigated by the NCP and almost imploded the SPLM/A. It was intended to pull the carpet out from under the feet of Dr. Garang, just as he was about to address a special session of UN Security Council in Nairobi on the eve of the signing of the Comprehensive Peace Agreement (CPA). The Rumbek Conference called to resolve the Yei crisis suppressed the crisis in favour of maintaining unity in the movement. Another contradiction arose in 2008 when the now-chairman of the SPLM/A, Salva Kiir, wanted Deputy Chairman Dr. Riek Machar and Secretary-General Pagan Amum Okiech removed from the SPLM hierarchy, triggering a political crisis in the SPLM. The resolution of the SPLM/A's Interim National Liberation Council to maintain the status quo defused the crisis. However, in 2013, barely three years into the independence of South Sudan, civil war erupted, pitting Salva Kiir against Riek Machar.

In fact, the dysfunction that has afflicted the SPLM/A from its inception in 1983 began at the time of its formation and, as I noted earlier, emanated from the structural weaknesses of the movement. It is not permissible to make the basis of a real contradiction magically disappear simply by not mentioning the contradiction. A debate evaded in the short run will, in fact, become a crisis in the long run, and will inevitably lead to a split. This was the reality in the SPLM/A. The absence of democratic structures and instruments of governance and public authority were the true drivers of the contradiction and conflicts in the liberation movement, not the personal differences between the leaders.

In my criticism of the Nasir Declaration in 1997, I was carried away by my anger against Dr. Lam Akol for detaining and sentencing me to life imprisonment in Tonga. I was also angry at the arrogance of Dr. Riek Machar. His refusal to re-join the SPLA mainstream triggered a rebellion in the SPLM/A – Nasir faction renamed South Sudan Independence Movement/Army (SSIM/A). This led to military action in which many able commanders, people like Peter Manyiel Kueth, Kong Bany-Piny, and others, were killed in action. In this way I missed, in my criticism of the debacle, recognition of some important aspects in the Nasir Declaration. This is an opportunity to discuss them with honesty and clarity.

The central point in the Creeping Revolution (stated clearly in Dr. Lam Akol's document, "Why Garang Must Go Now") was the need for democratisation of the SPLM/A. By this was meant building democratic political institutions, structures, and instruments of governance through which to exercise the SPLM's public power and authority. Only a politically illiterate or ignorant person would have an axe to grind with Dr. Lam Akol on this fundamental principle. In fact, it was the very mention of it and the removal of the main human obstacle to its realisation in the liberation movement that prompted me to support the Nasir Declaration, and my decision to return to the liberation movement after I had left it for academia. When I went to teach in Asmara, I did not think I would again return to the SPLM/A, and that was why I attempted to secure the status of 'asylum-seeker' in Germany. I changed my mind to return to the struggle only after I learned of the coup that purported to have toppled Garang. I then hoped to participate in a democratized SPLM/A. But this was again a disappointment.

The practice in the Nasir faction did not tally with the main thrust of the Nasir Declaration. I went to Nasir in January 1992 to see for myself how the tenets of the creeping revolution were taking root. Dr. Lam, the diligent architect of the move, had travelled to Europe. Meanwhile, four months into the "revolution," no structure or instrument of governance had been created except an

imaginary committee of the so-called founding leaders of the movement. Like the SPLM/A's High Command, it never met again after
release of the declaration of its creation. Dr. Riek was in Nasir but,
in a mirror image of Dr. Garang's leadership, he alone managed the
faction. No wonder that the Nasir commanders split and started to
fight each other along ethnic lines, and fractal militarised politics
began in earnest in South Sudan.

In Tonga, where Dr. Lam Akol established himself as the chairman and commander-in-chief, from his jail, I was better able to
closely follow how he was managing his SPLM/A–United. I did not
witness any difference in leadership style. What Dr. Lam established
in Tonga was a replica of Dr. Riek Machar's regime in Akobo, itself
a carbon copy of Garang's one-man-no-system-rule. This system,
political and military at the same time could not accommodate
democratic institutionalisation. For the system to function effectively, as it did through the agency of "Top Secret" radio messages,
it must operate opaquely at every level, and members must remain
suspicious of each other. This lack of transparency and mutual
suspicion became the energy that drove the system rather than
democratic organisation. This may explain the split that occurred
between Dr. Lam Akol and his deputy lawyer Peter Abdalla

In all decent respect, there is no better way of categorising the
Nasir Declaration and its so-called sweeping revolution to democratise the liberation movement than that it was a façade, and a
clever spin to provide a smokescreen for the SPLM/A's internal
power struggle. The commanders in Nasir were not democrats
but putschists who wanted a shortcut to power. No democratic
principles bonded them, as a result, they split into miniatures of
the same vacuity. It must be stated that failure to build democratic
structures in the SPLM/A, even after its final reunification in 2003
was syngenetic. It stemmed from its dual character as a political as well as a military organisation, and the incompatibility of
their respective modus operandi. In the army, it was commands,
orders and instantaneous obedience to execute these orders; in

the political organisation it was debate, discussion and building consensus around ideas. Neither the Nasir faction, the SPLM/A-United, SSIM/A nor the later versions of the original SPLM/A broke with this practice; they all ended gravitating back to the mainstream in the context of peace agreements.

The second message of the creeping revolution was the question of the inalienable right of the people of southern Sudan to self-determination. It is still being peddled even now, fifteen years after the CPA, that Dr. Riek Machar was the first southerner to raise self-determination in the face of the NIF regime. This couldn't be further from the truth. In the Parliament in 1958, Fr. Saturnino Lohure articulated self-determination as a right of the people of southern Sudan by virtue of being a free people. In 1965, at the Round Table on the Problem of Southern Provinces of the Sudan, the Southern Front presented plebiscite, its main position in the conference, as a means for the people of southern Sudan to exercise the right of self-determination. How then could Riek Machar be the first southerner to raise self-determination and only in 1991? It was a cheap stratagem to hoodwink southerners to support the Nasir Declaration.

The question of respect for and promotion of human rights in the liberation struggle was a central point in the opposition to the one-man dictatorship Dr. Garang exercised. Long-term detention without trial of individuals and extrajudicial executions were rampant in the SPLM/A. Immediately after the premature announcement of Garang's ouster, a number of loyal officers, most of whom were Dinka, were executed in Nasir. We never heard of any later trial of those who were responsible for these killings. The "sweeping revolution" did not introduce a fair regime that respected or promoted human rights. My incarceration in Tonga epitomised the reality that they had only raised 'human rights' tacitly only to put the other side in bad light; the practice demonstrated that they did not subscribe to its principles.

In view of the above discourse, a question imposes itself: Did the leaders in Nasir—Dr. Riek Machar and Dr. Lam Akol—by their action in releasing the Nasir Declaration really intend to democratically transform the SPLM/A? I would shout an emphatic no. It was more about usurping power. Dr. Lam Akol, unlike Riek Machar, had grown up politically, so to say, in the northern Sudan cultural environment with its relatively developed political culture of organisation and action. He was conversant with the culture of political organisation and struggle. They could have adopted a more strategic method of clandestine organisation to democratically transform the SPLM/A. Since they commanded a large number of troops, they could have put Garang on the spot, forcing him to commit himself to change by refusing to obey his commands, as a form of militarised civil disobedience. They could have postponed the announcement of the move and the military action against Garang until the new situation the SPLM/A and the people of southern Sudan were in, after the demise of the Derg, had changed and become predictable. I am convinced in the absence of external support Garang's would have acquiesced to the demand for re-organising the liberation movement. The release of the political prisoners including Kerubino, Arok, Alfred Lado-Gore, Amon Mon Wantok, George Maker Benjamin among others could have further weakened Garang's hold on power. It could have transformed the political military dynamics and any infighting could have been prevented or could have emerged on completely different contour lines.

A question may arise from the preceding paragraphs: Why were those ideas not presented in the political discussions that were undertaken in order to avoid the carnage that occurred in the liberation movement? The question would definitely be pertinent and valid. Before the SPLM/A's sudden withdrawal back into southern Sudan, there had been discussions, albeit discretely and only between trusted individuals, within the movement at large. These discussions centred around the need to democratise the SPLM/A and to build institutions and instruments of governance. The discussions were in fact meant to enlighten the people politically and to raise their social awareness However, due to the excessive repression in the movement and in society, it was impossible to reach the wider reaches of the organisation. Moreover, the idea of a military action against Garang in the manner it played out, was not part of the discussion. Dr. Garang himself defiantly described as "theatrical" the Nasir Declaration thus precluding any constructive discussion between the two factions. Immediately war erupted between the two factions, discussion of these ideas had become untenable.

I have described the Nasir Declaration as an illusion driven by ambition for power, not democratic change precisely because neither Nasir faction, the SPLM/A-United and SSIM/A nor all the splinter groups that sprang up in the course of thirty years emerged as genuinely as a democratic organisation. The contradictions among the different SPLM/A factions was triggered and driven by their struggle for personified not institutionalised power. And personified power in order to facilitate primitive accumulation of wealth.

Chapter 16

Political & Civil Society Activism

Attempts to Challenge Repressive Militarism
in the Liberation Movement & Society

*L*ike a botched putschist move, the Nasir Declaration, notwithstanding the split it caused in the national liberation movement and the immense suffering it caused in southern Sudan, triggered changes. Though short-lived, the changes permitted or enabled critical thinking to permeate the rank and file in the SPLM/A's factions. There was no way of going back again to the old methods of stifling opinion and free speech. This was especially so after the two factions started peace and reconciliation negotiations in Nairobi under the aegis of the National Council of Churches of Kenya (NCCK) and People for Peace in Africa (PPA). This process of reconciliation confirmed the separate existence of the two movements and served as a prelude to political pluralism.

In a nutshell, the ground was set for political and civic activism, initially in the Kenyan capital but slowly spreading into the areas controlled by the respective factions.

The shift from Ethiopia to Kenya as the operational base of rebel movements destroyed the iron grip that the SPLM/A's militarism had on the lives of people. Each faction now tried to demonstrate it was different from what the SPLM/A had been under the Derg. The resultant apparent liberalisation in the mainstream SPLM/A enabled officers and soldiers and/or their families to settle in urban centres in Kenya and Uganda, or even migrate further afield as refugees to Australia, North America, and Europe. It also allowed South Sudanese to establish indigenous NGOs as a means of redistributing the humanitarian cake provided by the international community. Hitherto, South Sudanese were not allowed to even work with the international agencies that controlled the multi-million-dollar industry.

Whenever, these agencies employed a South Sudanese, the SPLM/A forced the agencies to remunerate their South Sudanese employees in kind—kilos of sugar and salt, bars of soap, litres of oil—instead of the monetary values of those items. It was difficult to understand the rationale of such a policy. Although, the SPLM/A encouraged dependence on relief and humanitarian assistance, because it provided means for supplying the army, the refusal to pay in monetary values of these items deprived it of an enlarged tax-base to support its foreign operations. It was honourable than begging from the same donors. A further example of this irrationality was the 1992 decision to prevent a senior UNICEF director, Dr. David Bassiouni, from entering the Kapoeta area, while allowing his deputy to do so, simply because Bassiouni was South Sudanese. I am not sure they would have treated a Dinka in the same manner.

The engagement with international humanitarian agencies spurred a qualitative leap in political thinking of many in the liberation movement. It enabled individuals to question certain policies hitherto pushed by the SPLM/A, including the above mentioned payment by relief agencies to South Sudanese employees in kind rather than in cash. It was a policy that made a foreign nurse senior to a South Sudanese medical officer in the management of a health-care programme provided by the relief agency. The slow relaxation of some of these absurd policies opened up the flood gates for individuals to demand the rights to free speech, movement, and association.

In the Nasir faction, my first assignment was to serve as editor of the bi-weekly newsletter *The South Sudan Post*, which I did with dedication and a commitment to truth-telling throughout 1992. This commitment to truth is what made me cross swords with some of the senior members of the faction. I tried my best to objectively publish news, features, and analysis of events in South Sudan. But the leadership of Nasir faction wanted a mere propaganda mouth-piece to spread lies, mis- or dis-information, particularly about the faction's relations with the NIF government.

This put me at loggerheads with Secretary for Information John Luk Jok, and I had to quit that assignment. Earlier, I had refused to travel to Abuja, Nigeria, to cover the peace talks between the govern-ment of the Sudan and the two SPLM/A factions. The continuous denial by the leadership that the faction was hand in glove with the NIF government made it difficult for me continue in the faction. There was no clear intention to democratise and build credible institutions and instruments of governance, as proclaimed in the Nasir declaration, and this triggered serious internal contradictions leading to individuals deserting or defecting to the mainstream SPLM/A. The faction was virtually in the shoes of its predecessor.

When I found it impossible to continue publishing the Newsletter, I shifted to work with Simon Mori Didumo in the humanitarian department, which was also by no means easy. By November 1993 I had decided to break loose of the SPLM/A-United but, unlike some, I hesitated to re-join the mainstream SPLM/A. Among those who had re-joined the mainstream SPLM/A were Deng Tiel Ayuen, Telar Ring, and Timothy Tot Chol. Although the political environment in Nairobi was different, nothing much had changed in the mainstream SPLM/A. This was the factor that had led me to enter academia, and I did not want to jump back into the mud. I wanted to enjoy freedom and therefore opted to establish a consultancy firm to undertake studies and research for the humanitarian agencies.

Many SPLM/A officers established indigenous NGOs to work with international NGOs in the delivery and distribution of relief and humanitarian assistance in southern Sudan. But they were soon in trouble with their foreign donors for their lack of transparency and accountability in their operations. It was more preferable for me to establish a consultancy firm, Larjour Consultancy, with the express objective of "contributing to South Sudan development goals from the side-lines." This would allow me the freedom and latitude to participate in the struggle for liberation without necessarily being attached to any faction.

This attitude stemmed from my personal definition of liberation as a process of achieving people's aspirations, including personal emancipation from community traditions and customs through conscientisation. It is worth reminding the reader that since 1990, when I went to teach at the University of Asmara and travelled to Germany on a DAAD sabbatical scholarship, I had emancipated, or detoxicated, myself from the culture of militarism. Engaging in consulting and research brought me into democratic and civic society activism within the liberation movement. It allowed me to travel in the liberated areas and conduct research which gave me not only access to grassroots organisations but also augmented my knowledge and understanding of social process. It also afforded me report writing skills on non-geologic subjects.

Having gone through some horrible experiences in the SPLM/A, and having understood perfectly well its shortcomings, the liberation movement and its different factions no longer appealed to me in the way it had when I was still teaching at the University of Juba. Working as a consultant rather than an NGO executive, I stood the chance of engaging political leaders, cadres and operatives of the SPLM/A in constructive dialogue that I thought would lead to influence them. It gave me the strength to say "truth to power" without having to pay allegiance to the military leaders. I then spent a few months doing my own things, taking care of my family. Then, Riek and Lam, the leaders of SPLM/A-United and the architects of the sweeping revolution split, Dr. Lam Akol sneaked into the Chollo Kingdom and took over the troops and declared himself chairman and commander-in-chief of the SPLM/A-United separate and independent of Riek Machar. This triggered the spectre of 1991 in Nasir whereby Garang's Dinka loyalist were killed in cold blood reoccurred this time round with Chollo officers and soldiers presumed to be supporters of Dr. Lam. This forced me back again into the SPLM/A-United as a strategy to stop any further spilling of Chollo blood. I travelled to Akobo to meet Riek Machar and managed not only to save a few lives but to save Cdr. Alfred Akwoch's son Nuer facial scarification by forcing Riek Machar to grant permission for him to travel to Nairobi.

In June 1994, the SPLM mainstream held its first national convention in Chukudum. In a manner that proved that Riek Machar had no ideas of his own, suggesting that most of innovative ideas in the Nasir faction including the declaration flowed from Lam Akol, it appeared that Riek wanted to mimic whatever Garang did in the mainstream SPLM/A. In September, at the close of a church-funded Lou–Jikany peace and reconciliation conference, Riek surprised everyone present with the announcement that he had decided to turn the peace conference into the founding convention of the SPLM/A–United. He wanted its leadership to legitimatise the change of name from SPLM/A–United to the South Sudan Independence Movement/Army (SSIM/A). Many of us in the SPLM/A–United leadership voted against this opportunism. But Riek was obstinate, snobbish and sought to impose his will against the opinions of the majority members. One of the resolutions of the Jikany–Lou reconciliation conference was to recall

SPLM/A–United forces from Equatoria. Ignoring the resolution, Riek prepared to send more troops to fight the SPLM/A mainstream.

Back in Nairobi, I attended to my consultancy outfit. It was now going to be my main pre-occupation. Simon Mori and Paul Anade Othow called a press conference to announce that they were quitting Riek Machar's newly formed SSIM/A. It was a move that was highly welcomed as a positive step towards the deligitimisation and demystification of militarism in the national liberation movement. Unfortunately, instead of joining forces with others in this struggle, the two surprised everyone by boarding a Kenyan Airways plane bound for Khartoum that same evening. They had changed sides for the worst.

Three years later, in 1996, in the Hague, the Netherlands, John Luk, Simon Mori and I sat down over a glass of beer. As if to politely snub our insistence that he should come back to the SPLM/A, Simon told John Luk and me that when he arrived in Khartoum in 1994, he had told Omar el Bashir, "With Garang in the SPLM/A leadership, I stood in attention. Now that I have come to Khartoum, with you I stand in full attention." "If I were Bashir," I told Simon, "I would have said that you were lying. Had you stood at attention; you would not have defected to me." We laughed it off and continued with our business. We were attending on the side of the SPLM/A, a training on conflict resolution led by the Harvard Group International and sponsored by the Dutch Government through UNESCO.

Larjour Consultancy engaged in studies that informed the policies of humanitarian agencies. For instance, the first study I undertook was for UNICEF/OLS to investigate employment practices of the international relief and humanitarian agencies in South Sudan. This study took me to Tonga, where I was detained by the SPLA-United. In all honesty, I did not need to travel to Tonga: only two NGOs, World Vision and MSF, operated in the Chollo Kingdom. But, in addition to the objectives set out in the terms of reference, I wanted to better understand how the SPLM/A's split had affected the unity of the people of South Sudan.

I wanted to know first-hand the situation in the Chollo Kingdom. The study helped me understand the impact of the importation of relief goods from neighbouring economies on the war-torn economy in South Sudan. It put to shame the SPLM/A policy that remunerated South Sudanese labour in kind rather than the monetary value of those goods. It served the economies of the neighbouring countries of Kenya and Uganda and worked against rehabilitating the economy of South Sudan, rendering it perpetually dependent on these economies.

The study led to an important decision by the UN/OLS, forcing the agencies to give monetary payment to their South Sudanese employees. Because of this monetisation of the local economy, the Sudanese pound (never mind the poor state of the paper currency due to the lack of new banknotes in the garrisoned towns) soon had more value than Kenyan or Ugandan shillings. However, this created another dynamic. The underlying reason for in-kind remunerations was to enable SPLA officers to individually access certain consumer items through taxation of the recipients. When remunerations were monetised, the SPLA administration introduced exorbitant taxes which, instead of helping, destroyed the local economy. The officers sent the taxed cash to Kenya and Uganda to support their families and purchase real estate, a phenomenon that continued even after the CPA, independence, and into the new civil war.

In 1995–96, Norwegian People's Aid (NPA) commissioned Larjour Consultancy to undertake a study on the impact of relief assistance on the lives of people in the Lakes region, in terms of coping capacities and resilience. It was interesting to note that because of its mandate the NPA did not mind our criticism of some aspects of its programme. Humanitarian intervention created two groups: the "beneficiaries" and the "compound people". The compound people were the *khawajat* and their African employees who lived in gated compounds; no locals entered those compounds. The beneficiaries were the objects of humanitarian assistance. They suffered the indignities of being formed into queues, whether old or young, society dignitaries or commoners, women or men, albeit against societal norms, to receive assistance.

This differentiation of people on the basis of whether or not they were receiving relief items affected the community's sense of solidarity and fraternity. Not only that, they started to despise each other and composed disparaging poems and songs. This fuelled animosities that invariably led to violent conflict, including destruction of life and property. This was one of the negative unintended consequences of international humanitarian intervention in South Sudan. Following the recommendations of our study, the NPA introduced ox-ploughing in Rumbek and parts of Yirol as a means of improving people's agricultural skills.

Conducting research for humanitarian agencies was a kind of civil society activism on my part. It enabled me to directly influence and change the false perceptions European and American NGOs came with, which more often than not were informed by academic studies undertaken elsewhere. This activism was no less in importance than the political activism we undertook within factions in the liberation movement. In addition to the *South Sudan Post* and *Sudan Update* newsletters, published by SPLM/A–United and SPLM/A respectively, other publications representing dissenting political views appeared. The New Sudan Law Society (NSLS) was initially established as an indigenous NGO; its membership included lawyers and intellectuals from other professions. If it was to have any impact it was important that its membership transcend the existing political divide. The NSLS lobbied the political movements to respect human rights.

Later on, under the leadership of Dr. Peter Nyot Kok and the young lawyers Dong Samuel Luak and Charles Abyei, the NSLS evolved into a powerful instrument, placing at the centre of its programme the struggle for political and civic freedoms in the liberated areas. It was a direct confrontation with the SPLM/A's repressive militarism. The struggle for social and political space, which Larjour Consultancy supported morally and by providing research studies, sometimes for free, led to the formation and proliferation of regional, community-based, and civil society organisations, as well as women's and peace advocacy groups throughout South Sudan.

Civil society activism led to close relationships between individuals who hitherto had not been in contact with each other. The more we won social and political space between and within the factions, the more we began to trust each other. One individual I will never forget is Mario M. Mour. I first met him in 1992 during the conference to reconcile SPLM/A–Torit and SPLM/A–Nasir. Mario was an outspoken and diehard supporter of Dr. John Garang. I remember that he told the conference, in one of his interventions, that he would not mind if Garang ordered the killing of a person every time the SPLM flag was raised. I didn't know exactly what idea he was trying to express but when we told him to start with himself, he laughed. Mour later became director general of the SRRA. He was a very honest, hard-working, trustworthy, and progressive man. I met him one day after he had been relieved of his assignment. He was removed in a way that suggested some sort of conspiracy. He came to my small office on the third floor of Asili Co-op House in downtown Nairobi and told me what had happened between him and his deputy, Deng Kut, which led to his dismissal by Dr. Garang. Instead of shedding tears with Mour, I told him that he should go back and apologise to Deng Kut, the old man he had slapped in the line of duty. Not that he would be reinstated but for decency's sake: the man was much older and deserved respect. Further, I told him not to regret his dismissal. It was an opportunity to rediscover his family, which needed him more because he had spent much of his time without them.

Three weeks later, Mario came back to me and thanked me so profusely that I was embarrassed. I wondered what thing I must have done for him. He told me that he had "discovered" that he had a family and that, since 1992, when he took over the SSRA field office, no one had ever spoken to him in the way I had. I accepted his thanks and we started to talk about the research I was doing in Larjour Consultancy. He said that he wanted to establish an NGO. I encouraged him and assured him of my support. In late 1998, Mario and other youth leaders founded the Bahr el Ghazal Youth Development Association (BYDA). It hit the ground in a big way, which shocked the SPLM leadership. Nearly everyone in the SPLM/A hailing from Bahr el Ghazal supported BYDA, echoing the deep sense of alienation they felt about Garang's leadership of the liberation movement. It was an honour for me to have been of service to BYDA in terms of research studies, and the civic education and training sessions I conducted with the BYDA's women and youth.

BYDA engaged in civic education to raise social awareness and political consciousness among the women and youth, especially in Bahr el Ghazal Region. It was by no means an easy task given the conservative nature of Dinka society, where traditional mores are deeply entrenched. It was difficult to discuss certain issues like gender equality, dowry, and education for the girl child. This was a sensitive area for many rural folks because of its economic linkage. It appeared to them like denying the family or clan their source of wealth. We worked to convince parents that an educated girl could fetch more wealth through her employment and would honourably make a family, just like the late Victoria Yar Arol, who was our peer at the University of Khartoum.

BYDA also mobilised, organised, and engaged women to promote such economic activities like harvesting shea nuts to produce edible oil, soaps, and body lotions. These products were later marketed in Kenya, Uganda, and far afield to generate financial resources for the women. BYDA's civic education programme aimed at identifying communities by the names they call themselves. Hence, use of the term *jur* (Dinka for foreigner) was completely discouraged in case it referred to the Lou and the Bele people.

The New Sudan Council of Churches (NSCC) played an important role in the struggle for human rights and civil liberties under the rubrics of having a voice for the voiceless. Sure, it was an abdication of revolutionary responsibility that it was the NSCC and not the SPLM/A, which supported respect for human rights in areas under the SPLM/A's administration. By 1997, the liberal changes that the SPLM/A's leadership had permitted to sprout following the Nasir Declaration had receded. Political leaders—including Martin Majier Gai, Malath Joseph, Bol Kur, Dr. Madut, and many others—were murdered in cold blood or disappeared without a trace at behest of SPLM/A leadership. This prompted the SPLM–Church Conference in Kejiko, Yei River District, in August 1997, in a bid to thrash out the difference. This conference invigorated the civil society leading to the Dinka–Nuer Peace Covenant in Wunlit, Bahr el Ghazal, in February 1999. The Dinka–Nuer Peace Covenant triggered the people-to-people peace process, and later the reunification of the SPLM/A. This in turn accelerated the peace negotiations between the SPLM/A and the government of Sudan, eventually leading to the Comprehensive Peace Agreement (CPA).

Democratic openings in the liberation movement were few and far between, and sometimes too narrow to accommodate our yearnings. Working within the NGO system and having foreign mentors in what was a struggle for destiny were something new. But some of us did have experience in the student movement and political parties at home, so we were capable of managing the struggle. Having been members of the liberation movement was an added advantage. However, at times it was dangerous to openly criticise what the SPLA did, including abusing the rights of people. It was therefore important to weigh our words with extreme care and caution. In the end, two main civil society groups joined to form the Federation of Sudanese Civil Society Organisations (FOSCO); SUPRAID served as the chair and Larjour Consultancy filled the role of secretary-general.

FOSCO was under the co-chairmanship of Dr. Peter Nyot Kok, from the New Sudan Law Society, and Mario Mour, from BYDA. The four organisations played a pivotal role in defining the ideological direction of FOSCO. The competing group was the NESI Network, or NESI, which operated in close cooperation with the SPLM mainstream. In FOSCO, our focus was more on enlightenment, to enable people to emerge from social and cultural backwardness, and to socially and political empower themselves in the tradition of the great Brazilian educator Paulo Freire, to conscientise around two key words: demystification and delegitimisation. In our case, this meant demystification and delegitimisation of the SPLM/A's totalitarian military dictatorship. This was to counter the notion then prevalent that military dictatorship—or the cult of personality of SPLM/A leader Dr. John Garang de Mabior—was part of the liberation ideology. This placed us in direct confrontation with the SPLM/A's hardliners, who now considered us to be opponents of the SPLM/A's leadership.

It was an interesting development since some of us had the support of the second man in the leadership, Cdr. Salva Kiir Mayardit. Kiir had, in fact, encouraged people like Dr. Peter Nyot Kok, Mario Mour, and Telar Ring Deng in the drive towards democratisation of the liberation movement. In 1999, for instance, Cdr. Salva supported the convening of the Dinka–Nuer peace conference in Wunlit, Bahr el Ghazal, against the expressed opinion of Dr. Garang. That conference and the Dinka–Nuer Peace Covenant it achieved had a resounding impact on the political and military dynamics of war. What flabbergasted me was that Salva Kiir did not stand by those comrades when Garang ostracized and excluded them from participation in SPLM/A functions, especially in negotiating peace with the Sudan government.

It was unfortunate that Mario Mour succumbed to his illness, but we continued the struggle to place FOSCO and civil society work at a high diplomatic level to defeat political exclusion and isolation. In this connection, in 2003, FOSCO engaged and encouraged its member organisations to register for the World Bank-sponsored "Development Market Place" for Ethiopia and the Sudan. The government of the Sudan did not recognise the NGOs and civil society organisations operating in SPLM/A-administered areas of the country. We had to argue our case and, indeed, we succeeded to win stands for FOSCO and the NESI Network alongside the Sudanese NGOs in the Development Market Place. Many of them won prizes and funding for their humanitarian activities in South Sudan.

NGOs and civil society organisations are important components in the struggle for democracy and good governance in the Horn of Africa. I came to Kenya at a time of intense political activity and movement for democracy, dubbed as the second liberation. It was the time of leaders like Jaramogi Oginga Odinga, Kenneth Matiba, Martin Shikuku, Raila Odinga, Gitabu Imanyara, and Paul Muite. They, and many others, were at the forefront of calls for democratic change in Kenya. We linked up with this struggle against the Kenya African National Union (KANU) and Daniel Arap Moi's totalitarian dictatorship, even though the Kenyan government was supporting the people of South Sudan in their struggle.

The difficulties faced by those working for democratic change in Kenya stemmed from the assumption that change could happen without changing the constitutional order of the country. It was not enough that President Moi removed section 2(a) to make Kenya a multi-party democracy; tenets of dictatorship remained entrenched in the rest of the constitution. Many Kenyan political and civil society activists did not get our point that a new political situation required a new constitution. President Moi would remain in power for the next ten years.

Political and civil society activism seldom continues after the political system the activists have struggled against has changed; in most cases, the activists move on to something else. Civil society activism resonated with opposition politics against the Moi regime. In 2002, with the defeat of KANU and the ascension to power of the National Rainbow Coalition–Kenya (NARC), most civil society activists joined the government and the activism ebbed. Similarly, after the CPA was signed, most of the activists joined the government in Khartoum, Juba, and in the states. Their NGOs and the organisations they initiated just died a natural death. Activism based on the work of NGOs, civil society, and community-based organisations are usually only extensions of the western NGO networks. While they distribute, or redistribute, development assistance, these NGOs are vehicles for the inculcation of values that are aimed at changing attitudes and social behaviours. This NGO activism differs to a large measure from activism based on trade unionism or student movements, which struggles for political and democratic change.

Chapter 17

The House of Nationalities

A Space to Preserve the Unity & Diversity
of the People of South Sudan

"Africans used to live as negotiating ethnicities before colonial rule turned them into competing tribes." These wise words by Prof. John Lonsdale couldn't have been more fitting for the situation in South Sudan, where the colonial legacy of violent conflicts still haunts the various ethnic communities. These conflicts, particularly heightened in the context of the war of national liberation, share two important factors: the struggle among the elite for power and leadership of South Sudan, and the availability and proliferation of small arms and light weapons, replacing the traditional stick and spear, which resulted in the destruction of life and property leading to revenge attacks, and a spiralling cycle of violence.

At a certain stage in the implementation of the Addis Ababa Agreement, sections of the Anya-nya officers and soldiers absorbed into the Sudanese Armed Forces became restive and revolted against their command. The mutiny in Akobo in 1975 was the most serious; the officers and their men withdrew into western Ethiopia and established what was known as Anya-nya II. By the time the SPLM/A formed in 1983, the Anya-nya II units were active in eastern Upper Nile and engaged the Sudanese army in battles. In fact, stories ran the rounds in Juba that the army top brass in Juba and Khartoum deployed Kerubino Kuanyin and William Nyuon to conduct a low intensity war against the Anya-nya II. The corollary of that war was the illegal wildlife poaching whose trophies (elephant tusks, leopard skins, python skins, etc.) were sent by Kerubino and William to Gen. Siddiq el Bana, the commander of Southern Command in Juba

The Ethiopian Derg was reluctant to give military support to the Anya-nya II, largely made up of Nuer ethnicity, because it was a separatist movement. However, the Derg willingly supported the SPLM/A, whose agenda was a united socialist Sudan. The struggle over the leadership of the new movement pitted the Nuer against the Dinka nationality and generated the animosity that still clouds, to this day, their relations. At the height of ethnic and community animosities, triggered by the splits and desertions within the liberation movement, especially towards the end of the nineties of the last century, "liberation" was perceived as acts of "shooting to chase away the enemy" from the garrisoned towns. This distorted perception conditioned the political thinking and actions of some powerful SPLM/A leaders, which engendered another false notion of 'we died in large numbers' for the liberation of this country.

The question of "which tribe" had contributed more to the fighting forces created a sense of entitlement and defined who (and from which tribe) should provide leadership of the country. This generated the psychological tendency among the Dinka, the largest single ethnicity in the movement, to dominate and hegemonise other ethnicities. In this connection, "liberation" ceased to be a process of freeing social, physical, and psychological energies to transform the oppressive reality. The act of "shooting to chase the enemy" is important, but it is only a small aspect of the whole liberation process.

Sixty-seven ethnicities or nationalities inhabit South Sudan. They are at different levels of socioeconomic and cultural development and varying demographic weights. These factors notwithstanding, these nationalities enjoy their sovereign independence as peoples socially and culturally distinct from others. In the context of the war of national liberation, they participated numerically in proportion to their demographic weight. There is no way the Aja or Bai in western Bahr el Ghazal could contribute the same numbers as the Rek or Malual sections of the Dinka nationality. In the same vein, the Tenet in eastern Equatoria couldn't be expected to send to the liberation movement equal numbers as the Otuho; it was impossible due to their small size. The small contributions these peoples made to the liberation process in South Sudan cannot be ignored or overlooked on account of their small numbers. This raises issues that risked disrupting social harmony and stability in South Sudan. The perception of ethnic dominance and hegemony on account of demographic or other factors engenders discrimination and exclusivity, which work adversely to the concept of national unity. Similarly, imposing national unity while ignoring factors of diversity leads ultimately to social friction, conflict, war, and fragmentation in the long run. The Republic of the Sudan is a living example of this eventuality. Therefore, balancing national unity and diversity, as per the concept of "unity in diversity", is necessary to ensure peace, social harmony, cohesion, and prosperity. This can only be achieved through democratic dispensation in the social, economic, and political spheres.

The struggle for national liberation, which the SPLM spearheaded, was a golden opportunity to cultivate and nurture the concept of unity in diversity. It drew together all the people of southern Sudan. However, the absence of a liberation ideology that spoke to the unity of the masses through progressive social and political engineering processes deprived the country of the necessary conditions. Thus, by 1996, some leaders and cadres, particularly from the Bahr el Ghazal subregion, were already loudly saying "*Awich ku angich ku,*" literally meaning, "We know what we want." This resonated with the already growing alienation within the liberation movement resulting from deliberate selective promotion of ethnic oral symbols in the running the liberation movement. This unintended act of discrimination rendered it difficult to ensure unity in diversity of the people in a situation where some members of the largest ethnic group openly spoke of knowing what they wanted to the exclusion of others.

The preceding lines form the background to a three-day meeting, funded by the Swiss Embassy, at Nyeri Club in Kenya in 2000. It was attended by a group of twelve southern Sudanese intellectuals chosen across political, social, and religious lines. This was the event that generated the concept of the "house of nationalities". The meeting discussed the national liberation process and the difficulties facing the movement, particularly the splits occurring along ethnic and territorial lines. The meeting established certain principles as the basis of unity in diversity. Instead of using the colonial construct of "tribe" we went for the use of "nationality", irrespective of demographic weights, and discouraged the use of derogatory names. The meeting recommended a study to inventorise all the nationalities to be presented at the next meeting of the group. The Swiss ambassador to Kenya, Josef Bücher, appointed the Swiss anthropologist Dr. Conradin Perner (known as Kwacakworo), who in turn recruited me to undertake a desktop study of the nationalities of South Sudan. With great luck I managed to find most of the anthropological references, in addition to the *Sudan Notes and Records* (SNR) at the library of the British Institute in East Africa in Nairobi.

But some of us started to question the interests of the Swiss government in South Sudan. The existence of so many ethnic communities was enough basis for introducing a federation of nationalities along the Ethiopian model of ethnic federalism. This perhaps may have been the undisclosed strategic objective of Ambassador Bücher, who initiated the idea, which paralleled the concept of Swiss cantons. I personally did not care whether we would have a federation or cantonisation. My interest in participating in this project was to fight the practice of hegemony and domination by large ethnic groups over other smaller ones. I preferred a situation like that of the United Nations General Assembly, where the big and the small have equal visibility although the larger ones like US, China, Russian Federation, UK and France contributed more to maintaining world peace and security than the smaller one. The fact that the Dinka and Nuer nationalities contributed more to the liberation struggle in proportion to their respective demographic weights didn't necessarily mean that they should dominate or hegemonise the rest.

The strategy, therefore, was to bring out into the open the anthropological configuration of southern Sudan in the context of the struggle for national liberation. The essence of national liberation was not "shooting to chase the enemy," as some people perceived, but to emancipate the mind from negative ideas and practices and create a society that valued all its citizens. In this context, South Sudan and its people did not require federation but a democratic transformation of their reality. This was the essence of the struggle for national liberation that the SPLM/A spearheaded. This entailed recognising and accepting the existence and visibility of each and every nationality as sovereign entity irrespective of their participation in the liberation struggle. That South Sudanese exist as nationalities does not contradict the imperceptible process of nation-building that occurs as a consequence of the liberation process. Ethnicity, like culture, is mutable. In the process of genuine national liberation, South Sudan nation could rise up from the deathbed of its constituent ethnicities.

The war of national liberation was a golden opportunity to accelerate the process of social and cultural mutability leading to the emergence of a nation encompassing the different identities of the people of South Sudan. Unfortunately, the SPLM/A lacked the perception, vision or a scientific understanding of the liberation process, which linked to nation building in a multi-national environment as southern Sudan. Thus, despite the large geographical territory the SPLM/A controlled, it failed to build a state that could attract diplomatic recognition from the African countries that supported it. The UN/OLS was a de facto recognition of the SPLM's authority on account of international humanitarian law and principles. The lands under its control included eastern and western Equatoria, Lakes, parts of Bahr el Ghazal, Jonglei, and Upper Nile, with a population of about five million people. The economy was best described as a "war economy," the operation of which was lubricated by international humanitarian relief intervention and assistance.

The study identified sixty-three nationalities inhabiting southern Sudan. Some of these nationalities were so small that several of them lived close together in one county or payam, while some were so large as to cover an entire subregion. The discussion of the report raised pertinent issues, particularly in eastern Equatoria, where some groups (Ifoto, Imatong, and Itahiela) who claimed separate identities had been denied a separate listing because they were considered sections of the Otuho nationality. Another difficulty arose in the question of whether or not Jieng or Monyjiang (Dinka) and Näädh (Nuer), who are in a continuous process of segmentation and live as federations of clans or sections, could be considered as single distinct nationalities or if their sections should also be considered as sub nationalities. The assumption that a Jieng section as large as Malual (Aweil) or Rek (Aweil, Gogrial, and Tonj) could not be counted as a nationality, even though people of the Bai, Aja, Tenet, and similar small groups were counted as sovereign nationalities caused serious difficulties when power considerations kicked-into the discourse. These were complex issues that challenged the very concept of sovereign existence outside the context of other factors of culture, language, and religion. We therefore needed much wider academic and political discussions.

The classic model of representative government was considered in the context of the social and cultural diversity in South Sudan. How would large nationalities like the Dinka, Nuer, and Azande be represented? Would they be considered equal to peoples from small nationalities like Bai and Aja when it came to decision-making affecting their lives? In this context, the idea of the house of nationalities (HoN) popped up as an innovative contribution to the debate. It was envisaged that the HoN could be part of the legislative organs of the state. As we envisioned it, the legislative organs would be similar to but different from the Westminster parliamentary system and the American Congressional system. By virtue of its representation, the HoN would occupy the upper house, which has the final say on legislation affecting the nationalities, including their social and cultural values and geographical territory.

Kwacakworo, Napoleon Adok, and I refined the report during a retreat in Davos, Switzerland. In a matter of weeks, the booklet, titled "The House of Nationalities: A Space to Preserve the Unity and Diversity of the People of South Sudan," had been published. The SPLM/A's leadership (Dr. Garang and Salva Kiir) reacted differently to the concept of the HoN. It is worth mentioning that Cdr. Salva Kiir supported the 1999 Dinka–Nuer conference in Wunlit, conducted on the basis of indigenous peace-making. The Wunlit brought peace to the Dinka and Nuer people on the basis of mutual acceptance and recognition as they shared the border area between Bahr el Ghazal and western Upper Nile. Some of the ideas that were used to reach the Dinka–Nuer Peace Covenant echoed the concept of the HoN. While Cdr. Salva Kiir supported the HoN and encouraged us to build it up, Dr. Garang rejected it as a diversion. In fact, he was hostile to the idea. This came out into the open one night in June 2004, when he actually tried to erase the four years of research, meetings, and workshops we had put into developing the concept of the HoN.

By June 2004, the peace negotiations had reached a critical point and needed only to be consolidated and finalised. The IGAD mediators and the Troika (special envoys from Norway, the United States, and the UK) shifted their focus to engage the two principals—Dr. John Garang and Ustaz Ali Osman Mohammed Taha—in the peace negotiations. Dr. Garang then spent most of his time in Naivasha, where the talks were conducted. It was clear that there would be no going back to war. The ceasefire still held. The SPLM leadership invited leaders of indigenous institutions of governance from all over rural South Sudan to a meeting at Natinga (New Site), Budi County, Eastern Equatoria State. Sometimes called "traditional leaders", included were chiefs, rainmakers, kings, *monyomoji*, *kuar-moun* and *beny-bith*. The SPLM leadership intended to use the occasion to thank the people of South Sudan, through their traditional leaders, for their support for the SPLA over the years of the war of national liberation. I was there as representative of the Federation of Sudanese Civil Society Organisation (FOSCO). To my surprise, I was informed that my accommodation for the conference would be a structure within Dr. Garang's compound. I assumed that it was to make it difficult for me to link up with other delegates from civil society organisations.

The conference had barely begun when the chairman was escorted out of the room and left Cdr. Salva Kiir to continue chairing the session. Traditional leaders spoke, expressing their gratitude but also voicing the complaints of their people for the behaviour of some SPLA commanders. When Dr. Garang returned he brought with him Josef Bücher, the Swiss ambassador to Kenya, Kwacakworo, and Andrea Semadeni, the young diplomat who was to handle administrative matters of the HoN project. The ambassador and his entourage brought along copies of the booklet, "The House of Nationalities: A Space to Preserve Unity in Diversity of the People of South Sudan," and bundles of "HoN" T-shirts, which were to be distributed to the conferees and members of the SPLM/A. But Dr. Garang stopped distribution of both the booklet and the T-shirts, ostensibly until after the conference deliberations. The ambassador delivered his speech and was escorted back to the airstrip to fly back to Lokichogio.

As soon as the sun set, Dr. Garang ordered that the four hundred or so copies of the booklet and the bundle of T-shirts be taken to a certain spot some half a mile away and burned. He assigned one of his loyal military intelligence officers to oversee the process. Nothing was heard again of the booklet or T-shirts. I was to learn later that someone had whispered in the ear of Dr. Garang that the idea of the HoN belonged to Peter Adwok Nyaba, who wanted "to wake up people who were still sleeping when the war was already won." It was a very dishonest exposition of the HoN issue. That my name featured as the researcher added another layer of problem for some chauvinistic South Sudanese intellectuals. It drew a lot of hostility and resentment, particularly when I argued that the essence of "liberation" was to wake people up, to raise their social awareness and political consciousness to enable them to perceive correctly their reality. To my mind, to leave some people still sleeping in ignorance was the antithesis of liberation.

The concept of the house of nationalities emerged in a context of fragmentation and high tension within the liberation movement. The issue that concerned many people, including foreign friends of South Sudan, was how a people struggling to construct a state could be so disunited and fight amongst themselves. The issue of unity in diversity was seen as feasible but required a democratic political system. The Swiss had been involved in South Sudan, particularly with the underaged soldiers (the SPLA's Red Army) in the refugee camps at Pochalla and Kakuma, and the ICRC Hospital in Lokichogio where injured SPLA were treated.

The diversity of South Sudan fascinated the Swiss. Perhaps Ambassador Bucher wanted to experiment with the Swiss system of cantons in South Sudan, based on nationalities in their different localities and cultural configurations. Swiss involvement in the project was in the context of this interest, although the idea and the concept of the HoN was entirely a South Sudanese construction. I undertook the research into the South Sudanese nationalities in their different geographical, demographical, and sociocultural dispositions, and in this Dr. Conradin Perner (Kwacakworo) assisted me. Napoleon Adok and Jacob Jiel Akol were involved in the design, construction, and management of the *Gurtong* peace project website, where the information about the nationalities was published and made accessible to the public.

Dr. John Garang died in a tragic helicopter crash on 30 July 2005. An impression had been created that Garang was the only individual opposed to the HoN. However, with the establishment of the subnational entity called the Government of Southern Sudan (GoSS), it turned out that none of the SPLM leaders was interested in installation of the HoN as a structure within South Sudan's governance system. The authorities in GoSS dragged their feet and made no concrete decisions, even though they had initially accepted and agreed to create the institute. The project management acted innovatively. Instead of waiting for GoSS to decide, they transformed the project into a vehicle for educating and raising the awareness of traditional leaders. They organised themselves into a Council of Traditional Authority and Leadership (COTAL) in South Sudan. With the assistance of Ghanaian Prof. Kwesi Prah and the Centre for Advanced Studies of African Society (CASAS), members of COTAL were able to visit and study corresponding indigenous institutions of governance in South Africa, Botswana, and Ghana.

Why did the SPLM leader, Dr. John Garang, loathe the concept of the HoN? I assume that the statement regarding the 'sleeping people' was not the basis of Garang's resentment towards the HoN. As the leader of the liberation movement, he wouldn't countenance that some people remained sleeping while the guns of liberation were firing. I assume also that Garang was interested in absolute personal power, bordering on totalitarian dictatorship. It would, therefore, mean that Garang wouldn't countenance democratic institutions like the HoN, which included the sixty-seven nationalities, to share sovereign power and authority. It is unfortunate that he did not live to tell the people of South Sudan that, to his mind, the HoN was a foreign concept. Dr. Garang did not want the concept of the HoN precisely because he believed it was a foreign idea intended to disrupt his designs for Dinka ethnic leadership and domination of South Sudan.

Pursuing this discourse on the basis of the statement above requires a long digression. This digression takes us back to the political events before, during, and after the formation of the SPLM/A in July 1983 and is related to emergence of Dinka ethnic nationalism and its ideology of hegemony and domination. In 1980, a contradiction emerged between Marshall Gaafar Nimeri and the political elite in the Southern Region over the location of the oil refinery. To have his way, Nimeri continued to interfere in the political and democratic process, engineering schisms within the political elite and encouraging competing ethnic coalitions and hostile divisions. This eventually culminated in the abrogation of the Addis Ababa Agreement and the dismantling of the Southern Region. Against this backdrop, an insurrection brewed in Bor, which eventually led to the formation of the SPLM/A.

Both Dr. John Garang de Mabior and the SPLM/A came from outside traditional southern Sudanese body politics, then organised along the lines of two political parties—Southern Front (SF) and Sudan African National Union (SANU)—and encapsulated within the Sudan Socialist Union (SSU). The politics practised in the Southern Region, a brand of liberal bourgeois democracy, was a subset of the totalitarian dictatorship. The SPLM/A arose amid the regime's acute social, economic, and political contradictions. It, however, subsumed the myriad of contradictions underlying the socioeconomic and political crisis of the May Regime and the immense political tensions in the Southern Region. The emergence of the SPLM/A purely as a military movement created a serious distortion and prevented the evolution of a genuine national liberation movement uniting all the people of Southern Sudan.

The outward consequence of this distortion was the emergence of Dinka ethnic nationalism. The numerical superiority of the Dinka nationality in the SPLM/A's rank and file, notwithstanding the methods by which it was engineered, was used to justify the fact that four out of five members of the Political–Military High Command (PMHC)—namely John Garang, Kerubino Kuanyin Bol, Salva Kiir, and Arok Thon Arok—all hailed from the Dinka nationality. Morality apart, such a leadership configuration in a national liberation movement in a country torn apart by ethnic schisms sent a false message, affirming Dinka domination and hegemony over other nationalities. In the context of low social awareness and political consciousness, the Dinka would be right to accept, and the others also right to reject, this leadership. In hindsight, the post-CPA socioeconomic and socio-political engineering of the subnational entity vindicated the claim some Equatorians made in 1983 that the birth of the SPLA was a Dinka reaction to the establishment of Equatoria Region.

The SPLM/A's leadership failed to rebut that perception or to problematise the political process leading to *kokora* and the redivision of the Southern region. Instead, it reinforced this perception by sending Dinka-dominated SPLA units to Equatoria where they committed egregious human rights violations. In response to these atrocities, the Mundari and the Toposa opted to establish their own ethnic militia. The Equatoria Defence Force (EDF) of Dr. Theophilus Ochang and Cdr. Martin Kenyi was born to resist Dinka (now both Dinka and Nuer) domination and hegemony. Most Equatorians, in their resentment, didn't differentiate between the Dinka and Nuer and, to some extent, the Chollo. The formation of EDF was essentially against the occupation of eastern Equatoria by the SPLA mainstream, which was perceived to be Dinka, and the SPLA–Nasir faction, seen as Nuer.

Had the SPLM/A's leaders problematised the *kokora* movement in central Equatoria, they would have discovered that it was part and parcel of what Dr. Garang categorised as a "minority clique" in opposition to the bulk of the Sudanese people. It was a contradiction borne out of political exclusion, economic neglect, and marginalisation, as well as social discrimination based on race, language, religion, and other cultural attributes. The absence of a democratic platform to address these concerns invariably pushed people to extreme political positions, including rebellion. The social and political environment in the Southern Region then, in which the winner had it all, was so suffocating that some leaders preferred throwing the baby out together with the bathwater.

The war of national liberation began against the background of painful divisions among the people of southern Sudan in which lives were lost and property had been destroyed. The SPLM/A's leaders should have been extra careful and considered all those factors of division in order to bring back the unity of the people. Through the SPLM Manifesto, they should have been courageous to recognise and accept the responsibility for mistakes of their predecessors, in order to regain the trust and confidence of people negatively affected. It is also important to understand the psychological makeup of the different social groups in South Sudan. The Dinka and Nuer are very close culturally and may better understand certain attitudes or behaviours. To some extent, the Chollo also share with the Dinka and Nuer certain beliefs, practices and taboos in issues of marriage, compensation for murder and payment of blood price. However, it was wrong to assume that the people in Equatoria would understand and accept certain Dinka or Nuer mores and attitudes. It would appear that the SPLA Penal and Disciplinary codes of 1984 was for the Dinka and Nuer nationalities. It, for instance, provides for a certain number of cows as penalty for murder; this law would not be applicable to the Azande, Moro, and Bele, who have no cattle but possess different measures and standards for such crimes. This demonstrated how oblivious was the SPLM/A's leadership to the social and cultural totality of South Sudan.

Military confrontation with the enemy apart, liberation, and the war of national liberation for that matter, presupposes the participation of all the people as a national project. This was the fundamental objective of the ethnographic study of the nationalities of South Sudan. I did this study with enthusiasm, prompted by the disturbing story of an incident that occurred in the Lafon area in 1995. I was then still considered part of the SPLM/A–United of Riek Machar, although in fact I was on my own as a civil society activist. The SPLM/A–United had deployed forces in Eastern Equatoria under the command of Cdr. William Nyuon Bany. The troops were starving and getting a horrible beating from the SPLA mainstream. They were completely demoralised and wouldn't subscribe to military discipline. Cdr. William decided to discipline the troops by executing one of the soldiers. The choice fell on a soldier from the Lou Nuer, but his relatives were up in arms against his execution and William backed down. He chose another soldier, this time from the Jikany Nuer, and again his community was up in arms. He finally found an Equatorian soldier and he was duly executed. He was completely innocent but no one put up a fight for him. Instead of acting in the manner the Lou and Jikany soldiers did, the angered and embittered Equatorian officers and soldiers deserted the contingent and later formed the Equatoria Defence Force under the leadership of Capt. Martin Kenyi.

Not only was the execution of an innocent Equatorian soul horrible, it indeed served no military purpose. Once the commander backed down from disciplining the recalcitrant Nuer, the threat of execution by firing squad no longer served any purpose. The execution of the poor Equatorian demonstrated how certain leaders or ethnicities in the liberation movement harboured a total disregard for other nationalities. This attitude of belittling groups of people to the extent of murdering them like insects parodied the concept of unity of South Sudan and its people. Sixteen years in the CPA, and eleven years into the birth of the republic of South Sudan, these attitudes and practices not only persisted but have also heightened in intensity in Central Equatoria [between Dinka Bor pastoralists versus sedentary Bari, Acholi and Madi communities] and Upper Nile [between Chollo and sections of Padang Dinka] on the question of land and its utilisation. It was in order to acquaint our people with themselves that we proposed the concept of HoN to augment and enhance the perception of liberation as a uniting rather than discriminatory process. The colonial policy of "divide to conquer" had separated and turned our people against themselves such that if they were not immediate neighbours, they would not know each other. The Nuer, for instance, called all Equatorians *ji Juba* or "the people of Juba," even though the Equatorians are not one nationality but made up of more than thirty different nationalities and social groups.

The concept of the HoN was intended as a departure from the conventional governance structure of the bogus liberal bourgeois democracy that Africans practice, a model that is separate from the prevailing social and cultural context. Most post-colonial African states are modelled on Westminster or the French multi-party parliamentary dispensation, which in fact is a charade. The sixty-plus years of flag independence have shown that multi-party democracy has not sunk into the African psyche. The experiment did not provide the necessary socioeconomic, political and cultural transformation of society that underpins a liberal democracy. We wanted, therefore, to be innovative and think outside the iron box of conformity. Emerging from the three failed experiments of liberal democracy in the Sudan—namely, the first republic (1956–1958), second republic (1964–1969), and the third republic (1985–1989)—South Sudan needed a political model that served its sociocultural multiplicities.

The difficulty of wholesale adoption of European models of governance in Africa stems from the fact that these institutions and instruments of power are based and legislated on values completely

alien to African thought and practice. The laws by which South
Sudan is governed of necessity should derive from the shared values
of its people in the totality of their different sociocultural configurations. Therefore, the idea was to organise the custodians of these
values in an institution that would legislate them into laws. The
organisation, composition, and scope of this institution would
be different from the parliamentary models based on geographic
representation: it would be based on nationality. This experiment
would be a process of collective discovery through which people
could recognise their commonality. It was false for anyone speaking
as a member of one particular ethnicity or nationality to say "*We*
liberated you" or "*We* are the liberators," as implied in the falsehood that those advocating for the HoN "want to wake up those
still sleeping when the war is already won." In fact, up to this point
in time the liberation has not been achieved.

Initially, because I conducted the research and many of the
intellectuals who supported the concept were civil society activists, rumours circulated within the higher echelons of the SPLM/A,
particularly among the wilfully blind and many who had surrendered their reflective faculties to the SPLM leadership, that the HoN
was an idea to counter the liberation ideology that the SPLM/A
spearheaded. In fact, since the 1997 publication of my book, "The
Politics of Liberation in South Sudan: An Insider's View", there
was an undeclared sanction against me, although no one has ever
confronted me for writing in such detail about the movement's
shortcomings.

The greatest drawback of the western education many of us
in South Sudan received is that it did not allow us to think for
ourselves. We always accepted what was given, without questioning
the motives behind it. Thus, in writing the transitional constitution of independent South Sudan, our lawyers went for a "cut
and paste" of other constitutions, without reference to either the
conditions those constitutions were written under and promul-
gated or the conditions under which South Sudanese live. These

lawyers, without envisioning that too much power could corrupt the leader, heaped excessive powers on Kiir, even though they knew he couldn't manage these powers due to his limited capacity. The idea of the Council of States in the national legislature came from the falsehood that the political system in the Sudan was federal, and therefore it was necessary to take care of legislation on the states. We tried to influence the lawyers, some of whom were with us in the HoN project, to think outside the box and consider the HoN as an alternative.

The hypocrisy of members of the South Sudanese elite appeared as soon as they ascended to power. When President Kiir was Garang's deputy in the bush he supported the idea of the HoN. It seems he suddenly suffered amnesia when he assumed the presidency and became concerned only about his own power. The people of South Sudan have battled the Arab-dominated northern political establishment for nearly six decades and yet when given the opportunity to create a political system commensurate with their reality, they gravitated towards a state and a governance system that engendered asymmetric power and economic relations.

Over the last fifteen years, we have witnessed the ruling elite's abandonment of the principles of justice, freedom, and fraternity, which underpinned and drove the war of national liberation. The reason is simple: when the political elite speak of nation or nation state, what is at the back of their mind is their own ethnicity. They, therefore, deliberately empower the members of their ethnicity both politically and economically in order to hegemonise and dominate the "others". We have witnessed the political and economic empowerment of the Warrap elite. They lead in the business cartels, particularly in the oil industry and road construction. They are the effective heads of the security and other organised forces with a revenue-collection mandate: customs, immigration and passports, and traffic police. They are chairs or members of the board of directors of nearly all parastatal corporations, including the Bank of South Sudan.

This monopoly of power and wealth militates against the principles of justice (equality and equity) and can be sustained only by means of brute force. The presidential guards and the national security bureau are there to suppress any attempt by the people to protest. The government spokesman once said they didn't have rubber bullets, only live munition to kill any dissenters. So, a country born after bitter wars of national liberation spanning several decades has reverted back to the starting point of 1983. The difference is that ethnic chauvinists in the name of the Jieng Council of Elders (JCE) have pushed the regime towards the drain. The bad ethnic politics led Kiir to decree the division of South Sudan into thirty-two states, giving the Dinka forty-two percent of the land, including ancestral lands of the Luo, Fertit (western Bahr el Ghazal), and the Chollo (Upper Nile). Although Kiir later repealed this decree to return the country to a ten-state structure, there is now bitterness and hatred between neighbours who had lived peacefully for decades if not centuries.

Kiir's determination to protect Padang Dinka interests, where they are a minority in Upper Nile and Unity states and in the Fangak area of Jonglei, against their neighbours—Chollo and Nuer—may spell doom for these groups when Kiir is no longer in power unless a genuinely revolutionary system is installed. This ethnic policy could boomerang in the same way that it has done in Ethiopia, where the former rulers of Ethiopia—the Tigrayan People's Liberation Front—have been forced into another rebellion, or even secessionist endeavour because power had shifted to the hands of their former subordinates.

It is impossible to wish away ethnic entities or nationalities: they will remain as long as their means of social production sustains them. However, ethnicity is mutable, and the South Sudan nation will definitely emerge one day from the death-bed of ethnicity. However, this will obtain only in the context of a democratic socio-economic and cultural development paradigm that puts *all* peoples *at par* with each other, and places them at the centre of building the state. In this connection, the HoN could intervene as a mediator of the national culture, encompassing as it would the peculiarities of the people of South Sudan.

Implementation of the Revitalised Agreement on the Resolution of the Conflict in South Sudan (R–ARCSS) invokes the process of making a constitution. This would involve all the different stake-holders and offer an opportunity to mobilise public opinion for establishment of the HoN as an integral part of the legislative authority in South Sudan. This would be the only credible way to involve South Sudanese in decision-making that affects their social, economic, and cultural development. South Sudan's experiment with state formation, if it is to be sustainable, requires statesman-ship not brinksmanship. It cannot be conducted on the basis of "trial and error" or *mangmanga* (colloquial Arabic for "wobbling"). This was the way the SPLA conducted the war: individuals made terrible mistakes and there was no accountability. In 2005, the SPLM accepted the ten-states model for Southern Sudan without studying its implications. The SPLM negotiators did not question the NCP's motives for the bogus federalism which concentrated Sudan's economic and political power in Khartoum.

After negotiating the IGAD-mediated Agreement on the Resolution of the Conflict in South Sudan (ARCISS) in 2014, Riek Machar presented a 21-states model. When questioned about the model, he said it was based on former colonial districts. But Riek erased the two Padang Dinka districts of Renk and Bailiet (formerly Abuong). In response, Kiir decreed a twenty-eight-states model based on recommendations of the Padang Dinka community, which dispossessed the Chollo of their ancestral lands on the east bank of the White Nile and along the Sobat River. This was further revised to a thirty-two-states model, which gave Dinka 42 per cent of South Sudan's land. It was later returned to the ten-states model.

These were political decisions cooked up by ethnic lobby groups and imposed by the power of the president, who happened to be a Dinka. Honourable members of the South Sudan Legislative

Assembly who opposed these decrees were censured. The Speaker of the Council of States signed without contesting the thirty-two-states system, even though it dispossessed him of his own land. Political expediency apart, I believe the authentic traditional, rather than political, representatives of the people would not have countenanced such a breach to the sanctity of their ancestral lands. This underlines the importance of the HoN as an authentic representation of the people of South Sudan.

Chapter 18

The Comprehensive Peace Agreement & its Aftermath

*M*any of us Marxists and revolutionary democrats who joined the rank and file of the Sudan People's Liberation Movement were committed to, and inspired by, the ideal of a complete transformation and reconstruction of the Sudanese polity. However, as earlier stated, I started to have serious doubts that the SPLM/A's leadership would deliver on this promise. It was therefore a matter of extreme consternation when, on 31 December 2004, the two nemeses—Omar el Bashir and Dr. John Garang—representing the opposite poles of the contradiction underpinning the conflict in the Sudan, announced the end of the war. Delegations of the parties to the conflict, regional mediators, observers, and the press had assembled in Naivasha to witness final agreement on the sticking points. This included security arrangements during the interim period and protocols concerning the three areas of Abyei,

Nuba Mountains/Southern Kordofan, and Funj/Southern Blue Nile. It was, therefore, a ceremony to celebrate the initialling of the most important protocols of the Comprehensive Peace Agreement.

The spontaneity with which the large crowd, made up of both camps of Sudanese, thunderously roared in approval, as if the agreement was a rebirth of the Sudan, sent a shiver down my spine. But it felt like an anti-climax. Deep inside me, I felt oddly bereft. The crowd had a point in rejoicing the end of the war, which had been devastating in loss of life and material destruction. But the crowd that celebrated that night in Naivasha was not the same crowd of ordinary Sudanese who bore the brunt of this destruction. In fact, many of them came from Khartoum, including southerners who, years before, had been part of the crowds that ululated as the mujahideen and the Sudanese Army marched off to their deployment in the war zone of southern Sudan.

Sometimes, history does appear to repeat itself. I was at the University of Khartoum in March 1972 when the May Regime signed the Addis Ababa Agreement with the Southern Sudan Liberation Movement. It was well noted that of all the people, South Sudanese were particularly upbeat that a peace agreement had been reached between the rebels and the government. This attitude suggested there had been no cause for the war, and that the suffering of the people had been for no clear objectives. Some were indeed ready to start quarrels with those of us who questioned the agreement's provisions. In particular, there was no political programme to address the issues of socioeconomic and cultural development, which were the fundamental contradictions that had triggered and driven the war in Southern Sudan, beginning with the 1955 mutiny in Torit. Members of the African National Front had the audacity to vilify us, branding us as Communists and people who were opposed to the May Regime.

These memories ran through my mind as we prepared to travel from Naivasha back to Nairobi. It had not taken long to discover the motives for supporting the Addis Ababa Agreement, particularly among the elite. The establishment of regional self-government offered opportunities for employment and economic benefits. In fact, most of the southern students were members of the Sudan Socialist Union, not because they believed in its principles and political programme but to demonstrate that they were part of the mass, indeed uncritical mass, that supported Nimeri.

The recent and contemporary history of the Sudan is awash with political compromises (agreements) once described, by the veteran South Sudanese leader Abel Alier Kwai, as "too many agreements dishonoured." These were liberal peace agreements, invariably and ostensibly signed by the protagonists to buy time and save face. These agreements indeed demonstrated that the parties were not honest: they signed them knowing that they would not subscribe to or abide by their provisions. To me, it was clear that the CPA intended to create a situation similar to 1972. This was because the SPLM/A had been forced to sign a political compromise which fell short of achieving anything close to its concept or vision of the New Sudan, and this despite the enormous army the SPLM/A had raised over the twenty-one years of war and the large areas it controlled in Southern Sudan, the Nuba Mountains, and Southern Blue Nile.

The concept and vision of the New Sudan attracted the equally marginalised African compatriots from the Nuba Mountains and Blue Nile/Funj to join the war of liberation in their tens of thousands. It was the ideal of building a new Sudan of freedom, justice, and prosperity that all those combatants sang in their *morale*-building songs. It was a marked departure from the goal of secession of southern Sudan, which southern politicians called for during the first civil war (1955–1972). It is worth mentioning that the ruling Arab-dominated northern political elite mobilised Africans in northern Sudan to fight the seventeen-year war on its behalf. This time around, it was different. The marginalised Africans in different parts of the country had become conscious of their social and political conditions; a correct enunciation of the oppressive reality in the country had created a kind of unity. Viewed from this perspective, the signing of the CPA before achieving a radical transformation in the country or creating the conditions for a radical transformation would appear to have been a betrayal of the cause.

As the saying goes, everything must have a reason; nothing can happen without a cause. And indeed, all of the negative things happening at the time of this writing, in 2021, whether in the Republic of South Sudan, or in the Nuba and Funj areas of the Republic of the Sudan, must be attributed to the premature truncation of the revolutionary process—to the betrayal that culminated in the signing of the CPA in January 2005. To understand how this occurred requires a deep digression into the history of the SPLM/A since 1983. The war broke out consequent to serious social, economic, and political contradictions in the May Regime. The Southern Region was the weakest point in the system and the eruption had to occur there, along the political fissures in the ruling political elite. As a result of this, a coterie of military officers linked to the regime took over the leadership of the nascent movement.

The emergence of the SPLM/A and its militarised leadership remains an unsettled mystery in the contemporary history of South Sudan. To many southern Sudanese, the rebellion in Bor did not herald a spectacular moment. Nor did it signal the end of political scrambles in the Southern Region. However, the SPLM/A was a qualitative lift from the politics and armed insurrections of the 1960s, although its strategic objectives and dynamics were known perhaps to only a very few people connected to Dr. John Garang. The SPLM's *Manifesto* of July 1983 claimed that there was a clandestine organisation of former Anya-nya officers absorbed in the Sudan Armed Forces that had taken advantage of the situation to start a war by instigating a rebellion in Battalions 104 and 105 in Bor and Ayod, respectively.

In *The Politics of Liberation in South Sudan: An Insider's View* (Kampala: Fountain Publishers, 1977) I refuted this story on the grounds that the war of liberation couldn't have been started by officers who operated directly under the army's top brass in Juba and Khartoum to crush the Anya-nya II operating against the government in eastern Upper Nile subregion. Moreover, as it was later learned, it was the theft of the battalion money in Bor that precipitated the fighting on 16 May 1983. No one in the SPLM/A leadership has ever challenged my analysis of this event. It is often much later that protagonists and historians of phenomenal events piece together the facts of such historical events. The same goes with the SPLM/A's story.

It is not surprising that most of what has been said, or is still being said, about the SPLM/A's formation—how it suddenly appeared on the Sudanese political stage—are mere recollections, some of them utter exaggerations, of what happened after the main event. In fact, the SPLM/A did not even exist on 16 May 1983. Its first spectacular combat action to announce its existence was in February 1984. Therefore, between 16 May 1983 and the SPLA's first action in Malakal and the camps of the French Compagnie de Constructions Internationales (CCI) at the Jonglei Canal was when most of the wildest and imaginative stories were spread. What did not add up in much of the official account was the statement in the SPLM's *Manifesto* that alluded to the existence of a clandestine organisation of former Anya-nya officers absorbed into the Sudanese Armed Forces in 1972.

This official account of the SPLM/A's formation and first days of life, for obvious reasons, completely ignored the Anya-nya II and the struggle it spearheaded in the eastern Upper Nile subregion. If the account had recognised the Anya-nya II it would have exposed the falsehood that Kerubino Kuanyin and William Nyuon were part of the revolutionary cells in the army that planned the rebellion. This falsehood was further revealed by the absence of an established leadership hierarchy in the supposed clandestine organisation and what transpired later in the SPLM/A's leadership. By virtue of his rank, Col. Dr. John Garang should have taken over the command immediately after the war broke out in Bor. That he did not, but had to wait until the intervention of the Derg's generals to confirm him as the leader of the infant movement, throws clouds of doubts on the authenticity and accuracy of the official account. The SPLM's *Manifesto* of July 1983 is enough to refute the official account. It was written in Itang and approved by Mengistu Haile Mariam, suggesting that the formation of the rebel army predated the formation of the political organ of the national liberation movement. This egg–chicken riddle of the history of the SPLM/A still lingers unresolved.

It was not enough to declare that one was a revolutionary and instantly be one. To be a revolutionary one must pass through long periods of training, education, and practical experience. Before his name entered the national and regional political scene as leader of the rebel movement, Col. Dr. Garang was not known in social and political circles in the country, save perhaps for a few of his colleagues in the army, former schoolmates, relatives, and people of Jonglei. He was and remains an enigma. His name will remain linked to the events in South Sudan into the foreseeable future, notwithstanding the fact that his demise occurred more than fifteen years ago.

The SPLM's political and ideological character also remains an enigma. A popular anecdote in the Sudan in the early seventies of the last century went like this: "Gaafar Nimeri, driving the revolution's vehicle, signalled to the left, but to the chagrin of all he turned to the right." In the same way, the SPLM started off in 1983 as a revolutionary socialist movement but by 1992 had made a paradigm shift to ally itself with imperialism. Someone, indeed an obfuscationist, referred to this ideological vacillation as Garang's "strategic ambiguity," as if to affirm and glorify Garang's political ingenuity. It reminds one of life in the villages, where some people succeed through dexterity and dishonesty. Whatever it meant, strategic ambiguity cannot be the basis for any revolutionary enterprise or relations between leaders and the masses of the people in a war of national liberation.

In a revolution and revolutionary action, relations between leaders and the people must be based on and marked by honesty, trust, and confidence. It is permissible to apply strategic ambiguity to relations with the enemy. Indeed, it is absolutely necessary and imperative to keep the enemy ignorant of our tactics and strategies, lest it counters them and defeats us. However, it would be a grave mistake to indulge with the masses in a dishonest and opaque way in matters that concern them. It is absolutely necessary to raise the social and political awareness of the masses through political education, enlightenment, and civic education.

In hindsight, it is now clear why the SPLM/A's leadership shunned the political education and ideological training of its cadres and operatives. It did not permit any political organisation or discussion whatsoever in the training camps, refugee camps, or liberated areas under the control of the SPLA. It forced a militarisation of social relations between the leaders and the soldiers: militarism was the modus operandi. It promoted a cult of personality: instead of composing morale songs for the revolution and the liberation process, SPLA recruits and officers sang songs glorifying the leader and his personality. This SPLA subculture of militarism and the cult of personality dampened rather than sharpened people's awareness and political consciousness.

It became clear, especially in the aftermath of the detention of Cdr. Kerubino and Cdr. Arok Thon, that Dr. Garang was determined to stifle democracy in the movement. The intention was to produce in the people of South Sudan a mass that was utterly uncritical of its social, economic, and political environment; a mass that was completely incapable of questioning any decision made by the leader, leave alone participating in its making. It was a serious contradiction of reality. Paraphrasing the Brazilian educator Paulo Freire, liberation is conscientisation. There must be access to the truth of a situation, whether individually or collectively, through the dual process of action and reflection. The practice of the SPLM/A, however, apart from its military action against the enemy, could be categorised in all measures as counterrevolutionary.

Thus, the political–military dichotomy, which was the SPLM/A, was a deliberate decoy to prevent the SPLM/A from evolving into a genuine national liberation movement. This was clear from the way it conducted the war and the relations that evolved within the movement between the leaders and members, between the officers and the combatants, and between the movement and the masses of the people. Because it was parachuted from outside society, the SPLM/A's leadership could not resonate with society's sensibilities and sensitivities. Militarism in the SPLM/A did not evolve out of nothing. It was the logical consequence of seeing itself as independent of the poor peasants who comprised the bulk of the movement. This was the source of the SPLM/A's inclination to dedicate itself rigidly to one particular form of struggle—military action and militarism. In this manner, the SPLM/A consciously deprived itself of other means and tools for winning the war of national liberation.

Political developments at the international and regional levels, which witnessed the collapse of the former Soviet Union and the Ethiopian regime—the SPLM/A's main benefactor— accelerated the rebel army's ideological shift, quickly exposing its vulnerability and binding it more tightly to imperialism. In the intervening period we witnessed the evolution of a tiny clique of young officers who were loyal to Dr. John Garang. This tiny class of political and military elites was interested in power and primitive accumulation of wealth. In the SPLA's oral history of those days, a differentiation or stratification insusceptibly occurred with the officers' ranks leading to the evolving of what popularly came to known as "small, big commanders" and "big, small commanders."

The "small big commanders" were mostly younger ambitious officers, many of whom had left school to join the ranks of the SPLA and been promoted into the movement's senior ranks; they lacked experience and knowledge of government, he "big small commanders" were older and were mostly former regional government bureaucrats. Dr. Garang favoured the "small big commanders" in terms of deployment, including assignments to positions of responsibility and authority, while the "big small commanders" were rarely put in positions of power or authority.

This bias played out negatively in the so-called liberated areas when these young and inexperienced leaders engaged with civilians on issues of democracy and governance. The mess that led to civilian populations deserting liberated areas, particularly in Equatoria and Upper Nile, for refugee camps in Ethiopia, Kenya, Uganda, and the Congo must be attributed to the bad politics played by these young leaders. Part of the general weaknesses of the SPLM/A, this inability to maintain the civilian population was a factor in the SPLM/A's political compromise with northern Sudan's Islamic regime. To sum up, the signing of the CPA, having noted its shortcomings, was a consequence of the SPLM/A's structural weaknesses, embedded in the absence of liberation ideology and the shunning of political education and organisation.

It was past midnight when we arrived in Nairobi. I had hardly slept as my thoughts kept rewinding back to the emerging situation. I could see the people of southern Sudan returning once more to the same oppressive reality they had struggled against for twenty-one years. As far back as 1987, in our clandestine discussion circles (clandestine because the SPLM/A had proscribed any kind of open political activity in Itang refugee camps), we defined the war of national liberation as the height of contradiction between revolutionary forces and the forces of reaction and oppression in the country.

Resolution of this contradiction presupposed defeat of the oppressive regime and a corresponding emergence of a counter-society built on the foundations of freedom, justice, fraternity, and prosperity for all. The civil society activism we engaged in was intended to broaden this perception of the revolution among the masses, to deepen the understanding of the liberation process, and perhaps resist any attempts at a liberal peace-making. But, as it turned out, we were daydreaming: the SPLM/A's leadership had already succumbed to international diplomatic pressure to end the war. In fact, by 2003 the war of national liberation had stagnated and this was reflected in the seriousness the parties attached to the peace negotiations.

It goes without saying that there is a time for everything under the sun. Even now in their wretchedness, occasioned by war and the phenomenal failure of their leaders to lead, the people of southern Sudan know that they will one day stand with their heads above their shoulders, like the rest of humanity. I am forced to say this because during the twenty-one years of war both the SPLM/A's combatants and the civilian population under their control were submerged in apathy, despair, and hopelessness. The war was fierce and destructive. More than two million people, according to conservative estimates, perished due to war and attendant causes. However, but even with these losses and serious political failings on the part of the SPLM/A leadership, the war of national liberation wouldn't have generated apathy and hopelessness among the people, had the SPLM engaged in political education and organisation of the people.

The people of South Sudan hold the dates of 9 January 2005 and 9 July 2011 as sacred in their hearts, and have reason to celebrate them annually. The signing of the Comprehensive Peace Agreement (CPA) on 9 January 2005 invariably brought respite to the people, particularly ordinary folks who had quietly suffered through the war and its difficulties. Given that the majority of the people in the towns and rural areas had lost track of the primary objectives of the insurrection, the CPA came at about the right time. It was a replica of the events in southern Sudan on the eve of the Addis Ababa Agreement 1972, when many southerners were fed up with a war that they had no control of and whose developments they had ceased to follow.

Unlike the Addis Ababa Agreement, however, the Comprehensive Peace Agreement was a gamechanger. Southerners, through the SPLA, had empowered themselves to the effect that the CPA transformed the power relations between themselves and the rest of the Sudan. It made Southern Sudan a sovereign state in waiting, its self-determination to be exercised in a referendum in order to acquire international diplomatic recognition. This constitutional disposition was already obvious, given the formal protocol that the Kenyan government officials extended to the SPLM/A's leader, Dr. John Garang. On 9 January 2005, it now became obvious to many southerner members of the NCP who came from Khartoum with President Omer el Bashir to witness the signing and celebration of the peace deal that it was only a matter of six years and South Sudan would become an independent country.

My family had been living as asylum-seekers in East Africa. It was by no means easy as life was clouded by complex social and economic difficulties. In order to escape these difficulties, many South Sudanese opted to emigrate. However, there were many who stayed on and bravely resisted the temptation to leave for America or Australia. Personally, I considered Australia and America as places too far away from home. My idea, from the time that I joined the insurrection, was to come back and rebuild the country if I survived the war. That the peace agreement found me still alive, gave me high hopes for a return home.

By January 2005, Mama Abuk, the children, and I had lived in Kenya for nearly fifteen years. We had failed to integrate into the Kenyan society and lived there loosely as asylum-seekers. I use the term "loosely" because we had UN travel documents issued by the Kenyan government which enabled us to travel back into areas of South Sudan under the administration of the SPLM/A. These were certain weaknesses in the international system which non-state actors or asylum-seekers could easily exploit to their own advantage. The end of the war couldn't have come at a more opportune time. We really longed to return home, to be with relatives who had survived the war. In May 2004, Abuk lost her mother to hypertension in Malakal and she could not travel to attend the funeral, adding to an already heavy load of grief in the family that followed the loss of our son, Maulana Payiti, who drowned on 20 January 2000 in the YMCA swimming pool while celebrating his eleventh birthday. It is difficult to explain the urge that prompted Abuk and me to come early to Nyayo National Stadium. We were not part of the organising committee. It was a vague feeling that the time had come to leave behind everything. It seemed that every southern Sudanese present in the stadium shared this feeling. There were tears of joy in the eyes of every woman and man, as if they were experiencing a sudden relief from a big burden.

For most of the time during the five years preceding the CPA, many of us were engaged more in civil-society activism, in defence and promotion of human rights and civil liberties in the SPLM/A-administered areas. This was something that placed us at cross-purposes with the SPLM/A authorities. I was paid back for this in an awkward manner when, at the CPA signing ceremony at Nairobi's Nyayo National Stadium, an SPLM/A operative slighted me by categorically refusing to grant me the badge that would allow me to sit among the VIPs. It was a rude reminder that even my rank in the SPLA (a commander) and membership in the dysfunctional National Executive Council were of no consequence since I was seen as a negative agitator. This was a standard SPLM/A attitude towards those categorised as "opposition to the leadership." The SPLM leadership treated its detractors in a vindictive fashion. They had reduced me to the status of Abuk's spouse and I was to attend the occasion as her guest. I marked this incident as a precursor of things I must anticipate in the coming period.

Indeed, it was not because I had a short memory but changed circumstances that later led me to change my mind. After my encounter with Garang in November 1988, after I had suffered the loss of my leg and he told me flatly that he had no assignment for me, notwithstanding my right to it, nothing could have brought me back into the SPLM/A had it not been for Riek Machar's clumsiness. I had already made up my mind to join academia but changed my mind when the Nasir Declaration provided some glimpse of hope for rejuvenating, revolutionising, and democratising the SPLM/A. But all those hopes were later dashed and we were forced to swallow our pride and rejoin the mainstream SPLM/A.

Although we were accommodated in the structure of the SPLM/A, it was not an honest and fullhearted welcome back into the fold. At times we found ourselves ostracised and marginalised, especially after the death of Cdr. William Nyuon at the hands of Riek's forces in Ayod. I believe Garang did not want us back. He never forgave me for publishing *The Politics of Liberation in South Sudan* in 1997. I believe he did not take seriously my presence in the movement. He ignored my proposals and did not give me any challenging assignments. This pushed me into civil-society activism as part of my efforts to take care of my family.

With the signing of the CPA, the six-month pre-interim period to prepare the country for its implementation began. During the interim period the parties had two immediate tasks: ratification of the CPA and promulgation of the Interim National Constitution (INC) through which the country would be governed. As a second-tier SPLM/A leader and cadre with knowledge of and experience in government, I expected to be included in one of the preparatory teams. Unfortunately, this was never going to be. Like other members of the SPLM/A, I travelled to Rumbek where the SPLM's National Liberation Council (NLC), the movement's legislative organ, was to ratify the peace agreement. To my dismay but not my surprise, the acting chairperson, the late Abraham Rock, informed me bluntly that I was not an NLC member. According to him, I had attended the previous NLC meeting, held in 1997, because I was then secretary for mining in the SPLM's National Executive Council; since I no longer held the position, I would not be allowed to attend the session that would ratify the peace agreement. This meant that the SPLM/A's operative at the Nyayo National Stadium, who had denied me a seat, had not acted on his own.

The second immediate task, as noted above, was promulgation of the draft text of the constitution. Months later I learned that my name was included on the list of the individuals appointed for this task. It was typical of the tactics of the SPLM/A's military intelligence: since communication within the SPLM/A was done through radio messages, most of the time marked "Top Secret," only the officer to whom the message was addressed could divulge the information or send me word of the assignment. I was not duly informed about this assignment and my participation, whether for the ratification of the CPA or in the drafting of the Interim National Constitution, was deliberately sabotaged.

In the months of February and March I was engaged in facilitating a conflict-transformation workshop in Pochalla. After the SPLM's Upper Nile Regional Conference in Panyagor in 2003, we established the Upper Nile Peace Centre in Pochalla. Ambassador Philip Obang Ojway was the chairperson; John Luk Jok and I assisted in designing and executing projects as part-time consultants, while still managing our own small businesses at the Centre for Documentation and Advocacy (CDA) and Larjour Consultancy. Since I was not involved in the SPLM's pre-interim processes, I decided to stay almost full-time in Pochalla. There, with Ambassador Obang, I led a series of peacebuilding and conflict-transformation workshops funded by Pax Christi Netherlands. These workshops brought together the Anywaa and Murle in Pochalla; Murle and Nuer in Pibor (Likwangole); and Murle, Kachipo (Suri), and Jie in Boma.

The engagement with communities in these workshops enriched my understanding of what should be done in regards to the implementation of the CPA. At that time it was still too early for peasants and pastoral communities to envision what the NGOs called "peace dividends". The CPA was nothing but a compromise at the political level, and therefore to bring it down to the level of the communities where most of the destruction had occurred required a down-to-earth, patient process in which elders, the custodians of communities' traditional practices and customs, participated in force. In the disorder of the post-war period, there were resource-based conflicts over access to water and pastures, which were reflected in cattle rustling and the abduction of children and women. I was present when Chief Ngantho in Pochalla made a satellite telephone call to the Murle militia leader Ismail Kony, then in Khartoum; their conversation averted a violent conflict and resulted in Murle herders returning the cattle and Anywaa children and women they had stolen.

Back in Nairobi I received an invitation to travel to Neuchâtel in Switzerland to attend a workshop on the House of Nationalities. This came a little less than a week after the international donor conference on South Sudan in Oslo, Norway, to which civil society groups were invited to attend. As secretary-general of FOSCO I could not miss the Oslo meeting but had to synchronise the Oslo meeting with a meeting in Utrecht, the Netherlands, to discuss the funding of a Chollo peace and reconciliation conference in Malakal with Pax Christi Netherlands. The UNDP footed the modest bill for the civil-society delegation to travel to Oslo. Mama Abuk led the SPLM's women delegation, which had a better hospitality at the Radisson Blu Hotel, only a short walking distance from the conference centre. I decided to exploit my family relations to enjoy the comfort of the Radisson for the two days I spent in Oslo. I was to travel from there to the Netherlands to meet the people of Pax Christi.

At the Pax Christi head office in Utrecht, I managed to secure preliminary approval for the Chollo peace and reconciliation conference in Malakal. I then proceeded to Switzerland. The meeting in Neuchâtel was part of the Swiss government's project to promote federalism in South Sudan. However, since the SPLM's leadership did not countenance the concept of the House of Nationalities (HoN), the idea then was to see how the funds could be channelled into organising traditional leaders into an institution that encapsulated the concept of the HoN. While in Neuchâtel, we got the sad news that Dr. Walter Kunijwok Ayoker had died in a Nairobi hospital. He had been sick since early March. Abuk had already returned to Nairobi and therefore represented me in the delegation that accompanied Kunijwok's remains to Tonga, where he was laid to rest in Nyibodo.

After a few days in Nairobi, news came from Malakal that my mother was gravely ill. The telephone system was one of the great achievements of the Ingaz government. In a conversation with my sister, I learned that unless I reached there within three days, I might not find her alive. I desperately wanted to see my mother before she passed on. The SPLM had ordered that no bona fide member was allowed to travel to government-held towns unless he or she had written permission from the chairman and commander-in-chief. Cdr. James Hoth Mai had come to visit my sister-in-law. I asked him to inform Cdr. Kuol Manyang Juuk, the head of the SPLM's advance team to Malakal, to allow me to travel with his entourage to Malakal so I could see my mother. I don't know how the request was relayed. Cdr. Kuol thought that I wanted to come as a member of the advance team, which could only be sanctioned by Chairman Garang, so he refused. I could not make it to see my mum before she passed on. Two weeks later I received the written permission from Chairman Garang, thanks to Comrade Cdr. James Kok Ruai, who volunteered to inform the chairman about my problem. He worked with Mama Abuk on the SPLM's Peace Desk and had regular contact with the chairman. At the same time, Cdr. Oyay Deng Ajak brought me the Ugandan passport I had applied for nearly two years earlier. I travelled to Khartoum where Joseph Bol Chan received me on the tarmac and invited me to stay with his family. It was a kind of reciprocation for the treatment we had given him in Nairobi, when we hosted him and Tabitha Gwang Awok in our Magiwa rented residence. Bol and I travelled together to Malakal and put up in his government house in Mudiria. He was then the deputy governor of Upper Nile State, as well as the state's minister of education and instruction.

My mother was buried on our plot of land in Dangershopi, which had now been surveyed and turned into a huge suburb. I was able to meet all the immediate and extended family members. My Aunt Nyatieno, my mum's elder sister, had come from Anagdiar and so I was able to meet her for the first time in many years. The last time we had met was in 1963, a few months before I went to Rumbek. The one week in Malakal was so short a time that I could not meet all of the surviving relatives. I also had to make time to visit my in-laws in Surat Malakiya, including Nyachil, the younger sister of Mama Abuk, her two uncles, and their families, as well as the grave of my mother-in-law.

I made use of the time in Malakal to also visit His Majesty Rath Kwongo Dak Padiet, the Chollo sovereign, in his royal village at Alaaki in Panyidway. I raised the issue of a Chollo peace and reconciliation conference to be convened sometime in June. He gracefully agreed be the chief guest. Thus, the visit to Malakal was a success. I returned to Khartoum, from where I proceeded to Nairobi to start preparations for the conference. I had two young men working with me in the Larjour Consultancy, Acwil Odhiang Akoch and Mojwok Aba Nyawello. As soon as Pax Christi Netherlands wired the funds to Nairobi, I engaged them in the necessary preparations for the conference, scheduled for 21–25 June. In Khartoum, the office of His Majesty the Rath, as well as the Upper Nile State government, assisted in the mobilisation for attendance at the conference. In Nairobi, we recruited the SPLM's Women's Desk, Dr. Charles Yor Odhok, and Kwanyikir Abdullah Zion, who also wanted to visit his family in Malakal and join us in the mobilisation. We contracted the 748 Air Services for a return trip to Malakal. Joseph Bol Chan, the deputy governor, quickly resolved the security concerns about landing raised by the civil aviation authorities in Malakal and we flew into Malakal on 18 June to an official and popular welcome.

Ambassador Philip Obang, chairman of the Upper Nile Peace Foundation, added national clout to what was essentially a limited ethnic Chollo affair, while Edwin Ruigrok, representing Pax Christi Netherlands, Solomon Asopa Oburu, a Kenyan Luo, and Ali Kur, a Kenyan Nuba of Chollo origin, gave the delegation an international and regional configuration. Ali Kur wanted to trace his roots and, indeed, which he successfully did with the help of Rath Kwongo, prompting his decision in 2006 to return together with members of his family to Malakal. Tragically, he died in Malakal after suffering a sudden and severe diabetic attack before he could finally relocate to Sudan. As planned in advance, His Majesty Rath Kwongo arrived in Malakal on Sunday 20 June and, on the following day, opened the Chollo Peace and Reconciliation Conference in a celebratory mood.

It was unusual and indeed traditionally unacceptable that not all the Chollo leaders attended the conference sanctioned by Wad Nyikango, Rath Kwongo Dak Padiet. A group of Chollo in Yei, mostly SPLM/A officers and soldiers boycotted the conference on the flimsy grounds that they had not been involved in its organisation. I suspected that they had been influenced by Dr. Lam Akol, who felt that he should have been the one to lead the process. If factional leaders had led the process, however, it would have defeated the very purpose for holding the conference; it required neutral people to organise and manage the Chollo conference.

The Chollo people, like other ethnic communities in war-torn southern Sudan, have been fragmented as a result of the division and internecine fighting within the rank and file of SPLM/A–United, forcing Dr. Lam, its chairman and c-in-c to rejoin the SPLM/A under the leadership of Dr. John Garang de Mabior in October 2003. Cdr. Pagan Amum and Cdr. Oyay Deng Ajak, meanwhile, considered themselves national leaders and did not want to be involved with grassroots politics. My participation was a kind of forward planning. I had warned them earlier that the way the SPLM/A, and the liberation process was being run—without a clear liberation ideology and having failed to create institutions and instruments of power and public authority—would not end well.

In this confused situation, the time was bound to come when each and every person in the SPLM/A would retreat to his or her own ethnic canopy. The conference, therefore, was a means for Chollo leaders in the liberation movement to come back and get re-acquainted with their constituency in the kingdom. In fact, when it came to selecting people for appointments to constitutional positions (as in the legislative assemblies at the national (Sudan), subnational (Southern Sudan), and state levels) the SPLM/A's leaders, cadres, and bona fide members had to be referred to their home turfs.

Over four days, the conference deliberated on a number of topics, the most important of which were the divisions and in-fighting within the SPLM/A–United, which resulted loss of life and burning of villages including shrines. His Majesty Rath Kwongo rebuked Cdr. James Othow, who recruited the Nuer militia of Gabriel Gatwech Chan (Tang-ginye) in the operation against the forces of Dr. Lam Akol, holding him responsible for burning the ten shrines in Lwak (southern Chollo). He was then ordered to pay a fine of one cow and one heifer for each shrine razed to the ground. The conference drew up resolutions and recommendations, some of which required government intervention for implementation. The conference deliberations concluded successfully with a full day of colourful celebrations in Malakal stadium. We had wanted Dr. Garang to address the gathering but due to a technical failure he could not. The success of the conference was a clear indication that peace was at hand.

The following day, as scheduled, the plane arrived to take us back to Nairobi. Everyone in the team was feeling upbeat after the success of the conference. Ambassador Philip remained in Malakal, in fact, the time was already edging towards 9 July, the day that Dr. John Garang would take the constitutional oath of office as the first vice president of the Republic of Sudan. It was therefore necessary for Philip to travel to Khartoum as he had started to develop an ailment that would eventually kill him just a few weeks later. On 27 June, thanks again to the help of Cdr. James Kok Ruai, I led a delegation including Mama Abuk, Dr. Charles Yor, and Oyit-Jwok Liebo to pay a courtesy call on Dr. Garang. It was my first time to see Garang since the signing of the CPA.

I knew his unease with me but there was no way he could avoid me. James Kok had been very influential with him when it came to such public relations matters. I wanted to use the opportunity to push my agenda on community peace and reconciliation. I briefed him on the Chollo Peace and Reconciliation Conference, emphasising the need to transform the CPA into a tool that would support peace and reconciliation among communities that had been divided by the war. Chairman Garang appreciated our efforts and promised to discuss this matter after he settled down to form the GoSS. The stage was now set for the SPLM leaders to travel to Khartoum for Garang's inauguration.

Most of the SPLM leaders who had been sent for training in South Africa had started to return. Although I would have refused had I been asked to attend that training, I deeply resented having been excluded and was left with the feeling that I would not be included in the anticipated SPLM administration in Southern Sudan. There was absolute secrecy about what was going to happen. The three processes set in place by the Rumbek Conference in 2004—reorganisation of the civil administration under Riek Machar; organisation and restructuring of the SPLM as a political party under James Wani Igga; and organisation, structuring, and professionalisation of the SPLA under Salva Kiir Mayardit—had all stalled. This was partly because those assigned to lead the processes did not know where to begin, and partly because all of the leaders and cadres had been whisked off to South Africa for training.

I did not have concrete plans on what I would do as soon as I returned home, or what would happen to my family. This uncertainty preoccupied my thoughts. As a family, we had stayed together in Nairobi, except for the children whom we agreed would study for their matriculation in Uganda. Keni, Pito, Kut, and Aboui Alfred Akwoch were all sent to boarding schools in Uganda to give them some sense of independence and individual personal responsibility. By 2005, all but one of our children had finished secondary school. Keni had graduated from the United States International University

(USIU) in Nairobi with a BA in International Relations. She was already working as an intern with a humanitarian development agency operating in South Sudan when the SPLM/A's leadership included her in a team sent for training in South Africa.

Kut had finished high school in Uganda and won a scholarship, in recognition of her basketball skills, to study "A" levels at Bishop Mazzoldi Secondary School in Kampala. Pito had joined the SPLA and was now deployed with the New Sudan Brigade in Eastern Sudan. Agyedho had just joined the USIU and was studying journalism. Suzan, our youngest daughter, was in primary school. The future of Suzan and Agyedho was a great concern if we were to decide to hand over the rented house in Magiwa Estate. Abuk and I decided we would keep the house until Suzan had finished her Peace Junior Primary School in 2007, after which she would be able to join a boarding secondary school in Uganda.

As 9 July approached, everyone was busy trying to position himself to best take advantage of the changed landscape. Those in Garang's good books were assured of being given executive and legislative functions in the new dispensation. I had nothing to hope for as many of my friends in the civil society groups seemed to be distancing themselves from me. I resigned myself to returning to private life. Still hopeful that friends would support me, I started to plan an expansion of the Larjour Consultancy. In the midst of this personal uncertainty, my name was included on a list of SPLM members chosen to travel to Khartoum to attend the swearing-in of Dr. John Garang as first vice president of the republic and president of the Government of Southern Sudan. We were directed to fly to Rumbek, and from there another plane would take us to Khartoum.

On the Rumbek airstrip, it was all hustle and tussle to board the plane. It was an embarrassing scene. There were too many organisers, and others who wanted their relatives to travel. An operation that could have been dealt with in thirty minutes became three hours. I found the same disorganisation in Khartoum. It had been a long time since I'd witnessed the deliberate refusal to subscribe to organisation and order in the SPLM/A. Even as it was close to establishing a government, nothing had changed or improved in the manner SPLM/A leaders, cadres, and operatives went about executing their orders. It reminded me of the saying "too many cooks spoiled the broth."

After a long struggle I managed to get accommodation at the Green Village Hotel and was given transport. The accommodation at the Green Village Hotel was many steps better than the accommodation at Soba Aradhi, the former training camp of the mujahideen south of Khartoum, where most of the people were accommodated. As soon as they dropped us off, the organisers told us to be ready at eight-thirty the next morning to welcome Chairman and Commander-in-Chief Dr. John Garang de Mabior at the Green Square. This was about five kilometres away from Green Village.

Given that tens of thousands, mostly marginalised Sudanese, were expected to turn up to welcome Garang, I wondered whether it was really necessary for me to go there, given my physical debility. I decided to watch the events on TV in the hotel room. It turned out to be a good decision. Others from our group who went there did not even get a glimpse of the events that occurred in the square. Apart from the huge number of security personnel present, the place was thronged by Sudanese from west, east, and southern Sudan who considered the CPA a rebirth of the Sudan. Their hope was that the end of the war and Garang's presence meant that they would no longer face marginalisation or discrimination on the basis of race, religion, or culture.

The next day, Sunday 9 July, was the day on which the Sudan would never be the same again. For the second time in Sudan's history, and from a position of political and military strength, a southerner would now share power with a northerner in a collegial presidency. The first time a southerner had exercised Sudan's sovereign power was in March 1965; the Arab-dominated political elite then conspired to amend the Sudan's Transitional Constitution

1956 to render permanent what was then a rotating chair of the five-man Supreme Council of the State, making Ismail el-Azhari the president of the Sudan.

The CPA provided for a collegial presidency until 9 July 2011, when the people of southern Sudan would vote in the referendum. The organisers picked us up and drove us to the grounds of the Republican Palace. The organisation and protocol arrangements of the event were superb. Among the foreign dignitaries were IGAD heads of state and members of governments that had been mediators to the conflict and Gen. Colin Powell, the US secretary of state. Sudanese singers and artists performed during the proceedings' intervals. The most remarkable thing about this ceremony was that it lasted exactly two hours.

The swearing-in ceremony heralded the start of the six-year interim period, during which Sudan was expected to achieve two important political developments: democratic transformation of the Sudanese polity, and a decision by southern Sudanese before the end of this period to either affirm Sudan's unity based on the successful conclusion of the democratic transformation or opt for secession. It was going to be an experiment in either statesmanship or brinkmanship. Members of Sudan's political elite are notorious for "too many agreements dishonoured." To many of them, an agreement serves only one purpose: to buy time or save face, the content is not important.

This was the topic of discussion when friends came to visit me at the Green Village Hotel. They had lived in Khartoum for most of the war and I had to assure them that the CPA, unlike the Addis Ababa Agreement, was watertight and made so by the existence of the SPLA as a separate army and the wealth-sharing agreement which gave Southern Sudan fifty percent of the oil revenue. The weakness of the Addis Ababa Agreement was the absorption of the Anya-nya into the Sudan Armed Forces and that the regional government did not have a separate source of revenue.

As I was preparing to travel to Rumbek, Joseph Bol called to inform me that Ambassador Philip Obang was seriously sick and being treated at the Police Hospital in Burri, a few hundred metres from my hotel. His cancer had spread and, sadly, had become a terminal case. He was already in a coma and passed on two days later, when I was already in Rumbek. Mama Abuk had decided to travel to Nairobi and I had to call to inform her that I would be travelling to Pochalla for the burial of Philip. The office of the first vice president provided a plane to bring Philip's body to Pochalla, and 748 Air Service flew Dr. Charles Yor and me from Rumbek, courtesy of John Mark, the director of the US Agency for International Development (USAID) for South Sudan. The arrangements had been made to take the casket to Ajwara, Philip's home village about twenty kilometres from Pochalla. Ambassador Philip was given a traditional as well as state honours, courtesy of the SPLA contingent in Pochalla.

The untimely departure of Ambassador Philip Obang shocked our small organisation. Without Philip we would not have dared to establish the Upper Nile Peace and Development Foundation. He was the pillar of the people of Upper Nile, in all their different ethnic formations, and there was unbridled respect for him. With his death, staying in Pochalla became untenable for me. The local political environment was toxic and hostile, shrouded in greed and personal rivalries among the functionally illiterate leaders who paid little or no respect to His Majesty Nyie Adongo Agada. I knew it would be impossible to remain, especially during those times periods when Nyie Adongo would relocate the royal village of Utallo. I handed over the organisation's assets to the county commissioner and travelled to Nairobi. The assets were mainly office furniture, a computer, a printer, solar panels, and a power inverter. The NPA in Nairobi had borrowed the foundation's vehicle and driven it to Pagak, where a community centre was being set up for training women and youth.

I seriously considered serving the people of Upper Nile as a state governor. Indeed, I lobbied for the position. In Rumbek, a few moments before boarding my plane to Pochalla, I asked Cdr. Salva Kiir to throw his lot behind my candidature. In a seemingly unconcerned tone, he just said, "don't you know the person who appoints?" Back in Nairobi, like many other SPLM/A members who had been elbowed to the margins, I waited for whatever reports came out of Rumbek, which had become the centre of SPLM/A operations. The offices of the first vice president of the republic and the president of GoSS operated from Khartoum, Rumbek, and New Site alternatively, at Garang's convenience. Garang had appointed Cdr. Salva Kiir Mayardit as vice president of the GoSS. The SPLM adopted the NCP's ten-state bogus federal system, and appointed members of the so-called Leadership Council as caretaker governors of the ten states that now constituted southern Sudan.

It was during this time of waiting that a thunderbolt struck the country. On Saturday 30 July, Dr. John Garang de Mabior, the first vice president of the Republic of the Sudan and president of the GoSS, was reported missing. He was returning to New Site from Entebbe in Uganda, where he had paid a personal visit to President Museveni. The presidential helicopter crashed a few kilometres from New Cush, killing all on board. This tragic accident sent the Sudan on a deep-drive plunge into the political abyss, and the SPLM/A into a state of confusion akin to that which besets orphans and widows. In fact, the country had an uneasy calm, the kind of calm that precedes a deadly storm. When it became clear, on 1 August, that Garang was dead, the calm erupted into an inferno in Khartoum, Juba, Wau, Malakal, and other smaller towns in which hundreds if not thousands perished. Property was destroyed in racialised violence between South Sudanese and northerners. The SPLM's leadership made frantic efforts to bring the situation under control. Suspicion remained high that the NCP had conspired to assassinate Dr. Garang in order to sabotage the peace agreement and return the country to war. It was of course an uneasy start to the CPA implementation and everyone on all sides of the political divide held their breath lest the agreement collapse.

Notwithstanding the absence of institutionalised political relations amongst themselves, the SPLM leaders, in the so-called Leadership Council, demonstrated the usual political equanimity. During a short meeting at New Site, they confirmed Cdr. Salva Kiir Mayardit as chairman of the SPLM and commander-in-chief of the SPLA. The arrangements for the burial of Dr. John Garang proceeded without a hitch, and on 11 August Salva Kiir took the constitutional oath of office as first vice president of the Republic of the Sudan. The tragic demise of John Garang de Mabior raised more questions than answers. He definitely had enemies, some inside and others outside of the SPLM/A. In writing my memoirs, I am compelled to attempt to answer a question raised by Comrade Ponto Ferro when I met him at the Central Committee of the Communist Party of Cuba in Havana. This is because neither the SPLM nor the SPLA's Military Intelligence, nor its external intelligence organ, ever launched an investigation into the tragic incident that killed its leader and founder. The movement's establishment accepted the findings of the technical report released by the joint Sudanese–Ugandan technical committee.

Some of us agitated for an independent investigation, particularly after an outburst by Cdr. Aleu Ayieny Aleu, in which he said that President Yoweri Museveni had killed Dr. John Garang. Aleu was then deputy minister of the interior in Khartoum and a member of the joint technical committee. This matter, like many others was poorly handled. Comrade Aleu Ayieny was temporarily dismissed from the SPLM/A but later reinstated. He was appointed minister of the interior in the Republic of South Sudan in August 2013, just months before the outbreak of the new civil war, which witnessed UPDF participation in support of the SPLA against the forces of Riek Machar.

On a flight from Khartoum to Juba, sometime toward the end of 2006, I had a conversation with Philip Mabior, a former colleague at the University of Khartoum. Mabior, who was in the company of Mulana Abel Alier, co-chair of the Sudan-Uganda joint technical committee, asked my opinion about the technical report. I took him to the back of the plane, to allow us to speak without anyone hearing us. "My friend, Philip," I began, "I believe Dr. John Garang was the victim of an assassination conspiracy." I went on to explain that the conclusion about the "human error" was true. However, "human error" is something that can be engineered for strategic political or economic objectives. My theory is that President Museveni assassinated Dr. John Garang de Mabior, exploiting an opportunity when Garang travelled not as first vice president of the Republic of Sudan but as a guerrilla leader visiting Museveni, his friend and former colleague.

Finding himself in such a situation, Museveni, to my thinking, could not resist the temptation to kill his supposed friend. What he needed to do was to order his pilot, Col. Peter Nyakairu, to go on a mission of no return. Had Garang not been so full of himself and travelled to Uganda under the protection of the Sudanese state security system, Museveni wouldn't have had the opportunity to commit the crime and the Republic of South Sudan would not have become Uganda's vassal state in the region. Mabior was not convinced by my theory, so we left it at that point. I later understood that senior members of the Bor community had decided to let the matter sleep as any unravelling would never bring Garang back to life.

I was confident about my theory because I had some background information in respect to the love–hate relations between the two former Dar es Salaam University colleagues. At a certain point in time, Garang had trained some anti-Museveni elements of the Obote regime alongside the SPLA. I don't believe Museveni had forgotten, or forgiven, that episode. Comrade Deng Alor Kuol, Garang's closest lieutenant, once told me after returning from a trip to Kampala that Museveni had told him that "Dinka were stupid." I tried to tease out from Deng what that really meant, but to no avail. It could have been an unintended outburst of some bitter hidden feelings, and could have meant, "You stupid people

trained my enemies and now you are here begging me for help."
While Ustaz Ghazi Suleiman and I agreed on the theory that Garang
was indeed assassinated, he blamed this conspiracy on radicals
within the SPLM who had not wanted to engage with the NCP in
the spirit and letter of the CPA.

It did not take much time after the burial of Garang and Kiir's
ascension to the helm before the ghosts of the Yei crisis started to
hover over the SPLM. In fact, no reconciliation had been achieved at
the Rumbek Conference. The SPLM/A suffered from fundamental
structural weaknesses that nothing short of radical transformation
could resolve. Had Garang lived longer he would have exploited
the new situation to fix those problems. Gen. Salva Kiir had neither
the political skill nor the charisma needed to draw the movement's
divergent groups together.

As soon as the politics of division burrowed into the SPLM,
three factions emerged, none of which showed a clear ideological distinction. Individuals were now considered on the basis of
their ethnicity, region of origin, or personal allegiance. The faction
around the leadership of Salva Kiir Mayardit, those who supported
him during the Rumbek Conference, were mainly from the Bahr
el Ghazal subregions and loosely organised as the Bahr el Ghazal
elders. These elders were led by Dr. Justin Yaac Arop, who later
became the minister for cabinet affairs in the GoSS. This group
wielded political and economic power and determined who would
be appointed and to what position in Khartoum, Juba, and in the
states.

The second group was made up of the "small, big commanders,"
who used to wield power but had now become known as Garang's
orphans. It was not as coherent a group as the first one: competition, rivalry, short-changing, and conspiracies characterised this
group. Under the changed situation, each of them manoeuvred their
way into personal favour with Salva Kiir, usually at the expense
of a colleague. The third group comprised independent-minded,
often critical, individuals. They were mostly leftists and did not

subscribe to the ethnocentric ideologies of the political right and the traditionalists. Because I belonged to this latter group, I was ostracised and elbowed out of political participation. The former SPLM–United held sway over the four Chollo counties in the appointment of representatives. They only thought of "parking" me in the Council of States, rather than give me an appointment to the National Legislative Assembly.

Indeed, it turned out the Council of States was a parking ground where both the NCP and SPLM kept their political reserves. There was nothing challenging in the proceedings of the Council of States, particularly after the debate and approval of the justices of the Constitutional Court. The National Legislature had two sessions of three months' duration each year. Little did my detractors know that as a former Communist and a practicing Marxist, I was capable of transforming an unfavourable situation into its opposite. I was able to spend six months a year in Malakal attending to my private or public issues. Things couldn't have been any better. This gave me the opportunity to run the Larjour Consultancy, now incorporated in the Republic of Sudan as Larjour Training and Consultancy Institution and put in place my plans for the first-ever cybercafe in Malakal.

It also gave me the opportunity to organise our supporters. This began with the struggle to capture the position of speaker of the State Legislative Assembly. The Chollo members of the SPLM were clearly divided into two camps, according to whether one had been in the former SPLM/A–United or in the SPLM mainstream before their reunification in October 2003. Of the ten members hailing from the Chollo constituencies, only two—Dr. Charles Yor Odhok and Santino Ajang Aban—were SPLM. It was an uphill struggle to defeat the SPLM's nominee for the speakership, Julian Nyawello Dak. It involved instigating a rebellion in both the NCP and the SPLM to enable Dr. Charles to be elected to the speaker of the 48-member Upper Nile State Legislative Assembly. This was an open defiance to the SPLM and more particularly to the vice-president of GoSS, Dr. Riek Machar and the conspiracy he and Lam Akol hatched to have their supporters in positions of power and authority.

These two giant political leaders, in collaboration with people like Dr. Justin Yaac Arop and with the tacit support of President Salva Kiir, seemed to have neutralised and elbowed out of SPLM affairs Pagan Amum Okiech, the designated SPLM secretary-general. I discovered this when I came from Khartoum to visit my spouse, Abuk Payiti Ayik, then member of the Southern Sudan Legislative Assembly, and chair of the Specialised Committee for Social Welfare, Gender, and Child Affairs. Both Abuk and Pagan had accommodation at the tent-city called Afex, on the banks of the White Nile River.

Pagan was so frustrated with the goings-on, and even confided in me that he feared for his life and that he wanted to leave the country to visit his family in Australia. I opposed the idea of him leaving before the situation had been resolved and encouraged him to meet in Malakal for Christmas. "If in Malakal you found no support from our people, then you could decide to travel to your family in Australia," I told Pagan, and he accepted my words. In December 2005 he received a huge popular reception by the people and government of Upper Nile State courtesy of NCP Governor Dak Diop Bichok. This gave Pagan a morale boost and the confidence to stay on, despite his problems with the SPLM's leadership. In fact, the massive support he got in Malakal forced Chairman Salva Kiir to affirm Pagan's appointment as the SPLM's secretary-general.

Pagan's confirmation as secretary-general gave those of us from Makal County the strength to continue our struggle against the violations of our political rights. I write here specifically about the connivance of Riek Machar and Lam Akol in recommending the appointment of Dr. Said Morgan as commissioner of Makal County, despite the fact that Morgan came from the Dinka-Ngok country of Bailiet. We had to wait until the convening of the SPLM's County Congress to vote him out of office, first as the county's SPLM chairman. This occurred as we strategised and immediately recommended his relief as Makal County Commissioner and his replacement by Chan Alaaki Amaiker. We succeeded in all these struggles, thanks to our organisational and political skills boosted by the determination of the county youth and women who stood firm in every action we demanded of them. In fact, in this campaign, we were able to capture all the four Chollo counties' delegates to the SPLM Second National Convention, held in May 2007.

Pertinent to the question above—whether the CPA signalled the end of the SPLM/A as a revolutionary entity—is the fact that, on paper, the SPLM/A is such a huge political organisation, with its tentacles reaching the smallest of villages in South Sudan. But in reality, it scarcely existed as an organisation. The SPLM had moved to the political right since the early nineties of the last century. Unlike leftist parties, right-wing parties practice democracy, if at all, in an authoritarian manner. Leaders plan and decide while the members just endorse what the leaders have decided. In leftist political institutions, especially those that practise democratic centralism, ideally, decisions are built up from the grassroots to the summit.

In the six years that I spent in Khartoum as representative in the Council of States or as minister in the government, I cannot remember having attended a formal and minuted SPLM meeting, whether at the level of the legislature or executive, in which as party members we discussed or debated policies were executed in the executive or defended in the legislature. We were, however, formed into committees, though none of them ever had a quorum. My colleagues were never short of reasons for cancelling their attendance at meetings that we had agreed would be regularly held on a certain day in the week. In fact, many of them didn't like attending meetings. They loathed discussing issues, fearing that their lack of correct understanding of political matters would be exposed. In this way, they missed an opportunity to learn and educate themselves. I would add that membership of the SPLM was little more than a formality. My experience in the Communist Party was that one would raise hell if cell leadership did not call a meeting, or in certain instances a member must have to explain in writing why he or she had missed a meeting for it was a right, duty, or obligation to attend party meetings, as spelled out in the party's regulations.

In August 2008, I was appointed minister of higher education and scientific research in the Government of National Unity in Khartoum. Nobody in the SPLM had the courtesy of consulting my opinion as was always the case. It was assumed that I would oblige. Had I turned down the appointment, it could have been a different matter. First, the appointing authority would take offence of this and would punish me for the embarrassment I had caused. Many people will not understand this behaviour and would definitely blame or condemn me. I was also not briefed on what was expected of me in the ministry as a SPLM member. In a coalition of that nature each party would caution its ministers so as not to put the party in bad light. However, after taking the oath before the president and the first vice president, I requested to meet my chairman, Gen. Salva Kiir Mayardit, who had flown into Khartoum from Juba for the occasion. I thanked him for the appointment and wanted to know if there were any special tasks, he wanted me to carry out. Speaking with his usual informality, Kiir said, "You will find your assignment in the ministry." It was my first shock of working with Kiir as my leader. I had expected him to instruct me to transfer the universities of Juba, Bahr el Ghazal, and Upper Nile back to their locations in Southern Sudan. They had been moved to Khartoum during the war. With the war over there was no longer a reason for them to remain in Khartoum. Regardless, I moved ahead on this project, hoping that the GoSS would support me.

It had not occurred to me, nor had I at any time lobbied for a ministerial appointment; if anything, I had in 2005 wanted the position of deputy governor of Upper Nile State after the NCP captured the gubernatorial position. The news of my appointment came like a bombshell. The good thing in Khartoum was the presence of a highly professional civil service. Matters went smoothly for the federal ministers and state ministers because memos were professionally prepared. This meant that their discussions at the level of technical committees, ministerial clusters, and in the cabinet did not take much time. My real worry in the ministry had to do with administrative matters, both at the ministry headquarters and in the universities and technical colleges. Some matters were straightforward and were easy to deal with, but some required policy changes, which became no-go areas for the NCP ideologues. One sticking point arose from the NCP policy of opening up higher education to the masses – massification of higher education, which involved opening regional university and turning school edifices into university campuses. It was impossible to reconcile massification with quality higher education; they were incompatible. Given the low level of economic and technological development in the Sudan, it was impossible to have the two together without one compromising the other, but the NCP ideologues wouldn't countenance change of policy.

Another policy issue I found difficult to change because of the NCP leaders, especially Ustaz Ali Osman Mohammed Taha, who supervised the functions of the government, was what they called "domestication of knowledge." This was, essentially, translating foreign language books and knowledge into the Arabic language. This "domestication of knowledge", undertaken by the Ministry of Higher Education and Scientific Research, saw educational standards plummet. Experienced academics left the public universities, including Khartoum, Juba, Gezira and the Sudan University of Science and Technology for private universities run by the same Islamic fundamentalist who crafted, but refused to apply these policies in their universities. Some of the best Sudanese universities that hitherto used to rank high in the regional and international universities ranking systems had by 2008 completely disappeared from the lists. The backlash from this development was that for instance, the government of the United Arab Emirates refused to recognise academic papers produced at some Sudanese universities, although it was Sudanese workmanship, expertise, and knowledge gained from those same universities that had contributed to building the UAE into what it is today.

The case of the Aviation College, a private institution of higher education, was perhaps what Gen. Salva Kiir meant when he told me I would find an unfinished task in the ministry, one that had remained unresolved by my two SPLM predecessors: Dr. Peter Nyot Kok (2005–2007) and Dr. George Bureng Nyombe (2007–2008). It was essentially a quarrel within the shareholders (a family company) that affected other stakeholders; namely, the Directorate of Private and Foreign Higher Education in terms of implementation of Higher Education Act and the Licence provisions, as well as the academic programme of the college. They had a case in the courts but the elder brother (considered to have more shares) wanted to shortcut the adjudication process. This family quarrel interfered directly with the academic programme of the college and the ministry had to intervene with an independent team of managers through the Directorate of Foreign and Private Higher Education. This was a procedure designed to keep the academic programme running while isolating the trouble-shooters. Incensed by the decision of the ministry, the elder brother locked all the college gates and dismissed the police guards, which the independent team had called in to prevent arson and lawlessness.

I tried to mediate by calling the shareholders to a meeting on a Friday hoping that they would respect the religious dimension. I was met with disrespect arrogance that tended to loudly insinuate that as a southern Sudanese I had no power over the matter, even after sternly warning them of the decision the ministry was likely to take. The guy was arrogant and adamant. I was left with nothing to do but to call to session the Committee for Private and Foreign Higher Education – an important committee of the National Council for Higher Education, the policy-making body of the ministry - which endorsed my recommendation to revoke the licence of the Aviation College. This step was publicly announced. We had already secured an alternative premise to house the college, in order not to compromise the academic programmes already approved and the rights of the students to their degree and diploma courses.

Two weeks after the revocation of the licence, the governor of Khartoum State, Dr. Muta'fi, came to see me in my office. The Sudanese are good at playing such intermediatory roles. He had come to inquire if it was possible to reverse the revocation decision and what the owners needed to do for the ministry to rescind its decision of revocation. He had already been to see the family, as he was related by marriage, and had asked the mother of the boys why they had slaughtered the cow that gave them milk. Indeed, they were going to lose a lucrative business. The ministry was in a strong position, but I thought it would be unfair, in fact vindictive, to insist on the decision.

"I am ready to change decision on the following conditions," I told Muta'fi. "First, all the brothers and their mother should not be seen on the grounds of the college. Second, they should leave the administration to the ministry's team until the problem had been resolved in the courts. Third, they should go to a lawyer, a commissioner of oaths, to pledge that they will abide by the regulations of the Ministry of Higher Education and Scientific Research. They then take that document to the Ministry of Justice for authentication and endorsement, after which they should bring it to the legal counsel in the ministry." The problem with the shareholders was resolved within the following week. However, to avoid such a situation again, I introduced a change in the law to give stakeholders a say in the administration of private and foreign institutions of higher education. This put me at odds with some powerful politically connected shareholders, nevertheless, the government would always be on a stronger side and we managed to enforce the change in the law.

I can't conclude my stint at the Ministry of Higher Education and Scientific Research without relating my experience with the vice chancellors of the southern Sudan-based universities, particularly

Dr. Timothy Telar, vice chancellor of Bahr el Ghazal University, because it involved ethnic politics. When I realised that the three vice chancellors were not ready to execute the ministerial orders I had issued, I recommended, in accordance with the law, their dismissal, which the president of the republic ascended to and then had them replaced. Prof. Telar complained to first vice president Salva Kiir that his dismissal as vice chancellor of Bahr el Ghazal University was tribally motivated - a Luo conspiracy according to him. His replacement was Dr. Constantino Lual Jervase Yaac, a Luo. To his mind, the Chollo and the Luo had conspired against him, a Dinka. I may have reconsidered the matter if Salva Kiir had asked me that the relief of Telar would create political difficulties for his presidency. Instead, I received a presidential decree reappointing Dr. Telar as vice chancellor of Bahr el Ghazal University. I was so cross as to think it was a stab in the back. I did not to relay the message to Telar in a congratulatory letter as was the practice.

Two months later I was called to the Palace to meet Gen. Bakri Hassan Salih, the minister of presidential affairs After some courtesies, Bakri turned to me and said, "Minister Peter, presidential decrees are for immediate execution." "Yes, Sayyed Bakri," I responded. He continued, "Why then did you not execute the presidential order re-instating the vice chancellor of Bahr el Ghazal University?" I told Bakri, "I will never execute that order, unless the clause 'based on the recommendation of the minister, you have been appointed' is erased or the person who recommended the appointment is mentioned. Didn't I recommend the vice chancellor's removal? Who is this minister again who recommended his appointment?" Bakri knew I was right, and presidential appointments are usually revoked after an elapse of six months. "My brother, be a politician," came Bakri again. I told Gen. Bakri point-blank that there was only one way out of this situation: President Bashir sounded ask his First Vice President Salva Kiir to dismiss me and end the standoff with the Palace. In fact, I was so angry with Salva for backstabbing me that I now wanted to be relieved of that ministerial position. We ended our encounter without agreement but with the understanding that he would report to the president. I left the palace in high spirits, having stood my ground with Bakri. I was ready to accept whatever decision came from Bashir and Kiir. To my surprise, the palace instructed the National Security Bureau to take Dr. Telar to the Bahr el Ghazal University Centre.

The more Salva Kiir Mayardit entrenched his power in government and in the SPLM, surrounded by Jieng ethnic barons, the less he believed in the political and democratic processes and deeper the SPLM sank into its internal tensions. After identifying a coterie of sycophants, Kiir went for a clean break with some members of the SPLM leadership. The SPLM Second National Convention was convened specifically to dismiss Dr. Riek Machar as vice chairman and Comrade Pagan Amum as secretary-general. This became clear at the meeting of the Interim National Liberation Council, called on the eve of the convention to adopt the agenda of the convention, an agenda which had been known only to the chairman and his confidantes.

The plot was transparent to see through. It was to play out in the conventional hall as follows: propose to reduce the three vice chairs to one and Yasir Arman to nominate James Wani Igga to that position. Once Riek Machar was out as first vice chair of the SPLM, he would automatically lose his position in the executive branch of government as vice president of GoSS, which then would be filled by James Wani Igga. A similar process would involve the removal of Pagan Amum as the SPLM secretary-general, and Taban Deng Gai would be nominated to that position. All this plot was on the flimsy grounds that Salva Kiir did not want to work with both Riek Machar and Pagan Amum in the SPLM leadership. This clearly was a move towards authoritarianism, and the democrats had to oppose it at all costs. We proposed that if Salva Kiir insisted on going ahead with his scheme we would nominate Dr. Riek Machar for the chairmanship. The political tension went to a high pitch. The southern veterans Mulana Abel Alier and Gen. Joseph Lago, who Salva Kiir had smuggled into the meeting, saw sense in what we were saying and advised Kiir to back down. The SPLM Second National Convention endorsed the status quo. This was not a solution to the structural contradiction afflicting the SPLM and society in South Sudan but was a stop-gap solution in the hope that matters would become clear for all to wake up and act appropriately

The resistance to authoritarianism in the SPLM had to be maintained and indeed strengthened because Kiir had more tricks lined-up his sleeves. He managed to neutralise Riek Machar, Pagan Amum, and many others who never envisaged Kiir's intentions after his defeat in the INLC. He planned to use the midterm to rid the SPLM of his detractors. Instead of allowing the SPLM General Secretariat to meet, he created the National Elections Strategy Committee (NESC) and appointed James Wani Igga to supervise the NESC. It was indeed an internal coup against many members who were not in Kiir's good books. As a result, many contested as independent candidates and trounced the party's candidate.

The SPLM's political bureau threw the regulations and guidelines to determine who could contest on the SPLM ticket into the dustbin. It instead approved the proposal, submitted by James Wani, for an electoral college, which became a political disaster. The electoral college in Malakal rejected my application for gubernatorial position because I had not appended my birth certificate. Kiir, meanwhile, won the contest against Dr. Lam Akol, who ran on the ticket of SPLM–Democratic Change.

I bring up this example to demonstrate that the SPLM was not disposed to democracy and democratic practices. This is why, after only a short time, the country returned to war. Democracy is not an overcoat one puts on only when necessary. It is way of life, a tradition or culture inculcated over time through training, learning, and unlearning. That the SPLM was not so disposed did not come out of the blue skies: it was the consequence of the movement's early shunning of political education and organisation; it was a consequence of militarisation, the use of only weapons to prosecute the war of national liberation, without a political or ideological context. As a result, it did not produce leaders and cadres versed in political work.

On 9 July 2011, the Republic of South Sudan was formally born as the 193rd member of the United Nations group of nations and the 54th member of the African Union. The independence of South Sudan marked the end of decades of hostilities with the rest of the Sudan. But southerners were still bleeding everywhere in Warrap, Jonglei, Lakes, and Central Equatoria. Ethnic groups were in conflict with their erstwhile neighbours, with people whom they had lived peacefully for decades if not centuries. A people who fought the common enemy together had turned against one another.

What happened? This question, and many others, rings and rings loudly, yet no one can give a satisfactory answer. I believe this question points to the main reason why the SPLM signed the Comprehensive Peace Agreement. The fragility of Southern Sudan was obvious to all. Indeed, friends of the people of southern Sudan were worried that the insecurity ubiquitous throughout the states and the conflict between ethnic groups and clans could jeopardise the conduct of the referendum. But the referendum's promise of self-determination meant that no one was interested in rocking the leadership's boat, at least not until the referendum had been successfully completed.

Chapter 19

The Independence of South Sudan

Betrayal of Hopes & Expectation

Comparing the socio-political developments in South Sudan in the post-CPA and post-Addis Ababa Agreement eras, I clearly appreciate Nimeri's wisdom in appointing Mulana Abel Alier Kwai instead of Maj. Gen. Joseph Lago Yanga to head the first High Executive Council (1972–1978) of the Southern Region. Gen. Joseph Lago was president of the Southern Sudan Liberation Movement and commander of the Anya-nya Land Freedom Army, while Abel Alier headed the Sudanese delegation to the Addis Ababa peace talks. Most of the people in southern Sudan had expected Nimeri to name Gen. Lago. Nevertheless, Abel Alier became the first president of the self-governing region of the Sudan. Five years later, in 1978, when Gen. Joseph Lago took over as president of the HEC under the rubric of "wind of change," he could not sustain his leadership of the region. The legacy of bush politics still held sway over him, that he was removed from power, in part because of his political naivety.

Mulana Abel Alier was a public servant but from a background of civility, transparency, and accountability in political life and judicial service. He was secretary-general of the Southern Front party and had political experience in Sudan's second republic before the leftist putsch in 1969. Like all mortals, he had weaknesses, including the weakness to make timely decisions to correct the shortcomings of some of his lieutenants in the government and security organs. Abel Alier's inaction led to explosive ethnic and regional frictions, cleavages, and security breaches, all of which was politicised and cost him the presidency of HEC and, eventually, led to the outbreak of civil war.

Joseph Lago Yanga, meanwhile, came from a military background. He was a career military officer in the Sudanese army who became the rebel leader of a separatist movement. Joseph Lago had no experience with organised politics or civil administration. This was the hole he fell into when a group of southern Sudanese politicians, disgruntled with Abel Alier's subservience to the dictator Nimeri, thought Gen. Joseph Lago would be the tool to remove Abel Alier from power. They were counting on the general dissatisfaction within the Southern Region over lapses in the implementation of the Addis Ababa Agreement. They couldn't have been more wrong in their political calculations.

I bring up this comparison to prove a point. The current context in South Sudan appears to be history repeating itself. As Karl Marx wrote, "History repeats itself first as tragedy, second as farce." But, more succinctly, the story of a Turkish sultan captures the point to which I am driving. The sultan asked for an engineer with the qualifications and experience needed to reconstruct one of his old castles. After the engineer completed the work, the sultan summoned him and said: "When you were destroying the old building, you used one set of workers, and when you rebuilt you employed a different set of workers. Why did you do that? The engineer, in his reply, told the sultan that for destruction and construction he needed different types of people, for those specialised in destruction were not appropriate for construction. The moral of this story is that the leaders of war and destruction seldom become the leaders of peace and reconstruction of a post-war country. We are now seeing this in South Sudan.

I am not sure how things would have played out in the same way had Dr. John Garang de Mabior lived. The CPA was crafted in such a way that the SPLM would become the ruling party in South Sudan, suggesting that the way it conducted the war of national liberation and the administration of the civilian population would continue as part of its normal practice. This is the proverbial elephant in the room. That the liberation was purely military and without a political ideology was its greatest disadvantage. It inhibited the liberation from learning and unlearning, and eventually led to the phenomenal failure to separate the military from the post-war politics.

The lack of a political ideology to define the nature of the liberation struggle, and absence of institutions and instruments of public power and authority, obstructed by militarism and a cult of personality, explains the ease with which the SPLM's public power and authority shifted to the ethnic, regionally based lobby groups and business cartels as soon as its leaders had assumed state power as an ad interim arrangement before the crystallisation and emergence of the parasitic capitalist class. The widespread sense of entitlement to power and wealth—an entitlement based on having participated in the war of national liberation—blinded many SPLM leaders, cadres, and even the foot soldiers into believing that they owned the country. Their arrogant manner mirrored that of the Arab-dominated northern political elite after Sudan's independence in 1956.

But it is a hollow vanity that is unlikely to last for long. The current civil war was precipitated by a naked power grab to control state resources, ignorance of how to manage state institutions, and competition and greed for the primitive accumulation of wealth. The state has become a totalitarian dictatorship. Three years into the civil war, Kiir's dictatorship no longer sought ethnic allegiance, particularly after his break with Paul Malong Awan, a Malual Dinka from Aweil. The power and influence that the Jieng Council of Elders (JCE) wielded in the Office of the President has now shifted to a parasitic capitalist class led by NCP operatives who are well trained in the art of leader worship, flattery, boot-licking, double-crossing, and intrigues. In this process, the SPLM missed the opportunity to build a strong, economically vibrant, and politically stable state in the nascent Republic of South Sudan.

President Salva Kiir came from a military intelligence background. He left school in 1964 to join the Anya-nya and in 1972 was absorbed as a corporal into the Sudanese Armed Forces. The SPLA/M insurgency found him at the rank of a captain, suggesting that his experience was at the tactical level of the intelligence apparatus: the level of gathering, collection, and collation, rather than analysis of intelligence. This was a modest experience. He did not have an opportunity to learn and internalise advanced and sophisticated political knowledge and skills. Nor did the liberation movement provide that opportunity, even though from 1992 Salva Kiir had been the effective number two in the movement. In a situation of structural dysfunctionality as in the SPLM, there would be no political actions from which to learn, draw lessons and internalise political knowledge or understanding of issues. Moreover, Dr. Garang managed the movement as if it were self-sufficient entity that did not require any learning or unlearning.

The SPLM had no constitution, no internal regulation, and indeed no functional structures. It had no programme encapsulating its political objectives, strategies and tactics. It was Garang alone acting: issuing orders and directives, suggesting that without him nothing in the SPLM/A could move or happen. Because the SPLM/A's public authority and power rested in just one person, when Garang died in that tragic helicopter crash on 30 July 2005, the entire SPLM/A was orphaned. Nonetheless, it took over the government of the subnational entity, the GoSS, and extended its bush-era organisational dysfunctionality to its state institution. In 1966, Dumont described the post-independence era as the "false start in Africa." Indeed, the post-CPA era was a false start in Southern Sudan.

The SPLM established a government that had no programme to address either the fundamental contradictions that underpinned the war of national liberation, or to enable state formation and nation building in South Sudan. The commanders in the bush became ministers, legislators, generals, and senior bureaucrats in the government, operating without reference to anything other than their personal considerations. A senior politician told the members of the Southern Sudan Legislative Assembly, who were preparing to impeach the auditor general, "Don't waste your time talking about auditing accounts. This will be done after 2011. This is payback time. It is money to help ourselves."

Another senior member of the SPLM's Political Bureau apologised for the greed at a September 2020 ceremony to honour wounded heroes held at the army's headquarters, saying, "We should have done this a long time ago. After the war, we came in like hungry and thirsty people. We found a lot of money and we started eating and forgot about you. This was because when we got satisfied, we began to throw to our relatives, and to buy villas and castles in foreign lands. I am sorry for that." The people of South Sudan expected from their leaders in the SPLM at least provision of basic education, health, and agricultural support. They expected socioeconomic and cultural development to transform the centuries-old condition of poverty, ignorance, and superstition. But, as Cdr. Kuol Manyang, the former minister of defence and veteran affairs, said, they forgot about the people.

What happened then? Tribalism (ethnic preference when distributing favours), nepotism, and corruption thrived at a rate unprecedented before in the Sudan. Senior individuals in government called their relatives to return from the diaspora to fill positions in the civil services as director, director general, and even ministerial undersecretaries, positions for which they were not qualified. Most of these returnees from western countries—the United States, Canada, Europe, and Australia—were employed there as farm workers, street cleaners, porters, or were unemployed and surviving on welfare.

They had no knowledge of, or experience in, government bureaucracy. Ignorance of the business of government accentuated the corruption and completely destroyed the bureaucracy. This was the essence of the false start: the upstarts messed up the nascent state from the centre to the states, to the counties, payams, and bomas. South Sudan was born a fragile state not because it had emerged from the long war of national liberation but because its leaders were ignorant, arrogant, and had no concern for the population. As UN Secretary-General António Guterres said in January 2018, "I have never seen a political elite with so little interest in the well-being of its people." This was a fitting description of the SPLM/A's leaders.

The civilian population in their villages spent the six-year interim period (2005–2011) in distress and agony. The competition among the elite in Juba for power and accumulation of wealth translated into insecurity in the villages and cattle camps, particularly in Lakes, Warrap, and Jonglei. Inter- and intra-ethnic section and clan conflicts spread; the elites supplied guns and ammunition for the people to settle scores that had nothing directly to do with them. One glaring example of elite-instigated intercommunal conflict was triggered by Salva Kiir's decision to create a Dinka Padang County—Pigi—on Chollo lands east of the White Nile, between Zeraf River in the south and the White Nile–Sobat confluence in the north. Kiir took the decision after lobbying from Dinka Padang elders and Jonglei politicians. Unsurprisingly, fighting erupted in the area. Angered by the government's action, the Chollo people rejected all Chollo SPLM candidates in the mid-term elections of

2010, but they also did not vote for Salva Kiir for presidency of the GoSS.

The most critical mistake President Kiir committed, perhaps because of ignorance or a sense of entitlement, was to ignore calls for a conference of all political parties and social forces to determine the nature of the state desired by the people of South Sudan. There was enough time, between 9 January and 30 June 2011, for such a process to be carried out. It was mistakenly assumed that the regime that governed southern Sudan during the interim period regime was acceptable. But there were different political opinions: some wanted a federal system of governance; others favoured an imperial presidency; some wanted a mixed and parliamentary system; and there were those who desired a parliamentary system with an executive prime minister. President Salva Kiir ignored these opinions and even bribed Dr. Riek Machar, who initially agitated for federalism, to drop his demands and push his supporters to vote for the so-called democratically decentralised system of governance.

The tendency to marginalise, exclude, and ignore the opinions of others was evident when President Kiir ignored an important provision of the Interim Constitution of Southern Sudan 2005. This provision states that if the result of the referendum is in favour of secession, it only requires an amendment to the text, substituting "South Sudan" or the "Republic of South Sudan" for "Sudan" and "Republic of Sudan" respectively. President Kiir instead commissioned a 45-man constitution committee, dominated by three SPLM lawyers, to write a draft constitutional text: the intention was to give the president powers not contained or envisaged in the Interim Constitution. I was a member of the committee. Because I was still a minister in Khartoum, however, I rarely attended the committee's deliberations. Suffice to say that the work of the committee proceeded, my absence notwithstanding.

Once the results of the referendum came out in favour of secession, the political mood in the country changed. Many northerners had not imagined that South Sudan would secede. NCP delegates on the committee to negotiate post-referendum issues, headed by the former South African President Thabo Mbeki, were adamantly reluctant to commit themselves to any agreement. I was on the committee on the Nile waters agreements and treaties of 1929 and 1959. A certain Dr. Mufti Ali, who was my contemporary at the University of Khartoum, made it difficult to reach consensus even on treaties that disadvantaged the Sudan. He did not seem to understand or accept my point that Sudan or South Sudan should not be bound by treaties signed when Sudan was still a colonial property of the Condominium. I thought it was a waste of time, and decided not to attend these meetings; as minister of higher education and scientific research, I still had the serious problem of relocating the universities of Juba, Bahr el Ghazal, and Upper Nile to their respective places in Juba, Wau, and Malakal. Rumour had it that the NCP authorities intended to impound the assets of the southern-based universities located in Khartoum. I had warned the vice chancellors that as South Sudan prepared to conduct the referendum on self-determination, they should race with time to relocate to the south as much of the moveable assets as possible. They did not heed my words and, as a result, Upper Nile University lost the river steamers donated to them by state, and Juba University lost both the land (a huge piece of land) and moveable assets at Kadro Campus, north of Khartoum.

One day, Ustaz Ali Osman Mohammed Taha, who supervised government matters, summoned me to his office at the Council of Ministers. He was responding to a statement I had made to the northern students and academic staff of the three universities after they came to the ministry to tell me that they would never relocate to southern Sudan. The NCP had decided to create a new university to be called Bahri University. It was to be based at the University of Juba campus in Kadro and accommodate the three southern-based universities once South Sudan became independent.

Although I was a government minister, I was helpless in the face of the reckless and illegal behaviour of the NCP leaders. One such humiliating action taken by the rogue state minister in the Ministry of Cabinet Affairs, probably on the instructions of Ustaz Ali Osman Mohammed Taha, was to impound my official car before I was formally relieved as minister. I retaliated by boycotting official functions, including the session of the National Council for Higher Education and Scientific Research, until the secretary-general came pleading for me to open and close the one-day occasion: I was still the chairman of the council and regulations did not allow any other person to perform that function. Out of respect for many of my colleagues in higher education, I obliged.

Immediately, I was set to leave Khartoum and had nothing but a suitcase to take with me. I did not want to remain in Khartoum until 8 July, the end of the interim period. The writing was already on the wall and a section of the NCP had become hostile to southern secession. It was difficult to predict what might happen. Perhaps, out of desperation, they could make it difficult to travel to the south. I went to see a former colleague at the University of Khartoum, the late Engineer Bior Ajang Duot, then working with Greater Petroleum Operating Company (GPOC). I asked him to help me book a seat on the company-chartered flight to Paloich, and from there onto a helicopter to travel to Malakal. He gracefully made the necessary booking, and on 29 June I landed in Malakal.

After six years of SPLM assignments, I was not ready for another round of stress, frustration, and uncertainty. I no longer wanted to work under a political leadership that had neither principles nor morality. I did not suffer from any sense of entitlement and did not expect to continue in government service simply by virtue of having been a member of the SPLM/A. If I could, I wanted to be just an ordinary member and enjoy the rest of my life as a private citizen. In fact, while in Khartoum I had prepared myself to be a farmer. I bought a tractor and its accessories through a hire-purchase arrangement with the Agricultural Bank of the Sudan. I planned to farm a range of different crops. Instead of the traditional sorghum or sesame, I wanted to farm onions, garlic, and beans (*jangaro*), crops that are not labour intensive and not threatened by pests. Little did I know that this was not to be.

I couldn't dare miss the independence celebrations and the raising of South Sudan's flag in Juba on 9 July. But more importantly, Abuk and I had been separated for almost six years, seeing each other only during the few trips I made to Juba. I booked a flight to Juba and for five days we were again together as a family. Our three children were involved in the celebrations: Keni and Agyedho were in protocol, receiving and seating guests, while Pito, now a helicopter pilot with the Air Force, was on the ground directing helicopters for the flyover at the celebration grounds next to Garang's mausoleum, later named Dr. John Garang's Memorial Park. The seats meant for members of the Legislative Assembly had already been occupied by guests, but we managed to get space on the empty stairs. We watched the presidents, prime ministers, diplomats, and other dignitaries as they took their seats. The place was full to the brim.

The 9th of July was above all an emotional day for the South Sudanese people and their friends in the region and in the international community. It would not be a figment of my imagination, nor a wilful exaggeration, to say that nearly all South Sudanese shed tears of joy when the flag of Sudan was lowered, and the new flag of South Sudan was raised. President Salva Kiir told President Omar el Bahir that the Sudanese flag would remain in Juba as part of the South Sudan archives. The common history between the two Sudan's has yet to be researched and recorded as honestly as possible. The day ended without incident.

As we waited for the car to take us home to Hai Malakal, the lyrics of a Louis Armstrong song— "The easy part is over, the difficult part remains: staying alone"— kept interfering with my thoughts. Indeed, the question of what would happen engaged our evening. We would wake up in the morning as citizens of an independent country—the newest in the world. But there were clouds on the horizon. The imposition of a wrong draft constitutional transitional constitution on the dissenting members of Southern Sudan Legislative Assembly had precluded a national consensus on the system of governance. This occurred because President Kiir promised to retain Dr. Riek Machar as his vice president prompting him and his Nuer supporters to desert the 'federation' group thus allowing the 'decentralisation' text to sail through. The independence of South Sudan felt somehow like an anti-climax after the twenty-one-year war of national liberation.

Many people in Equatoria and parts of Upper Nile were bitter that a bad system has been imposed without allowing more debate in the chambers or in the society. Some regretted having voted for independence in the referendum. It was not difficult to discern what underpinned this negativity. During the interim period, power had been distributed according to ethnic demographic weight. This was a system that ingrained inequality. An attitude echoing. "We were the ones who died in the war" started to emerge mouthed by even very senior members and was strengthened, as mentioned earlier, by the bringing of people from particular communities back from the diaspora to take positions in government.

In this configuration, the Dinka were the dominant ethnic group followed immediately by the Nuer; for the third party, the rest of the nationalities were lumped together as "Equatorians". This followed the logic that Salva Kiir (a Dinka) was the president, Dr. Riek Machar (a Nuer) was vice president, and James Wani Igga (an Equatorian) was the speaker, and there was even a suggestion that this arrangement be made permanent. It therefore took quite a while for the government to be formed. Those who had mismanaged the subnational entity during the interim period continued to make mistakes.

One such error was the printing of a South Sudan currency and banknotes before most of the post-referendum issues had been settled amicably with the Sudan. When Bank of South Sudan printed its own currency, the billions in Sudanese pounds, banknotes and metal coins, circulating in South Sudan lost their value because immediately Khartoum rejected the idea of buying them back. If South Sudan had not printed its own currency, the banknotes belonging to the Bank of the Sudan would still have value, even after South Sudan became independent. South Sudan lost billions of dollars in the process. The currency decision was a show of not only political immaturity but also ignorance of economics.

One of my former colleagues in the Government of National Unity, the state minister in the office of the first vice president in Khartoum, Joseph Lual Acuil, must have told President Kiir about the mistreatment meted out to South Sudanese ministers and state ministers in our last few weeks in Khartoum. This infuriated the president and he ordered that each of us be paid a SSP150,000 (then equivalent to US$60,000) gratuity and given one of the latest-model Toyota Land cruisers that had been used for transporting guests during the independence celebrations. There couldn't have been a more valuable gift for some of us who had been receiving peanuts in Khartoum. In fact, Abuk and I put this money and her gratuity from the Legislative Assembly together to build a house in Hai Jebel, Juba, in which we still reside. The decision to build this house came as a result of pressure from our land lord to vacate the house and the refusal of Salva Kiir to release to me the ministerial house occupied by relatives of a minister who had died five years earlier. In hindsight, I don't know how we could have managed had we not made that decision.

When the first independence government of the Republic of South Sudan was formed in September 2011, I was appointed minister of higher education, science, and technology. I was about to decline the appointment. First, I had my own plans and did not want to be in the government. Second, I had not been consulted: they assumed that I would eagerly accept any appointment. Abuk advised me against making an enemy of Salva Kiir, saying that he would not appreciate my reasons for declining his offer and would likely take offence. I accepted her advice and went to take the oath of office. The GoSS had, in fact, established a Ministry for Higher Education, Science, and Technology in 2010, after the midterm elections. The mandate of higher education was then still the responsibility of the national government in Khartoum, which meant that the ministry in Juba functioned without a legal framework.

Since there was no government policy paper for the new born republic of South Sudan, I had to race with time to make a policy statement to the Council of Ministers outlining the objectives of the ministry, which foremost was about achieving quality higher education, technological innovation, and promotion of science, technology, and mathematics (STEM). This required a legal framework. I requested that the cabinet approved the draft Higher Education Bill we had submitted to the Ministry of Justice for legal framing. The Higher Education Act would provide for the establishment of the National Council for Higher Education as the policy making entity within the ministry. The Council of Ministers approved my policy statement-cum programme, made the necessary improvements and presented it to the Legislative Assembly in December 2011. Six months later, in June 2012, the president of the republic signed into law the Higher Education Act, and immediately approved the National Council for Higher Education. Through this law, I closed down all thirty-six bogus universities, owned by some powerful individuals in government and the army, that had mushroomed in South Sudan.

My intention was to turn the public universities into self-administering, self-funding democratic entities with little or no government interference or funding after the successful implementation of the fifteen-year strategic plan (2012–2027). The objective of the plan was to transform the five public universities of Juba, Bahr el Ghazal, Upper Nile, Rumbek, and Dr. John Garang into world-class campuses. The idea underpinning this plan was that higher education has become a lucrative business worldwide, meaning that the universities could become self-financing if the government provided funds for developing the physical, technical, academic, and administrative infrastructure. In this respect, we presented a budget of US $2.5 billion over a period of ten years. In fact, the whole higher education plan was intended to abolish the ministry and instead promote the National Council for Higher Education, headed by its secretary-general, who would be the link to the government and other state institutions.

But, as they say, old habits don't die. It was fascinating that the SPLM/A's subculture of intrigues, untruths, disinformation, double-crossing, blocking, competition, and prejudices in the bush still persisted and had become even more pronounced six years after the war's end, that colleagues in the same party and government work to undermine and fail each other. Many of us who had been deployed in the executive and legislative organs of government in Khartoum did not have an opportunity to witness or experience it first-hand. Back in Juba and at independence, it was impossible to take anything at face value. I witnessed members of the same political party—the ruling party—undermining themselves to the point that comrades enjoyed seeing a colleague in government fail. I still remember hearing the raised voices that bitterly opposed the plans I presented as my programme to the cabinet. I wondered how people in the same government could be at such cross-purposes. This must explain why South Sudan has remained a fragile state; ministers presented cabinet memoranda of which their undersecretaries or senior officials in the ministry had no prior knowledge, having employed foreign consultants to do the job.

I received a communication from the Office of the President. The letter, signed by a junior officer, requested me to travel to Kampala, Uganda, to officiate at a student function. My undersecretary had no knowledge of the matter. I called the minister in the Office of the President to ask how a junior officer could write directly another minister as to even give me an assignment. He apologised and asked me to forget about it. On private investigation, I discovered that a large part of the higher education budget without our knowledge or agreement had been diverted to the Office of the President to fund the education of students hailing mainly from Warrap in Uganda and Kenya - enrolment of students from the president's home turf—Warrap State—in universities and secondary schools, primary schools, and even kindergartens. Only President Salva Kiir could answer my questions but meeting him was impossible. In fact, for just under the two years I was in government I found it impossible to get an appointment for official or personal matters with President Kiir. I got so depressed and frustrated that at a certain point I wanted to resign, but again my wife restrained me warning against taking that action.

I was the happiest person on earth when President Salva Kiir dismissed the entire cabinet on 23 July 2013. It was a blessing in disguise: I had been saved the trouble of resigning and becoming an SPLM outcast. It was during the peak of a dispute that had been simmering for some time between Chairman Salva Kiir, Deputy Chairman Dr. Riek Machar, and Secretary-General Pagan Amum Okiech. But President Kiir's dismissal of the entire cabinet, including his deputy, seemed to close all avenues for political consultation and discourses as the SPLM did not have a tradition of democratic dialogue or consensus building. Indeed, Kiir had been mobilising for a military confrontation with the support of a JCE-built private army—known as Dotku Beny—and on 15 December 2013 war erupted. At the time of writing these lines, more than seven years later, South Sudan has spiralled down the drain, sliding from fragility to the total collapse of state institutions.

The subtitle of this chapter— "What, Really, was the Point?" — refers to the long bitter struggle for the independence of South Sudan in which more than three million perished and the current reality in the country. The Republic of South Sudan evolved on our watch—all of us, whether or not one did or didn't participate in the war of liberation—into a country ruled by a totalitarian dictatorship. At its apex is a close-knit cartel of relatives, business associates, and a coterie of political patrons. The system is buttressed by a ruthless security apparatus, the Presidential Guard, a toothless Legislative Assembly, a dysfunctional judiciary, and a corrupt and ineffective police and civil service.

There is no "standing army," as is normally found in a nation state. The SPLA and the tribal militias absorbed into it have disappeared into the civilian population. They are involved in the informal market in Juba and other towns, or in the charcoal-production industry, destroying forests and the environment. Many of them cannot say when they last received their salaries. Their commanders own the water tankers that criss-cross Juba all day, driven by Ethiopian and Eritreans. In some areas of Juba, a town which until 2006 had water running in its pipes, the price of a two-hundred-litre plastic barrel is around SSP1,000.

Agriculture, the mainstay of South Sudan's economy, both livestock and crop sectors, remains subsistence in nature. Even where there may be surplus production, particularly food crops like maize, sorghum, cassava, millet, and fruits, the lack of good roads makes access to the markets difficult. South Sudan therefore depends entirely on its oil revenue, and because of bad economic policies has turned the US dollar into a commodity traded in the official as well as parallel (black) market. Traditional food-producing areas in central Equatoria have been destabilised and people scattered by war and insecurity. In Upper Nile, there is mechanised sorghum and sesame production, but it is difficult to bring this food southwards to Juba due to insecurity on the White Nile.

As a result, Juba and other towns have become markets for agricultural produce from Kenya and Uganda. Ugandan businesswomen control the food and vegetable markets in Konyo -Konyo and Sherikat in Gumbo, while Dar Furis control of the market for foodstuffs flown or trucked in from Khartoum. Somalis run the market for fuel and building materials, including steel rods, cement, and corrugated iron sheets. Kenyans are found in banking and air transport. Lebanese, Ethiopians, and Eritreans are in catering and hotels. What, then, do the South Sudanese do? That is not a difficult question to answer: they are employed in government but hardly work. You would find many of them, including those with no business in government, lingering at the Ministry of Finance and Planning, carrying bogus claim papers for services that may not have been delivered. One day, while passing near the Ministry of Finance, my friend Maker and I met a young man carrying a document. Maker told me it was a claim for US$2million coming from one of the states in Bahr el Ghazal.

The young man did not appear like someone who could handle that amount of money. Indeed, he received the money, and three days later he looked much the same. Nothing had changed for him, suggesting that he was just a middleman. The false claim belonged to a senior person who did not want to be seen queuing at the Ministry of Finance. The many ordinary South Sudanese in Juba and other towns, including those in the UNMISS protection of civilian camps, spend their days hustling around, running tea and food kiosks, or sitting idle under neem trees, gossiping, rumour-mongering, complaining, or playing dominoes and cards. Those in the villages rear their animals, which they will never sell, preferring to ask their kin in government to provide for their needs. In this way, corruption spreads through the communities.

Since September 2018, South Sudan has been in a transition to peace and normalcy, but peace in South Sudan is as elusive as a mirage. After resigning from the SPLM/A–IO, I charted my own way to the country and arrived in Juba in November 2018. I had believed that implementation of the Revitalised Agreement on the Resolution of the Conflict in South Sudan would proceed without obstruction. I planned to return to Watajwok to rebuild my life. I still had enough physical and intellectual energy to do something for myself. Peter Orat Ador and I travelled to Khartoum to sound out His Majesty Rath Kwongo Dak Padiet about the revitalised peace agreement. We thought it was an opportunity for the Chollo people, displaced by war and living under difficult conditions in the Sudan, to return to their villages and rebuild their lives. Rath Kwongo Dak accepted our intervention, and left Khartoum to relocate to Pachodo. However, the process of helping the refugees to relocate to South Sudan, we had hoped for, did not materialise; someone none other than president Salva Kiir developed cold feet. And, therefore, the process flopped.

Attempts to fix an appointment with President Kiir came to nothing and we gave up. This setback for Peter Orat and me suggested two possibilities: either President Kiir had listened to and endorsed Padang Dinka demands that the Chollo not be allowed to return to their villages, or he had duped us because of his apparent reluctance to share power with Riek Machar. The idea of five vice presidents was something unprecedented and anomalous. That Salva Kiir could in 2018 accept the ARCSS with five vice presidents, when he in 2015 had rejected ARCISS with only Riek Machar alone as the vice president, cast doubts on Kiir's genuine acceptance of peace in South Sudan.

I really feel bitter about all of this. In retrospect, my disappointment shows that I had not carefully considered all aspects of the matter when Salva Kiir and I met in December 2018 to discuss the idea of travelling to meet Wad Nyikango in Khartoum. First, I seemed to have forgotten or chosen to ignore Kiir's motives for igniting the civil war in 2013. Kiir had paralysed the political and democratic processes in the SPLM to avoid convening the SPLM's Third National Convention in 2013. This would then ensure that the presidential and general elections would not be held, as scheduled, in 2015. Kiir was not sure of being returned as president of the republic. That Kiir desires unaccountable power has not changed. His rule is now a totalitarian dictatorship whereby he governs by presidential decrees and orders, and does not see anything beyond this horizon.

Second, I naively believed that Kiir had forgiven me for joining Riek's rebellion and for sneaking out of the country in 2014 in breach of security protocols. Third, Kiir resents organised systems like that of the Chollo Kingdom. At the same time, the kingdom has only a small role nationally, thus Kiir half-heartedly entrusted it to me. I should not have expected Kiir to behave in an honourable way. But bitterness against a situation does not resolve the problem. It is like crying over spilled milk. Resigning oneself to become a passive spectator in this revolutionary situation is a crime and against human fraternity.

Returning to the issue I raised earlier, there was a point, indeed an important point, in joining the armed struggle: to achieve the vision and concept of New Sudan. Notwithstanding the deficiencies of the revolution's leadership, which became more acute after 2005, it was and remains a revolution that must be taken to its logical conclusion. The SPLM/A was a phase in the revolutionary process; it did not live up to its mandate due to objective factors, including the weakness of the forces and because they were not politically organised.

Cultural underdevelopment meant that ethnic sensibilities and ideologies were more powerful than the national liberation agenda, and therefore distorted the revolutionary trajectory of the national liberation movement that culminated in the independence of South Sudan in 2011. It was a historical mistake, indeed, opportunism, that led the SPLM's leadership to pursue the independence of South Sudan rather than the democratic transformation of the Sudan. This is proven by the continued and persistent struggle of the Ngok people of Abyei, the Nuba, and the Funj. It is also proven by the phenomenal failure of state formation and nation-building projects in South Sudan, which plays out as insecurity, which is now ubiquitous throughout the country, including communal conflicts, corruption in government, and the collapse of state institutions.

The SPLM/A is an example of armed struggle conducted outside a political or ideological context. In addition to the massive destruction of life and property, the war also produced an elitist (political, military, and business) class whose socioeconomic and political interests do not resonate with those of the masses of the people it purports to represent. This applies also to the faction which broke rank in 2013, later to be known as the SPLM/A–In Opposition

(SPLM/A–IO), to lead an insurgency. Its leaders later negotiated their way back into a position of power in the very system they blamed for the massacre of innocent Nuer in Juba. When SPLM/A member Gen. Taban Deng Gai failed to be given the petroleum portfolio, he cut a deal with Salva Kiir and Paul Malong Awan to drive Riek Machar out of Juba, and then took over Riek's position as first vice president.

The independence of South Sudan brought on its wings the betrayal of people's expectations for social and economic development; for peace, social harmony, and cohesion; and the rule of law and enjoyment of civic rights and freedoms. Many South Sudanese, particularly those who participated in the war of national liberation, have been bewildered and indeed perplexed by the turn of events. They did not expect President Kiir to provide such irresponsible leadership, which has led to systemic dysfunction and obfuscation. There is now an unprecedented degree of inequality in the distribution of power and wealth in favour of individuals from his home turf. The country is sinking and people outside the wealth orbit fear they will die of hunger rather than Covid–19, and therefore breach medical and WHO procedures and guidelines, risking infection to look for food. One day, as I sat chatting with a group of legislators under the tree in the NLA's compound another honourable member of the Legislative Assembly complained that he had not eaten for three days. Before any of us could say anything, he collapsed and upon reaching the hospital he was pronounced dead. If a lawmaker can perish in such a manner, what will be the fate of the ordinary folks? The situation has choked many people to the point of apathy.

In January 2017, Dr. Riek Machar, chairman and commander-in-chief of the SPLA–IO, was put under house arrest in South Africa, with guards restraining his daily movements. Despite no sign that he would be released, Riek insisted on leading the opposition from his place of detention. I was of the opinion that a committee comprising members of the political bureau and the military council should manage affairs. Dr. Riek would not hear of this and dismissed it as an attempted coup against his leadership. I decided to travel from Nairobi to Khartoum, and from there to the Chollo Kingdom. Forces under Cdr. Johnson Thubo (Olony) Dak, a militia by the name of Agwalek, were in control there as part of the SPLM/A–IO. My objective was to see for myself if the Agwalek, the only organised unit of the SPLM/A–IO forces, was capable of continuing the struggle. Gen. Johnson Thubo was just a warlord, however, serving the interests of Sudan's military intelligence, which provide him with armaments. In a clever way, he had used the Chollo land dispute with the Padang Dinka to build a fortune for himself. He resented educated people and liked to boast that he had a doctorate in the military. To my dismay, I quickly saw that Agwalek was not a military force. I came back disappointed and this perhaps accelerated my decision to call it quits with the SPLM/A–IO. But the deciding factor was Riek Machar's insistence that he could lead the movement from his incarceration in South Africa.

President Kiir, Riek Machar, and the opposition groups would appear to be implementing the Revitalised Agreement on the Resolution of the Conflict in South Sudan (R–ARCSS), albeit in a very reluctant and slow manner. The hidden secret seems to be that they have no intention of implementing important provisions, including security arrangements leading to the unification of forces, the establishment of a hybrid court for South Sudan, and writing a permanent constitution. Kiir was in no mood for any changes that would disturb the power configuration and his authority to issue presidential decrees.

Meanwhile, Riek was content with being the first vice president as long as he was not returned to house arrest in South Africa. All the other opposition leaders had no qualms about their continued participation in what had become an unrealised peace. In fact, many of them were grateful that the IGAD mediation had included them in the talks. The betrayal of people's hopes and expectations is likely to continue as the trend has been to leave things as they are until the transitional period expires, making its extension inevitable because the R–ARCSS will not have been fully implemented.

This gave credibility to the hold-out groups, organised under the South Sudan Opposition Movements Alliance (SSOMA), who rejected the R–ARCSS on the grounds that it did not address the fundamental issues underpinning the war. Agwalek in the Chollo Kingdom, whose political objectives are not clearly spelled out, split from the SPLA–IO and created another dynamic in the area. In parts of Central Equatoria, the National Salvation Front/Army (NAS) sporadically engaged in combat with the South Sudan People's Defence Forces (SSPDF), as well as the SPLA–IO, keeping the area in a state of insecurity and forestalling peace. Unable to rebuild their lives in the villages, many people had been displaced to Juba where acute economic difficulties made their lives miserable. The acute economic crisis, exacerbated by the corona virus pandemic, makes it imperative that the peace agreement is implemented. I made the move to quit the SPLM/A–IO and to come back home to participate in peace-building and, indeed, I took practical steps to achieve it by engaging with the Chollo Kingdom. There will be setbacks in these efforts but in the end, peace will prevail in South Sudan. Peace is imperative as it creates conditions conducive for social and economic development and qualitative change in the lives of the people. This helps raise their level of social awareness and political consciousness. A conscious and critical mass is difficult to ensnare and betray, or fragment on the basis of ethnicity or region.

The independence of South Sudan was the culmination of relentless struggle for freedom, justice, fraternity and prosperity. However, the struggle for power and control of state resources among the political, military, and business elites was transferred to their communities. People who were once good and peaceful neighbours started to battle it out among themselves along ethnic and clan lines. A people who fought the common enemy together had turned against one another. What happened? This answer to this question points to the character of the SPLM/A and its leadership. As Amilcar Cabral has written:

> *[No] matter how high the degree of revolutionary consciousness of the sector of the petty bourgeoisie called on to fulfil this historical function, it cannot free itself from one objective of reality: the petty bourgeoisie, as a service class (that is to say that a class not directly involved in the process of production) does not possess the economic base to guarantee the taking over of power. This means that in order to truly fulfil the role in the national liberation struggle, the revolutionary petty bourgeoisie must be capable of committing suicide as a class in order to be reborn as revolutionary workers, completely identified with the deepest aspirations of the people to which they belong.[1]*

The SPLM's leaders remained true to their class character. Since 2005, they have implemented liberal economic policies dictated by the Bretton Woods Institutions. The result is that the policies have pauperised the masses and rendered South Sudan economically speaking a vassal state of its neighbouring countries of Kenya, Uganda and Sudan. South Sudan is a country and a people whose economic strength could have been in the development of all sectors of agriculture and its industrialisation has been run down by ignorant and visionless leaders to the extent that the country must import food from its neighbours. It is heart-breaking that when the Juba-Nimule Road closes down for whatever reasons, or Kenyan and Uganda truck drivers go on strike and would not drive their trucks beyond Nimule in protests against the killing of their

---

1 "The Weapon of Theory," an address delivered to the first Tricontinental Conference of the Peoples of Asia, Africa, and Latin America, held in Havana in January 1966.

colleagues by bandits, whoever they are, food and fuel prices hick in Juba and other towns. Everything has an end. It is now beginning to dawn on many people, especially those who blindly supported the regime, and are beginning to realise that their leaders have betrayed them. This betrayal has different forms and dimensions.

South Sudan started off almost better than many sub-Sahara African countries in terms of its economic and financial resources. Between 2005 and 2011, the South Sudanese economy received something in the range of US$600 million each month. It was huge money, and the small economy could not absorb it. The result was unprecedented losses due to corruption. The SPLM/A political and military elite stole the money and failed to provide economic development or social service in health and education. Instead, these leaders sent their children and relatives to schools in Uganda and Kenya, even down to the level of kindergarten, and sought medical attention in hospitals in Kenya, Uganda, and further afield, in India, Germany, Thailand and the United Kingdom.

In a half-hearted response to the outcry against official corruption, President Kiir wrote a letter to the seventy-five former and (then) present officials to return the money they may have taken. For the whole of the interim period, I was in Khartoum and therefore had no connection with the corruption in Juba, yet I received that letter addressed to me personally. I thought it was a tailing-cutting exercise ostensibly make it very difficult, if not impossible, to catch the actual thieves. President Salva Kiir knew of the dura saga which cost GoSS more than US$ 4 billion and the many exponentially over-priced government contracts that his business associates took and did not deliver.

The other area of betrayal was in the failure to implement certain provisions of the comprehensive peace agreement. The CPA and the interim constitution of Southern Sudan, also transplanted to the states' constitution, provided for reconciliation and national healing to mitigate the consequences of the war and the inter- and intracommunal conflicts that resulted from the political splits and internecine fighting within the SPLA's factions. This was a necessary condition for social harmony and coherence, and to enable the people to benefit from peace dividends. The SPLM, like the NCP, ignored the importance of community peace and failed to implement this constitutional provision. The result was that in most instances the inter- and intracommunal conflicts were rekindled, stoked by the competition and power struggle among the political and military elite. This elite supplied small arms and light weapons to their home communities, creating ethnic or sectional lobby groups that sought political patronage.

The worst betrayal took place in 2014, when the SPLM's power and public authority shifted from the general secretariat through the office of its chairman to the Jieng Council of Elders, and the formation of the presidential militia known as Dotku Beny. This militia was complementary to the Presidential Guards, often referred to as the Tiger Battalion and mostly composed of men from President Kiir's home turf of Gogrial. This was in the context of a parochial project to promote an ethnicised ideology that would support Jieng hegemony and domination and establish a Jieng state in South Sudan. That Salva Kiir accepted this madness was the height of betrayal of the people of South Sudan, including the Dinka people who did own up to this nonsense.

It was obvious from the very beginning that the idea of a Dinka state in South Sudan could not survive for more than three years. It was an idea peddled by some backward and illiterate individuals in 2012, and had no scientific basis. It may be traced back to the crisis within the SPLM/A in 2004 which has been misrepresented as a problem between Dr. John Garang and his deputy, Cdr. Salva Kiir. There was no way of resolving that contradiction without addressing the structural weaknesses in the SPLM/A. Dr. Garang died in a tragic helicopter crash before that issue had been addressed. When the SPLM/A took power in 2005, there were already two competing camps: the camp comprising what was called Garang's orphans and the camp around Salva Kiir, mostly made up of Bahr el Ghazal elders. Garang's orphans eventually lost out and the Bahr el Ghazal elders won, later transforming themselves into the Jieng Council of Elders (JCE).

As I mentioned above, the idea of Jieng state, arising from the Dinka ethnic ideology of hegemony and domination, is bound to fail because it is peddled by people who are socioculturally backward and control no means of production. The use of Dinka ethnicity was in fact a strategy to allow the emergence of a parasitic capitalist class that has benefited from state resources in the name of the Dinka people. This class is made up of the SPLM/A's political, military, and security elite that led the war on national liberation, their business associates and relatives, elements of the merchant class that ran the war economy in the garrisoned towns, and NCP operatives. The parasitic capitalist class has installed a totalitarian dictatorship buttressed by a brutal and repressive national security apparatus modelled on the NCP's national intelligence and security organisation, which protected Beshir and his regime.

The betrayal, therefore, plays out through the promotion of economic policies that have heightened inequalities in society. The silver lining of this growing polarisation engendered by primitive accumulation of wealth on one side and pauperisation and impoverishment on the other side will definitely be the emergence of only two tribes: the haves and the haves not. This would rid the society of secondary contradictions and the masses of the people would focus their attention on those who through extraction and plunder have looted the resources of the country. This would be the genuine basis for a sustainable revolutionary change in the republic of South Sudan – Halleluiah!

Chapter 20

Whither I Stand, Between Chollo & South Sudan

My Life's Main Purpose

*I*dentity is a central theme of a person's life, and an individual may have several identities by which he or she is known or identified. Identity may be biological, social, professional, and also could, in certain circumstances, define one's character, which speaks to a combination of traits and qualities distinguishing the nature of a person. What I have tried to understand about myself is whether or not identity and character are synonymous. If they are not, how does this dichotomy play out in the context of freedom, justice, and fraternity? These were the categories I had set up myself to achieve and live by in all my life.

I ask this question as part of an attempt to define my life's purpose, which I believe must be something inborn and engrained in one's psyche. It plays out externally in attitudes and behaviours, and gives meaning to certain moral claims. It is an intrinsic part, if not all, of one's character. In writing this autobiography, I am aware that the reader may want to dig out more to discover the kind of person I am or was, to reveal my life's main purpose. But that has not been my raison d'être. In all honesty, it never occurred to me that I would one day write something that concerned me or my life.

Over the course of my life, I acquired many different identities. One such identity—as a writer—took me to some high places which I wouldn't have dreamed of. As a Noma Award winner for publishing in Africa (1998), I travelled in February 1999 to Maputo, Mozambique, to receive the award from President Joachim Chicano. I was given a Japanese flag, noting the award's Japanese origins, and a cheque for ten thousand dollars. I doubt that if I had not ventured in the SPLA, where the loss of a limb forced me to become a student of society; had I remained a geologist, for which I trained as a profession, writing a text to be published by an African Publisher, this winning of the Noma award could have occurred. Another identity was as a member of the SPLM/A. This enabled my appointment as representative of Upper Nile State at the Council of States in the national legislature, and as minister of higher education and scientific research in the Government of National Unity in Khartoum. This would have been impossible had I been an ordinary Chollo peasant in Watajwok, which also would have been my other identity as a citizen had my father not sent me to school. These experiences tell me that if one could, one would engineer one's identity either consciously or as an unintended consequence of one's interaction with society.

In 1993, while in Kenya, I met the Swiss anthropologist Dr. Conradin Perner (Kwacakworo), who was then an employee of the International Committee of the Red Cross (ICRC). He was working with the young SPLA soldiers, popularly known then as the Red Army or Al-Jeish al-Ahmar in Arabic. I don't exactly remember the circumstances of how we met but I believe it was in the Kakuma refugee camp, where these small soldiers were settled after their evacuation from Pochalla. Simon Mori Didumo and I were working for the humanitarian department of the SPLM/A–Nasir faction, and we had gone to Kakuma to settle a dispute between the different factions, which led to the partition of the camp. Kwacakworo taught me a lesson in sociology; why the Nilotics in general don't have an equivalent of 'thank you'. It is not that they don't appreciate the good done, but that it has no meaning if one was expected to reciprocate for that good thing in one way or the other.

Simon Mori knew Kwacakworo well. He had obtained his doctorate in anthropology studying the Anywaa people, and was staying with Mori's maternal uncle, Nyie Agada Akwai Chaam in Utallo, the royal village. Kwacakworo and I eventually became friends, a friendship we upgraded to an intellectual and cultural association that saw the publication of a booklet titled "The House of Nationalities: A Space to Preserve the Unity and Diversity of the People of South Sudan." Through this project, I was able to visit him in his home city of Davos, Switzerland.

Kwacakworo never liked my political writings and constantly pestered me to write folklore and stories from my village. When he realised that I was not interested in folklore, he shifted to suggesting I write something about my life. "It would be useful. Your children and grandchildren will remember you not because of the political books you have written, but for the story you tell about yourself," he would say. The idea of writing an autobiography appealed to me but I kept putting it off, making false promises that I would start as soon as the opportunity availed itself. The last time I met him was in Juba, in January 2020, after an elapse of almost twelve years. I was surprised that he still harboured the same sentiments. Napoleon Adok, a mutual friend, and I were talking about my recent publication. "All these political books you have written are useless," Kwacakworo said, interrupting us. To placate him, I promised him that he would soon see the first draft of the book.

It was about the time that the Corona virus pandemic was under way, killing some of my colleagues in Juba. The possibility of becoming a victim of Covid–19 started to dawn on me. I started to take seriously the words that Kwacakworo had repeatedly told me. Writing my autobiography is essentially an attempt to selectively narrate what I have done in my active life. It would not be possible to remember everything in the order that events unfolded. But I believe I could share some of my life experiences, and define the principles and social values that guided me as I moved through society, beginning from village life in Kwogo and Watajwok, through to my studies at Dolieb Hill, Atar, Rumbek, and the University of Khartoum, and to my workplace in Port Sudan and Juba University, as well as my political life in the Communist Party of the Sudan, and in the SPLM/A during the war of national liberation and after the comprehensive peace agreement.

These were chapters in my life, including things I was obliged to perform by virtue of societal demands or I did out of my own volition. The border line between societal obligations and one's own volition could be blurred to the point that it does not exist, merging the two sides into each other in the same way we see clouds in the sky change in their shape and colour. In this context, I would agree with my friend Kwacakworo that memories of certain people and great events in our lives, some of them despicable, must be kept alive in books, films, soundtracks, and now videos. In oral societies like Chollo village life, songs and folktales store these memories. Life, in general, is a unidirectional superhighway on which people are continuously arriving (being born) and passing on (dying), and no one has ever come back to relate his or her life experience. We do it while we are still experiencing this life.

In the words of an Arab poet, whose name has eluded me for quite some time now, "How will those who come after us know that we have gone this way if we don't leave our footprints?" This suggests that the footprints I leave on society's sand, in terms of academic or professional achievements and actions in society, would be my life's purpose, translating into how in my active life in society I dealt with certain categories of concepts like freedom, justice, and fraternity; and social values like integrity, dignity, valour, kindness, honesty, cruelty, and greed; and certain political principles like patriotism, democracy, civic and political freedoms, responsibility, accountability, criticism, and self-criticism. This presupposes three different levels at which I have interacted with life processes; namely, the personal, social, and political levels.

The *personal level* entails dealing with the immediate and intimate environment—family (parents, siblings, wife, and children), the clan (great-uncles and great-aunts, uncles and aunts and their children), and Chollo ethnicity (Chollo royalty and loyalty, village, *podho* or province, and the kingdom)—which overlaps with the social level. This relationship and level of interaction begins with life itself at birth and ends with death. It is of course simple but can also be complex, underpinned by a code of conduct that changes according to one's age and gender. The code of conduct demands personal integrity, dignity, honesty, responsibility, selflessness, fraternity, valour and bravery, and loyalty to the Rath. Integrity and dignity become synonymous in respect to the rights of the elderly and particularly women. As a child I was taught what I could or couldn't do in public.

Someone might ask what happened when I found myself at odds with these values. The Chollo justice system is retributive rather than punitive. In some cases of homicide, however, both clans (that of the murderer and that of the victim) have to report the crime to Pachodo, and the culprit may lose his liberty and become an open-air prisoner in Pachodo. I call it open-air prison because there are no guards. The strength of tradition and the possibility of collective punishment of the clan by the sovereign restrains the person from escaping from Pachodo – some heartless people do exactly that escaping to northern Sudan (podhi-bwonyo) and the hatchet falls on the clan or the whole village in terms of cattle fines or labour in Pachodo.

In my hamlet, I was considered to have committed a misdemeanour by befriending Prince Kwongo. But instead of punishing me, it was my father who took the verbal battering from his peers and elders. While rearing goats, sheep, calves, and cows, I was expected to exercise a degree of responsibility to protect them and to prevent them from destroying other people's crops. I would be punished in the form of lashing or a beating if I failed in that responsibility. If substantial damage had occurred, my father would be expected to compensate the owner of the crops destroyed.

The *social level* of interaction, I would say, began at about twelve years of age, when I came into contact with persons outside my hamlet of Watajwok village, Chollo ethnicity (or race, for that matter), and geographical area (Upper Nile Province). This occurred in the cattle camp and educational institutions like Atar Intermediate School, where I encountered for the first time members of other ethnicities in Upper Nile: Nuer, Dinka, Anywaa; in Rumbek, where I encountered virtually all southern Sudan ethnicities; and Khartoum University, which represented the whole of Sudan. In all of these situations, principles of freedom, justice, and fraternity, and such values as integrity, dignity, kindness, honesty, and valour kicked in and come into play in my relations and interactions. In the school and in the wider society, I was obliged to act positively towards what was considered the necessary public convenience or common interest. Never at any point in time did I act in contravention of the will of my colleagues, so as not to become a blackleg. The main concern was about building a likeable image of myself. The elements of my character and social identity evolved and began to stick.

At the *political level* interaction occurs at a certain level of political consciousness, although there were times when I acted or took part in actions which I did not know were political. The Sunday strike of 1960 was a political action but I doubt if I was ever conscious of it as a political action. The same could be said of the failed expedition with the Anya-nya to the Congo, although my motives were more about chasing education than becoming a rebel. Support for the Southern Front was a more emotional feelings driven not by knowledge and understanding but by mob sentiments, which I wouldn't countenance being different and separate from my peers, this pushed me to participate in political activities like the demonstration against the promulgation of the Islamic Constitution in 1967/8. I would say that it was only in the final years of secondary school that I was introduced to some right-wing political teachings mixed with Christian indoctrination.

It was in the Communist Party of the Sudan that my political thinking matured. I would say that if I hadn't been a Communist, I would not have joined the war of national liberation, and I would not have twice joined Riek Machar in his adventurous endeavours to reach the top echelon of power in South Sudan. These choices were not taken because the Communist Party endorsed my decisions but because I responded to my scientific knowledge and evaluation of the situation; from the party's standpoint, I was seen as undisciplined and rebellious. I was not the first to act in this way. My contemporary at the University of Khartoum, the late Ustaz el Khatim Adlan, left the party almost for almost the same reasons. In fact, at the political level, particularly when comrades engage in sterile debates or discourse that reference practices that have proved unworkable, I believe personal considerations must be taken into account to forestall a split and to keep unity of purpose. Currently, I am not connected to any faction of the political left partly due to stifling of democracy nevertheless when it comes to major national challenges, I am open to compromise and cooperation but on matters on which fundamentally we don't differ. This means that political opinions based on personal considerations are important and should never be overlooked.

I have discussed the issues of identity and character and therefore would like to project the two categories onto the positions I took on ethnic, regional, and national issues in South Sudan, at least to find justification for whatever position I took as fulfilling my life's purpose. With the tragic death of Dr. John Garang, the SPLM began to politically wobble in its internal relations, not to mention its relations with the NCP and other political parties. The difficulty was that, more often than not, these divisive issues were discussed in small, closed circles of friends and confidantes; any decisions reached were communicated to the general meeting for endorsement. It was invariably the wrong way to manage public affairs.

In 2007, almost two years into the implementation of the comprehensive peace agreement, there were serious disagreements in the Government of National Unity, which necessitated a meeting between the NCP and the SPLM to evaluate the progress of CPA's implementation in order to clear the hurdles and improve the working relations between the two partners. The SPLM–NCP meeting took place against a backdrop of a serious political crisis in the SPLM leadership. The crisis was between the "Garang orphans"— Pagan Amum, Deng Alor Kuol, and Kuol Manyang Juuk—and the Bahr el Ghazal elders. The elders included Dr. Justin Yac, Dominic Dim, Telar Ring, and Aleu Ayieny (plus Dr. Lam Akol Ajawin and John Luk); this was before the creation of the Jieng Council of Elders. Kiir resolved the crisis tactically by appearing to side with the Garang orphans, which led to a reshuffle of SPLM ministers in December 2007 to accommodate them in those portfolios vacated with the shuffling out of government: Lam Akol (cabinet minister for foreign affairs), Timothy Tot (state minister for trade and industry), Aleu Ayieny Aleu (state minister of interior), and Telar Deng (state minister in the presidency). It was a game of shifting chairs for Malik Agar, Kosti Manibe, George Bureng Nyombe, and others.

I did not see anything in this NCP - SPLM get together, save to smokescreen the plot to shuffle out of the cabinet, Dr. Lam Akol as minister of foreign affairs portfolio on the grounds that he was implementing the NCP's agenda in the ministry. This of course was an extension of the division within the SPLM since 2005 that fitted Justin Yaac, Arthur Akuen, John Luk and others against the so-called Garang orphans. Deng Alor was appointed minister of foreign affairs and there was an immediate negative change in the performance of the Ministry of Foreign Affairs. In fact, Dr. Lam Akol had been ranked as the best Arab foreign minister by President Omar el Bashir. This was perhaps what infuriated the Garang orphans, triggering the intrigue and forgetting that the president of the republic directed the foreign policy of the Sudan, not Dr. Lam Akol.

In fact, his purported political crime could be said of all the SPLM ministers, who invariably implemented policies laid down by the NCP. The SPLM had no policies which its ministers could implement. After I took the oath of office as minister of higher education and scientific research in September 2008, Gen. Salva Kiir told me in no uncertain terms that I would find what to do in the ministry. In fact, the SPLM had no input on the policies the Government of National Unity. Kiir's words to me suggested that the SPLM had no blue print of its own not only for the Ministry of Higher Education but for the whole GoNU. As earlier noted, the SPLM, as a party, lacked policy and guidelines on which to operate. The issue of relocating southern Sudanese universities now based in the north required a policy decision at the level of the SPLM Political Bureau; this was what I had expected Salva would tell me when he appointed me to the position. Inevitably, when I used my own discretion to make changes, I ran into trouble with NCP hardliners.

I would say that Salva Kiir's leadership of the SPLM and South Sudan, flanked by the so-called Bahr el Ghazal elders, exacerbated the schisms within the SPLM. His inability to make decisions or take decisive action against misdemeanours in the party and government led to the widening of the gap between Garang's orphans and Kiir's loyalists. This paralysed the SPLM, preventing it from performing its political functions, both in the Government of National Unity and GoSS. The split and eventual eruption of violence in 2013 may be attributed to this style of leadership, which relies not on formal and open communication between members of the same party but on gossip and intelligence gathering. The NCP exploited this weakness to burrow deep and widen the cleavages within the SPLM.

On 9 January 2009, members of the Government of National Unity and the Government of Southern Sudan gathered in Malakal to celebrate the third anniversary of the CPA. Just as the ceremony was about to commence, a security breach occurred. The Chollo and Padang Dinka cultural troupes began violently skirmishing over who should lead the procession. This was the first time in the history of Malakal that ethnic squabble occurred over such an event. In the past, the surrounding Chollo villages of Watajwok, Obwaa, and Makal had provided the entertainment at such celebrations.

That night, following the event, while President Bashir, First Vice President Salva Kiir, and Vice President of the GoSS Dr. Riek Machar were in the town attending others events in the CPA celebration, Padang Dinka soldiers of the SPLA, police, wildlife, and civil defence razed two Chollo villages: Anagdiar, on the Sobat River, and Abelnimo, north of Malakal. This crime, in which lives were lost, has not been investigated to date. The Chollo people including their sovereign, Rath Kwongo Dak are still awaiting government's explanation of the incident.

In April, three months later, President of GoSS Gen. Salva Kiir Mayardit, at the head of a huge delegation, came to Malakal, the capital of Upper Nile, for a conference of reconciliation of two Padang Dinka sections, the Paweny and Luach. The two sections had been feuding over the location of their county. The two sections, however, do not belong to Upper Nile but to Jonglei State. In reality, this reconciliation conference should have been held in Bor, the capital of Jonglei State. To add insult to injury reflecting nothing but ethnic arrogance, Kiir decreed Pijo, a boma of Panyikango County in the Chollo Kingdom located at the confluence of the White Nile and Sobat rivers, as the county and declared its capital under the administration of Jonglei State.

The Chollo people, including the Rath, made no public comment about Kiir's position. Indeed, they failed to digest that the president of the country was instigating conflict rather than peace and social harmony between people who had lived peacefully as neighbours for centuries. When no explanation was forthcoming from the government, the Chollo took the law into their own hands to avenge the killings in Abelnimo. In June, they assassinated Thon Wai, the paramount chief of the Dongjol, in an attack on the village that avoided harming his family. Perhaps it was intended to be a message to the authorities and those who had earlier burned down and killed people in Abelnimo.

In November, Johnson Thubo led an insurrection at Pijo, killing the designated county commissioner. This county commissioner, a man by the name of Othethi, was of mixed ethnicity. His murder escalated the conflict in the area until it linked up with the civil war in 2014. Notwithstanding the GoSS' lack of policy, and the provocations against the Chollo in Pijo, Anagdiar, Abelnimo, and other areas, I was one of the people who opposed the insurrection. This was on the grounds that the NCP could easily exploit the insurrection to prevent the holding of the South Sudan referendum. Many Chollo people, blinded by Kiir's callousness, refused to consider our reasons. We were already considered traitors to the Chollo cause for taking positions in the government (I was then an SPLM minister in Khartoum). In the general and presidential elections of April 2010, Chollo residents made their feelings known by rejecting all the Chollo SPLM candidates in favour of candidates from the SPLM–Democratic Change, which had split from the SPLM and established itself as a separate party in 2009.

It was on 23 July 2013 that President Salva Kiir finally jettisoned all principles of democratic governance in the SPLM. Of course, it could be said the SPLM, from its inception in 1983, had never followed democratic principles. The only difference between Garang's leadership and that of Kiir, although both hail from Dinka ethnicity, lay in the coterie of associates or confidantes in the circle around each of them. While Garang operated with lieutenants drawn from all the ethnicities of South Sudan, Salva Kiir was surrounded by his mainly Dinka elders and clan chiefs, essentially from Warrap and Aweil states in Bahr el Ghazal.

By unceremoniously dismissing his deputy, Dr. Riek Machar, and the entire cabinet, Kiir sent the message that he was ready for a showdown. The SPLM internal contradictions simmered quietly at the summit while the base remained silent. The confrontation quickly spread and turned violent, moving along consequent to ethnic or clan lines rather than any notions of ideology. Many of my former colleagues in that now-defunct cabinet were bitter. They complained against the president and challenged his decision. Because they were members of the SPLM, they were entitled to retain their positions in government. However, as I earlier argued, appointment to and, disappointment from, the cabinet was a presidential prerogative. In this respect, entitlement to a ministerial portfolio solely on the basis of being an SPLM member was not a strong case. What should have concerned bona fide members was whether or not the SPLM was in the driver's seat and its policies being implemented in the interest of the people of South Sudan.

These political developments came against a backdrop of paralysis in the party and state institutions. Kiir had deliberately engineered this paralysis over a period of six months in collaboration with the Jieng Council of Elders (JCE), which had now expanded from its original composition of Bahr el Ghazal Dinka elders to include the Padang and Bor Dinka sections. With the help of James Wani Igga, the president rendered toothless the South Sudan Legislative Assembly, reducing it to a rubber stamp for all his decisions. In collaboration with Chief Justice Chan Reech, a member of the JCE and chairman of the Aguok community, Salva Kiir emasculated the judiciary.

The SPLA and the other security organs had already been corrupted by their respective generals; efforts to transform them into professionals had failed. Thus, in the absence of strong oversight institutions and a standing army imbued with national symbols and military doctrine, Salva Kiir was able to recruit a private army, Dotku Beny, which he deployed to massacre innocent Nuer in Juba between 15 and 18 December 2013, which triggered the civil war. This was the lowest point Kiir's presidency has descended in the eight years since he had assumed leadership of the SPLM.

Sometimes human instincts can be more powerful than ideological or political considerations. The sight of the corpses of innocent Nuer on the streets of Juba overwhelmed me. I renewed my communication with Riek Machar on the grounds that this was an opportunity to undertake what the SPLM/A had failed to do in the twenty-one-year war of national liberation. However, we did not need physical fighting to achieve that. My idea was to close down the oil fields to deny Salva Kiir resources for prosecuting the war, with the assistance of President Museveni. Without money from the oil, Salva would have no means to pursue a military solution, something which he had planned for a long time.

In this situation, Riek would withdraw to the countryside and isolate it completely from the urban centres; mobilise, enlighten, and organise the masses into productive units in their villages; establish an administration based on principles of justice (equality and equity), freedom, and solidarity in areas under the control of the opposition; and defend it against any incursion by government troops. I advised Riek not to engage Kiir in peace talks and particularly not under the aegis of IGAD, which through Uganda was a party in the war. Riek never demonstrated a commitment to the ideas I raised, and soon sent a delegation to the IGAD-mediated peace talks in Addis Ababa.

Liberal peace-making favours the incumbent government—in this case, the aggressor—and invariably maintains the status quo, while the rebels are absorbed into the system through the rubrics of power-sharing. Riek Machar spoke of reforms to the system while we spoke of transforming the system. This was the difference between Riek Machar and those of us in the SPLM/A–IO who favoured a radical transformation of the contradictions that afflict the people of South Sudan.

"Too many agreements dishonoured" was the conclusion Mulana Abel Alier Kwai came to after Nimeri's abrogation of the Addis Ababa Agreement. Liberal peace agreements end up being dishonoured after serving their purpose: saving face and making time while engineering other policies. President Kiir dishonoured the Agreement on the Resolution of the Conflict in South Sudan (ARCISS) just thirty-five days after signing it on 26 August 2015 when he decreed the executive order that established twenty-eight states. The agreement finally collapsed on 10 July 2016, when the SPLA launched a full-scale offensive, using tanks and helicopter gunships, against Riek Machar as a follow-up to the skirmishes at the Republican Palace, known as J–1, on 8 July.

The SPLM/A–IO became divorced from all theory, from all rational synthesis. Riek's cynicism could only be matched by his colleagues' scepticism of his ability to deliver on either his political ambitions or people's wider aspirations. Riek had a poorly concealed sense of superiority. When he dealt with comrades, he often used threats of excommunication, ultimatums, and insults rather than engaging in political discussions. To paraphrase Debray, the terrorism of political impotence sought to avenge the political impotence of terrorism. It therefore became impossible to continue in the same organisation with Riek Machar as the leader. I called it quits and decided to return to Juba to pursue my private life, unhinged to any political party or organisation. I didn't want to re-join the SPLM from which I resigned in June 2014 just before sneaking out of the country to join the SPLM/A in opposition. I only met and interacted with Salva Kiir in his capacity as president of the republic and with others only on social basis.

But after many years of political activism, it was not easy for me to avoid public discourses no matter their content and ideological orientation. As Einstein once said, life is like riding a bicycle, to keep your balance you must keep moving. It may appear that

I would only quit political activism on death. The Ebony Center, an intellectual thinktank run by South Sudan Economic Society, managed an online platform called Development Program Forum. On this platform, South Sudanese intellectuals, professionals and their foreign friends discussed all kinds of issues on South Sudan. Dr. Lual Acuek Deng moderated the forum, and wouldn't countenance any discussion of a national democratic revolution as an alternative to the prevailing neoliberal economic system pursued by the government of South Sudan. It was possible to discuss politics rationally with many on the forum who readily resort to insults and name calling. I ended my participation in the forum.

My conscience remains troubled that I find myself helpless and can't do anything in the midst of enormous human suffering in South Sudan and Juba in particular, where the contradictions stare one in the face. The situation in Juba is such that everyone is suspicious of each other. In the absence of minimal trust and confidence between people, there is little or indeed nothing they could do collectively whether it is in their common interest or not. Sometimes I do ask myself whether or not I have reached the end of my road at the age of seventy-six with still enough physical and intellectual energy. What was the meaning of the struggle if in the end one has to fend only for himself? One day while exercising my limbs I came across a former SPLA combatant. We had trained together in the Sonke Battalion in Bonga, western Ethiopia. He wanted assistance from me. He could not believe it when I told him that my children and I were financially dependent on my wife, a member of the Legislative Assembly, which had not paid the members for eight months.

"Is this what we sacrificed for, Adwok? he asked me. I told him no, but we must admit our mistakes in what is going on. Admitting mistakes corresponds to what in Marxist literature is called criticism and self-criticism. It occurs at, and reflects, a very high level of social awareness and political consciousness. In this respect, only a few people have recognised and accepted their part in the damage that has been done. I count myself one of these people. Throughout my life I have not been afraid of admitting my role in certain events, even though it may have resulted in beatings and other serious punishments. I grew up conscious of my role to do what is good and desirable and would follow the steps required.

The only time something forced me to lie was when I decided to spend the night in Adodo, a few kilometres from my home in Watajwok. I left Atar in the morning and by sunset was in the last village of Adodo. I could even see the first hamlet of Watajwok, but I pretended I was tired and could not go any further. Without shame, I told the people gathered around a fire in the middle of the hamlet that I was headed to another destination, to a place called Lul, forgetting that one or two of them could have known me. What really scared me were the stories of wild animals, said to rush to the river through the gap between Adodo and Watajwok at that particular time of the day and in the early morning as they return to their abode in the forest. I did not want to be caught up in it. I could negotiate the journey in the morning. For my hamlet, it was considered an embarrassment that I would choose to spend the night in Adodo.

Nurturing, cultivating, and doing the right thing—things that conform to the fundamental human principles of good and morality, whether for myself or desired by the wider society, including taking part in life-risking endeavours like the war of national liberation—remain what I consider my life's main purpose. I grew up ever ready to sacrifice, to volunteer, and contribute to the public good. I have committed my life to noble causes that linked the Chollo people with all the other nationalities of South Sudan; something that glorified Chollo. Now, as an emancipated intellectual, I don't consider cultural differences as a dividing line between these peoples: culture, like ethnicity, is mutable.

I consider the *malakiya,* the social group which emerged in urban centres in South Sudan as a result of the mixing of cultures, as a more progressive culture that must be promoted. I despise and reject the notion that considers the *malakiya* less than the ethnicity from which the individuals originated. I believe that ethnicity in South Sudan has endured partly because of absence of socioeco-nomic and cultural development and partly because the SPLM/A prosecuted the war of national liberation outside its ideological and nation-building context. National liberation has an inbuilt ideol-ogy of uniting the people. That the SPLM/A's leadership failed to inculcate and nurture the notion of a cultural melting pot was its worst omission. This allowed the most backward and reactionary social forces to thrive and capture the state and push the people back into their ethnic cocoons, making it difficult, if not impossible, for progressive forces to emerge.

Yes, we have contributed to the liberation of the country, and many people make reference to this contribution. But between me and the rural village I was raised in, there is not much of a story; after my initiation into adulthood, I no longer had time for the village. In July 2005, as we drove back to Pochalla from Ajwara, where we had laid to rest the remains of Ambassador Philip Obang, the scene we left behind struck me like a thunderbolt: a lone grave under a solitary neem tree, without so much as a hut nearby. It looked familiar but it felt strange to realise that many of us—the elites who served the state, whether Sudan or South Sudan—end up in villages that have no experience of the state. The thought of what I could do for Watajwok village, which neither the state in the Sudan nor South Sudan had done anything to elevate, occupied my thoughts in Pochalla and Nairobi.

It was a duty, a right, as well as an honour to serve the country. Some of us who were beneficiaries of the welfare state have a duty to pay back for the education we got through the agency of the state. It would be a measure of patriotism to serve in different capacities and in different locations in and outside the country. Sometimes the demands of government job don't allow one to visit the village, or one may develop a distaste for the village and therefore spend one's holidays in the city. Nevertheless, relatives would still insist on bringing your remains to be buried in the ancestral home. This is what happened with both Obang and Mori: they were buried in the home they had not seen in decades.

I saw this phenomenon in Kenya, where I stayed as a refugee for fifteen years. Every weekend people would be transporting the remains of their loved ones to their ancestral homes. I knew that I wanted to do something for my village before my bones were put in the ground. The issue of the socioeconomic development of Watajwok had engaged my thoughts for some time. When opportunity presented itself during the Chollo peace and reconciliation conference we conducted in Malakal in June 2005, I started sounding out the sons and daughters of Watajwok on the need to plan for the village now that there was peace in the country.

However, I soon discovered that the war-engendered dependency syndrome was not confined to the SPLM-administered areas. It was also prevalent in government-controlled towns, including the capital Khartoum, where many people were involved in the informal sector of the economy. Their expectation that "somebody" would augment their meagre resources was overstretched out of all cultural proportion. They also wanted only short-term solutions to their problems. This definitely clashed with my thoughts about transforming the reality of socioeconomic underdevelopment and cultural backwardness that has submerged many of our people. It required me to be present, on the spot in the village, in order to push my ideas. Many of the older generation who would have supported me have sadly perished from natural and other causes.

The parasitic capitalist class at the helm of power in South Sudan will not provide any meaningful socioeconomic development paradigm for the country, least of all to peripheral areas like Watajwok. It will therefore require the efforts of its sons and daughters to take up the issue of developing the area's natural resource potential in agriculture (crops and livestock) aquaculture, business (trade and commerce), and cottage industries with the express goal of creating wealth for the people of Watajwok.

The area of Watajwok, encompassing the hamlets of Kwogo, Adhikong, Dot, Adáng, Olelo, and Pakoy, covers about four hundred square kilometres. It extends from the border of Southern Kordofan in the Sudan in the west, to the dividing line separating Watajwok from Konam in the east. This is a large area and resources therein are common assets, with the whole population being stakeholders in these resources. This means that the development paradigm would be different from the system whereby land is divided or subdivided into small family holdings, as in Uganda or Kenya. We have the advantage that land is communally owned or held in trust of the people by Wad Nyikango.

The idea, therefore, would be to organise the population into a cooperative society in which all these resource potentials become their collective shares valued in monetary terms. It is assumed that all the people will accept the idea, given that these resources are commonly owned and no single person or group of individuals could separate themselves from the rest. The cooperative society could be organised either on the basis of individual households or hamlets, depending on whichever is appropriate for the best management. It is envisioned that the cooperative society would continue to exist through successive generations of the people of Watajwok, and therefore would respond accordingly to the country's changing socioeconomic and socio-political conditions.

What I am now engaged in thinking aloud, as a contribution to the development of this concept, is to sound out and mobilise as many sons and daughters of Watajwok as possible to accept the idea that Watajwok, as an entity in the Chollo Kingdom, could create a development path that allows its people, without prejudice to Rath Kwongo or any other neighbouring villager, to benefit from the resources available in its territory. The next step in the process would be to invoke legal instruments and establish institutions to implement the concept and make it a reality. In this way, I would feel satisfied that I fulfilled my obligations to the people of Watajwok, which in a sense would mean I had achieved my life's purpose.

Postscript

The Southern Progressives & the Struggle
for National Liberation in South Sudan

$\mathcal{I}$n my self-evaluation, I feel that in life I traversed different social, cultural, ideological, and political terrains, though with nothing much to show or to speak of. One of these terrains was the group known as the Southern Progressives. I think it's necessary to say something about it before exiting the stage, and nowhere would it be more appropriately said than in my autobiography. Whatever has occurred, I am still a revolutionary democrat, a Marxist, and therefore nothing hinders me from being truthful and credible when I speak of my social and political experience. Revolutionary life is indeed complex, loaded with powerful messages of episodes, ideas, and relations when unceremoniously ended as though of no consequence, remains embedded in the memories of those who witnessed the actions and relations constructed in the course of the struggle.

This is my humble attempt to celebrate the lives of comrades in arms and struggle: Edward Lino Abyei, Amon Mon Wantok, and George Maker Benjamin, who respectively left a year, four month, and two months ago as of today, 14 June 2021. Glory and honour to their memory. Long live their memory. Their passing in succession of each other over a period of less than a year was ironic but affirms that historical selection, unlike biological selection, fails to ensure the survival of the politically and ideologically fittest.

The manner the six of us came to know each other in 1972 was by chance. George Maker had just been released from Kober Prison, after his arrest in Wau for taking part in a demonstration that called for the head of Nimeri on 22 July 1971. Edward Lino had been in the Democrat Front since joining the University of Khartoum in 1967. The events of July 1971 were so searing as to put my sympathies with the Communists. I had just started to read Marxist literature, on the recommendation of a northern Sudanese student leader I met while on a train travelling to Port Sudan.

I believe it was not the strength of ideology but the wider emotions, sentiments, and reactions to the events in the just-established Southern Region that must have pushed us together. Atakdit Mawien, Karlo Kiir Deng, and Edward Lino Abyei (all law students), Bol Kolok Manjing (biology), George Maker Benjamin (political science), and myself (geology) established the Southern Progressives as a student activist group within the African Nationalist Front (a southern Sudanese student organisation) at the University of Khartoum.

It would be presumptuous to say that we Southern Progressives knew the direction where we headed, suffice only to say we were left-leaning in our thoughts and had great enthusiasm for taking part in political activism. I must admit I was then still green, in both ideological and political terms, but I wanted to learn. The Southern Progressives established, owned, and published a wall-paper, *The Alternative*, in the students' standing club. The wall-paper published scientific analysis and features on the political situation in the then Southern Region. It attracted the attention of political leaders in Juba, as well as elements of the national security organ in Khartoum.

As a result of our activities, Edward Lino later found it difficult to get employment with the regional government. Our student activism ended when we graduated from the university. Atakdit joined the judiciary and Karlo joined the Attorney General's Chambers, both in Khartoum. George Maker took a position in the Ministry of Information in Juba, while Edward Lino and Bol Kolok taught at Rumbek Secondary School. It was easy for them to link up and continue with political activism in the Southern Region. As for me, my profession took me to the Red Sea region, into a different ideological and a political zone outside the Southern Region's politics, where I joined the Communist Party and began a deep learning experience.

The Southern Region, during the eleven years of its existence within the political realm of the Sudan, was nothing but a subset of the May totalitarian dictatorship. However, the southern petit bourgeois organised their politics through clandestine parties (Southern Front and SANU), albeit within the Sudan Socialist Union (SSU), the only legal party in the country. In 1978, a group of politicians rallied behind Joseph Lago in an effort to wrest the presidency of the High Executive Council from Abel Alier, and they succeeded. Amid Nimeri's constant and unprovoked interference in the political and democratic processes, the removal of Abel Alier transformed the Southern Region's political dynamics.

A few days ago, in a ceremony to mark the fortieth day since George Maker's passing – what they these days call the prayers for the soul of a departed relative - someone who was not part of our group at the university recounted how the Southern Progressives were the founders of the National Action Movement (NAM), and that they had approached Capt. John Garang to lead the resistance to the regime. I had heard this story from Joseph Bol Chan in 1980, when I was in Budapest, Hungary. The names of such leaders as Benjamin Bol Akok, Malath Joseph, Matthew Obur Ayang, and Sir el Khatim Makuen Anai were mentioned. I did not hear any of the names of my colleagues, which is why I took the story of recruiting John Garang with a pinch of salt.

Benjamin Bol Akok and Malath Joseph were later assassinated by the SPLA, possibly on the orders of Dr. John Garang. If the story that NAM leaders approached Dr. Garang to lead an insurrection was to be believed, then it was a repeat of the mistake made by liberal democrats that put Joseph Lago at the helm of power in the Southern Region in 1978. It couldn't have been anything but political naivety, the work of novices who were poorly organised and had no commitment to a defined political ideology.

When I returned to Juba in 1982, I did not get first-hand information about any relationships between my former colleagues, members of the Southern Progressives, and the NAM leadership. In fact, NAM was no longer in the political lexicon of that time, dominated by politics of division and unity of Southern Region. It would appear, like in any political situation that brings together people of different ideological hues, that this cooperation was intended to create political space for collective struggle. Most of my colleagues were civil servants who could not play politics in the open, therefore NAM was the creation of liberal politicians but solicited the support of leftist ideologues.

I would say that when Edward Lino, George Maker, and myself, as elements of the Southern Progressives, regrouped in Khartoum in 1984, it was in another context of joining the war of national liberation spearheaded by the SPLM/A. Edward was then a member of its clandestine cell. George Maker was coming from Wau and travelling to Cairo, Egypt, and would travel from there to Addis Ababa. I had come from Juba. None of us ever again spoke of the Southern Progressives and although we knew that each of us had links with the Communist Party. Nevertheless, we spoke highly of the SPLM/A and in the context of southern Sudan but not as an element in Sudanese national politics.

Of the six of us, George Maker was the first to become a *bona fide* member and combatant in the SPLM/A. There he met Alfred Lado-Gore, Amon Mon Wantok, Marco Machiec Chol, Daniel Abudhok, Mayom Kuoc Malek, Kok Apollo, Chol Deng Alaak,

Deng Alor Kuol, and a few others who had formed a ring of progressive (revolutionary) officers around Dr. John Garang. The idea was to protect the revolution by forming a closely knit group that spoke to itself, rather than propagating the ideology among the masses. This soon translated into discord as the members spied on each on each other and engaged in backbiting and double-crossing. Under the pressure of reactionary forces in the leadership, the group disbanded. I was the second after George Maker to report to the SPLM/A, and found no trace of the group. Nor would Maker tell me what had happened. However, from Amon Mon Wantok, who was the area commander in Itang, I could gather some pieces or glimpses of the situation. When I met Maker in Addis Ababa, he warned me to be careful about whom I spoke with.

Edward Lino finally arrived at the SPLM/A general headquarters in 1987, after it became difficult for him to continue his clandestine activities under the democratically elected regime of Sadiq el Mahdi. It was not possible to revisit our former political outfit, the Southern Progressives, because the new militarist environment would not allow it. Moreover, one was in the SPLM/A without reference to prior political experience. It was not necessary. This was the essence of populism: you dealt only with the present. In fact, Dr. John Garang de Mabior wanted us—former Communists and revolutionary democrats—only as objects to be used, not as subjects in our right as political thinkers. This is where the contradiction arose. As long as we remained individuals without organisation, not only were we now vulnerable but the populist leader preyed on every one of us to implement his reactionary policies. This further alienated us from ourselves.

I was seriously wounded during fighting in Jekau and immobilised. George Maker, Amon Mon Wantok, Chol Deng Alaak, Alfred Lado-Gore, Daniel Odiech Abudhok, and other so-called progressive officers languished in the SPLA's jail in Boma for six years. It was only after the Nasir faction demanded their release, in 1992, that they were freed. Edward Lino was spared arrest and detention, but was deployed as director of the SPLA's external security, something for which he never received an honour or even acknowledgement. President Salva Kiir chose to mourn and lower the South Sudan flag in honour of the northern Sudanese SPLM member Dr. Mansour Khalid but not for Edward Lino Abyei, who served the SPLM/A with dedication to the point of bitterly parting ways with Maker and me because we had supported the Nasir Declaration.

The greatest weakness of those on the southern Sudanese political left was that they operated as individuals without an organisation to bind them politically and ideologically. In the Southern Progressives, we engaged with politics as students. As soon as we left the university there was a need to link ourselves to a political outfit to continue the struggle at another level. This was what I did in Port Sudan when I joined the Communist Party. My colleagues in the Southern Region remained as social democrats. The first generation of southern Sudanese leftists appeared on the political map of the Sudan in the 1950s; nevertheless, the footprints are scarcely visible. The dichotomous relationship between northern and southern Sudan contributed to this erasure of historical knowledge.

The socioeconomic underdevelopment and cultural backwardness of southern Sudan meant that the masses had no political or ideological tools. As such, their struggle was absorbed in a violent yet essentially passive political struggle. In an environment of low social awareness and political consciousness, it was easier to mobilise people for war and violence than for political struggles. This is what right-wing politicians have been doing since the Torit mutiny in 1955. It explains why it has not been easy to engage in organised political action in the Southern Region. In this way, left-wingers have always tried to ally themselves with populist leaders in political or military adventures, only to find themselves betrayed and abandoned.

It is safe perhaps to say that the Southern Progressives melted into the National Action Movement and later ended up in the SPLM/A seeking space for political and ideological action; in northern Sudan, where my profession took me, I joined the Communist Party, but also ended up in the armed struggle. There couldn't be any explanation other than the reality that most of us, notwithstanding our internationalism were still strongly attached to our roots. Ethnicity and provincialism remain strong forces in South Sudan and this could be explained as a result of its socioeconomic underdevelopment and cultural backwardness. And no matter how politically conscious a person maybe he will still gravitate towards ethnic sensibilities. It is not surprising that some SPLM cadres who received political and ideological training in Cuba and Ethiopia ended up as leaders of ethnic community associations and/or councils of elders.

As I write these lines, South Sudanese, without exception, are organised as communities or community associations, headed by elders who may be senior individuals in government to act for political leverage and patronage. Thus, when President Kiir removes a constitutional post-holder, like a state governor or county commissioner, in less than three months of his or her appointment it is likely because the community associations or councils of elders have been at work in the Republican Palace, known as J–1. Political parties, including the SPLM, have become irrelevant. This reality is a serious challenge to state formation and nation-building in South Sudan.

I have always maintained that the SPLM did not exist as a political outfit, with a constitution, political programme, functional structures, and instruments of public power and authority. It was an afterthought dictated by the reality that as a liberation movement, it is primarily political/ideological and then military. But even when its leadership accepted the idea of being both political and military, the military remained dominant instead of the political. Thus, the SPLM/A developed like Siamese twins conjoined at the head. This was the difficulty that the SPLM/A lived with until

2005, rendering it impossible to separate them into their professional domains. However, the SPLA was changed into South Sudan People's Defence Forces (SSPDF) without necessarily undergoing the process of de-politicisation or professionalisation. The SPLM failed to demilitarise itself, and therefore retained the rigid militarist command structure, rendering it impossible to function genuinely as a political and democratic party. This is a confirmation of the notion I developed in my previous writings that the separation of the SPLM/A into its professional domains would result in their mutual death.

That only external enemies united South Sudanese is verifiable in the case of the SPLM. This stems from its deep roots in traditional society, where power and authority are personified rather than institutionalised. The political–military character of the SPLM/A resonated with traditional society, where leadership is not shared. Thus, when Dr. Lam Akol and Dr. Riek Machar came up with the idea of collective responsibility, it quickly degenerated into a split in the movement. Dr. John Garang's intellectual and political dexterity had enabled him to weather the contradictions the configuration engendered. But as soon as he was no longer around, relations in the SPLM collapsed and triggered the civil war.

The split within the SPLM leadership—pitting Salva Kiir against Riek Machar, Pagan Amum, and the so-called Garang's orphans— was essentially about power. It had no ideological overtones or underpinnings. This is why the SPLM's well-wishers, namely the Ethiopian People's Revolutionary Democratic Front (EPRDF) and South Africa's African National Congress (ANC), in January 2014 thought it could be handled with ease. But it wasn't the case: the personal schisms ran deep and seemed unresolvable.

Failure of the intra-SPLM dialogue meant that the late Seyoum Mesfin, IGAD's special envoy ambassador, had to push for peace negotiations. President Salva Kiir initially rejected the Agreement on the Resolution of the Conflict in South Sudan (ARCISS), his reason being that he did not want to work again with Riek

Machar. While the IGAD-mediated peace process remained on track, another initiative on intra-SPLM dialogue for reunification of its three factions—SPLM in government, SPLM/A–IO, and the SPLM–Political Leaders, former political detainees—kicked off in Arusha, Tanzania, under the auspices of Tanzania's ruling party, the Chama Cha Mapinduzi (CCM). This was a joint CCM–ANC initiative supported by the presidents of Uganda and Kenya.

The initiative appeared to side-line Ethiopia, which chaired the peace negotiations. Indeed, it was difficult to determine how the SPLM reunification process would affect or impact the peace process after the signing of the agreement on Cessation of Hostilities (CoH). The political gerrymandering involving the CCM, ANC, and the two SPLM factions (namely, the SPLM–IG and SPLM–PL) ensued with the intention to elbow the SPLM/A–IO out of the process. Underlying this was Kiir's resentment towards and his refusal to work with Riek Machar.

CCM Secretary-General Abdulrahman Kinana travelled to Pretoria with the delegations of SPLM–IG and SPLM–PL. After this, the SPLM–PL travelled to Juba in December 2015 to join the government, and Pagan Amum was reinstated as the SPLM secretary-general. Salva Kiir, with the assistance of the CCM and ANC, had succeeded in completely isolating the SPLM/A–IO from the SPLM reunification process. However, less than a month later, Pagan Amum stormed out of Juba, accusing President Salva Kiir of a lack of commitment to the SPLM's reunification. This precipitated a split in the SPLM–PL: Deng Alor, John Luk, and Madut Biar remained inside as an entity, while Chol Tong Mayai left them and joined the SPLM–IG. Nyandeng Garang, Oyay Deng Ajak, Kosti Manibe, Cirino Hiteng, Pagan Amum, and Majak de Agoot stayed on in Nairobi as a separate group. Like the SPLM–PL, the SPLM/A–IO also suffered from division and many of its generals and political leaders abandoned Riek Machar.

Kiir's political heavy-handedness and readiness to spend public resources to buy his way rendered impossible the SPLM reunification. This begs the question of why Kiir asked President Jakaya Kikwete to start the process. In August 2014, the IGAD special envoys toyed with the idea of Kiir and Riek being kept out of the transitional government. This angered Kiir and he wanted to leave the IGAD mediation. On the side-lines of the UN General Assembly, he met Kikwete and requested his help. I would also say that the request was not made in good faith, but Salva Kiir had his mentor, President Museveni of Uganda, to bail him out of any inconveniences accruing from his political miscalculations.

I led the SPLM/A–IO delegation to Arusha, and before leaving I asked Machar about what he wanted to achieve from the SPLM reunification: he had no idea except that he was responding to the invitation of a head of state. Daniel Awet Akot led the SPLM–IG delegation, and Pagan Amum led the SPLM–PL. The meetings were cordial and the final communique reflected the desire of ordinary people in South Sudan to reconcile and unite the fighting factions, and to restore peace to the country. On 17 and 26 August 2015, the parties respectively signed the Agreement on the Resolution of the Conflict in South Sudan (ARCISS). On 26 April 2016, Riek Machar took the oath of office as first vice president, as per ARCISS, and on 29 April the cabinet was sworn in. None of the SPLM factions made reference to the Arusha Agreement on SPLM reunification. I reluctantly accepted to occupy the higher education docket. I had thought I would not work under President Salva Kiir again.

Barely three months into the ARCISS implementation, the agreement collapsed, mostly because of Riek Machar's lack of strategic political thinking. He could have prevented Taban Deng Gai and Salva Kiir from engineering a coup against him by appointing Taban Deng as the minister of petroleum. Taban had skirted the process provided by ARCISS because he wanted the petroleum docket for himself. Now Riek Machar denied Taban the portfolio and instead gave him the mining docket, and then hell broke loose. The events of July 2016 are reminiscent of the SPLM/A's internal workings before the CPA, which were characterised by intrigue, backbiting, double-crossing, lies, spying on each other, and innuendo. No credible or sustainable relations could be built in such an environment, where everyone is suspicious of the other and ready, out of self-interest, to destroy the common good.

The price for Riek's complacency was a forty-day journey to the border of the Democratic Republic of Congo under hot pursuit by Gen. Paul Malong, Blackwater drones, and helicopter gunships. More than half of Riek's forces perished and he was lucky to have survived. Taban Deng Gai supplanted him as first vice president. Alas! If he had only listened to our words. President Salva Kiir Mayardit has turned out to be a superb strategist, combining military intelligence, patience, little talking, cool calculation, and ruthless action in order to achieve his objectives. He is interested only in power, and personal power for that matter, in the same manner that Dr. John Garang de Mabior managed the SPLM/A until he got rid of his detractors in the leadership. Salva Kiir has dismantled Garang's power base, removing his supporters and protégés, and allowed power to shift from the SPLM to the JCE and its Jieng state project. Most of the JCE members, although are bona fide members of the SPLM, operate as an ethnic lobby. This has led to the functional demise of the SPLM.

In December 2017, Salva Kiir commissioned the so-called National Dialogue, which was essentially a fact-finding exercise at the grassroots level. Belatedly, these leaders realised that the problem in the country was Salva Kiir himself and his ambition for personal rule. They recommended that Salva Kiir and Riek Machar should not contest elections at the end of the transitional period. Their call for the effective end of Kiir's rule has, as a consequence, affected their close relationship with him, and possibly interrupted the Jieng state project.

In eight years of fratricide, from 2013 to 2021, the SPLM has split into a number of factions. There are no political beliefs or ideological leanings to bind them together except what they call responsibility sharing (power-sharing) at all levels—national, state, and county—in the now-bloated government. That responsibility sharing is not closing the political gap between these leaders. Inequality in distribution of national wealth (oil and non-oil revenues) has increased to a phenomenal level. Individuals linked to the centres of political and economic power have grown rich while the masses of the people have been pauperised. The country is heading towards a radical change that must involve all social and political forces opposed to the burgeoning parasitic capitalist class now in control. My humble assessment of the political situation in South Sudan is that the SPLM may not sustain itself after the current leadership is gone. Old ties may never bind again.

Pictorial Glimpses

Waat, Jonglei, December 1992
*With Cdr. Simon Mori Didumo: Emerging from a meeting of the
SPLM/A Nasir faction*

Delivering my speech accepting the
Noma Award for Publishing in Africa, 1998

Posing with the President
President of Mozambique, Joachim Chisano in the middle. On his left: Madame Mondlane, the widow of Edwardo Mondlane, the first president of Frelimo, Simon Tumusiime, Managing Director of Fountain Publishers, Kampala, Mary Fay, the Director of African Book Collectives, London, chair of the Mona Award Committee. On the right. Myself, the representative of Noma Publishing Company in Japan and Dr. Walter Bgoya

Strolling back from launch with Kwacakworo

Davos, Switzerland, 2002

Marling at the snow-covered landscape around Davos

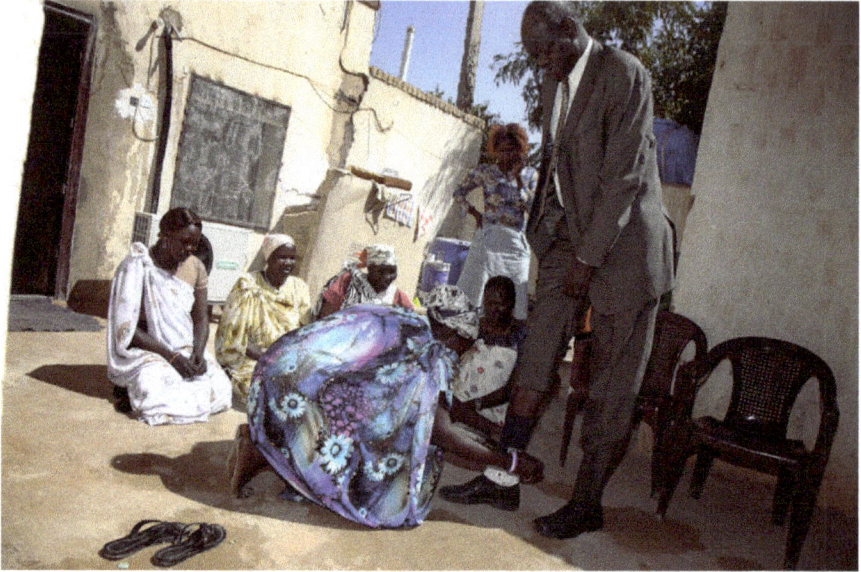

Fatiab, Omdurman, September 2008
Shilluk ritual of white-bead-tying ceremony on occasion of my
appointment as Minister of Higher Education and Scientific
Research in the Government of National Unity, Khartoum

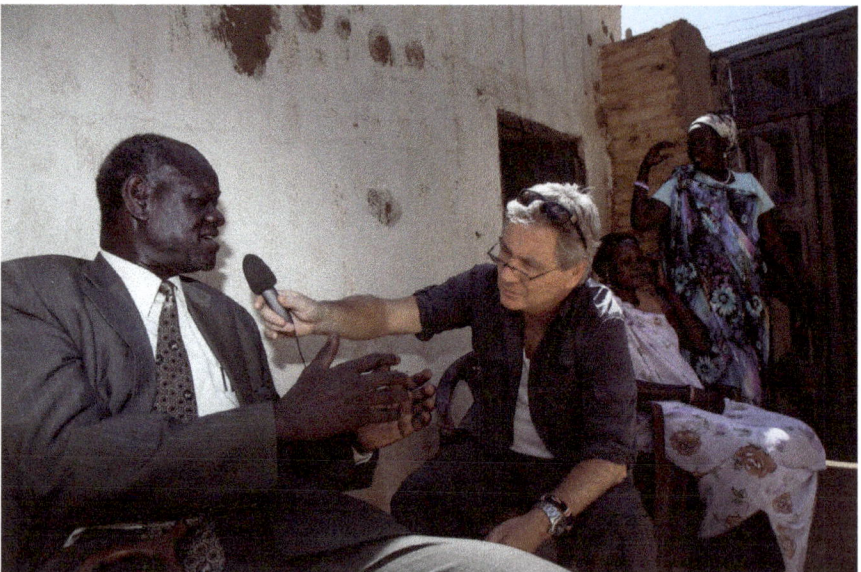

Immediately after the ceremony Koert tied me down to an interview

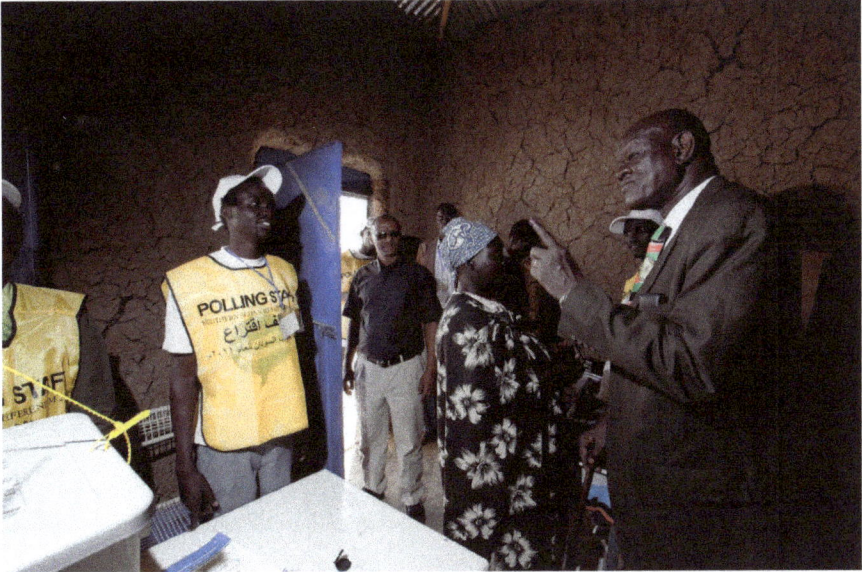

Malakal, Southern Sudan, 9th January 2011
Waiting to cast my vote in the Southern Sudan Referendum on self-determination

HM Rath Kwongo Dak Padiet poses with Jean Francois, Juba, 2013

Gordon Eric Wagner worked for the USAID office of Southern Sudan. He was a great friend indeed, Nairobi, Kenya

Rev. Canon Clement Janda was a friend and colleague in the struggle for the liberation and independence of South Sudan. We became members of the Council of the States in the National Legislature in Khartoum.

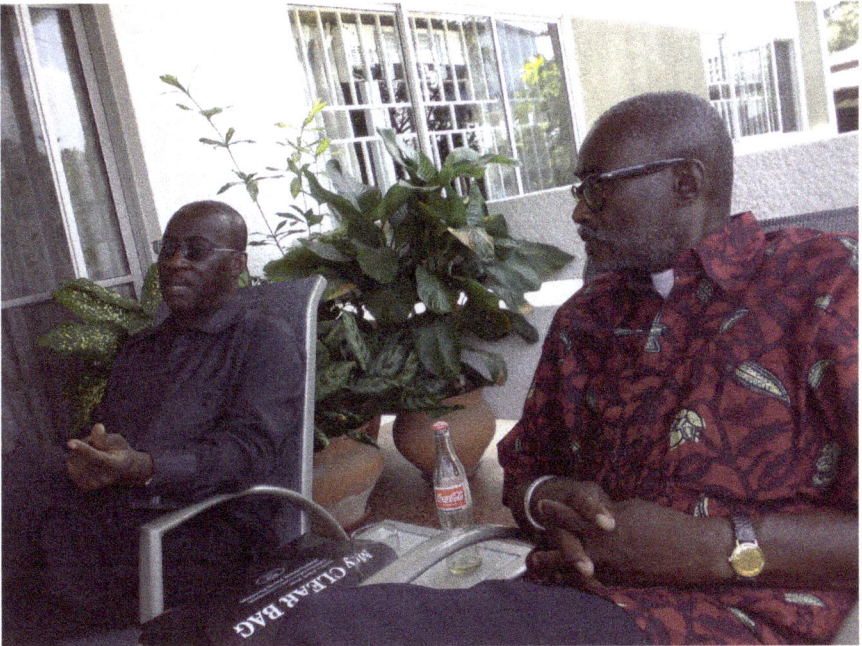

*Banke Foster Bankie and Prof. Karikari in Accra, Ghana, 2007.
In January 2017, Bankie and I travelled to West Africa in what
was a campaign to raise awareness about South Sudan, which
took us to Ghana, Nigeria, and Serra Leone. BF Bankie was
a great Pan-Africanist, who worked tirelessly for Pan-African
Movement. He worked for the Government of Southern Sudan
(2006-2008), died in Windhoek, Namibia in August 2017.*

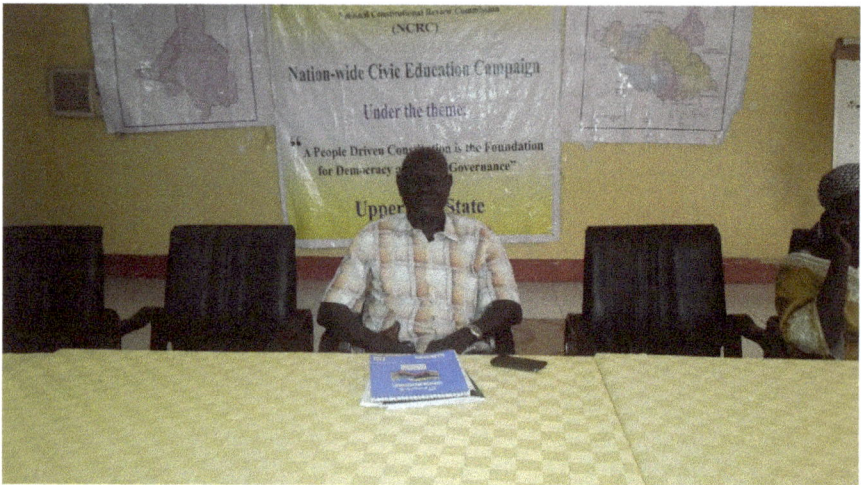

Reviewing the South Sudan Transitional Constitution [2011]
*As member of the National Constitutional Review Commission,
in August 2013 I led the delegation to undertake Civic Education
in Upper Nile State. This picture was taken just before beginning
a meeting in Malakal.*

Juba, South Sudan, January 2014
*In my reading, I spent the six-months house detention in the
aftermath of the violent eruption on 15th December 2013 and
where I wrote the book, South Sudan: The Crisis of Infancy
published by CASAS in 2014.*

Epitaph of Political Failure
Protection of Civilian Centre, under the auspices of UNMISS, Bentiu, Unity State, January 2014. It depicts the sad ethnic divisions that occurred in the aftermath of the eruption of violence in Juba in December 2013.

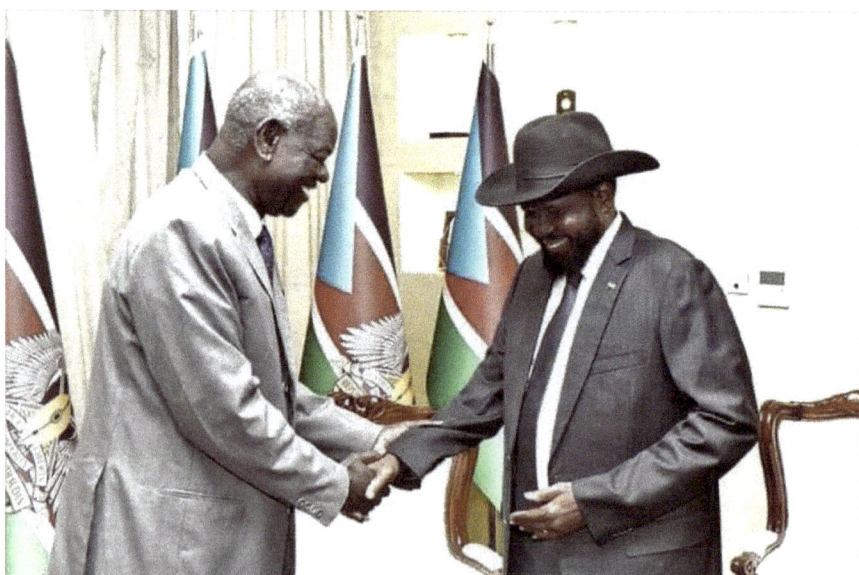

Return to Juba, November 2018
Cordial encounter with President Salva Kiir Mayardit in State House, Juba, December 2018

My daughter, **Keni Adwok Nyaba,** *who was First Secretary in the Embassy of South Sudan to the European Union and the Kingdom of Belgium. She was dismissed from job together with many other diplomats on account of supporting the rebellion. She passed on in April 2016.*

Vice President, Ministers & Deputy Ministers of the Republic of Southern Sudan Retreat, 21st-26th Nov, 2011, MSA Kenya

*Retreat for Vice President, Ministers & Deputy Ministers of the
Republic of South Sudan, held in Mombasa Kenya,
21st-26th Nov, 2011*

Retreat for Vice President, Ministers & Deputy Ministers of the
Republic of South Sudan, held in Mombasa Kenya,
21st-26th Nov, 2011

Retreat for Vice President, Ministers & Deputy Ministers of the Republic of South Sudan, 21st-26th Nov, 2011, Mombasa Continental Resort, Kenya

Retreat for Vice President, Ministers & Deputy Ministers of the Republic of South Sudan, held in Mombasa Kenya, 21st-26th Nov, 2011

Peter Adwok Nyaba

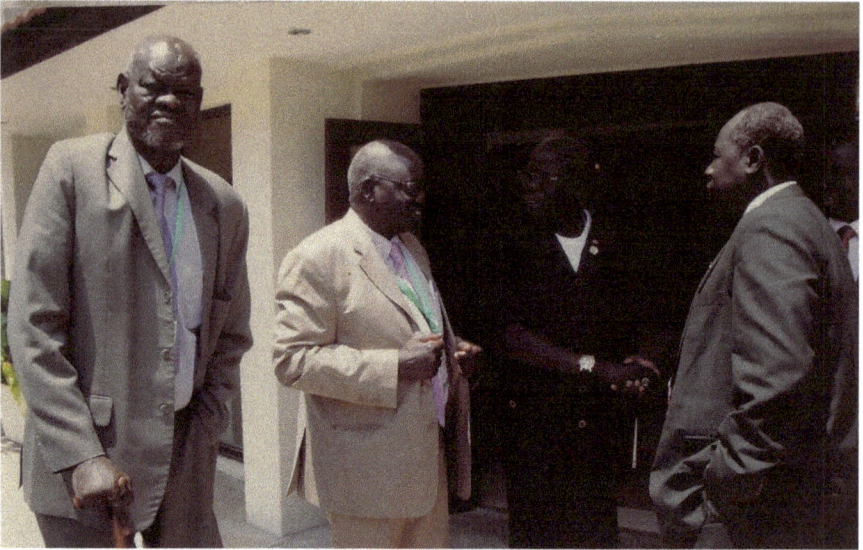

Retreat for Vice President, Ministers & Deputy Ministers of the Republic of South Sudan, held in Mombasa Kenya, 21st-26th Nov, 2011

Watajwok village on the west bank, courtesy Encarta 1995

With Hon. Abuk Payiti Ayik

4th September 2019, after being decorated by the
then Minister of Defence and Veteran Affairs

Index

Akobo 41, 45, 48, 59, 222, 282, 293, 301, 312
Akoch 21-22, 31, 70, 117, 347
Akok 184, 229, 284, 417-8
Akoka 81
Akol xi, xii, xx, xxi, xxi, 221-2, 262, 271, 273, 286, 288, 290, 292-3, 295, 301, 320, 348-9, 360, 368, 403-4, 422
Akolong 2
Akon xix
Akorwa 112
Akot xxi, 72, 253, 424
Akuch 235
Akuen 403
Akujok 24
Akuot 184, 253
Akwai 222, 398
Akway xix
Akwoch 167, 287, 350
Alaak 211, 218, 220, 418-9
Alaaki 347, 361
Alan 76
Aleijok 103
Aleu xv, 214, 254-5, 356, 403
Alexander 187
Alfred 206, 289, 295, 301, 350, 418-9
Algeria 173
Algerian 177-178
Ali 53, 55-6, 148, 160, 235, 261, 318, 347-8, 363, 377-8
Aliab 90
Alier 83, 182, 184-5, 333, 356,

367, 370-1, 409, 417
Alitalia 170
Allam 178
Alor 249, 257, 260-1, 264, 357, 403-4, 419, 423
Aluong 243
Alwin 42
Amaiker 361
Amal 271
Amarat 182
Ambrose 201
Amer xix, xxi
America 166, 234-5, 276, 278-9, 298, 341, 392
American 17, 23-5, 27-30, 32, 34, 36, 54, 107, 116, 133, 175, 179, 195, 234, 236-8, 259, 304, 317
Americans 29, 66, 189
Amid 417
Amilcar 232, 392
Amin 179
Amon 116, 210-2, 229, 295, 415, 418-9
Amos 32, 117
Amsterdam xxi
Amujo 17
Amum 29, 43, 67, 77, 82-3, 140, 167, 169, 179, 183, 207, 238, 241, 291, 348, 360, 367-8, 384, 403, 422-4
Anade 302
Anagdiar 3, 24, 347, 405-6
Anai 417

Bareth 51
Bargo 42
Bari xv, xvi, 3, 42, 219, 222-3, 226, 228, 250, 288, 325
Baro 218, 223, 254-6
Bashara 235
Bashir 302, 331, 341, 366-7, 404-5
Bassiouni 298
Bata 117
Battalion 156, 199, 207, 214, 254, 394, 410
Battalions 334
Bavaria 172
Bayuda 271
Bazilio 208
Beirzansky 175-176
Beja 149, 159
Bele 306, 323
Belgian 95
Belgium 439
Beloved 76
Ben 183
Beneath 184
Benedict xxi, 243
Benjamin 138, 140-1, 143, 184, 208, 229, 251, 284, 295, 415-8
Bentiu 42, 57, 83, 155, 195, 250, 438
Beny 201, 394, 408
Berger xxx, 157
Berlin 270-274
Beshir 84, 395
Bethuel 266

Bey 36-37
Bgoya 429
Biar 423
Bichok 360
Biel 248
Bieler xvi
Bileu 223
Bilpam 222, 229, 251-2, 255
Biong 209
Bior 378
Birkat 55
Bissau 234
Blackwater 425
Blu 345
Blue 66, 114-5, 127, 157, 162, 227-8, 254, 332-3
Boeing 143, 231
Bol 16, 31, 37, 70, 117, 130, 138, 167, 172, 174-5, 179, 184-5, 189, 216, 227, 229, 239, 252, 282, 284, 290, 307, 322, 346-7, 353, 416-8
Bole 204-205, 229, 231
Bolivia 171
Boma 229, 231, 239, 245, 251, 344, 419
Bona 290
Bong 78
Bonga 209, 213, 216, 218, 254, 285, 410
Bonn 176, 272-3
Booker xxi
Bor 11, 45, 48, 59, 72-3, 90-1, 98-9, 104, 106, 120, 133-4, 156,

Machar xi, xii, 186, 273, 286, 289-292, 294-5, 301, 324, 329, 356, 360, 367-8, 376, 380, 384, 387, 389-390, 402, 405, 407-9, 422-5
Machiec 418
Machuei 130, 169
Macpilo 115-116
Madi 325
Mading 272
Madrid 242
Madut 258, 307, 423
Mageed 148, 150, 166, 171
Magiwa 269, 346, 351
Magnun 214
Magog 104, 106
Magok 223, 275
Magui xix
Mahdi 151, 249, 419
Mahdist 10
Mahgoub 85, 136-7, 152, 235
Mai 251, 346
Maj 93, 100, 137, 185, 206, 218, 220, 223, 249, 254, 257, 260-1, 282, 370
Majak 271, 424
Majesty 347-349, 354, 386
Majier 284, 307
Majok 224, 275
Majur 221
Makal 3, 10, 12, 360-1, 405
Makuei 290
Makuen 417
Malakal xxi, 2, 6-10, 12-4,
18-9, 22-3, 31-4, 43-5, 48-9, 51, 55, 58, 61-2, 64-7, 71-2, 74, 77-8, 80-3, 85-7, 92, 96, 99-100, 103, 107, 110-3, 118-124, 130, 133-4, 136, 139-140, 144, 150-1, 167-8, 172, 179-180, 184, 186-8, 193, 209, 225, 227, 252, 335, 341, 345-9, 355, 359-360, 368, 377-9, 405, 413, 433, 436
Malakiya 120, 140, 347
Malath 184, 284, 307, 417-8
Malek 25, 41, 48, 89-90, 98, 100, 258, 418
Malik 253-254, 403
Malith xix
Malok 275
Malong 373, 389, 425
Malou 77
Malual 256, 272, 290, 313, 316, 373
Mama 235, 341, 345-7, 349, 354
Manaqil 114
Manchol 172
Mandela 258
Mangalla 63, 72, 96
Mangar 212-213
Mangok 254
Manibe 403, 424
Manjing 138, 416
Mansour 420
Manyang 346, 374, 403
Manyiel 292

465

www.ingramcontent.com/pod-product-compliance
Lightning Source LLC
Chambersburg PA
CBHW052009030426
42334CB00029BA/3139